Queer Premises

Queer Premises

LGBTQ+ Venues in London Since the 1980s

Ben Campkin

BLOOMSBURY ACADEMIC
LONDON · NEW YORK · OXFORD · NEW DELHI · SYDNEY

BLOOMSBURY ACADEMIC
Bloomsbury Publishing Plc
50 Bedford Square, London, WC1B 3DP, UK
1385 Broadway, New York, NY 10018, USA
29 Earlsfort Terrace, Dublin 2, Ireland

BLOOMSBURY, BLOOMSBURY ACADEMIC and the Diana logo are trademarks of
Bloomsbury Publishing Plc

First published in Great Britain 2023

Copyright © Ben Campkin, 2023

Ben Campkin has asserted his right under the Copyright, Designs and
Patents Act, 1988, to be identified as Author of this work.

For legal purposes the Acknowledgements on p. xi constitute an extension
of this copyright page.

Cover design by Adriana Brioso
Cover image: First Out Café, image adapted from 10th Anniversary Party invitation design
by Alex McFadyen, 1996.

All rights reserved. No part of this publication may be reproduced or transmitted
in any form or by any means, electronic or mechanical, including photocopying,
recording, or any information storage or retrieval system, without prior
permission in writing from the publishers.

Bloomsbury Publishing Plc does not have any control over, or responsibility for, any
third-party websites referred to or in this book. All internet addresses given in this
book were correct at the time of going to press. The author and publisher regret any
inconvenience caused if addresses have changed or sites have ceased to exist,
but can accept no responsibility for any such changes.

A catalogue record for this book is available from the British Library.

A catalog record for this book is available from the Library of Congress.

ISBN: HB: 978-1-3503-2486-2
PB: 978-1-3503-2485-5
ePDF: 978-1-3503-2487-9
eBook: 978-1-3503-2484-8

Typeset by Deanta Global Publishing Services, Chennai, India
Printed and bound in Great Britain

To find out more about our authors and books visit www.bloomsbury.com and
sign up for our newsletters.

In memory
Judy Campkin (1946–2015)

Contents

List of figures	viii
List of plates	ix
Acknowledgements	xi
List of abbreviations	xiv
Introduction	1
1 Queer urbanism	7
2 Perverted purposes	27
3 Mainlining pride	47
4 Rupture and repair	67
5 Seeking closure	95
6 Sui generis	119
7 Macho city	147
8 Pandemic premises	171
Notes	179
Select bibliography	258
About the author	269
Index	270

Figures

Cover: Adaptation of First Out Café, 10th anniversary party invitation, 1996. Original design by Alex McFadyen

2.1	London Lesbian and Gay Centre, rear elevation drawing, 1984	28
5.1	Planning application, 190 West Lodge, Euston Square, 9 April 1996, completed by Elaine McKenzie, with sketch indicating conversion from offices to a bar	105
5.2	The Astoria, 2008, with announcement for G-A-Y	107
5.3	First Out Café, concept sketch, Mark Bullus, First Out Coffee Shop Business Plan, 1985	112
6.1	The Black Cap, 2011	121
6.2	The Royal Vauxhall Tavern, London, still image from a laser scan produced between Covid-19 pandemic lockdowns, 2020	126
6.3	RVT Future, 'Who are RVT Future?' flyer, 2015	127
7.1	David Pollard, 2010	149
7.2	The Joiners Arms, plan, undated	151

Plates

1 London Lesbian and Gay Centre, leaflet, 1985
2 Sketch proposals, London Lesbian and Gay Centre, basement, 1983
3 Exterior of London Lesbian and Gay Centre, 1985
4 *Changing the World: A London Charter for Gay and Lesbian Rights*, 1985
5 London Lesbian and Gay Centre, *Newsletter*, No. 1, November, 1988. Cover with cartoon section by NINE
6 London Lesbian and Gay Centre, 'Buy Our Centre', leaflet, 1990
7 London Partnerships Register, first ceremony, attended by Mayor of London, Ken Livingstone, 2001
8 Mayor of London Boris Johnson tries on a pink cowgirl hat at London Pride, 2008
9 Mayor of London Sadiq Khan shakes hands and takes photos with organizers before London Pride, 8 July 2017
10 Map showing locations of LGBTQ+ venues and clusters of venues in London, 1986
11 Map showing locations of LGBTQ+ venues and clusters of venues in London, 1996
12 Map showing locations of LGBTQ+ venues and clusters of venues in London, 2006
13 Map showing locations of LGBTQ+ venues and clusters of venues in London, 2016
14 The Bell, King's Cross, 1981
15 The Glass Bar, Euston, 2007
16 First Out Café, 2005
17 Map of venues affected by Crossrail 1 [Elizabeth Line] Tottenham Court Road Station redevelopment
18 Protest vigil outside The Black Cap, October 2015
19 Her Upstairs, Camden, 2017, stage
20 The Joiners Arms, Hackney Road, 2012
21 Mural by David Shenton, The Joiners Arms, 2012
22 The Joiners Arms 'completely trashed a few days after the closing night', 2015
23 Friends of The Joiners Arms, poster for public meeting, 2017
24 Frame from *Will You Dance With Me?*, 2014, shot in Benjy's, 1984
25 Frame from *Will You Dance With Me?*, 2014, shot in Benjy's, 1984
26 The Backstreet, Mile End, 2018
27 The Backstreet, Mile End, 2018
28 The Royal Vauxhall Tavern, London. Still image from a laser scan produced between Covid-19 pandemic lockdowns, 2020

x   *Plates*

29   The Royal Vauxhall Tavern, London. Still image from a laser scan produced between Covid-19 pandemic lockdowns, 2020

30   The Royal Vauxhall Tavern, London. Still image from a laser scan produced between Covid-19 pandemic lockdowns, 2020

Acknowledgements

From dance floors, cabaret stages and protests, to planning inquiries and archives, the journey of researching and writing this book has taken me down many unexpected paths, prompting me to make connections across disparate spaces and to question my assumptions on the way. It would not have been possible to pursue my curiosity about queer premises, or to complete this project, without the patience and support of family, friends, colleagues and students. I am deeply grateful for the multiple ways that their insights, conversations and collaborations have spurred me on.

I have been fortunate to encounter generous encouragement and inspiration from many students and colleagues while at UCL. I would like to thank, especially, James Agar, Sabina Andron, Pushpa Arabindoo, Nishat Awan, Matthew Beaumont, Kara Blackmore, Iain Borden, Sebastian Buser, Barbara Campbell-Lange, Brent Carnell, Daniel Ovalle Costal, Edward Denison, Michael Edwards, Ginger Farbrother, Adrian Forty, Haidy Geismar, Matthew Gandy, Andrew Harris, Jonathan Hill, Rebecca Jennings, Rían Kearney, Amy Kulper, Paola Lettieri, Christoph Lindner, Leah Lovett, Sian Lunt, Sé Mali, Clare Melhuish, Sophie Mepham, Robert Mills, Chi Nguyen, Barbara Penner, Joe Penny, Jordana Ramalho, Peg Rawes, Sophie Read, Jane Rendell, David Roberts, Jennifer Robinson, Jordan Rowe, Pablo Sendra, Tania Sengupta, Anthony Smith, Nathaniel Télémaque, Stephen Vaughan, Nina Vollenbröker, Stephen Wall, Tim Waterman, Marco Venturi and Henrietta Williams.

I owe a particular debt to Johan Andersson for sharing his passion for and deep knowledge of queer scenes, and for generously commenting on the entire draft. To Lo Marshall, I would like to express deepest thanks for the volumes I have learnt through our joint endeavours. Some of these projects are described in the book, and they inform its arguments in a multitude of ways. Our daytime forays into planning databases and our occasional fieldtrips have added much joy to the research process.

UCL Urban Laboratory has provided material help through supporting a decade and a half of programming on queer urban themes. For their contributions to these research activities and events, I would like to thank Jo Alloway, Tom Bolton, Robert Clinton, Chryssy Hunter, Chi Nguyen, Filippos Toskas and Rachel Tyler. Special thanks to Cristián Valenzuela for coding survey data; to Chris Storey for producing digital maps and cluster analyses; to Cath D'Alton for producing maps; to James White and Lucca Ferrarese for digital laser scanning; and to Tom Kendall for editing and visualisation of scan data. Heartfelt and suitably awkward thanks and respect to my partners in crimes against millinery and planning, Fabulous Façades, who gamely paraded queer architectural histories with me: Gabrielle Basso Ricci, Sebastian Buser, Tom Kendall, Zia Álmos Joshua X, Lo Marshall and Sé Mali; and to Ben Walters (aka Dr Duckie) for nurturing our research and participation in Queer Fun at the RVT. I am grateful to Clare Melhuish and our students for lively seminars, which provided opportunities to think deeply about London heritage.

Some of the chapters of *Queer Premises* developed from earlier essays published in *Sexuality and Gender at Home: Experience, Politics Transgression* (2017), *The Routledge Companion to Urban Imaginaries* (2020), *Queer Sites in Global Contexts: Technologies, Spaces and Otherness* (2021), *Queer Spaces: An Atlas of LGBTQIA+ Places and Stories* (2022) and *Urban Omnibus* (2018). Thank you to the editors of these works for their insightful feedback: Caroline Ellerby, Adam Nathaniel Furman, Christoph Lindner, Joshua Mardell, Miriam Meissner, Mariana Mogilevich, Sharif Mowlabocus, Jacob Moore, Regner Ramos and Olivia Schwob.

Chapter 4 draws on the survey and workshops undertaken as part of the UCL Urban Laboratory project *LGBTQI Nightlife in London*, initiated in May 2016, which I co-designed with Lo Marshall, and with Ben Walters and Tim Other of RAZE Collective and Queer Spaces Network. This research led to two reports: *LGBTQI Nightlife in London: From 1986 to the Present* (2016) and *LGBTQ+ Cultural Infrastructure in London: Night Venues, 2006–Present* (2017). The 2017 report and the production of a dataset of venues 2006–17 were supported by a small grant from the Greater London Authority. Whitechapel Gallery's exhibition *Queer Spaces–1980s to Today* (2019) provided an opportunity to exhibit archival and audio materials from case studies Lo Marshall and I had compiled through this research. I am grateful to Nayia Yiakoumaki, Vassilios Doupas and Cameron Foote for the opportunity to collaborate in co-curating these materials, and to Cameron for meticulous image research.

Thanks to all those who have generously given their time and trust in sharing stories of London LGBTQ+ venues, including Dan Beaumont, Raf Benato, Reggie Blennerhassett, Simon Brooksbank, Simon Casson, Kimberley Clarke, Malcolm Comely, Jarlath O'Connell, Peter Cragg, Peter Davey, Madam Defarge, Samuel Douek, Rob Downey, Carla Ecola, Kell Farshéa, Stuart Feather, Christina Gawne, Lyall Hakaraia, Richard Heaton, Steve Hignell, Jeffrey Hinton, Phillip Inglesant, Duncan Irvine, Anton Johnson, Andy Jones, Robert Kincaid, Ash Kotak, Amy Lamé, Ralph Lane, Jeremy Atherton Lin, James Lindsay, Frank van Loock, Andrew Lumsden, Jim MacSweeney, Elaine McKenzie, Veronica Mckenzie, Fiona McLean, Meth, Raja Moussaoui, Dan de la Motte, Kevin O'Neill, Susan Orr, Joe Parslow, Rob Pateman, Giuliano Pistoni, David Pollard, Helen Tejada Randall, DJ Ritu, Amy Roberts, David Shenton, Wayne Shires, Terry Stewart, Jay Sutherland, Maria Tejada, Karl Thomas, Stuart Walker and Oscar Watson.

I am grateful to all those who have kindly provided and allowed me to reproduce images. Thanks to the following organizations, networks and archives for access to materials, image permissions and other support: Bishopsgate Institute Archives, especially Stefan Dickers; Black Cap Foundation; Camden Council, especially Sharon Dunn and Andrew Triggs; Camden Local Studies and Archives Centre, especially Daniel Croughton; Central Station; First Out Café; Friends of The Joiners Arms; Gays the Word; Greater London Authority, Culture and Creative Industries Team and LGBTQ+ Venues Forum; London Metropolitan Archives; London Night Czar; London School of Economics Library and Hall-Carpenter Archives; Planning Out; Royal Vauxhall Tavern; RVT Future; Society of Architectural Historians of Great

Acknowledgements xiii

Britain LGBTQ+ Network; and qUCL. Ron Peck (1948–2022), kindly provided stills from *Will You Dance With Me?* He and Sandro Kviria generously talked with Urban Lab staff and students about Ron's work and their collaborations. The Bartlett School of Architecture, Architecture Research Fund, UCL, funded the reproduction of two commercial stock images.

Funding from the European Union Humanities in the European Research Area Collaborative Research Project, *Nightspaces, Migration, Culture and Integration in Europe* (NITE), provided the opportunity to research LGBT citizenship within urban governance in London since 2000, the subject of Chapter 3; and the resources to produce the digital laser scan of the Royal Vauxhall Tavern, discussed in Chapter 8. I am so grateful for the generous collaboration of the NITE network through a pandemic that changed (but far from scuppered) our plans: Sara Brandellero, Manuela Bojadžijev, Ailbhe Kenny, Seger Kersbergen, Alessio Koliulis, Laura-Solmaz Litschel, Lo Marshall, Derek Pardue, Kamila Krakowska Rodrigues and Katherine Young.

For their inspiration, friendship, instruction and collaboration on queer space projects, special thanks to: Sam Ashby, Stav B, Garrett Burns, Tom Frederic, Celeste Gattai, Amin Ghaziani, David Gissen, Tony Hallam, Max Hill, Alan Hollinghurst, R. Justin Hunt, Rafael Pereira do Rego, Cat Rossi, Timothy Smith, George Taxidis, Mark Turner, Ben Walters and Stamatis Zografos.

Huge thanks to Kim Walker for commissioning the book, to Olivia Dellow and Sophie Campbell at Bloomsbury and Mohammed Raffi at Deanta for steering it to completion, and to the reviewers of the proposal and manuscript for their thoughtful feedback. Kate Lindesay of Echo Transcript's meticulous work has been invaluable in processing many individual and group interviews undertaken during the research.

Finally, deep thanks for their sustained support and encouragement to David John – who read the manuscript and gave much helpful advice to improve it – Rebecca Ross and Victoria Grimwood; and to my father, David Campkin and all my family.

Abbreviations

ACT-UP	AIDS Coalition to Unleash Power
ACV	Asset of Community Value
AIDS	Acquired Immunodeficiency Syndrome
BAME	Black, Asian and Minority Ethnic
BDSM	Bondage, Discipline, Sadism and Masochism
CAMRA	The Campaign for Real Ale
FOTJA	Friends of the Joiners Arms
Friends of the RVT	Friends of the Royal Vauxhall Tavern
GBA	Gay Business Association
GLA	Greater London Authority
GLC	Greater London Council
GLF	Gay Liberation Front
GVA	Gross Value Added
HAART	Highly Active Antiretroviral Therapy
HCA	Hall-Carpenter Archives, LSE Library
HIH	Her Imperial Highness
HIV/AIDS	Human Immunodeficiency Virus
HM	Her Majesty
LAM	London Assembly Member
LASM	Lesbians Against Sadomasochism
LCC	London County Council
LGBTQ+	Lesbian, Gay, Bisexual, Trans, Queer, plus
LGSM	Lesbians and Gays Support the Miners
LLGC	London Lesbian and Gay Centre
LMA	London Metropolitan Archives
LSE	London School of Economics
LWT	London Weekend Television
MP	Member of Parliament
NTE	Night Time Economy

Abbreviations

S106	Section 106 Agreement
S/M	Sadomasochist
SPAB	Society for the Protection of Ancient Buildings
QR Code	Quick Response Code
QSN	Queer Spaces Network
QTIPOC	Queer, Trans and Intersex People of Colour
RAZE	RAZE Collective
RVT Future	Royal Vauxhall Tavern Future, the campaign to secure the use of the RVT as an LGBTQ pub and queer performance space
RVT	Royal Vauxhall Tavern
UCL	University College London
UNESCO	United Nations Educational, Scientific and Cultural Organization
WLM	Women's Liberation Movement

Introduction

How have London's diverse queer populations embedded themselves into urban space, governance and planning? To address this question, this book looks at how bars, cafés, nightclubs, pubs, community centres and hybrids of these typologies have been imagined, created and sustained from the 1980s to the present. I ask how, where and why these venues have been established, how they operate, the purposes they serve, what challenges they face and why they close down. Venues are studied in different material dimensions: as proposals and planning applications; as buildings and spatial layouts with rooms that have been designed, decorated and iteratively adapted; as locations, situated in and shaped by constantly changing urban environments; as legal entities, defined through land and property ownership, subject to governance, planning, lease and licensing arrangements, and the flows of property and consumer markets; as sites of everyday use, work, leisure, intimacy and pleasure; as incubators, platforms and mirrors for culture, collectives and social change; as nodes within local and international networks, mediated and extended by changing communications technologies.

Queer premises include venues that lesbian, gay, bisexual, trans and queer people have identified with, and which connect with and facilitate the social movements of these groups.[1] They comprise a vital and distinctive social and cultural infrastructure – a *queer infrastructure*, I argue in Chapter 1, where I chart the interrelations of queer theory and practice with urban policy, theory and activism. These venues connect between different locations, facilitating the movement of resources, across and beyond the city. Carefully planned, spontaneous (or both), they are produced within and compromised by material constraints, whether socio-economic, political, architectural or urban – factors that influence their distribution, social value and longevity. They extract from, are embedded within, are contingent upon and are compromised by their settings, even while they sometimes offer transport to alternative conditions.

In this book you will encounter just a sample of the typologies of 'gay space' or 'queer space'. The extended histories of these terms are the focus of Chapter 1. The chapters that follow it consider a variety of examples using evidence in multiple media. These include state-funded community centres, socialist cooperatives and collectives from the 1980s, commercial nightclubs and multipurpose pub-club-cabaret venues from the 1990s and 2000s, and examples from today's dynamic scenes – from fetish clubs to pop-up parties, to the campaigns linked to venues recently closed, or threatened with closure, by large-scale redevelopment. These scenes and venues reflect and shape the priorities of different groups and generations. They also connect across them, and allude to multiple times, places and cultures, transforming in response to changing externalities. The empirical scope of *Queer Premises* ranges from the early 1980s, when plans were underway for the London Lesbian and Gay Centre, to the very recent past and the impacts of the Coronavirus pandemic. The case studies were selected for their potential to illuminate the changing relationships between LGBTQ+ venues, planning and governance. Rather than tracing a linear evolution, or a rise and decline, the book follows iterations and interconnections, moments of reproduction, redirection, resistance and innovation throughout this period.

Research on queer space has often focused on the experiential, spontaneous and underground qualities of night-spaces. In this book, the histories of individual venues are linked to wider trends in culture and urbanization. Changing qualities and provision reflect not only the preoccupations of LGBTQ+ people at given moments, but the ways these populations have been addressed or overlooked. I ask how these venues have been planned at different scales, by individuals or through collaborations between community organizations and activists, artists, entrepreneurs, businesses and the state. I look at how LGBTQ+ communities and campaigns have interacted with local and metropolitan-level governance, under both radical socialist and neoliberal models.

The chapters detail and compare case studies to trace how queer heritage surfaces – if it surfaces – in planning processes. They show how LGBTQ+ venues have been imagined and specified; the ways these populations have been addressed in urban policy, within imaginaries of the local, global and cosmopolitan city; and the tactics used to create, archive or hold on to venues. My interest is in how venues – and more recently campaigns to protect them – have attached to, traversed and sometimes contested dominant modes of urbanism, in ways that include the predictable, normative or homonormative, as well as the queerly eccentric and the utopic. If venues often reproduce dominant power relations, including wider norms of sexuality and gender embedded in and reproduced by cities, the creative queering of urban spaces and political structures by minoritized groups and counterpublics has also challenged the status quo.

In my research, whether on regeneration, housing or queer heritage, I see urbanism as a collective project, a set of practices that traverses different forms of knowledge and goes beyond the singular concerns of any discipline or profession. This book contributes to an international, transdisciplinary field of queer urbanism. Here, scholarship across multiple disciplines and varied forms of cultural work, including activism and art, intersects with urban policy, planning and heritage practices, with the imagination, creation and sustenance of everyday spaces of community and culture, and the lifeworlds they support.

Substation

In 1994, when I moved to London at eighteen years of age, I was just beginning to tiptoe out of the closet. Crossing the threshold of a gay bar would have been a far too brazen step. Like many before and since, my migration was from a small-town life, experienced as prohibitively straight. For me, the movement was a mere 40 miles from suburban Reading. The back and forth of that journey continues to be one of reconciliation between my sexuality and the cultural, family and religious expectations of my upbringing, and my acquired, and changing, sense of belonging in London. For many queer people, of course, moving to London is a migration from places where direct and extreme violence and danger, as well as discrimination and discomfort, are regularly experienced. Such journeys are not a simple or one-way escape. In London, as elsewhere, safety is relative and conditional, and unevenly experienced by LGBTQ+ people according to how they present, or pass, as they move through the world, in ways that are shaped by their prior experiences. The qualitative accounts of LGBTQ+ venues presented in this book elucidate these negotiations with identity, subjectivity and place.

The Black Cap, a long-running cabaret bar in Camden, was close to my student hall of residence and became an early landmark in my sparse mental map of queer London. But I was not brave or out enough to go in. Shame suppressing curiosity, I would scuttle past its ornate façade as I walked to university each day. Living in Bloomsbury a couple of years later, I had a growing collection of discreetly hidden queer literature, but I would not dare to look too closely into the conspicuous shopwindow of Gay's the Word bookshop on Marchmont Street, let alone go inside. I was certainly not educated enough to know the important role the shop had played in lesbian and gay liberation since its establishment in 1979. I now know that if I had entered, I would have had the friendliest reception, and a conduit to so many lesbian and gay groups, and so much queer culture, past and present. Despite my reticence, queer desire had compelled my move to London, where I imagined I would meet other gay people. My knowledge of a gay community, of the scenes and spaces gay people frequented, may have been vague, but I was driven, as is common, by the promise of new freedoms and intimacies, and the anonymity to experience them.

The battle cry of gay liberation in the 1970s had been, 'out of the closets, into the streets!' My early encounters with London gay life were instead underground and in the dark. While writing this book, hazy memories of one of my earliest visits to a gay nightclub were sparked as I pored over faded club flyers in public archives. I remembered how, emboldened by alcohol, I had followed a backstreet that branched off Charing Cross Road. Steps to an anonymous basement delivered me from the throngs of tourists to the dance floor of Substation Soho: a thick fog of dry ice, cigarette smoke and techno cut by strobes. It was practically empty – I must have arrived, completely uncool, not long after the doors opened – but the relief of being submerged in that cocoon was immense. Perhaps I had looked up the address in *Time Out's* Gay and Lesbian listings: an index of London's gay bars and networks where the briefest entries of names, locations and one-line descriptions had the power to evoke new worlds for me. Within a few years of living in London, coming out and in and out, I had acquired much more tacit knowledge of the bars, clubs and cafés and cruising sites that made up London's scenes and was reliant on them.

My accounts of many of the venues in the following pages are informed by first-hand experience. But in most cases I was not attending them as a researcher, and my encounters are not part of the method, in the way that they would be if this were an autoethnography or memoir. Nor are my own experiences held up over other forms of evidence. As a white, cisgender, able-bodied, middle-class, mainly straight-passing gay man, my experience of venues and my perspectives on them have been shaped by intersecting forms of embodied privilege. Most commercial venues in the late 1990s and 2000s were accessible to me – more so than to many LGBTQ+ people. I include important venues that I have no direct experience of and which were explicitly created by, or actively addressed, people with different identities, backgrounds and embodiments. I have not always been conscious of, or attentive to, how intersecting privileges shape experiences of venues, or how these venues reinforce those privileges and power disparities. Although the book considers a wide range of venues, it has a focus on the most formal ones: licensed premises. The process of researching these has been one of learning about how they reflect and reproduce wider societal inequalities as well as modelling, at times, different and fairer realities.

One such venue, discussed in detail in Chapter 2, is the London Lesbian and Gay Centre, which closed just before I arrived in London, in 1992. This multipurpose facility was an incubator of numerous vital initiatives. The Centre was initiated by the Greater London Council in collaboration with local authorities and gay and lesbian organizations. Although I was not aware of its existence, I directly benefitted from some of the resources accommodated in the Centre: PACE – the Project for Advocacy, Counselling and Education, which I accessed for affordable therapy in the late 1990s, by which time it had relocated to north London. More recently, I have drawn upon the Hall-Carpenter Archives, originally housed at the Centre, in researching its history, and have frequented Gays the Word, which temporarily set up shop there. The Centre displayed many contradictions that require careful deciphering. Here, as in other cases, *Queer Premises* examines the limits of venues, the ways they concretize the past, how they fail to meet needs or expectations as well as how they offer opportunities to shape different futures.

Accommodating an impressive breadth of activities, the Centre existed during from the early 1980s to the early 1990s – a decade of huge socio-economic and political change that followed the social movements of the 1960s and 1970s. It endured through a transitional time of crisis, featuring extreme homophobia, biphobia, transphobia, and social and legal discrimination. These were the years of the AIDS epidemic, prior to the introduction of combination anti-retroviral drugs (HAART) to treat HIV in 1996. The devastating impacts were still unfolding, with many sick and dying. Queer communities were in a state of emergency, which necessitated modes of care and survival, mourning and activism. The 1980s and 1990s AIDS crisis in the UK, which was most acutely concentrated in London, continues to shape experiences. The AIDS Memory UK project, which has recently secured a site for a monument near London's Tottenham Court Road, frames this project as one of collective memory and ongoing support, connecting between the past, present and future.[2] The memory and trauma of the 1980s and 1990s, as well as the collective action, HIV prevention and care that emerged in response, are deeply interwoven with the histories of many of the venues in this book. By the late 1990s, in the wake of the acute stigmatization associated with AIDS, LGBTQ+ rights and social acceptance began to take a more positive trajectory. But lived experiences do not straightforwardly evolve, generations are not neatly defined and rights have not unfolded evenly across these diverse communities.

The funding and governance models of a period of radical state innovation in support of oppressed groups would be decimated in the late 1980s and 1990s. The Centre's switch from grant-funding to social enterprise reflected a pattern as the commercial gay scene expanded apace, mirroring cycles of boom and bust that followed the 'Big Bang' and the deregulation of financial markets. It was not until 2000, in the New Labour era, that London once again had a central governing body, the Greater London Authority, now with a directly elected mayor. The successive phases of London governance since 2000, and the ways that these phases have shaped and been influenced by LGBTQ+ politics and venues and have conditioned their relationships with wider politics and economics, are the subject of Chapter 3. I ask how each mayor has defined 'social infrastructure', and how they have oriented themselves towards LGBTQ+ populations. What ways of engaging with these groups did they initiate or oversee? How did they use their convening power, and that of their administrations, to further equality, especially for intersectionally marginalized groups? How have their attitudes and policies on citizenship, sexual orientation and gender aligned with their conceptions of culture, or their approaches to urban change, or the management of the city at night? If queer venues have long been objects of scrutiny, on the radar of urban authorities, including the police, there has been a gradual recognition in City Hall of the wider and positive ways that they have been generative. The activities of campaigners have led to improved understanding of how these venues comprise heritage as artefacts of the past and present that are vital to supporting LGBTQ+ people into the future. This is reflected in governance structures and practices, and in the use of legislation and planning tools, albeit with varied outcomes.

Surface

From Chapter 3, I discuss how, since the mid-2000s, spates of venue closures have brought these spaces to the surface through widespread media coverage and a lively intra-community discussion about their qualities, their distribution and their inclusiveness or exclusivity. This has featured critique of the exclusions reproduced within dominant commercial scenes. *Queer Premises* does not offer a romantic or nostalgic account, but rather attempts to bring out these qualitative differences and the overall diversity of venues. This includes venues that are among the most radical, queer, socially and culturally distinctive and inclusive, architecturally and aesthetically interesting, altruistic and anti-normative. It also involves investigations into some of the most commercial venues, and their alignments with identity, property and power.

The research for this book emerged from public debate and activism prompted by the venue closures and threats of redevelopment and changes of use that intensified from the mid-2010s. *Queer Premises* contributes to the recent and ongoing collective effort to understand, document and sustain queer venues in London, in parallel with other cities. It draws together a constellation of evidence from plans, maps, archives and ephemera, to interviews, questionnaires, workshops, public events and artworks. It takes its lead from the many campaigns for better scenes and spaces, where queer venues are understood as a vital resource for the present and future.

From Chapter 5, I ask why venues have closed, and examine the consequences of closure. I discuss the distinctive cases of some formative venues in the central neighbourhoods of King's Cross, Angel and the West End. I scrutinize the controversial large-scale redevelopments that prompted the first online activism against closures, and the responses in policy and planning, in the mid-2000s. I consider three radical community-generating venues – The Bell, The Glass Bar and First Out Café – which were initiated or operated by and for women, as well as 'polysexual' nightclubs in the warehouses of ex-industrial King's Cross, and one of London's most commercial LGBTQ+ franchises: G-A-Y.

By the mid-2010s, campaigners were working determinedly to prevent further closures, to protect venues deemed to have community and heritage value, and to reopen some that had already closed. These dedicated volunteers helped to reframe media coverage which had been quick to declare the death of gay space, and which had conveyed losses in too simple terms. The various campaigns nuanced the interpretation of closures and made the case for the continuing need for LGBTQ+ venues. Chapter 6 centres on two long-standing pub, drag and cabaret venues – The Royal Vauxhall Tavern and The Black Cap – which have both been claimed as London's or the UK's first gay pub. It looks at the actions that cohered around threats to these notable venues in the mid-2010s.

Conventionally, as I discuss in Chapters 1 and 4, gays have been associated with pioneer gentrification: they are perceived as establishing creative and residential clusters and increasing property value through processes of renovation. The cases I present in Chapters 5 and 6 suggest that these dynamics demand re-evaluation. In response to the crisis of closures and the threats of redevelopment, some politically eclectic, collaborative and reparative forms of queer preservation have emerged, which contest the aggressive tendency of neoliberal urbanization to consume deeply embedded cultural venues. Propelled by a huge voluntary effort by campaigners, this has involved new uses of planning and heritage instruments; attempts to sustain intergenerationally important sites of sociality, including those marked with significance as sites of historic struggle; and a more visible assertion of some elements of London's queer infrastructure.

As evidence of the oversimplification of commentary on the decline or death of queer space, *Queer Premises* offers case studies of individual venues. By looking from the 1980s to the present, and at a variety of types, it covers an area that has not yet been a central focus for historians of queer London. Placing specific cases of multipurpose venues within a historical understanding of shifts in the structures of urbanization in London over time, it suggests both what is exceptional about LGBTQ+ venues, and how they fit within the wider dynamics of the capital, including its demography, property and the changing values attached to built heritage and social and cultural infrastructure. What are the material circumstances in which venues and scenes have been founded, have flourished or floundered? How do they connect or diverge across distinct communities, periods and functions? What do crises over venue closures suggest about the value of these spaces, the risks that continue to threaten them, and emergent queer collectives and subjectivities? How has the Coronavirus pandemic impacted queer scenes and what typological and programmatic transformations are taking place? Rather than suggest that these crises, or venue closures, point to a neat conclusion, the final chapters of *Queer Premises* offer a more open-ended reflection and discuss nascent venues and the latest interventions to protect extant ones.

1

Queer urbanism

'Gay space' and 'queer space' are terms that have been conceived through a diversity of models and scholarly and activist debates from the 1960s to the present.[1] These discussions have been shaped by the specific social, political and economic settings of different cities, neighbourhoods, venues and social movements, and through transnational exchanges. Venues have featured prominently within the currents of empirical research and theory, as new social imaginaries have been produced between the academy, legal and governmental institutions, and other sites of activism. As premises open, operate or shut down, they have been influenced by wider epistemological and discursive shifts in society, in academic disciplines or in practices of urbanism. There is no single neatly evolving line of debate. Rather, specific preoccupations come into view at given moments, with connections and divergences between scholars and activists in different locations, and new pathways forged through intra-community critique, diverse subjectivities and embodied experiences and changing political and socio-economic conditions.[2]

In this chapter, I foreground the empirical chapters on London venues from the 1980s to the early 2020s by drawing selectively from the long-running debates on gay and queer space. To set the scene I begin with early attempts to account for the presence of gay and lesbian populations from the 1960s, focusing on how venues featured as part of urban networks which had social, geographic and temporal dimensions. I then consider queer space as expanded transdisciplinary fields of debate and praxis after the emergence of queer theory in the 1990s; before turning to queer scholars' interrogations of subjectivity, the social and relations between time and space under neoliberal urban governance in the 2000s. I draw out some tensions between urban and queer theory and engage in detail with a number of methodologically inventive writers from queer, literary, philosophical and performance studies. Driven by the elimination of urban spaces of queer sociality, and attentive to questions of history, memory and social reproduction, my contention is that these authors' work holds potential to inform urban practices, including heritage and planning. This is a response to critiques of planning as a heterosexist domain, which has neglected LGBTQ+ issues.[3] My intention is to contribute to growing scholarship which highlights the potential for queer studies and praxis to generatively disrupt and positively inform urban fields.[4]

In the final part of the chapter, I bring these discussions together and contribute to recent models of LGBTQ+ venues and clusters by arguing that, in London, the diversity of scenes and venues across different periods, generations and geographical locations can be imagined as a dynamic queer infrastructure. LGBTQ+ venues have often been embedded in the everyday and ex-industrial physical infrastructure of cities. They extend across media, through the print and communication technologies of the day. They have international reach through exchanges in culture and activism. Recent threats have shown how their locations in gentrifying neighbourhoods have left them vulnerable within the capital flows of global property portfolios. In response, they have been designated as part of London's 'social infrastructure' in planning and policy. Grounded in the book's profiling of different premises and planning contestations, queer infrastructure encapsulates the variety and layering of scenes and the ways that venues, groups and individuals are subjected or attached to, traverse, or disrupt, dominant models of urban development and social reproduction.

Occupations

North American and European civil rights movements intensified from the middle of the twentieth century, through claims on streets and squares. Grounded in the radical Marxist-infused student movements, gay liberationism in the 1960s and 1970s was inherently a politics of space. It involved the congregation of lesbian and gay populations in specific neighbourhoods; the creation and inhabitation of designated venues such as commercial bars, clubs and community centres; new forms of domesticity that contested cisheterosexist norms; visible appropriations of the street through demonstrations and marches through public space; and the pushing of legal and social frontiers, through the inhabitation and remoulding of institutions of governance, the law and the media.

The gay liberation movement was inextricably linked to other rights-based movements, including currents of feminism where sexuality and gender were positioned as fields of power and utopian imagination.[5] In contesting patriarchy and heterosexism, many of those involved in these movements made it their priority to challenge and subvert the restrictive, disciplinary functions of normative classifications of gender and sexuality under capitalism. Distinct identity-based rights movements deployed resonant arguments and tactics, even if there were antagonisms and numerous objectives within and across them. These movements played out in varied ways, and in some cities with newly visible concentrations of lesbian and gay people, they were embedded in clusters of residences, businesses and services. They included heterogeneous groups and a mix of liberal and radical agendas that were critical of or aligned with capitalism to different degrees.[6]

Memoirs by Gay Liberation Front (GLF) members emphasize that this was a political movement that, having crossed the Atlantic from the United States, saw the advent of a more defiant and concentrated taking of space by distinct groups, as well as the forging of coalitions across them.[7] These accounts stress that the GLF was founded out of dissatisfaction with the existing commercial gay scene in London. Noting the lack of gay media in the late 1960s, GLF activist and historian Lisa Power remarks that:

The bars were no better. At the time of the founding of GLF *Time Out*, the underground-affiliated new listings magazine, listed no bars as 'gay'. It offered a small handful of drag pubs scattered across the capital, as much for the voyeurism of straight tourists as gay men. They included The Black Cap in Camden and the Royal Vauxhall Tavern. Other than this, there were a few known gay pubs in Earls Court, the Salisbury in central London [. . .] and a few members-only drinking clubs in Soho. In any case, you could be rejected for the slightest sign of affection towards another person of the same sex. Time and again, GLF people speak of the unfriendliness of the bars, their 'meat market' quality. Sex was hard to get, but easier than conversation with another homosexual.[8]

Presenting extensive oral testimony, Powers emphasizes the desire to create new social venues. Her book and GLF member Stuart Feather's more recent memoir, *Blowing the Lid,* document how this happened through claiming space in institutions. This included the GLF's first meeting at the London School of Economics (LSE) in 1970.[9] In the following months and years, the spaces of municipal governance would also be repurposed, with the first large-scale dances being held in Kensington Town Hall, and in the buildings of other boroughs sympathetic to the gay cause.[10] GLF demonstrations and protests used the spectacle of drag and theatre to occupy space. As Powers suggests in her reference to *Time Out*, these activities would connect to other localities and extended internationally through the print and telecommunications technologies of the time.

I draw out these themes because they signal some preoccupations that recur through the following chapters. First, that new night scenes are forged out of a sense of dissatisfaction with the commercial provision of venues of the day. Second, new venues are produced through collaboration with activist groups mobilizing connections to other institutions, such as local government and universities. Third, they are formed and extended through inventive multimedia practices and uses of technology.

Networks

In Britain in the 1960s and 1970s, historians and sociologists debated homosexual identity and the politics of visibility.[11] They articulated, in new ways, what Mary McIntosh, sociologist, lesbian, feminist and one of the founding members of the GLF, described in an influential paper, 'The Homosexual Role', as the 'groups and networks of homosexual subculture'.[12] In England, McIntosh argued, these had their roots in the seventeenth century, when the distinct male 'role' of the homosexual emerged.[13] This role adapted to prevailing cultural conceptions, networked into a 'complex of institutional arrangements', including the structures of stigmatization and criminalization that upheld heterosexuality.[14] McIntosh's paper is celebrated as an important milestone in the theoretical and activist social constructionist debates of the 1970s and 1980s.[15] These debates served to dislodge essentialist understandings of sexuality and pathologizing medical and psychiatric accounts through conceiving of homosexuality as a socially produced category, with a controlling function in society.

In *The History of Sexuality*, translated into English in 1978, Michel Foucault used a similar network metaphor, describing sex as:

> [. . .] a historical construct: not a furtive reality that is difficult to grasp, but a great surface network in which the stimulation of bodies, the intensification of pleasures, the incitement to discourse, the formation of special knowledges, the strengthening of controls and resistances, are linked to one another, in accordance with a few major strategies of knowledge and power.[16]

Foucault, like McIntosh, was invested in the revolutionary potential of sexuality, and in the historical project of understanding the production and disciplining of sexual subjectivity at specific moments. Although Foucault's work has had wider visibility and impact, including in urban studies, McIntosh and other authors were coming to similar conclusions about the social construction of sexuality, and in the process generating new understandings of urban order, everyday life and the categories, discourses and technologies of social control.[17] Pointing to the urban dimensions of McIntosh's work, sociologist Jeffrey Weeks, another leading contributor to social constructionist debates, notes how her Marxist framework embedded the homosexual role in 'material developments, especially the clear link suggested between urban growth and subcultural evolution'.[18]

Such accounts opened avenues for lesbian and gay scholars to undertake new empirical research in a range of urban fields. Studies focused specifically on gay and lesbian space began to be published in geography and sociology in the late 1970s and 1980s in the United States. They first mapped spaces associated with gay men and then lesbians.[19] Earlier scholarship had focused on homosexual subculture, the 'gay world' and the interplay between external stigmatization and group identification in producing feelings of difference and alienation.[20] The new studies placed more emphasis on methodically gathered empirical evidence and were less inclined to moralize or pathologize.[21]

Martine Levine's study of US cities, for example, drew from Chicago School sociologists' theories of urban analysis and methods of mapping, fieldwork observation and interviews. Levine developed the concept of the 'gay ghetto', aligning homosexual culture with other stigmatized and segregated groups, such as immigrants.[22] This work was based on classic urban sociological interests in the definition of, and interactions between, social groups and their establishment of specific cultures and institutions. But it also involved novel conceptual formations and methodological challenges. For example, Levine recognized the 'well-known sampling problems' of researching dispersed and historically hidden gay populations which necessitated a 'multi-faceted research strategy'.[23] Whereas maps had until this point been used as a tool to police queer bodies, they now began to be used to produce evidence to better understand homosexual culture and articulate its relationships with place.[24] These methodological challenges continue to be relevant in the production of knowledge about queer urban phenomena today.

Geographer Barbara Weightman developed a sophisticated 'geography of the gay community', introducing a new vocabulary of 'gay spaces', 'gay place' and the 'gay landscape'.[25] The bar was a key site:

Gay community elements include time, space, interaction and relationships, along with knowledge of the straight (heterosexual) world and certain unique psychic and experiential dimensions of the gay world. Certain institutions are important in this community. Of primary importance is the gay bar – the most common element of the gay landscape. Other institutions include baths, bookstores, theatres, churches, community centers, hotels, clothing stores and a variety of others which cater to the gay population.[26]

Through the imagination of a network of actors and institutions, these early studies contained claims to the tangibility of gay community, in contrast with earlier understandings of a gay 'underworld where membership is "attained through psychopathology"'.[27] Weightman points to how communities were being formed through a rapidly expanding 'organizational network' of activists, contending that these offered geographers possibilities to understand 'evolutionary and structural patterns'.[28]

Sociologist Manuel Castells' study of the Castro district in San Francisco mapped the newly visible gay male community in comparison with straight-dominated neighbourhoods.[29] He concluded that

Men have sought to dominate, and one expression of this domination has been spatial. [. . .] Women have rarely had these territorial aspirations: their world attaches more importance to relationships and their networks are ones of solidarity and affection.[30]

Castells' study argued that women's networks were less traceable because of an imbalance in property ownership. To note the patriarchal lineage of property was not controversial. But feminist and lesbian scholars were critical of the essentialization of feminine attributes and Castells' suggestion that lesbian spaces and cultures were not empirically knowable.[31]

In this early period of dedicated scholarship, which traversed different scales, discussions revolved around gay and lesbian groups' concentrated presence, their networks of designated spaces and their practices and impacts on the character of neighbourhoods and cities. This included attempts to delineate these populations' relationships with economic markets: as sometimes challenging or interrupting norms of binary gender and sexuality, reproduced through property ownership, marriage, inheritance, or modes of domesticity.

By the mid-1980s there was an emergent focus on gays as agents of change, imbricated within processes of renovation, preservation and gentrification – innovating and reproducing distinctive cultures in ways that both reflected and redirected wider urban dynamics.[32] The range of emergent scholarship in the United States acknowledged what Mickey Lauria and Lawrence Knopp called the 'gay factor' in urban renaissance – meaning the interplay between gay (mostly male) identities, gentrification and redevelopment.[33] But these scholars critiqued the lack of any in-depth analysis of this topic and set out to interrogate it. Knopp studied gay identities and networks as they are produced within and against capitalist modes of production and reproduction, upheld through monogamous heterosexuality and patriarchy.[34]

Queer Premises builds on the insights of such work, understanding venues as part of a network of relations, which is dynamic, with scenes that overlap and cross-reference different times and places, rather than evolving in a linear fashion. The following chapters further underscore the patrilineal networks that have shaped scenes and venues and emphasize the cultural and nightlife innovations that have been propelled through spaces set up by and for women. In similarity with earlier studies, queer counterpublics' own mapping and publishing practices, including political pamphlets and city and bar guides, are important sources, alongside a variety of qualitative and quantitative evidence in different media.

Turning space

From the 1990s, scholars from a wider range of disciplines paid increasing attention to sexuality, gender and space, the categories through which they were understood, and the intersections between them. Queer scholars' deconstruction of texts and institutions opened new potentials for thinking about cities, architecture, space and place, and the concept of 'queer space' emerged.[35] New scholarship in architecture and geography was infused by works now celebrated for the ways they propelled queer studies, such as Judith Butler's *Gender Trouble: Feminism and the Subversion of Identity* (1990) and Eve Kosofsky Sedgwick's *Epistemology of the Closet* (1990).[36] These texts problematized binary categorizations and the ways these were naturalized, re-read canonical texts alert to new cadences and radically contested normative heterosexist and patriarchal constructions of sex, sexuality and gender.

The word 'queer' had been a term of insult but was reappropriated by gay and lesbian activists in the 1980s.[37] The formulation 'queer theory' was initially intended as a provocation, used by the cultural theorist Teresa de Lauretis as a conference title in 1990.[38] Queer was a political orientation that troubled the fixity of categories, including identity classifications, and called for definitions to be destabilized.[39] It soon became institutionalized, as if its meaning were agreed. Gender and queer theorist David M. Halperin has written about the contradictions and confusions that arose as 'queer' became understood as a postmodern identity, a presentation that was implicitly more advanced than lesbian or gay.[40] Queer scholarship's focus on the organizing structure of discourses on gender and sexuality means that the terms and categories used are always a matter of debate, as are the inclusion and representation of different groups and political orientations. The literature on queer spaces is one prism through which these debates can be viewed. *Queer Premises* considers how these terms and categories circulate between venues, urban governance and planning.

In the UK, geographers David Bell, Jon Binnie, Julia Cream and Gill Valentine experimented with Butler's ideas in urban analysis to elucidate how sexual identity influences the use and interpretation of space, and how the social production of space influences the performance of sexual identities.[41] These researchers highlighted that the straight default of urban space was not an essential attribute but was actively produced. They posited 'queer space', appropriated by queer bodies, as an alternative to, or reclamation of, heterosexual space.[42]

In *Queer Constellations*, literature scholar Dianne Chisholm presents an expansive synthesis of the geographies, sociologies and histories of sexuality to foreground analyses of queer novelists' evocations of cities and urban life.[43] She looks to the ways that interdisciplinary writers and curators proposed queer agendas for architecture and urbanism in the 1990s, in parallel with the scholarship that was emerging in geography. At that time, alongside feminist scholars and practitioners, queer designers and curators advanced the discourse on sexuality and gender in architecture through speculative writing, designs and installations and attempts to queer the architectural canon.[44]

The multimedia exhibition *Queer Space* (1994), at Storefront for Art and Architecture in New York City, was an important site for these discussions. It was organized by a collective of theorists and practitioners from architecture, literary studies and queer studies who had a shared interest in the relations between gender, sex, sexuality, queerness and the built environment.[45] The plans were not fully realized due to practical constraints, but the exhibition – a springboard for discussion and an exercise in multimedia and transdisciplinary curation – was influential in shaping subsequent accounts of queer space in multiple disciplines.[46] The architectural theorist Oliver Vallerand has recently noted that the group used the exhibition to create a queer space, which extended across different media and into the city, fostering discussion across different publics, sites and historical contexts. Storefront, as a public gallery with a porous and interactive street frontage, was ideal for this. The project exemplifies transdisciplinary queer urbanism: a praxis which traverses activism, theory, history, art and built environment expertise and spatial practices.[47]

Chisholm sets queer space debates within the framework of the poststructuralist 'spatial turn' in urban theory, in which Henri Lefebvre's *The Production of Space* (1974, translated 1991) and Michel Foucault's concept of 'other spaces' or 'heterotopias' (1986) were important markers.[48] She points to Lefebvre's interest in the appropriation of the city, as liveable space, through the body, and his call, in her queer reading, for 'coming revolutions to take back the city for nonreproductive (homo?)sexuality'.[49] The 1990s work on sexuality, gender and space drew on these texts, as well as the longer trajectories of critical writing about the urban experiences of marginal or dissident groups in the work of the Frankfurt School. Chisholm follows queer space back to these authors' Marxist and psychoanalytically informed accounts of the materiality and experience of the early twentieth-century city. In the queer literature she studies, she pays attention to the interweaving of collective memory, specific cities and sites, and sexual subjectivities.[50] Arguing that 'when the archaic and enduring can no longer be sighted amidst renovations, the cue to remember, remembrance itself, is lost', she points to the colonial and amnesiac tendencies of late-twentieth-century urbanization. This operates primarily through modes of clearance, destroying 'lively gay space' – spaces of cruising and intermingling.[51]

In response, Chisholm takes up Walter Benjamin's writing as a critical method that mirrors the fragmentary, vivid, multidirectional, polytemporal and experimental accounts of the city in works of twentieth-century gay and lesbian literature.[52] In Benjamin's writing, constellations illuminate the contradictions of capitalist cities and processes of urbanization, without resorting to totalizing interpretations.[53] In queer urban writing, Chisholm finds parallels with Benjamin's preoccupations and his montage-like dialectical images.[54] The texts she works with 'glimpse utopia, dystopia and heterotopia at once, foreseeing with hindsight the idealization and ruinization of what the city could become, as well as the fetishization and fossilization of what it never really was'.[55] Samuel Delany's *Times Square Red, Times Square Blue* (1999) – an autoethnography and theorization of the loss of spaces of social 'contact' through the elimination of porn cinemas associated with the redevelopment of Times Square in New York – is an exemplar held up by Chisholm (and other theorists of queer space) for its account of the implications of such profit-driven urban purification processes for queers.[56] For Delany, such venues, commercial as they are, create opportunities for social 'contact' which are deeper in the democratising and utopian political possibilities they offer than mere networking. He is one of several novelists Chisholm selects who attend to the city as an erotically charged terrain, where 'perversity [. . .] characterises social-sexual relations in commodity exchange and circulation'.[57] Their accounts render queer sexual subjectivities that are constructed within and disruptive of the phantasmagoria of the gentrifying, deeply commodified, late capitalist city.[58] They articulate unofficial, overlooked histories, which counter the myths of linear progress bound into urban renewal, through fragments, layering and sensitivity to perceptual saturation and multi-sensory encounters with the past.

Out of time

Chisholm's reflections on the entanglements of commodity capitalism and gay spaces and practices point to a long-running debate where urban and queer theory intersect. This revolves around the extent to which neo-Marxian analyses of urbanization, with their focus on political economy, capital and class, have appropriately integrated the insights of queer, feminist, critical race and postcolonial scholars on questions of social difference and the divergence of experiences. This debate features feminist and queer responses to geographies of postmodernism the 1990s and early 2000s, and recent critiques of 'planetary urbanism', one of the dominant theoretical discussions in contemporary urban theory, which is grounded Lefebvre's work.[59] It goes beyond urban theory, however, in that it includes critiques of the heterosexist foundations of Marxism, psychoanalysis and social theory.

Michael Warner's influential and still vibrant anthology, *Fear of a Queer Planet* (1993), which took stock of lesbian and gay and queer politics after the postmodern turn, is an important reference in these debates. Warner critiques not just the neglect of sexuality, but the active presence of heterosexism and homophobia in social theory. In psychoanalytic and Marxist conceptions of the social he locates blind spots on sexuality and gender, which pose problems for feminists and queer scholars alike.[60] 'Marxist thought', he writes, 'is embedded in a history of sexuality, reproductivism, and homosociality in a way that prevents it from grasping these problems as conditioning its own project'.[61]

Taking stock of lesbian and gay and queer politics, Warner also points to several internal contradictions and questions. These resonate with the debates that will be encountered in *Queer Premises*. First, he notes tensions caused by the disparate politics of those involved in the drive for lesbian and gay rights: from the conservative to the liberal to the radical. The experience of being queer, for Warner, requires the creation of a social space to exist. But not all those invested in gay and lesbian politics ascribe to radical queer politics propelled towards fundamental social change. Second, he observes that while social constructionism generated specific accounts of the formation of sexuality, the fundamental question of how the social is defined, and by whom, was neglected. In these debates he notes the dominant voice of white, middle-class, gay, male activists. Third, he points to the ways that contemporary struggles are characterized by tensions between local constructions of sexuality and universalizing rights agendas. Hence, he calls for queer theorists to 'be more alert to the globalising – and localising – tendencies of our theoretical languages'.[62] Finally, despite the dominance, in Anglo-American discourse, of a concept of 'gay and lesbian community', Warner questions what this refers to, arguing that 'much of gay and lesbian history has to do with noncommunity' or with an imaginary of dispersal rather than localization.[63] With such themes in mind, in this book I look at how LGBTQ+ collectivity has been shaped or expressed by venues (or threats to them) at specific moments; their distribution and the ways they locate migrant and displaced queer subjects; and their materialisation of interacting local and global forces.

For Warner, the different relationships that people with minority sexualities and gender expressions have with place, often involving dislocation or relocation, is a complicating factor in the possibility for these groups to imagine and create community. As with earlier studies of gay place, and histories of gay and lesbian liberation, venues were central in his account:

> In the lesbian and gay movement, to a much greater degree than in any comparable movement, the institutions of culture-building have been market-mediated: bars, discos, special services, newspapers, magazines, phone lines, resorts, urban commercial districts. Nonmarket forms of association that have been central to other movements – churches, kinship, traditional residence – have been less available for queers. This structural environment has meant that the institutions of queer culture have been dominated by those with capital: typically, middle-class white men.[64]

Licensed premises, like the dance floors of nightclubs studied by dance and club culture researcher Fiona Buckland, are an important component in 'queer lifeworlds', defined as 'environments created by their participants that contain many voices, many practices, and not a few tensions'.[65] In the London context, from the days of the GLF to the present, paying attention to the ways that market capitalism has shaped specific urban movements, identities, spaces and media has been vital as activists have worked to deconstruct exclusions, create counter-scenes and imagine better worlds. Yet, as Warner suggests, generalizing theories have been limited in elucidating these entanglements, underscoring the need for detailed case studies, such as those presented in the following chapters.

Feminist and queer responses to some of the dominant Marxist accounts of postmodernism followed similar lines to Warner's critique.[66] At the beginning of the 1990s, writing on the work of urban and cultural theorists David Harvey and Fredric Jameson, the art historian Rosalyn Deutsche challenged the idea of 'postmodernism as an embracing historical condition in which the valorization of difference conceals the spatioeconomic relations that underlie the totality of late capitalist society'.[67] Her position was that in their totalizing theories, Harvey and Jameson demonstrated a 'refusal of difference', and of feminists' accounts of representation, disavowing their 'own partial and fragmented condition'.[68] The neglect of social difference, and the homogenization of 'social movements', simultaneously limited studies of postmodernism, and limited understandings of history, constructing this as somehow 'constituted apart from subjects'.[69]

In gender, sexuality and queer studies, other writers whose work is important to my framing of Queer Premises, such as gender theorist Jack Halberstam and Cuban American performance theorist José Esteban Muñoz, were also sufficiently troubled by these (straight, white, cismale, universalizing) geographies of postmodernism to write extensive critiques. Halberstam's In A Queer Time and Place: Transgender Bodies, Subcultural Lives (2005) contested the contention that sexuality was an obstruction to 'the "real" work of activism'.[70] He takes issue with the superficial attention to the politics of sexual identity. Instead, he calls for a more nuanced understanding of queer lifeworlds, formed through specific historical contexts and traumas, which re-script space and time in eccentric ways – refusing or disrupting normativity and the structures of power which are produced by and sustain capitalism. Halberstam critiques Marxist accounts of postmodernity for neglecting queerness, sexuality and gender as they seek to denaturalize constructs of time and space: they are dependent on Foucault and his analysis of power, but neglect the discussions of queer kinship and networks put forward in The History of Sexuality.[71] In response, Halberstam's theory of queer time and space sets out to show how queer subjects disconnect from normative logics of lifecycles, inheritance, progress and success.[72] These insights inform Queer Premises' analyses of venues, the activities and campaigns linked to them, and the outcomes of urban redevelopment upon queer subjects.

Muñoz also responded to Harvey's A Brief History of Neoliberalism (2005) for its dismissal of queer and feminist 'struggles for sexual liberation' as a 'demand for lifestyle diversification'.[73] For Muñoz, Harvey is an exemplar of white Marxist scholarship, which neglects the Frankfurt School's 'interest in the transformative force of eros and its implicit relationship to political desire'.[74] Harvey's position is that identity-based social movements lead to individualistic politics that weaken union solidarities, undermine the importance of the state and are easily co-opted and depoliticized within neoliberal consumerism.[75] For Muñoz, Harvey's reductive treatment of sexuality and gender as 'narcissistic' concerns of 'bourgeois urban culture' is indicative of leftist North American thinkers' disregard of 'the experiences of working class and ethnic-racial queers'.[76]

It is uncontroversial to say that identity politics, including sexuality and gender, are commodified in consumer culture. Yet Harvey's account of the rise of neoliberalism in the United States and United Kingdom shows little awareness of the history and character of gay and lesbian or queer social movements. He points out that 'a noble rearguard action against (Thatcherite) neoliberal policies was mounted in many a municipality', citing the radicalism of the Greater London Council under Ken Livingstone.[77] But he neglects to detail the specific forms of strongly identity-based gay and lesbian, feminist and anti-racist New Left socialism of this period, and the ways in which these radical politics were embedded in local government institutions, seeding, or accelerating, important civic society organizations and attitudinal change. These topics feature in the next chapter, in my account of the history of the London Lesbian and Gay Centre.

Hopeful transport

As discussed earlier, Warner's account of queer politics and social theory in the early 1990s suggested that queer experience, and the production of the social, are shaped by rejection and 'noncommunity'.[78] In the 1990s and 2000s, a debate sometimes referred to as the 'anti-social thesis' in queer theory raised similar questions regarding the possibilities of queer social reproduction, property, kinship, community and civic participation and the rejection of heteronormative models for understanding psychic and social life. Literary theorist Leo Bersani's *Homos* (1995), and its challenge to a 'rage for respectability . . . in gay life today' was one of the earliest propositions in this discussion.[79] Bersani's provocation was that homosexuality 'necessitates a massive redefining of relationality', through embracing a position of social and political unacceptability, and he therefore treated the drive for marriage and parenting rights with suspicion.[80] This prompted multiple reflections on queer social reproduction, on relations with the past, present and future.[81] The debates in the 1990s and early 2000s included radical queer critiques of the drive for particular rights and modes of assimilation in the LGBT movement. Lee Edelman's *No Future: Queer Theory and the Death Drive* (2004), for example, rallied against the pursuit of 'generational sameness' and argued for 'disidentification from the promise of futurity'.[82] Mainstream identity politics were argued by Lisa Duggan to be 'homonormative', and to promote neoliberal forms of newness, hope and progress in place of radically queer social relations.[83] These ideas are valuable for their potential to inform discussions of queer social reproduction through venues and other forms of built heritage.

As a queer studies text within these debates, Muñoz's *Cruising Utopia: The Then and There of Queer Futurity* (2009) demonstrates how embedded in the urban they were: in the impulse of neoliberal governance to eliminate queer space, and in the continuing possibility for queers to construct hopeful 'urban landscapes of astonishment' within the cracks of the quotidian city.[84] Muñoz's work responded to the threat to public sex cultures and tightening of regulation of bars and cabaret venues prompted by the policies of Rudy Giuliani during his tenure as mayor of New York City (1994–2001).[85] *Cruising Utopia* critically engaged with these pressures on New York City at the turn of the century via reflections on the 1950s and 1960s, around the moment of the Stonewall rebellion in 1969. Illuminating queer histories, struggles and utopian imaginations, Muñoz discusses a wide range of periods and places, rendered through visual artworks, performance, poetry and ephemera.

Delany, Halberstam and Chisholm are also critics of what the latter calls the 'sterile rezoning policies' of Giuliani's mayoralty, enacted through licensing and policing.[86] These queer responses to the sanitization of New York offer an alternative to dominant Marxist urban theory. Simultaneously, they challenge a 'merely identitarian logic' in pragmatic, assimilationist, homonormative gay and lesbian politics.[87] Muñoz describes such gay identity politics, which predominantly serve the white gay male majority, as 'basic networking', and suggests how such politics might underpin the mode of neoliberal urbanization threatening queer venues.[88] A departure from the uses of the network metaphor discussed earlier, here it illuminates qualitative differences in the forms of support and kinship across LGBTQ+ populations, forged through varied relationships with power and capital.

The politics of 'basic networking' are, for Muñoz, embedded within – if not determined by – the logics of certain night-spaces, from the regulations that govern them, to the fashion and dancing styles of their patrons.[89]Against the rigid linearity of straight time, neatly articulated through licensing laws, the fixing of venues in normative exercises of zoning or mapping and their potential extinction, Muñoz emphasizes the multidirectional ways that queer venues and practices 'transport' minoritized subjects.[90] To subvert the 'attack on cultures of sexual dissidence' – which continued under mayor Michael Bloomberg – he looks to German idealism and the Frankfurt School.[91]

Muñoz 'create[s] an opening in queer thought' via the Jewish German Marxist philosopher Ernst Bloch's writing on utopia, and his treatise *The Principles of Hope* (1986), largely written in exile on the US East Coast, during and after the Second World War.[92] In these volumes Bloch compares different ways of engaging the past, present and future in Marxist materialism, German Idealism, psychoanalysis and Romanticist and Expressionist art. Core to his work is an idea which he had articulated by 1907, of the 'not-yet-conscious', the preconscious of the past, present and future, which intellectual, political and cultural work or events have the capacity to illuminate.[93] In Bloch's conception of heritage, the past has 'undischarged hope-content', which can elicit fresh meaning in new contexts. The concept also refers to the possibility of articulating that which is otherwise obscure in the present, and to open thinking and experience beyond perceived horizons, through premonitory 'forward dawning'.[94]

Against 'banal optimism', and the politics of pragmatism or individualism, Muñoz takes up Bloch's 'concrete utopias', as a methodology of 'educated hope'.[95] Concrete utopias are differentiated from mere wishful thinking detached from material conditions. They are also pitched against narrow or depoliticized empiricism, venturing beyond the status quo, in ways that are 'relational to historically situated struggles, a collectivity that is actualized or potential'.[96] It is easy to appreciate Muñoz's attraction to Bloch's work, which he takes up brilliantly in relation to queer art practices. He turns to Bloch's writings in an empoweringly open and flexible mode of critical engagement, and one that challenges knowledge hierarchies between philosophy, art practice and everyday activism.[97]

Bloch had an idiosyncratic, expressionist way of writing and was undogmatic in his approach to different intellectual and artistic movements. He was also an exile who was somewhat ostracized within the Frankfurt School. These factors, and the delay between the original publications and translated editions, meant that his work was not taken up as much as some of his peers. The polytemporality and musicality of his writing, and his focus on the imagery of light, twilight and night-light, on mysticism and transcendence, connect well with Muñoz's interests. For him. queer modes are modes of potentiality and anticipation. These aesthetics and practices create 'networks of queer belongings', which draw from the past to survive and critically engage in the present, while offering hopeful transport to illuminate better futures (the 'not-yet-here').[98]

Muñoz models a nuanced approach to identity and attachment, for what he terms 'minoritarian subjects' and counterpublics – specifically queer people of colour and performance practitioners. For him, identity is a site of struggle, which becomes 'formatted' in specific places and times. It involves both attachment to 'subcultural circuits', and the 'survival strategy' of *dis*identification – that is, necessary but semi-detached relations with 'toxic' representations, such as cliched popular culture stereotypes of minority sexualities. As Laurent Berlant notes, disidentification for Muñoz is not simply the opposite of identification.[99] This rejection, within the anti-social debate, of the binary identification/disidentification, is useful. My investigations in *Queer Premises* are informed by Muñoz's reading of venues as at once entangled within the neoliberal dynamics of urban governance and LGBTQ+ politics, offering spaces of hope and transport, and causing frustration, disappointment and disidentificatory responses across heterogeneous populations.

Muñoz was one of those who detected an underlying conservatism in the politics of Edelman and Leo Bersani and others.[100] He named the anti-social thesis the 'gay white man's last stand', considering it a reaction to perceived contamination of sexuality by other lines of difference, such as race and gender, and he critiqued the rejection of coalitionist politics.[101] *Cruising Utopia* did not straightforwardly reject proponents of the anti-social stance, instead proposing a 'reparative reading'.[102] Problematizing the romanticization of the negative, and the acceptance of 'no future', through Bloch he instead proposes queerness as collectivity and historically and politically situated utopian futurity.[103] He writes:

> Some will say that all we have are the pleasures of this moment, but we must never settle for that minimal transport; we must dream and enact new and better pleasures, other ways of being in the world, and ultimately new worlds. Queerness is a longing that propels us onward, beyond romances of the negative and toiling in the present. Queerness is that thing that lets us feel that this world is not enough, that indeed something is missing.[104]

Muñoz's study of cabaret scenes in New York City illuminated the radical queer politics that were embedded in venues, ephemera and performance practices. But it also suggested how these fragile resources were being restricted, and incrementally eliminated, suggesting a need to protect them and activate their possibilities as conduits for historical knowledge and social change.

Queer feminist philosopher Sara Ahmed shares with Muñoz an understanding of queerness as affect rather than individual identity, a hopeful and collective political project oriented towards radical horizons.[105] Ahmed's *Queer Phenomenology* (2006) opens new avenues into the work of philosophers who have been influential in discussions of architecture and spatial theory, such as Martin Heidegger and Edmund Husserl, by incorporating evidence from the lives and embodiments of subjects – queer, migrant, lesbian – who have conventionally been excluded from this canon.

20 *Queer Premises*

Like Halberstam and Muñoz, she articulates queer temporalities that are at odds with 'straight time'.[106] Following lines, Ahmed writes:

> [. . .] involves forms of social investment. Such investments 'promise' return (if we follow this line, then 'this' or 'that' will follow), which might sustain the very will to keep going. Through such investments in the promise of return, subjects *reproduce the lines that they follow*. In a way, thinking about the politics of 'lifelines' helps us to rethink the relationship between inheritance (the lines that we are given as our point of arrival into familial and social space) and reproduction (the demand that we return the gift of the line by extending that line). It is not automatic that we reproduce what we inherit, or that we always convert our inheritance into possessions [original emphasis].[107]

For Ahmed, queer subjects are often dislocated by 'sideways moments', which involve loss and trauma, but which are generative.[108]

Muñoz and Ahmed enrich our understanding of the embodied experience of place and the queering of practices of social reproduction. They contribute to a trajectory on affect and language in queer theory. Following Butler's interrogation of categories of gender, sex and sexuality as they perform in different legal, philosophical, political and social frameworks, they engage linguist J. L. Austin's analysis of speech acts.[109] Austin draws attention to the 'felicitous' or 'infelicitous' qualities of language. Speech acts have the power to *do* something as well as say something, but they always eventually fail. Muñoz uses these ideas to argue that hope is an important structure. Since disappointment is built into hope, 'affective reanimation needs to transpire if a disabling political pessimism is to be displaced'.[110]

One aspect of Ahmed's work that is especially relevant to *Queer Premises* focuses on the function of diversity categories as they attach to institutions and bodies.[111] She argues that, in considering diversity policies and practices, we need to 'think about words, texts, objects, and bodies, to follow them around, to explore what they do and do not do, when they are put into action'.[112] These insights are useful in paying attention to the operations of identity categories and vocabularies in the institutions of urban governance, and in the debates within and across queer communities about different spaces. They underpin my analyses of LGBTQ+ venues as they are discursively produced in different contexts.

As this chapter has shown, lesbian and gay and queer scholarship has long had an empirical focus on urban sites, and on the investigation of networks that are both spatial and temporal. In recent years, however, there has been a renewed interest in the materiality of queer spaces, whether neighbourhoods, buildings or landscapes, as places of embedded memory and heritage that are identified with past and present-day LGBTQ+ populations and social movements. If earlier discussions of lesbian and gay space focused on the visibility of these groups, their occupations of space and their involvement and agency within urban change, there is now a growing body of work which, in common with Muñoz, is propelled by the effects of neoliberal urbanization processes in eliminating established venues and clusters.[113] Against this backdrop, queer heritage has become one of the most transdisciplinary, international and dynamic axes in academic, public and policy debates and activism on LGBTQ+ issues.[114] The remaining chapters of *Queer Premises* contribute to these discussions, detailing how conflicts arise when queer sites are threatened, overlooked or misunderstood within the conventional practices of planning.

In their book *If Memory Serves: Gay Men, AIDS and the Promise of the Queer Past* (2011), literature and visual culture scholars Christopher Castiglia and Christopher Reed advance understandings of queer heritage through theoretical and empirical contributions. They critique a 'denial of memory sites' in queer theory following the AIDS epidemic of the 1980s and 1990s, linking this to a form of collective amnesia and commenting that

> [. . .] the sacrifice of spaces and rituals of memory to the lure of amnesia has weakened gay communities, both our connections to one another and our ability to imagine, collectively and creatively, alternative social presents and futures for ourselves.[115]

For these authors, a 'de-generational unremembering' of the past, in which social struggles and traumas have been sanitized, has been driven by a neoconservative, homonormative agenda of social acceptability.[116] They argue that theories of queer space, wary of essentialism, have overemphasized its fleeting, appropriative, performative and embodied qualities, locating it always in a perpetual present or the future, neglecting the ways that identities are historically and geographically embedded.[117] They look to a selection of US and European sites and monuments to consider how these can activate historical knowledge and collective memory.

These authors concur with Muñoz's claim for the potential for pre-AIDS sexual cultures to nourish utopian possibility in the present (the mid-2000s).[118] They share Muñoz's celebration of the affective power of memory but are keen to draw some distinctions with their own position. They argue that Muñoz's understanding of the past is 'defensive and ambivalent' and that he overemphasizes the role of memory work to reimagine the future, rather than to remake the present through processing loss. It is right that Muñoz emphasizes lack, rather than loss, in accounting for the ways that marginal subjects construct what he terms a 'queer relational orbit, a force field of belonging.'[119] Yet loss, or imminent loss, of spaces of contact through urban redevelopment are at the foundation of his study. His is very much a project located in archives, including those of losses wrought by HIV/AIDS. He also attends to the 'formalizing and formatting of gay and lesbian identities' in earlier social movements, in ways that seem aligned with Castiglia and Reed's call for attention to memory sites.[120] To suggest that this work is too invested in futurity, or denies historical sites and connections, is to overlook Muñoz's emphasis on working with artworks and ephemera to understand the 'particularity of the Greenwich Village lifeworld of the 1960s', and the ways that he grounds analyses of queer sites in his own lived experience and emphasizes, via Bloch, the importance of the past to survive in or illuminate the present.[121] It may also be to fetishize certain archives and typologies of monument over those that Muñoz invokes: the intangible traces of 'urban landscapes of astonishment', and the networks of those precarious queer subjects whose foothold in property is least secure.[122]

Muñoz's method and the range of evidence he engages align with Chisholm's call for historical approaches that push beyond 'more traditional, empirical (demographic and geographical) demarcations of queer space'.[123] Such approaches open possibilities to recognize and articulate overlooked queer urban histories: a concern central in this book. They offer a way of bridging between the earlier empirical studies of the physical spaces linked to lesbian and gay populations with later poststructuralist theories of queer space as 'a practice, production and performance of space beyond just the mere habitation of built and fixed structures'.[124]

Queer infrastructure

Discussions of queer heritage and memory, have informed geographer Johan Andersson's work on London and other cities. In a body of work that has taken shape since the mid-2000s, Andersson has examined interactions between neoliberalism, queer nightlife spaces and gay identity politics. His archival research and cultural analyses have focused, for example, on the gay media, the aesthetics of venue interiors, and the elimination of cruising spaces within heritage-driven processes of urbanization.[125] His analysis brings Muñoz's critique of Harvey, Duggan's conceptualization of the neoliberal shift to homonormative politics, and accounts of the interplay between AIDS, gentrification and memorialization in New York, to the London context.[126]

The empirical work I present in *Queer Premises* builds on these accounts. It similarly moves beyond binary categorizations of commercial venues as either radical or homonormative and shares an understanding of London's heterogeneous local scenes as being shaped by transnational exchanges in culture and activism. It further considers the intertwining of global and local forces that shape venues through focusing on planning and governance in the 1980s, and around two waves of venue closures in the mid-2000s and mid-2010s. I focus on the collaborations and interventions that were instigated in attempts to improve, protect, archive, reactivate and establish venues.

I have set out some of the different positions within the anti-social thesis debate as it provides a useful frame to consider the varied preoccupations and actions of the LGBTQ+ campaigners, artists, businesses and communities, policy makers and professionals involved with the venues discussed in the following chapters. These are groups that have responded to venue closures, the conditions that threaten them and the pressures experienced by LGBTQ+ populations, by engaging with processes of heritage and community designation in planning. How does the activation of heritage and planning instruments within urban governance sit with radical queer politics? Can these systems be queered? Or do they always protect the status quo, reproducing established relations of dominance and subjugation?

Read literally, works that adopt a negative, anti-social stance imply that there is *no future* in making alignments with practices of social reproduction that have often been used conservatively. We should note, though, that the proponents of anti-sociality were critiqued for flattening the distinction between 'structural claims about the unconscious from empirical claims about culture'.[127] Within these debates, and in the work of Halberstam, Muñoz and Ahmed, especially, there are signposts towards affirmative approaches, which recognize the need and opportunity for groups to connect and sustain themselves into the future, through material connections with the past and the messy, contradictory present. I use the term 'queer infrastructure' to indicate these dynamic relations, which include and extend beyond venues.

Infrastructures, conventionally speaking, are highly charged symbolic networks that bring people and services together. They are physical, fixed and materially layered, but also conduits for transport. They are characterized by replaceability, adaptiveness and extendibility. Through its historical associations, this collective term for substructural parts signals both underground spaces and defensive fortifications.[128] These resonate appropriately since the spaces that have served queer uses and LGBTQ+ populations have often had to be defensive and subterranean. They still are, of course, in many places. They have often been situated in physical infrastructure or ex-industrial sites, camouflaged within the everyday fabric: some of the examples explored in the following chapters include nightclubs in nineteenth-century railway arches, canalside storage warehouses and Victorian stables. Infrastructure also helps to understand how these venues are networked, more than the sum of their parts, to provide collective resources, albeit that these resources are limited, precarious and diffuse.

Queer infrastructure connects policy and theory, too. In urban scholarship, and in many areas of the humanities and built environment, there is a current theoretical interest in infrastructure. In postcolonial urban theory, infrastructure expands to articulate not just physical systems but forms of collaboration among marginalized people who are most likely to be both the producers and precarious inhabitants of those systems.[129] This recent extension of the term sees it deployed to envisage the dynamic interactions between technologies, subjectivities, forms of collectivity, care and urban space.

How do queer scholar-activism and other forms of cultural work connect to these discussions? For queer theorist Laurent Berlant, writing in the context of austerity politics in the United States, in transitional times, times of crisis, glitches reveal infrastructural failures. Berlant argues that *infrastructures of the social* arise in the 'hoarded infrastructure of capital', supporting life where capital and the state have failed, pointing to new ways of being together.[130] 'Queer' is one of many prefixes used by Berlant to open out from the concept of infrastructure.[131] They contrast the movement of infrastructure with the repetition and congealing functions of institutions. In Berlant's poetic analysis, infrastructure is a flexible concept, which includes a sense of dynamism and structure and practice. Berlant's recent discussion can be connected back to the earlier empirical studies of newly visible lesbian and gay urban networks as complex systems of material and immaterial things, institutions and interactions.

Infrastructural categories, as they are articulated in legal and policy discourse, have recently provided opportunities for queer subjects. Under the latest mayoral administration in London, 'LGBT+ night-time venues' have been designated as 'social and cultural infrastructure'. In Chapters 2 and 3 I trace this category back to New Left notions of 'infrastructures of cultural distribution' in the 1980s and through politically distinct iterations in the London Plan from 2004 to the present version. The current 'Cultural Infrastructure Map' places LGBTQ+ venues alongside a wide range of typologies, from cinemas and museums to community centres, attributing cultural, social and economic value to resources that are often precarious and overlooked.[132]

As a policy metaphor, 'community infrastructure' has a longer history. At the start of the 2000s, urban planning historian Michael Hebbert accounted for London's waves of migration by describing how different populations have cumulatively built 'community infrastructure' and 'fixed social capital', over long periods, through diasporic exchanges with other places, including former colonies.[133] Hebbert did not consider migration, or social infrastructure, in relation to sexual and gender diversity, however. Writing about cosmopolitanism in Spitalfields, East London, in the early 2000s, these were aspects that geographer Gavin Brown took up in a discussion that referred to a 'small and relatively diffuse *infrastructure of gay venues*' [my italics].[134] Although he did not develop this idea, it is suggestive of a model of queer space that is both more dynamic and flexible than the 'evolutionary model' of gay districts that economist Alan Collins proposed to describe the different stages in the formalization London's Soho as a gay district.[135]

I extrapolate from Berlant's analysis that queer infrastructure is what diverse inhabitants of the city are making through the creation of venues, networks and events. It works with and against the types of built fabric, and other structures and media, that these have inhabited. In today's terms, LGBTQ+ venues are the most visible, formal examples, and this is what I mainly focus on in *Queer Premises*. But Berlant's theorization of infrastructure and the commons suggests that queer infrastructure creates and anticipates new ways of being together, which might riff from as well as challenge historically formatted identities and would trouble the alignment and co-option of modern Western identity categories with capitalism as it manifests in different times and places.

Queer infrastructure extends from earlier models of LGBTQ+ venue networks and cluster formations. These conceptualisations have recently been moving away from the enclave conception, inherited from Chicago School urbanists, of bounded (if porous and changing) formations which evolve in a linear developmental fashion.[136] Rather, they use the metaphor of a mosaic, a series of archipelegos, or more dynamically, for the planner Petra Doan, a 'solar system' subject to 'orbital dynamics'.[137] In Doan's model, centrifugal forces pull LGBTQ+ populations to urban clusters while centripetal flows, such as the atmospheres of exclusion experienced by minorities in mainstream scenes, or the the negative impacts of redevelopment, disperse or repel them. Queer infrastructure builds on these spatial models. It suggests the interconnectivity of dispersed and constantly shifting LGBTQ+ venues. It points to the ways that resistance to closure, sale and redevelopment has complicated linear developmental models, and further emphasises the temporal dimension underplayed in spatial or economic interpretations of the rise and decline of scenes, recognising the role of interdependent venues as dynamic sites of heritage and as connectors between the past, present and future.

Today's policy use of the term 'social and cultural infrastructure' to mark the venues associated with LGBTQ+ populations, along with other typologies of vulnerable social and cultural space, comprises an explicit recognition within urban governance, meaning that they are more legible, and have material weight in planning. The policy mapping of licensed venues is just the most visible surface, the most formal. It suggests that *some* parts of London's queer infrastructure have come into view. This expansive notion might also encompass much activity that eludes official surveys. Nonetheless, as everyday spaces of imagination and creativity, venues play important connective and enabling roles in processes of social and cultural reproduction towards the sustenance of queer lifeworlds.

2

Perverted purposes

The ambitious London Lesbian and Gay Centre (LLGC) operated in Farringdon, in the Labour-controlled London Borough of Islington, from 1983 to 1992.[1] Those involved had imagined

> a central community-based centre run by lesbians and gay men for lesbians and gay men, providing a relaxed alternative to the commercial 'scene', which often excludes women, older and younger people, and those without much money.[2]

How was it, then, that by 1989 such an admirable vision had mutated into what the Centre's general manager described as a 'strange beast, a monster which needs constant attention and feeding to keep it alive'?[3] 'It's devoured people, money, time and energy', he continued, 'and every conceivable resource imaginable.' But in many ways it is remarkable that the Centre was able to keep going until 1992, through a tumultuous and traumatic decade, outliving the Thatcher government, which had both inadvertently funded it and then held it under siege.

First imagined by activists, plans for a 'Gay Centre' were developed under the auspices of the Greater London Council (GLC) through its Gay Working Party, chaired by GLC member John McDonnell.[4] As they began to search for premises, the group envisaged both a Central London facility and a network of local centres in other boroughs.[5] The project was realized in collaboration with Islington, in dialogue with varied gay and lesbian groups. A capital grant was awarded and administered via the GLC. At the time, ex-industrial spaces and publicly owned land and buildings were readily available. Aided by the GLC and Islington, a former 1930s poultry processing facility was identified as a suitable property for this radical social project. The building was spacious enough to accommodate multiple uses. Coinciding with a time when the gay and lesbian community was battling AIDS and extreme homophobia, for many, even during its short lifespan, the Centre became an important site of social and political life and for explorations of identity. It was a space for activism, education, publication, debate, performance, artistic production, dancing, cruising, mourning, exercise, sex and much more. The Centre would become a platform upon which intra-community lesbian and gay politics, and the wider politics of sexuality and gender, would be enacted. The dominant issues of the day were woven into its constitution and everyday use. These discussions revolved around the possibilities and pitfalls of coalitions across different social movements, political agendas and identities, who

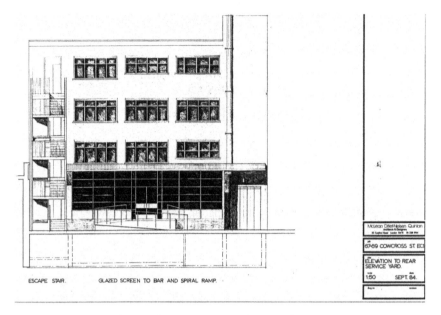

Figure 2.1 London Lesbian and Gay Centre, rear elevation drawing, 1984. Fiona McLean, McLean Quinlan.

and what should be included and prioritized, discouraged or excluded. The focus was on the boundaries of acceptability and rules required to promote equality, serve the distinct needs of multiple groups and provide shared space for a heterogeneous lesbian and gay community.

The Centre also became a heated ideological battleground for party politics as the Tories and Labour fought over the organization of local government and the provision of public services. The GLC's equalities policies and funding of social projects were easy targets for its detractors. The Centre drew national attention to the New Left GLC's radical support for minorities. Its agendas were shaking up the old Left and were emblematic of everything the Conservatives deplored. Even so, political and media attacks strengthened the resolve of the GLC to support the Centre, accelerating its establishment as an independent entity. High-profile criticisms of the GLC by the Conservative government, led by Margaret Thatcher in her second term as prime minister, the withdrawal of funding and the GLC's abolition in 1986 were the overriding factors that ensured the Centre's equally rapid demise.

The decade of the Centre's existence, following the revolutionary movements of the 1960s and 1970s, marks an important period of transition in lesbian and gay politics. It was initially set up as a workers' cooperative. Such arrangements were at odds with the Conservatives' enterprise-driven approaches, which in urban development were proceeding through the accelerated sell-off of public land, property and utilities. Subjected to funding cuts and rhetorical attacks, and under pressure to generate income, in the late 1980s the Centre was forced to shift to a commercial model, with a new board dominated by businesspeople. Did this mean that the original radical ambitions were simply lost, or diluted to give way to a more mainstream and individualistic politics? What can we learn from the way that the Centre was designed, the different phases of its operation and the debates that ensued? In this chapter I present evidence from archives and oral testimonies to evaluate the intentions and realization of the Centre, its use and closure.[6] From multiple perspectives, I draw out the significance of this high-profile but ultimately short-lived experiment. I consider the structure, governance model and membership; the design process and adaptation of the building; the various groups that used the Centre or were allocated space and their activities; the ways that it featured in mainstream politics and the media; and the ways that it is understood by those who were there, today. It provides a precedent for more recent collaborations to create community-oriented venues explored in other chapters.

Rehearsing representation

On 9 September 1982, the GLC's Grants Sub-Committee awarded a grant to the London Lesbian and Gay Centre Steering Committee, convened under the GLC's Gay Working Party. This would provide for the employment of two development workers to advise on the establishment of the Centre, which 'would offer recreational, cultural and educational activities, a meeting place, and an information and gay rights service'.[7] By 1983, with plans taking shape apace, a packed open meeting, with a reported 100 attendees, took place at County Hall, then London's city hall. This assembly included a declaration of the Centre's constitution 'for the advancement of lesbians and gay men, regardless of age, sex, race, ethnic origin, creed or disability'.[8]

Dissatisfaction with dominant and extractive commercial scenes has long driven innovation for new types of venues, and this remains as true today as in the 1980s. An early pamphlet explaining the Centre was disparaging about commercial venues, casting the scene as 'predominantly a service facility for fairly affluent middle-class gay men', with 'still very few places for lesbians, the disabled, those who are not rich enough to afford pubs and clubs etc. to meet, let alone participate'.[9]

If these early conversations defined the project against the commercial gay scene's inadequacies and exclusions, they also emphasized who would need to be kept out of the Centre to achieve an inclusive environment for lesbians and gays. A question recorded in the notes of the open meeting summarizes some of the concerns: 'What specific provisions should be made about who can use the centre? Can it exclude certain groups e.g. Tories, religious groups, TV/TS [Transvestite/Transexual], Paedophile Groups[?].'[10] Where, in other words, should boundaries be drawn or alliances formed? Given the variety of activities and uses that co-existed, and the tensions they created, it was prescient that the planning conversations focused on 'how one centre could cope with the differing interests and needs of the lesbian and gay community'.[11] Some of the lesbians in attendance were part of Women's City, a collective who were planning a separate women-only centre in Holloway, North London, and there were those who argued that their efforts should be concentrated towards this.[12] Others noted the risks in political compartmentalization or in over-stretching scarce resources, or felt that both centres were needed.[13] Although Women's City was never built (see Chapter 5), some spaces within the LLGC were assigned solely for use by women.[14]

The County Hall meeting, at which a Steering Committee was elected, was dominated by gay men, prompting complaints that women's groups had not been properly notified, leading to a low turnout.[15] Taking this into account, after the election of five men and one woman, a further six places were reserved for women. The Steering Committee oversaw the election of a voluntary Management Committee through a carefully worked out and highly elaborate democratic process. An Electoral Reform Society worker referred to the structure as 'one of the most complicated he had ever seen'.[16] There were ongoing controversies over representation through the Centre's lifespan. Peter Davey, who wrote the original proposal for the centre in his bedroom with Bob Marshall, notes that the Management Committee was 'incredibly representative', with spaces reserved for women, ethnic minorities and young people, but jokes that it 'couldn't manage its way out of a paper bag'.[17] This emphasizes a perception that inclusivity and operational inefficiency were linked.

The Centre was constituted as a 'Company Limited by Guarantee Not Having Share Capital', meaning that shares were not distributed to members.[18] It would operate independently from the GLC, and there was a commitment, if not a requirement, for it to support other autonomous 'self-help' initiatives.[19] In 1983, the voluntary members of the elected Steering Committee were formalized as a Board of Directors and an elected Management Committee was instituted. An application for charitable status, with the financial advantages that would bring, was refused. A pompous, tortuously expressed letter from the Charity Commission to the LLGC's solicitors set out multiple reasons why 'homosexuals and lesbians are not a charitable class *per se*'.[20] Instead, the Centre had to operate under a club licence, following the precedent of the Institute for Contemporary Arts, one of the many cultural venues that were researched.[21]

The staffing model was that of a workers' cooperative. Everyone was paid the same. There were twelve full-time staff when the Board took formal possession in January 1985, in advance of the official opening, on 9 April.[22] In theory, the structure was non-hierarchical. One member of the original team reflects, however, that 'the most strategic and powerful positions in the workforce were done by men, and none of them had ever worked in a collective or in a cooperative way'.[23] Those involved in the workers' collective observe that it was difficult to make it financially viable and that discussions underpinning decision-making could be time consuming. A user of the Centre who was involved in political campaigning and was a member of another workers' co-op at the time, recalls, with humour, the absurdity that 'you spend a lot of time having arguments about how you're going to run the thing and not an awful lot of actual [time] doing things, and they are always on a shoestring'.[24] The difference from other workers' cooperatives, he notes, was that the LLGC was not just intended to be an egalitarian work environment, but also became vital to deliver acutely needed resources during the AIDS crisis, and at a time of widespread discrimination and intense political and media hostility. When the Centre's management was accused of a lack of transparency in decision-making, even in the planning stages as early as January 1984, their quite reasonable defence was that under the mounting pressure of the GLC's impending abolition, they had to prioritize *doing* over talking.[25]

Individual membership was eventually opened to all who supported the Centre's aims, and comprised individuals and representatives nominated by lesbian and gay groups.[26] A celebration first birthday pamphlet records 1,400 registered members and offers a generous estimate of 500,000 visitors annually.[27] The organizational structure set out to widely represent different user groups, and there were attempts by the Steering and later Management Committees to include women, ethnic minorities and older and younger people, and to accommodate meetings of organizations representing these groups.[28] The discussions of who was being included or excluded – as workers, committee members, members or organizational members – were impassioned throughout the Centre's lifetime. In 1986, for example, the management and staff were criticized for failing to reach out to Black and ethnic minority lesbians and gays.[29] Frank discussions ensued, along with a motion to appoint two Black outreach workers. At this juncture, the newly appointed Management Committee took the opportunity to define themselves as agents of change, labelling the Centre 'racist' and tabling a motion to take reparative actions to address criticisms.[30]

Building resolution

The five-storey building purchased to accommodate the Centre in 1983, at 67-69 Cowcross Street, is adjacent to the ancient Smithfields meat market, in Farringdon (Plates 1–3). Formerly a frozen poultry processing facility, its conversion was overseen by Fiona McLean of McLean Ditlef-Nielsen Quinlan Architects. McLean was just starting out in her career and was contacted via a professional register to which she had subscribed, and on the back of her *pro bono* involvement in Women's City, which had instigated a lot of meetings and discussion, even if it had not ultimately been realized.[31] The LLGC commission was an exciting and unusual one for a young architect, sizeable in volume, with a decent budget and strong connections with the vision for Women's City.[32]

As an architectural project, the Centre faced significant advantages and challenges. The weight of the GLC's support, as well as Islington Borough Council's pro-lesbian and gay attitude, was beneficial. But there was inevitably still opposition. A climate of homophobia in the construction industry, political hostility towards the GLC and Islington, and criticism of their funding of initiatives for minority and stigmatized groups, presented a series of barriers. Structural engineer Frank van Loock, who worked on the project, conveys the multiple and subtle ways, alongside overt expressions, in which homophobia and ideological opposition manifested at the time. He refers to 'a spirit of – shall we say – not *full* cooperation from [. . .] the District Surveyor's department', and goes on to say that 'The general attitude I *got* – although there was no obstruction [. . .] there certainly wasn't 100 percent enthusiasm'.[33] At a time of scarce resources there was also a 'certain feeling of envy that [. . .] a special user group [should] get money'.[34] Van Loock expresses some surprise, in retrospect, that in this climate the contractors, Woodwards, came on board, having won the project through a competitive tender.[35]

The building itself was in many ways well suited to its new purpose. Looking back, the Centre's users stress that the fact that it was a run-down industrial facility added to the sense of potential, describing it as a 'wonderland' and 'more than we could ever hope for' now (in 2018).[36] Major structural changes were neither necessary nor affordable within the budget. The site was dominated by infrastructure, with railways at the rear. Brick built, the facility had large open spaces. The top storeys were converted into simple cellular units, and the ground and basement levels, accommodating the more public areas, were kept open. At ground level, the view to the west was glazed, while the eastern facade, at the front, was intentionally anonymous. The industrial feel of the building was accentuated, with a half-built blockwork wall in the entrance becoming part of the aesthetic. Relatively cheap conversions of ex-industrial space were more feasible in the 1980s, under the less stringent building regulations of the time. This meant that space could be maximized for the intended social uses rather than for engineering and other services; on the other hand, running costs were high because of the lack of insulation.[37] Two notable external features were the installation of a large Crittall – steel framed – window on the rear west side of the building, overlooking a service yard and on the same side an external spiral ramp, for direct wheelchair entry to the bar (Figure 2.1).

The processes of briefing and design were well documented. Archival sources demonstrate a high level of engagement to understand the anticipated needs of the building's future occupants. This was mediated by an Architects Liaison Group from the client's side, led by the two Development Workers, who had been installed in a nearby office allocated by the council.[38] McLean notes that although she did not directly liaise with the GLC, she was aware that the brief was being generated by its equalities agenda and that these policies were controversial. She recalls: 'we could tell there was quite a lot of politics going on, and in a way as an architect you're there to interpret and come to a resolution [. . .] *in the building*.'[39]

If the GLC's New Left radicalism shaped the overall vision, the detail of the brief was complex, reflecting the multifunctional programme and diversity of users. It had to be inclusive and welcoming overall, to offer spaces for specific groups, some with specialist fit-out requirements, and to provide security, at a time when lesbian and gay venues were frequently attacked. The mix of spaces and services offered in one building was unique. The lower floors included a basement disco with exposed brick walls painted black, a bar with dark wood features on the ground-floor facing west, well-lit through the Crittall windows and with coloured spot lighting. Above this, there was a café, bookshop (run by Gays the Word), the women-only lounge and coffee bar (The Orchid), a crèche, meeting rooms and workshop spaces, a shop, and a printing and typesetting workshop with its own printing press. The latter was used to generate posters, pamphlets, flyers and other publicity materials on site. The upper floors included a photographic studio and darkroom and the offices of lesbian and gay community organizations on both long- and short-term leases. The Hall-Carpenter Archives was another important resource allocated space and storage units after detailed briefings.[40]

At the local, city, national and international scale, the Centre provided a powerful materialization of the GLC's priorities. The vision was to 'help all sections of the community, especially those suffering hardship, handicap, disadvantage and discrimination'.[41] In developing the design, and in the Centre's operation, accessibility featured prominently. This was embedded into the practices that underpinned the Centre's development, with an emphasis on holding planning meetings in accessible venues. The prioritization of access was facilitated by the GLC, with the direct involvement of Ken Livingstone.[42] The intention was to provide unlimited access to wheelchair users on the ground floor, and access for four users on the other floors, which required substantial alterations to the existing lift and the addition of half-hour doors (a type resistant to fire for thirty minutes). The external ramp was particularly important to the Centre's initiators who were insistent on a gradient favourable to wheelchair users.[43] Wheelchair-accessible toilets were also included in the design.[44] Flyers and other records show great attention to detail in describing the venue and its spaces for accessibility purposes.[45] Once it was up and running, practical issues inevitably had to be worked through. Some of the adaptations failed, and discussion focused on how to make the basement disco more accessible.[46] The lift was unreliable due to regular flooding, and there was no other means for people with mobility issues to exit (or escape from) the building. The gay men's disability group judged access to be 'severely restricted'.[47] Tracing these discussions through archival materials conveys both the sense of optimism and purpose as well as the barriers and disappointments that were encountered.

Changing the world

The GLC's vision for lesbian and gay human rights was expressed in a comprehensive manifesto, which was launched at the Centre: *Changing the World: the London Charter for Lesbian and Gay Rights* (Plate 4).[48] The Charter, like the Centre, was a project of the Gay Working Party. In his preface, Livingstone comments on the latter's completion against the odds: 'the first regional lesbian and gay centre has been built and is now operational, surviving the government's last-minute attempt to shut it down by cutting off GLC funding'.[49] This was selective with the truth, however, since the Manchester Gay Centre, established in a basement in the 1970s, had been a pioneer and had received Urban Aid programme funding by 1978.[50] The South London Gay Community Centre had opened in a Brixton squat in 1974 and Birmingham Gay Community Centre ran from 1976 to 1979.[51] Nonetheless, the LLGC marked a significant moment in the formalization of the typology of a multipurpose gay and lesbian centre, through the extensive and collaborative redesign and refurbishment of an entire building, with substantial state support.

Changing the World is meticulously designed and visually dynamic. It aimed, as the title suggests, to promote a widespread change of attitudes to fight heterosexism.[52] Through abundant, impactfully organized images and text it distils complex challenges, while promoting a positive understanding of life within, and diversity across, lesbian and gay communities. In forty-eight pages it presented 142 recommendations, detailing multiple discriminations experienced by lesbian and gay communities on a range of socio-economic and welfare issues, from housing, to employment, family, health, immigration and media representation. Discriminatory stereotypes were challenged both through the content and form of the Charter. '[W]ords and tones can break your bones [. . .] and images can hurt you', the subtitles cautioned. In response, a variety of visual materials are used affirmatively. These include cartoons, photographs – with an emphasis on the representation of lesbians, Black and disabled people. In addition to its representation of individuals and groups, the Charter documents rallies, marches, discos, banners and billboards. The texts, captions, graphics and layouts combine to communicate the recommendations in a highly effective manner.

The pamphlet was collectively written by the Gay Working Party, including ex-GLF members, with inputs from the wider lesbian and gay community.[53] Its authors invited feedback and comment. The Charter compiled both the policies and actions of the GLC to fight discrimination and change attitudes, as well as negative responses to this work. A later reprint points to the ways that it had already prompted several progressive local authorities to set up offices and policies in support of lesbians and gays.[54] It reflects, and helped to shape, the affective political charge of the day, with an energy that still emits from archival copies. Even so, the missionary zeal reads as naieve today when we consider subsequent critiques of crude attempts to export Western conceptions of liberation and constructs of sexuality and gender.[55]

A summary of the Charter was produced in 16 languages, and in braille and on tape, with over 10,000 copies printed.[56] The Centre followed the GLC's model in prioritizing accessible dissemination for diverse audiences.[57] The Centre's constitution emphasized a commitment to the 'advancement of lesbians and gay men "regardless of age, sex. Race, ethnic origin, creed or disability"'.[58] Official publications, such as *Centre News*, had a distinctive, accessible visual identity throughout the Centre's existence (Plate 5). These bulletins displayed creativity and a propagandistic tone that complemented the DIY aesthetics of the pamphlets, posters and flyers associated with specific groups, hand-drawn or printed on site.[59]

The Centre had been envisaged as a generator and distributor for information. It was understood that substantive resources had to be invested in producing counter-publicity to redress the homophobia of mainstream media and politics. The initial concept note had specified a 'typewriter and duplicator' among the resources.[60] Ultimately, these facilities expanded to include print preparation, a graphics and layout workshop, dark-room, screen printing, badge-making machine and display screens, with the idea of assembling many of these resources in proximity, and close to the Hall-Carpenter's archive.[61] The co-location of these facilities with the Centre's other uses helped to stimulate a social media environment, providing a focus for planned and unplanned collaboration and information exchange.[62] Such resources provided the means to achieve a level of autonomy from the mainstream media; they saw a hybridization across artistic, activist and bureaucratic practices, and enabled the creation and migration of the Centre's identity, and the scenes it fostered, through print, post and telephone trees.

In the Centre's original visual identity, the inverted 'pink' triangle used in the logo, was a dominant motif, although not always in colour (Plate 1). Formerly used by the Nazis to badge homosexuals, it was widely reclaimed in the 1980s.[63] Repurposed, it conveyed the memory of historical violence, invoked international frontiers in gay and lesbian rights, and connoted political resistance. In the Centre's official publications, the triangle was liberated, taking the form of a kite, sometimes flying above the London skyline (Plate 6). This was a powerful act in placing the Centre and lesbian and gay communities within the imaginary of the modern and historic metropolis.[64] The Management Committee complained about the logo's impracticality, but overall the visual identity was effective.

If *Centre News* and other publications were one line of distribution, the parades and the spectacle around them were another. The LLGC was the symbolic heart of both Pride and Lesbian Strength marches in the 1980s. On these occasions, the variety of autonomous organizations that operated there were brought together under the Centre's banner. These marches were followed by rallies, discos and ambitious programmes of events and activities, attracting thousands from London and further afield.[65] Central London Pride events were coordinated with activities in local boroughs. A Pride 1991 flyer records a sample of what was by then a formal programme for a ticketed 24-hour 'Fabaganza', with music, live bands, a barbeque, comedy, karaoke, bingo, poetry reading, a healing workshop, a Terrence Higgins Trust event, mixed men's and women's dances and the café and bar open throughout.[66] The programme of Pride events increased visibility of the Centre and its community locally and helped with fundraising. It provided an opportunity to connect the Centre, and the GLC's drive for lesbian and gay equality, to international campaigns and the commemoration of the Stonewall uprising. This saw the realization of the early vision, which had emphasized potential international significance, and the creation of a focal point for overseas visitors.[67] Part of the argument then, and in the framing of the *Charter*, was that Britain lagged behind other European capitals, which already had centres, and that London needed to raise its game.

Amazing resource

The Centre accommodated and actively fostered an array of autonomous organizations offering hugely important services to gay and lesbian communities dealing with the stresses of queer life in the 1980s and early 1990s. These included, for example, mutual care, organizing and campaigning in response to the AIDS crisis, or other health matters, and on the full range of issues highlighted in *Changing the World*, whether employment rights, housing or police monitoring. Spaces were allotted to a variety of organizations dedicated to communication and education. Many of these, including the Hall-Carpenter Archives, Gay's the Word bookshop, and the Lesbian and Gay Switchboard (now Switchboard), remain essential to LGBTQ+ communities today. They operated alongside other important telephone-based and in-person information and support services that have since disappeared, such as the Camden Lesbian and Gay Telephone Trees, and GLAD, a legal advisory group which operated services for those with legal issues related to being lesbian or gay.[68] Some initiatives formed at the Centre. In 1985, for example, the Project for Advocacy, Counselling and Education (PACE), a volunteer-founded charity, was set up to promote mental health in recognition of the challenges lesbians and gay men faced due to homophobia.[69]

Throughout its existence, the Centre was a hub for political meetings and activism for a wide range of groups and organizations. Its function as a meeting, conference and exhibition venue is one of the main ways that it is remembered.[70] There were rooms and facilities for a wide range of voluntary sector initiatives promoting collective and self-care. The arts programme was very active. Cultural and leisure organizations and creative practitioners used the space; artists were encouraged to exhibit their work; music and drama productions and performances took place, as well as video screenings and arts festivals, often promoted around particular cultural or national identities.[71]

In the planning and earlier operational phase of the workers' collective, the meetings were dominated by the concept and design for the building and the management structure. The governance structures of the Labour-led GLC, with its Gay Working Party, other working groups and groups associated with the Labour party, such as the Labour Campaign for Lesbian and Gay Rights, set the tone. When it was in full operation, external organizations who were otherwise critical of the GLC, such as the Lesbian and Gay Youth Movement, also used the space.[72] During the Centre's lifespan, membership rules became less proscriptive. Radical activist groups, such as ACT UP London, were allocated space on a consistent basis and at affordable rents.[73] For these groups, offices and meeting rooms at the Centre were vital as they mounted campaigns and supported those who were sick and grieving. In 1990, there was a campaign to create a permanent exhibit in memory of those lost to AIDS, in the form of a photomontage.[74] It was initiated following the suicide of Simon Ra-Orton, a twenty-year-old ACT UP activist who had been diagnosed with HIV the same year, and whose health had quickly deteriorated. The recruitment flyer for this project emphasizes the importance of the Centre as a site of care, grief, memory, solidarity and creativity.

For Outrage! – a 'broad based group of queers committed to radical, non-violent direct action and civil disobedience' – being located at the Centre helped to facilitate and amplify campaigns, and enabled interaction with other groups with complementary agendas or useful resources.[75] One Centre member, who spent considerable time attending political meetings there, recalls participating in Thursday Outrage! meetings 'with possibly over 100 people there [. . .] predominantly gay men'.[76] He notes the connection between cruising, sex and politics in the Centre's daily operation: 'people did hook up at those meetings, but it created something, and it actually put issues on the front pages of the newspapers'.[77] These meetings took advantage of the basement disco for large gatherings. This was a safe space for such discussions to take place, it is recalled as an arena of high passions, where disagreements unfolded and physical fights sometimes took place.[78]

Those who were involved in running and using the Centre emphasize that it induced a powerful sense of belonging, even for those who only experienced it for relatively brief periods. Photographs of the interiors of the more public areas evoke a vibrant and social atmosphere. Walls were covered with community notices and artworks, and it was furnished with comfortable chairs and tables adorned with houseplants, emphasizing – as former members testify – that this was 'meant to be some sort of *home*' or a 'second home' for the lesbian and gay community.[79] This was especially the case for those who were involved directly as volunteers, DJs, activists or in other roles.[80]

For many, these positive associations contrasted with the commercial nightlife scenes of the time, as one member emphasizes:

> I thought it was an amazing place, and I *much* preferred going there to – and there weren't that many commercial places even in Central London – Brief Encounter, Comptons and the bars that would have been in Earl's Court; but you know, I was never sure what to do with myself in those places. So, it was a nice place to go after work before a meeting, or just going for something to eat. And it *was* an amazing resource. I still think the café was brilliant. I *loved* the café; you could get simple food and it was at a very cheap price. But there was always somebody there that you knew that you could talk to.

The definition of the Centre as distinct from dominant forms of nightlife was also important for DJ Ritu, who was the Centre's resident DJ from 1986 to 1991:

> the wonderful thing about going to the LLGC – as we called it – was that out of *all* the places we could go to there was daylight, for starters, as opposed to being in a dank, dark basement or an upstairs room in a pub. And it felt really, really welcoming – for *me*, anyway, it felt very welcoming – you didn't have this thing of being stared at the minute you walked into the room because people were too busy eating their lentil bakes or having a drink at the bar.

Ritu was instrumental in establishing Shakti in the basement of the Centre in 1988. This was a 'bhangra disco for Asian lesbians and gay men and their friends', with music and food, from which grew a long-term social network.[81] Ritu's comment that the feeling of inclusivity was subjective, acknowledges that others remember it differently. The separate Black Lesbian and Gay Project was felt by many to be a necessary alternative.[82]

The Centre, and in particular the basement disco, played an important role in fostering innovative and radical nightlife and performance events, framed thoughtfully around the needs of specific groups. Nights at the Centre became as popular or more so than those hosted in popular nearby venues, such as The Ace of Clubs in Piccadilly, or The Bell in King's Cross, where the clientele, counterculture and politics overlapped (see Chapter 5).[83] In recalling the Centre, those involved highlight the popular Saturday night women-only disco that ran from 1986.[84] The provision of space for groups with specific heritage, including Shakti, for South Asian community members, as well as 'mixed race', multicultural, and 'world music' nights, are all notable.[85] A volunteer at the Centre, who later worked behind the bar, notes that these nights would not at the time have been successful in obtaining space in mainstream clubs.[86] Others recall how such events enabled new cultural encounters.[87] Alternative drag cabaret and tea dances also featured, such as Jo Purvis's popular Tea Dances.[88] The longevity of nights such as Pink Jukebox, which began life in the Centre's basement and continues to thrive today, far outlasting the Centre itself, is testament to their popularity, the sense of community they engendered, and their agility in adapting over time and to different locations.[89] Yet many events were transient, including benefit discos held to support causes like the Legislation for Lesbian and Gay Rights Campaign.[90]

The LLGC hosted many lesbian and gay campaigns and organizations that were set up on a voluntary basis. A community also formed around the Centre because of the many volunteers required to support its own operations. Volunteering was a route for individuals to form a meaningful attachment with the Centre, as part of a process of constructing their own identity, their identification with the lesbian and gay community, and with the specific organizations that nested there. Recalling his time in the Workers' Collective, a former finance officer at the Centre notes:

> certainly, for the people that I know who volunteered when I was working there, some of them wouldn't be here today if they hadn't had that opportunity to engage with the Centre; you know, these were very vulnerable people coming into a safe space.[91]

Vulnerability, in this context, could include those who had newly arrived in London and were in the process of coming out. Recalling the Centre today, a volunteer in various roles during the mid-1980s describes how he went to the Centre on his first night in London, having moved from South Wales as a shy young man who was not out to anybody.[92] Others recount how the opportunity to volunteer and socialize in a space where one could just *be*, without drinking, was important on their journey of recovery from alcoholism.[93]

The Centre provided opportunities for affirmative everyday contact and conversation within and across different social groups for the communities that used it.[94] Another former volunteer and bar worker remarks:

> I used to go to the Lesbian and Gay Centre on a Sunday and talk to women and men who had been *out* as gay and lesbian – or it wasn't called 'out' in those [days] but – in the '40s *during* the Second World War and would talk to me with *stories* about how they operated in *their* lives, and they were very white [. . .] working-class Londoners.[95]

Those coming to the Centre to use counselling services to help them cope during the AIDS crisis also reported the positive experience of being able to volunteer and to be in a social space that was different from, and in some ways an antidote to, the commercial nightlife scene.[96] Less reliance on volunteer labour would have allowed for a more disciplined operation. Yet this aspect was clearly very important to the Centre's social contribution, at a time when discrimination against lesbian and gay people in the workplace was a major issue, as *Changing the World* highlighted.

Disgraceful waste

In parliament, the GLC's use of public funds was controversial long before the Centre opened its doors. In 1982, Thatcher had referred to initiatives for sex workers, lesbians and teens as 'a disgraceful waste of money and a disgraceful imposition of increases on the tax burden'.[97] Islington, the borough in which the Centre was located, was a hotspot in the battle of ideologies. The battlelines between the Conservative government, the New Left GLC and the GLC-supporting Labour-led boroughs were drawn over the spending of rates on public services and financial support for inner-city minority community groups. As peers and MPs vented their outrage that their constituents' rates could be spent on such 'perverted purposes', the Centre and minority groups being supported by the GLC were repeatedly referenced.[98] 'I defy anyone to tell me why my constituents should pay taxes to subsidise those groups', remarked John Maples, the Conservative MP for Lewisham West, in one parliamentary debate in which the Centre was singled out in January 1984.[99] The Centre, and activities in Islington, became emblematic in mainstream political and media debates to signify all that was wrong with Livingstone and the GLC's radical and provocative agenda. Spiteful attacks were directed at organizations at the frontline of the AIDS crisis, or at organizations undertaking research to understand the reasons why women went into sex work. '[T]here can seldom have been a local authority that has been more maligned and vilified by Ministers and their friends in the press than Islington since the 1982 elections', the MP for Islington North, Jeremy Corbyn, declared angrily in 1984.[100]

The discourse of moral outrage and indignation was accompanied by strategic political moves to abolish the GLC and curb the powers of local councils to subsidize external agencies. In a speech central to the 'Control of General Expenditure Powers Debate', Allan Roberts (1943–90), the Labour MP for Bootle, made an impassioned defence, questioning, organization by organization, why the Conservatives would be against the causes the GLC' were supporting:

> They are scratching the surface of racialism, ruthlessly exploiting sexism and prejudice against gays and lesbians and are appealing to the worst elements and prejudices in society in a manner worthy of the worst sort of Right-wing extremists, which they are doing their best to prove they are.

> We should not apologise for our controversial grants. They are pioneering grants and they help people in the greatest need. They help to create a better, more just, and equal society. If central Government will not do that, it will continue to be the role of local government, as it has traditionally been.[101]

Even if it did continue to be local government's role, capacity would be greatly diminished.

Apart from the narrative about squandering public resources, and with the abolition of the GLC on the horizon, the Centre's management had to navigate a bleak landscape of funding cuts more generally. The GLC tried to raise awareness of what the impacts of withdrawing funding from lesbian and gay groups would be, alongside the damage to other voluntary sector organizations they supported. A press release in 1984 highlighted, for example, how the London Gay Teenage Group Research Project would have reduced capacity to understand, convey and make policy interventions to improve the experiences and mental health of people aged between sixteen and twenty-one.[102]

Swirling politics

The LLGC functioned as a theatre for the sexual and gender politics of the day within and across the feminist, lesbian and gay movements and for discussions of marginalisation and rights within these communities. Complex dynamics and conflicts between different ideologies were inevitable in the operation of a venue that ambitiously incorporated so many groups and activities under one roof. With its unique combination of uses, the Centre became an important space for live debates to play out. This meant that intra-community political discussions were amplified, staged in a high-profile and already controversial setting, at the risk of feeding homophobic and other discriminatory tropes. Some of the controversies revolved around sex, and what was permissible on site. The Centre, as discussed earlier, was framed in opposition to a commercial scene that was at the time dominated by cruising bars for gay men. But cruising and sex on the premises were important features of many of the events that it hosted for women, men and mixed crowds. At the limits of the building, favourite places for people to have sex included the fire escape – an appropriate, liminal 'backroom' for emergency times – and the basement.[103]

In 1985, led by Lesbians Against Sadomasochism (LASM), a battle ensued over whether lesbian sadomasochist (S/M) groups should be allowed to meet at the Centre. This was written up at the time by socialist lesbian feminists Susan Ardill and Sue O'Sullivan, two friends who were directly involved and who published their account in *Feminist Review* the following year.[104] By grudgingly permitting some SM meetings to take place at the Centre, in a spirit of liberal tolerance, the Management Committee created a space for what was a much wider and international debate to play out.[105] Ardill and O'Sullivan place the episode within wider contexts of lesbian feminism and lesbian and gay politics, writing evocatively that 'different eddies and currents already swirling elsewhere in the WLM [Women's Liberation Movement], settled on the Centre, with histories already in the process of gelling'.[106] Fault lines were drawn around attitudes to sexuality, its relationship with the patriarchy, and the different forms and political possibilities of erotic desire and sex between women. The battle over S/M practices at the Centre was, Ardill and O'Sullivan relate, reflective of wider Anglo-American debates and campaigns around a range of taboo sexual practices and identities, which also included bisexuality, transexuality, prostitution, paedophilia and promiscuity.[107]

Ardill and O'Sullivan make several points that are salient to the interpretation of the Centre beyond the recollection of these specific angry scenes. First, that the venue was an opportunity for a new coalitionist approach to sexual politics, but that clearly not everyone within the feminist and lesbian and gay movements was supportive of this. Second, that the controversies highlighted that individual experience and structural social forces of racism, sexism, class exploitation and imperialism should be understood as interactive.[108] Third, that the new awareness to positionality, and interconnected oppressions, raised important questions of social difference and empathy, with implications regarding the understanding of other peoples' sexual practices which were being thought through.[109] Fourth, that the battle at the Centre was an attempt to come to terms with these 'politics of experience or "identity"' at a

Perverted Purposes · 41

time of criticism of the inadequacy, and inaccessibility, of feminist and Left political theory, in their engagement with questions of social difference.[110] Evoking the S/M debates, in retrospect, a founding GLF member raises the ways these were filtered through class and educational privilege. He is critical of middle-class and 'academic' Marxist socialist women spreading the rumour that 'gay liberation was publicly pushing for sadomasochism' – which was 'not the case at all [as] gay liberation was open to everybody'.[111] This suggests how the debate hinged on a perceived contradiction between being 'open to everybody' and 'publicly pushing for sadomasochism'.

The Centre was therefore an important site for the various debates that were taking place in what has been termed the Feminist Sex Wars, where different positions were being adopted by those within the women's movement, gay liberation movement and lesbian feminisms, on pornography, sex positivity, sadomasochism, sex work and transgender inclusivity. Historian Susan Stryker has noted, in her history of LINKS S/M parties in San Francisco in 1989, that

> The AIDS pandemic was in full swing in those years before the anti-viral cocktails, and S/M seemed situated at the very crux of the crisis – its precepts of negotiation and consent, its panoply of techniques for eliciting bodily sensation without exchanging bodily fluids, its meticulous disarticulations of erotics from genital sexuality, all promised a viable future.[112]

At this moment of the emergence of new queer politics, theories and identities, and of attention to intersectional oppressions, Stryker demonstrates the importance of such parties as places of corporeal, subjective and epistemological transformation, communality, conviviality and negotiation.[113] Her assertions are elaborated in the context of exchanges that were happening between queer theorists and Marxist urban theorists discussed in Chapter 1. Stryker writes against the universalizing assumptions and unmarked embodiments of white, cismale, Marxist theorists of postmodern space, who reject or underplay the importance of the local. In this she draws on Doreen Massey's embodied, feminist geography as offering alternative understandings of place and connectivity. She contends that in S/M the dungeon and the body were sites of experimentation that were at once local and global. The Centre can also be understood as a site of embodied improvisation where local and global forces and practices coalesced.

Another archive of these debates can be found in an impassioned letter to the LLGC from a member who writes as a lesbian-identified post-operative transexual – the poet, novelist and critic Roz Kaveney. The letter expresses anger at the Management Committee's decision to 'ban SM dykes and the SM support group from holding meetings at the Centre'.[114] It vigorously dismantles the arguments justifying the ban and the undemocratic processes through which it was enacted. Kaveney expresses the discomfort she felt in using the Centre, as a transexual, and someone aware that their right to use the women's floor may be deemed 'contentious'.[115] Kaveney's perceptive letter also highlights how the divisiveness around such issues distracted from more pressing matters, including securing the Centre's future when it was under continual threat.

42   *Queer Premises*

The controversies affected day-to-day proceedings. Of the gender politics, one ex-employee recalls:

> the people involved in the users' committee, trying to decide which groups would be allowed or not allowed to come in [. . .] decided it was okay for transvestites to come in, even though there was some disquiet about that because they were clearly copying and parodying women [. . .] but transsexuals were one step too far. And [. . .] there was a meeting where a woman stood up and said, 'I'm a hermaphrodite, am I banned too?' and then they had to have a whole discussion about whether or not someone who was intersex should be allowed in or not. [. . .] Later on, by the time we get to the days of Outrage! and Act Up and stuff, the atmosphere was very different. I think to begin with it was quite proscriptive in terms of who was allowed in to the lesbian and gay community.[116]

In the later life of the Centre, controversies over S/M inclusion were articulated through debates on whether Sadie Masie's, one of the first lesbian and gay S/M clubs in Britain, should be accommodated.[117] Oscar Watson, who became manager in 1989 and was in office until 1991, recalls that he did not permit Sadie Masie's to run during his tenure because he worried that it could be alienating for users who were uncomfortable with the commercial scene – and that being seen to be permissive of events oriented around sex could fuel negative stereotyping.[118] This is understandable given that Watson's tenure was towards the end of the Centre's existence, by which time the attacks had hardened, and it was struggling to survive.[119]

Feeding the monster

Government and media attacks on the Centre and cuts to its grant funding tested the viability of the Centre's already complex operating model. In 1985, it came under attack from Kenneth Baker, the minister for Local Government in Margaret Thatcher's second Conservative government, who refused consent for the GLC to make a grant to the Centre.[120] Valerie Wise, chair of the GLC's Women's Committee, and the LLGC's information officer, Spike Aldridge, pointed in response to the negative consequences for the Centre's eleven full-time employees and the 'hundreds of volunteers' who would be affected, as well as the waste of public investment.[121] The role of voluntary labour became a source of increasing controversy. The high number of volunteers put stress on the elaborate organizational structure. Paid in tokens for soft drinks and meals, towards the end of the Centre's life, volunteers, along with employees, were frequently accused of theft, in what became an increasingly pressured, distrustful and acrimonious atmosphere.

In 1986, the GLC was finally dissolved under the Local Government Act, in line with a commitment in the Conservative Manifesto on which Margaret Thatcher's government had been re-elected in 1983.[122] When this came to pass, the building was offered for the Centre to purchase from the London Residuary Body, set up to manage the GLC's assets. But the Centre had fallen into a debt crisis by 1988, as well as suffering cuts to the grants it, and the organizations it accommodated, relied upon. By 1989 there was a funding campaign underway towards the purchase of the building.[123] Once the GLC was disbanded and local authority grant funding ceased, there was a shift to a board structure and a more commercial approach. The Centre was now framed as a 'social enterprise'.[124] The Gay Business Association provided a bailout.[125] The new focus on economic viability shifted things away from the political positioning of the early years. There were changes in the allocation of space, such as the use of the second floor as a gym, The Farringdon Works. This operated, like the Centre, on a subsidy, rather than on a market-rate membership fee model.[126]

In this period, taking up his role as general manager, it was Oscar Watson who had referred to the Centre as a monster that devoured energy and resources.[127] His frustration was that, despite these resources, the Centre was still easily destabilized, and the aims of its proponents sabotaged: 'all it takes is a letter in a paper or a tiff in the bar and it needs major surgery'.[128] Watson became the subject of controversy himself through a bitter and public exchange with the Board of Directors about the Centre's finances. The Board saw a discrepancy between his approach and the urgency to increase profit, and he was dismissed in 1991.[129]

In retrospect, Watson understandably highlights the intense pressure created by government discrimination around the time that the GLC was abolished and which continued until the Centre closed.[130] He observes that when the GLC's assets were transferred to the London Residuary Body and buildings were offered for purchase or rent to GLC-linked organizations, this was mostly for a peppercorn rent or less than market price. The Centre, on the other hand, was offered for sale at a commercial – and therefore prohibitively expensive – price:

> The LLGC was the *only* former GLC building that was asked to come up with its commercial value. So, if you [. . .] put that into context for an organisation that was started with a big annual subsidy, to suddenly sort of *spin round* and say, right, you've now gotta [clicks fingers] buy your building, and you've [clicks fingers] got to pay all your rent, *that* was an unrealistic ask.[131]

Archives suggest that the valuation was lower than the market price, yet still unaffordable without significant capital.[132] Nonetheless, in this hostile context, alongside the mocking and shaming discourse in parliament, despite the energy that went into fundraising, it is not surprising that the financial problems worsened over time and that the Centre closed in 1992. The effect on many of the organizations that it hosted was devastating, with many community services and campaigns diminished. Where they continued, they moved to other venues, with several groups using the newly opened gay pub, Central Station, in King's Cross.[133]

Bittersweet

How have those who experienced the Centre remembered it? How do they articulate their memories? One founding GLF member sees the Centre as mirroring a wider depoliticization of the movement, and labels those who used it 'politically correct': 'they were ignorant politically, and so they just invented anything that they had a prejudice about and decided that they were against that [. . .] They had no politics whatsoever.'[134] In this take, the GLF's radical liberation agenda, which had been driven by working-class members, had been replaced by a new generation who wished to distance themselves from the gay liberationists' revolutionary tactics and were more conservative, trans-exclusive and misogynistic.[135] Following the end of the GLF, by the beginning of 1974, in this commentator's view there had been a shift away from a revolutionary agenda that was inclusive of sexual subcultures and in which transexuals had played a leading role.

For those everyday users whose identity was not contested, it was, of course, possible to use the Centre and remain blissfully unaware of the controversies and wider political debates. As one former member, a white gay man who used the Centre in its closing days, puts it:

I was totally *oblivious* to all this stuff that was going on, because I was taken there by somebody I fancied and I was looking at them and I wasn't paying [. . .] I couldn't tell you what the place *looked like*, you know [laughter].

This highlights that the venue was experienced just as part of the everyday fabric of gay life, as a space of joyfulness and escape, which had important political functions beyond organising, campaigning and debate.

A *Vice* feature of 2016, 'Remembering the 1980s Lesbian and Gay Centre That Didn't Last a Decade', gathered reflections from various people who had worked at or used the Centre, including Lisa Power, also a GLF member, who is also disparaging in her testimony. In the article there are various references to the political infighting, critiques of staff being chosen for specific political affiliations and being over-generously paid, flawed financial management, theft, the policing of the use of internal spaces for those with the sanctioned identities and the programming which provoked tensions between groups.[136] The reality, those quoted suggest, directly contrasted the positive 'symbol of lesbians and gay men working together on such diverse issues as women-only space, AIDS, childcare and services for gays' celebrated in a pamphlet published for the Centre's first birthday.[137] Overall, though, if the Centre is presented as a failure, with a strong sense of disappointment, it is also articulated by those who were closely involved as a 'lifeline', 'fantastic', a 'great way to integrate yourself into a community', in a building that was well structured for multiple experiences. Those quoted suggest that it was 'ahead of its time', 'of the time' and 'its demise was too soon'. The article asks why the Centre was so quickly forgotten. The raw feelings about it, and the traumas that surface in recollecting it, help to answer this.

Interviewed as part of an oral history project on the GLC, Femi Otitoju, who worked there and was on the original LLGC Steering Committee, and who was later involved in the Black Lesbian and Gay Centre project, gives a frank evaluation of the 'painful' process of setting up the Centre, among groups who 'were not very used to being together cooperatively' in a project that 'tried to be all the things to all the lesbians and gay men'.[138] Her overall assessment is finely balanced:

> There were hassles about everything. 'Oh, S&M dykes were coming in, that's awful, oh, they're doing poppers, that's awful, everybody's racist . . .' There were rows about absolutely everything. Nonetheless, it was an amazing resource, absolutely phenomenal.[139]

The debates of the time resurface in such testimonies today, with the LLGC a vehicle to project different views and feelings.

Commentaries on the Centre also express the desire to connect these historical moments, and the revolutionary gay and lesbian politics of the 1970s, with today's moment of trans-visibility and the struggle for trans rights. One ex-employee reflects on the way that discussions around who was welcome or prohibited reflected wider feminist politics that are still resonant:

> Sadomasochists were seen as fascists, bisexuals were seen as traitors, trans women were seen in exactly the same way trans women are seen now, actually – as being . . . you know, I mean some things haven't moved.

She notes, in this period just prior to the internet, that the Centre provided a physical venue for debates that parallel those that take place on social media today.[140] Negative evaluations are counterbalanced by recognition of the pioneering, experimental and radical nature of the underpinning vision, and of the array of groups and activities that the Centre facilitated. Several characteristics of the urban imaginary embodied within the GLC's policies and the Centre are worth noting. First, the inclusion of diverse groups with overlapping but distinct agendas and interests and attempts to address what might now be discussed as intersectional differences in terms of access to and need for the space and associated resources. Significant attention was given to minorities within the diverse London lesbian and gay community, with attempts to direct funding to understand varied experiences and needs through research and meaningful consultation. Second, the ethos of cooperation underpinning the Centre as it was conceived and operated, evidenced in both a municipal operational structure and accommodation of informal or DIY approaches. Third, the powerful co-location of services, research and communications in order to gather and disseminate evidence and counter the misinformation and homophobia of the time. Fourth, the strong connections to borough-level local government in Islington and, through proactive seeking of resources and access to other local government funding streams, to other administrative districts. Fifth, there were ongoing issues regarding the fragmentation or joining up of scarce resources. Acknowledging the difficulties and complexity that engulfed the Centre and led eventually to its closure, it is important to see these in the context of the time. Interestingly, as the following chapters will discuss, the LGBTQ+ community centre has re-emerged as a typology in London, led by grassroots campaigners, and once again facilitated by the city authorities.

3

Mainlining pride

The Conservatives' abolition of the GLC left the capital without a city-wide government for fourteen years. As part of a wider devolution agenda, the London mayoralty and Greater London Authority were established under New Labour in 2000. The new administration was again led by Ken Livingstone, now elected mayor. Other individuals and organizations from the GLC days took up appointments and regained influence. Under the GLA, sexual orientation and LGB equality were soon reinstated as key strategic areas in London politics. The radicalism of the feminist, lesbian, gay, Black and disability social movements of the 1960s, 1970s and 1980s had helped instigate a broader shift in Western democracies towards the inclusion of sexual and gender diversity within governance frameworks in the 1990s and 2000s.[1] Policies and practices in these areas were now driven by and constrained within the orthodoxy of neoliberalism.

The GLC's social policies and support for lesbian and gay rights, gender equality, environmentalism and opposition to racial discrimination had been controversial and subject to intense stigmatization by Conservatives, some Labour factions and the media. Doreen Massey, who advised both the GLC and GLA, observed that perceptions of a deluded 'loony left' endured long after the GLC's abolition and had a lasting legacy of disempowerment.[2] Yet, as communications theorist James Curran has recently remarked, many of the ideas pushed by the radical New Left had soon been accepted into the mainstream.[3] He points to main party policies that gradually became more socially liberal, and to statistical evidence of steadily increasing societal acceptance of same-sex relationships.

The New Left's rights agenda of the 1980s had been intrinsically urban. It was linked to an interventionist regional economic approach that was international in its outlook and democratizing in its attitude to culture. As we saw in the previous chapter, under Livingstone's leadership, GLC-based lesbian and gay activists had expressed zealous hopes for London to be a beacon that would 'change the world', and such hopes included progressive plans for London's postcolonial transformation. The GLC's vision differed from the Thatcher government's attempts to promote London as a post-industrial global city through the deregulation of financial and labour markets, and committed instead to the public economy and 'popular planning'.[4] As an alternative to Thatcherite monetarism, the GLC had provided a fine-grained sector-by-sector plan for the modernization of London's industrial core, aiming to replace 'the anarchy of the market economy with justice and fairness'.[5] It recognized the significance of a growing tourism sector and outlined strategies to make it fairer.[6] It promoted approaches to the cultural sector that recognized London's national importance, incorporated popular cultural forms, new media and independent cultural industries with their 'real base' in the 'practice of everyday life' – a phrase resonant with the Marxist urban theories of Michel de Certeau and Henri Lefebvre.[7] This meant 'investment in the infrastructures of cultural distribution', and recognition of the increasing 'transnationality' of cultural industries alongside their technological democratization.[8] Recently evaluating the GLC, architecture critic Owen Hatherley writes that as well as building alliances across feminist, anti-racist and anti-homophobic politics, the GLC's efforts can be seen as 'the start of the creation of the multicultural capital of the creative industries'.[9]

Still, as Curran puts it, the Left was 'comprehensively defeated in the area of the economy', since 'neoliberalism reigned supreme under both New Labour and Conservative governments'.[10] The deregulation of financial industries (the Big Bang), the opening up of foreign exchange trading, the use of financial instruments and computing technologies that accelerated global flows of capital, the deregulation of labour markets facilitating transnational movement, the growth of the financial and services sectors and the private sector-led and state-facilitated speculative redevelopment and gentrification of former industrial and working-class neighbourhoods were all distinctive features.[11] By 2000, London's characteristics as a global city, networked and competing with other global financial centres, were fully evident.[12] A new urban optimism was oriented around an assumption of growth, a 'diplomatically motivated obsession with the global city', and an enthusiasm for large-scale property-led regeneration and infrastructure development, where the public benefits would trickle down to those in need.[13] As Massey argues, the local and global were deeply entangled, and London as an experimental ground for neoliberalism was deeply entwined with other regions and cities in the UK and internationally.[14]

Evaluating the new London governance structure in 2004, policy analysts noted that, although the GLA Act 1999 had been grounded in the pursuance of 'sustainable development', the GLA had been constrained in achieving this for a variety of reasons.[15] These included its limited powers, the 'diffuse' mode of governance that resulted from a need to negotiate with diverse partners and interest groups, its inability to mount a material challenge to an underlying growth-based, competitive economic model and the political priorities of the mayor himself.[16] London continues, today, to be positioned as a pro-business 'global city', where the financial sector and property speculators have enormous influence.[17] Following the loss of the local government funding of the 1980s, property- and infrastructure-led approaches to urban change have been facilitated by the mayors and local authorities, with huge benefits to developers and property owners. In short supply, land and buildings formerly held in public ownership have been sold off and, with inflated values, have been turned to profit to the benefit of their new owners and developers with well documented adverse impacts on the capital's social sustainability and cultural life.[18]

Even under consistent neoliberal, global city logics, however, the specific contexts shift constantly, and we can detect changes of emphasis under each mayoral administration. The wider economic picture at any given moment, the political priorities of each mayor, the direction from national government, international relations and inter-city competition have all had an impact. Analysing the GLA after its first decade, geographers Ian Richard Gordon and Tony Travers drew on the concept of urban 'ungovernability' formulated by political scientist Douglas Yates.[19] London fitted, they argued, with Yate's understanding of large cities as fragmented entities conditioned by their uneven historical development, the multiple and conflictual demands of urban service delivery, and the reactive, problem-oriented design of policy. Gordon and Travers noted that city governments, including the GLA,

> are called on to manage exceptionally complex systems. Complexity here is not just a synonym for difficulty, but relates to the combination of unusually high levels of diversity (of both people/cultures and business activities) and a very strong potential for interaction (among actors and issues), with knock-on effects making problems hard to disentangle, and greatly increasing the likelihood that policy has unintended consequences.[20]

This is a useful framework through which to consider how, since the mid-2000s, activities on LGBTQ+ equality have increasingly intersected with a broader cross-section of policies and practices on 'social infrastructure'. This term, as I explore in this chapter, is present in all the London plans since 2000, but it shifts across the mayoralties, intersecting in different ways with approaches to equality and diversity, heritage and culture, night-time governance, planning and redevelopment.

During the first decades of the twenty-first century, these have been increasingly lively areas of policy and practice internationally. For example, there has been a growing attention to heritage associated with minoritized populations, and a recognition that heritage is linked to the advancement or maintenance of rights and should be central within practices of sustainable urban development.[21] Governance of night-time economies and attention to nocturnal cultures has also moved higher up the agenda in many cities.[22] From the late 1990s to the present, discussions of cities at night have gradually shifted from discourses of harm, and a narrow interpretation of the costs and benefits of the night-time leisure economy, to a broader focus on culture and social justice at night.[23] Recently, in the London context, this has been linked directly to the well-being and livelihoods of LGBTQ+ populations and other minorities, together with a growing awareness of the cultural innovations associated with venues they have created and used.[24]

In this chapter I consider how policy and rhetoric on social sustainability, minority rights and diversity have materialized through changing approaches to LGBTQ+ citizenship and heritage. I highlight and compare some of the key statements and actions that each mayor has taken in their engagements with LGBTQ+ communities. Following Massey, I am interested in the disparities between political rhetoric on London as a global city, the legacies of the city's imperial past on which these are built and mayoral positioning on the city's diversity, cosmopolitanism and accommodation of difference. Massey considers, but only tangentially, the interrelations of world cities and the 'sphere' of 'gay and lesbian networks', with reference to Sydney.[25] I take this as a prompt to focus on how LGBTQ+ equalities agendas have been embedded in urban governance and planning since 2000. I examine the mechanisms, level of formality and proactivity of engagement with LGBTQ+ populations, and how the range of interacting organizations and individuals have shifted in response to the mayors' changing tone and political inclinations. What are the relations between LGBTQ+ communities, the politics of sexual citizenship and urban governance? How have radical queer activism and City Hall interacted? With the radicalism of the GLC of the 1980s interrupted, did the 2000s simply see an increasing homonormativity, in parallel with the ever-deeper embedding of neoliberal policies?[26] To address these questions I follow election manifestos, speeches, events, policy documents and equalities practices.

World-class gay rights

In the first London mayoral election following the establishment of the GLA in 2000, Ken Livingstone stood and won as an independent candidate. Livingstone was not only the first mayor to lead the GLA but also the first directly elected mayor in England. In this period, the personalities of mayors and mayoral candidates took on a heightened importance.[27] Livingstone entered office in 2000 with a record of activism for lesbian and gay rights. He had also used his power as Leader of the GLC to support radical feminism and anti-racism. Having been caricatured by the press in the GLC years, he courted controversy once again, using the media spotlight to emphasize his independence and increase his popularity.[28] Local government analyst Tony Travers observes that the stigmatization of the GLC had been underpinned by a misrepresentation of Livingstone as a rigidly ideological figure.[29] He notes that 'new Ken' was able to easily win the inaugural election even without the support of Labour, and with his association with the old guard. Contemporary commentators observed that Livingstone had gained broad appeal relative to the candidates from the established parties.[30]

With a number of the same personalities involved, including the new mayor, some continuity with the GLC period might have been expected on issues of equality and minority rights. By 2000, the legal and social frontiers had moved on, and in the decade that followed there were key legal gains nationally.[31] Evidence from polls suggests that the HIV/AIDS crisis of the 1980s and early 1990s had negatively affected public opinion on homosexuality and gay rights, but this improved in the late 1990s and 2000s.[32] From the 1990s, the concept of equalities mainstreaming shaped the UN, European Council and other international institutions' work on gender and sexuality, and informed tone and practice within British legislative and policy frameworks.[33] The theory and practice of mainstreaming represented a shift from an approach focused solely on anti-discrimination measures. It proposed that equality should be an aim of decision-making, with this objective integrated into all aspects of an organization's operations.

Mainstreaming, in theory, sought not only to consider the outcomes of decisions from minorities' perspectives but actively to involve those groups through participation in the decision-making process. The GLC had pioneered such approaches, albeit using procedures that were criticized for their elaborate complexity. In the early 2000s, overseeing key public bodies, the mayor of London was once again in a good position to embed equalities practices.[34] The institution of the mayoralty provided renewed opportunities in the drive to improve rights. Sexual orientation, understood specifically through the prism of lesbian, gay and bisexual equality, became a key focus for Livingstone and the GLA.

The introduction of the Civil Partnership Act (2004) in the UK stemmed directly from actions in City Hall.[35] Livingstone pledged to establish a London Partnership Register in his first manifesto.[36] Its introduction underscored a renewed commitment to advancing lesbian and gay rights under the new administrative structure of the mayoralty and assembly. In 2001, with the mayor present, two couples – Ian Burford and Alexander Cannell, and Linda Wilkinson and Carol Budd – became the first signatories (Plate 7). They held ceremonies at the GLA's Visitors' Centre, presided over by GLA officials. As the first lesbian couple to become registered partners, Wilkinson and Budd remarked:

> We are not doing this to ape heterosexual marriage. We are doing this because we believe it is another nail in the coffin of the prejudice that denies us our fundamental rights as human beings and makes us second class citizens in our own country.[37]

Somewhat defensive, they may have felt it necessary to clarify their reasons due to an association of partnership and marriage rights with the aim of assimilation within heterosexist, patriarchal traditions sanctioned by the state. In the context of the United States this logic was subsequently termed 'homonormativity' by Lisa Duggan.[38] The decision of these couples to register reminds us that rights have been achieved incrementally through the opportunistic insistence on the recognition of queer relations within complex institutions, including the institutions of urban governance. Some three hundred couples registered in the first year.[39] Although not yet a legally recognized status, documentation of these partnerships confirmed same-sex couples' relationships in ways that held legal substance. The register had an affective value, too, by raising awareness of same-sex partnerships and contributing to the momentum that would change the law. When the register was initiated, Peter Tatchell, the prominent human rights and LGBT campaigner, pushed the mayor to ensure that the rights it bestowed would be 'more than a symbolic gesture', and would apply to workers in the public bodies he oversaw.[40] Setting benchmarks has been one of the mayor's and GLA's routes to instigate change.[41]

Tatchell has been a dominant voice in debates about mayoral powers and decisions across Livingstone's and Boris Johnson's administrations, and into Sadiq Khan's. He was just one of several campaigners active in the GLC era who continued to play an important role. His has been a sustained voice in debates about the mayor's position on human rights, free speech, cultural difference and the role and character of annual Pride events. In the 2000s, Tatchell was still part of Outrage!, the direct-action group he co-founded at the London Lesbian and Gay Centre in 1990, and which continued to campaign until 2011.[42] Following the establishment of the partnership register, Outrage! pushed further than the mayor on partnership rights. It ran campaigns for gay civil marriage, and for heterosexual couples to form civil partnerships. These rights were enshrined in law in 2013 and 2018, respectively.[43]

Public spats in which Livingstone and Tatchell were central reflect the ego- and media-driven politics fostered by the mayoral system. In 2004, Livingstone drew criticism by inviting the controversial Islamic cleric Sheikh Yusuf al-Qaradawi to City Hall, and for describing his 'honored guest' as a 'man of tolerance and respect'.[44] A dossier collated by Outrage! challenged the mayor about al-Qaradawi's association with extreme views, support for violence and for the capital punishment of LGBT+ people.[45] This was sent to London Assembly members, who debated a motion proposed by the Green Party's Darren Johnson condemning the mayor. The criticisms, synthesized by Tatchell in an article for *Labour Left*, created a media storm.[46] The mayor refused to meet with the dossier's authors but defended himself in a lengthy written response.[47] He disputed the portrayal of al-Qaradawi's views, downplaying these as equivalent to those of many religious leaders, including those who had objected to the recent repeal, in 2003, of the infamous Section 28 of the Local Government Act 1988 (which prohibited the 'promotion' of homosexuality by local authorities) in England and Wales.[48] Livingstone contended that it was his duty to host religious leaders, including those he disagreed with, but this did not placate those who accused him of being 'too accommodating to "contemporary Islam"' and 'taking sides on the Palestine/Israel question'.[49]

After the announcement on 6 July 2005 of London's successful bid to host the 2012 Summer Olympics, and in the wake of the 7/7 London terrorist bombings which happened the following day, in his second term there was increasing pressure on Livingstone to articulate his vision of global London as a place of respect across difference. Massey, who had been a member of the GLC's Enterprise Board and remained active and influential in London politics in the first phases of the GLA, reflected positively on Livingstone's approach in *World City* (2007). Considering his statements on the bombings, on Iraq, Islam and the al-Qaradawi affair, she concludes that there is 'an attempt to construct not a bland diversity so much as a recognition of differences with all their conflicts and problematical implications'.[50] Although Massey does not focus on sexuality, the exchanges between Livingstone, Outrage!, and other commentators highlight that sexuality was central in the navigation of the different conceptions and lived realities of the cosmopolitan city. Such dialogues exposed fault lines regarding free speech and in understandings of the mayor's role. They demonstrated the need for careful thought and nuance in negotiating what Massey refers to as London's 'astonishing multiplicity of ethnicities and cultures'.[51] Gender and sexuality have continued to be important to the mayors' positioning.

Michael Keith, another urbanist associated with Labour, also contributed to public debates on diversity in London in the early 2000s. Like Massey, Keith bridged urban theory and practice, drawing from his research on racism, migration and urban change, and his experience as a former councillor and leader of the London Borough of Tower Hamlets. Like Massey, he emphasized that in a culturally diverse city one of the main roles for the mayor must be the establishment of public spaces to facilitate engagement across social difference. For Keith, tensions inevitably arise between an abstract, liberal ethics of citizenship, constructs of 'the community' as a social unit and 'source of moral value' at a local level, and the broader recognition of cultural difference in an increasingly diverse, postcolonial city.[52]

In the wake of the 9/11 attacks in New York City, and 7/7 bombings in London, such debates were framed against a backdrop of rising Islamophobia. Livingstone emphasized this factor as he defended his invitation to al-Qaradawi.[53] In this case, both the mayor and the objectors to the meeting he had set up (Tatchell being the most prominent) affiliated themselves with Muslim groups, Left-wing politics and the international movement for LGBT rights. The exchanges that unfolded highlight that in interactions with the LGBTQ+ population, the mayor and GLA have needed to look beyond the local, neighbourhood scale of community imagined by Keith. These groups represent a dispersed population, characterized by multiple established and transient networks, transnational identities, internationally mobile cultures and politics, and minority sexual and gender expressions that intersect with a wide range of other variables. The debates during the early years of the GLA demonstrate the ways that, as Michael Warner suggests, LGBTQ+ populations challenge normative theorizing, and by implication policy making, in their association with dispersal, and their disruption of received understandings of community.[54] He writes that queer sexuality is 'a political form of embodiment that is defined as noise or interference in the disembodying frame of citizenship'.[55] The trajectories of debate in London reinforce this, and support Jack Halberstam's claim that in researching sexuality and space a 'complicated picture of globalization and the relationships between the local and the global' emerges.[56]

During Livingstone's period in office, the GLA's approaches to sexual orientation equality were justified firstly on grounds of local inclusivity for Londoners, and secondly through suggesting that London had a wider role in addressing homophobic discrimination and violence as an international issue, and as a matter of competition with other global cities. For example, in 2007, in an article he wrote on the fortieth anniversary of the partial decriminalization of homosexual acts between men, Livingstone couched the importance of London in leading on gay rights in terms of the capital's role as a 'world-class benchmark', in competition with New York.[57] This demonstrates overlaps between the sphere of gay (cismale, white, wealthy) networks Massey alludes to in her comment on Sydney, and the aspiration of moving London up in the world city league tables.[58] Where urban governance and international rights agendas come together so directly they can reflect a neo-Imperialist desire for 'global gay rights' which projects hegemonic constructions of sexual and gender diversity and is inattentive to contextual variation or the violence of what Jasbir Puar terms the 'homonationalist' state.[59]

Beyond the external relations aspects of the mayor's engagements, driven by global city aspirations, it is notable that the first London Plan, published in 2004, was explicitly inclusive in addressing the capital's lesbian, gay, bisexual and trans people, under the policy 'Addressing the Needs of London's Diverse Population'.[60] This gave these populations a material presence alongside other minoritized groups. The plan determined that these groups' needs should be identified and addressed in borough-level plans to ensure they were not further disadvantaged due to general policies or those specifically on 'social infrastructure', 'the public realm, inclusive design and local distinctiveness'.[61] Importantly, it determined that: 'Existing facilities that meet the needs of particular groups should be protected and where shortfalls have been identified, policies should seek measures to address them proactively'.[62] The statement on LGBT people recognized discrimination based on societal attitudes to homosexuality, the existence of 'gender identity discrimination', and the impacts of hate crime and poor service provision. In line with the GLC-era approach, the Plan recognized that negative

54 *Queer Premises*

issues were 'compounded further for Black and minority ethnic lesbians, gay men, bisexuals and trans people'.[63] Emphasizing the primary role of the GLA as determining strategic direction, with the plan as a lobbying document, it called for 'further research and supporting data on the experiences and needs of lesbians, gay men, bisexuals and trans people'.[64]

From isolation to inclusion?

Along with public exchanges in the media about the mayor's duties and decisions, and the tone-setting London Plan, lower profile mechanisms of LGBT engagement were also introduced under Livingstone's tenure. Practical steps included the GLA's employment, in 2002, of a policy adviser, Rob Downey, a gay man with campaigning and policy experience gained working on HIV/AIDS, homophobia and policing.[65] In 2004, Downey helped initiate what would become a barometer of the mayors' approaches to LGBT inclusion: an annual Pride reception, at City Hall that brought together a variety of organizations. A regular LGBT Forum was also established, with an invitation to 'lesbian and gay groups [. . .] to meet GLA officers roughly every quarter to discuss issues of concern'.[66] There was therefore an open-door approach, but one that was reactive and problem-based, and linked to individual job roles, rather than strategic, proactive and change-focused. Criticisms were raised about the appointment of an unelected chair, Anni Marjoram, a Policy Advisor, who did not identify as LGBT, and who was perceived to be in Livingstone's closest clique.[67] The purpose and operation of the Forum were also questioned, since it had no powers to propose resolutions or hold votes on policy recommendations.[68]

Towards the end of Livingstone's first term a full-time LGBT Equality Coordinator post and a quarterly LGBT Forum accompanied a wider mainstreaming agenda stressing shared responsibility for equalities across the GLA.[69] The push to mainstream LGB equality manifested in a detailed strategy, *Sexual Orientation Equality Scheme: From Isolation to Inclusion*.[70] In contrast with the London Plan, this document did not include trans people. Pale in comparison to the fiery radicalism of the GLC's *Changing the World*, the tone and aesthetic contrast between these documents illustrates the shift to a more managerial governance approach. Nonetheless, *Sexual Orientation* was just as wide in scope. It elaborated issues signposted in the London Plan, detailing key challenges for LGB people in terms of employment, homophobic crime, education and bullying, homelessness, health and mental health, and service provision. It provided an overview of terminology, community history, legal contexts and other resources. Its main purpose was to set out the mayor's responsibilities for equality under the GLA Act (1999), to identify key personnel, and to provide a framework for measurable goals. The document treated 'LGB' communities under one umbrella for strategic purposes. Like the London Plan, it evidenced nuance in understanding different experiences and disadvantages within these groups, acknowledging the 'compounded discrimination and isolation from both the mainstream and LGB communities' faced by – in the terminology of the time – Black and minority ethnic LGB people.[71] As often with strategies and policies, including the London Plan, it was somewhat out of sync with the political cycle. As a directive for the GLA's public-facing work with LGB groups, and to shape its internal culture and employment practices, it covered the period 2005 to 2008, but it was only published as a draft in 2006. This highlights policymaking as a dynamic, iterative activity, pulled by the tides of elections and fluctuating political will.

In the final period of his administration, during the run-up to the election of 2008, Livingstone made a number of moves intended to respond to critics who sought a more direct approach to tackling disadvantages and discrimination experienced by LGBT populations.[72] In the process he received further criticism for electioneering. An LGBT advisory panel was established. It was chaired by Ben Summerskill, chief executive of Stonewall, and included Black Lesbians UK, the trade union UNISON, Polari, a network for older LGBT people, REGARD, an LGBT group for the disabled, and Imaan, a Muslim LGBT group, whom Tatchell had criticized Livingstone for failing to engage.[73] The advisory group met only once before Livingstone's term ended. It would be immediately disbanded by his successor, Boris Johnson.

Pride in a pink stetson

As an MP, Johnson had voted for the Civil Partnerships Bill (2004). He had been notably absent from other key votes on LGBT equality, such as the Equality Act (Sexual Orientation) Regulations (2007). He also came to office with a long record of misogynist, classist, homophobic and racist statements made during his journalistic and political career.[74] Although ostensibly the approach to mainstreaming LGBT equalities would continue, his tenure saw the retraction of established engagement structures, and heightened contradictions between rhetoric, policy and practice.

As Johnson restructured the GLA to create his team, equalities roles, such as Women's Adviser, were discontinued, with gleeful Conservative commentators capitalizing on the chance to disparage their existence as a 'throwback to the eighties GLC'.[75] The *Sexual Orientation Equality Scheme* was also scrapped. The dissolution of the LGBT advisory group provided an early opportunity for Johnson to distinguish his position from that of his predecessor. A spokesman pointed to the mayor's intention to 'use a range of channels to consult with the community, not least through the members of his team that happen to be gay'.[76] This characteristically flippant and inflammatory comment marked a deeper shift: a dilution of equalities mainstreaming, which distanced Johnson from past attempts to use City Hall as a vehicle for the progressive change sought by identity-based social movements. This is encapsulated in the replacement of an external expert panel – chosen specifically to represent a multiplicity of LGBT-identifying groups, and especially those marginalized according to their age, ethnicity, ability and religious beliefs – with unspecified consultation channels; and the assumption that LGBT Londoners, imagined as a homogenous gay community, would be adequately represented by privileged City Hall employees.

Unsurprisingly, the LGBT advisory panel Johnson disbanded condemned this decision.[77] Outrage!, however, supported it, using its platform to criticize the panel's establishment as an electoral tactic, and something it believed to be an 'elitist, unelected, unaccountable and undemocratic' group, handpicked by the mayor [Livingstone] and 'not necessarily representative of the LGBT community'.[78] Such calls of cronyism have echoed throughout all the mayoralties. Rather than being specific to LGBT engagement, specialist advisory groups are characteristic of the shift between the GLC era and the GLA towards a networked, partnership-based mode of governance. After the GLC was disbanded, the political vacuum was necessarily occupied, or partially occupied, by informal special interest groups. In 2000, the partnership-based governance approach became a defining feature of the North American-style executive-mayoralty that New Labour instituted, where the mayor and London Assembly's function was primarily to envision strategy.[79] Keith observes that the diminishing of democratic checks and balances in such mayoral systems meant that they were ill-equipped to deal with the complex and competing interests of different groups.[80] Outrage!, therefore, had a fair point. However, Johnson was not proposing any new accountable body to replace Livingstone's LGBT Advisory Group.

Since the establishment of the London mayoralty and GLA, participation in Pride has been an easy vehicle for the mayor to signal LGBTQ+ support. Pride marches – annual commemorations of the Stonewall uprising organized in London since 1972 – have become important hooks from which to fly rainbow flags, for mayors and many other urban interest groups, including grassroots activists and big corporations. Official and media sources evidence the handling of Pride by urban authorities and are a barometer of changing approaches to LGBTQ+ engagement. They reveal how issues of equality and public commemoration are regularly politicized by the mayors and mayoral candidates to shape their own image and manage external relations.

The 2008 Pride season saw Johnson host the annual Pride reception at City Hall and lead the march, donning a camped-up pink cowgirl hat (Plate 8). He did so against the advice of his LGBT advisor.[81] Many concerns would have been valid: Would it be seen as cultural appropriation, and hypocritical? Reportedly, he had also refused the requests of the GLF, who had led the first London Pride march in 1972, to march behind them: a decision which still smarted in 2022 when the group recounted it at Khan's celebratory reception to mark the fiftieth London Pride.[82] The image of Johnson and the pink stetson, concurrent with the retraction of LGBT engagement structures under his leadership, neatly symbolizes his ambivalent political persona: superficially light-hearted, but fickle and untrustworthy.

In queer culture cowboy iconography connotes and parodies masculine archetypes.[83] Carried by a white, cisgendered straight mayor leading a march to commemorate an uprising led by working-class trans people of colour against US state and police violence towards queers, the gesture suggests the form of cultural appropriation termed 'pinkwashing'. This has been central to lively recent debates about the devaluation of London Pride as an act of protest, remembrance and community: a critique, that is, that institutions and corporations benefit from association with diversity initiatives even while their practices work against or fail to contribute to positive structural change.[84]

Two speeches given by Johnson at the Pride receptions in 2008 and 2009, which can be viewed on YouTube, display similar contradictions. The 2008 event, sponsored by Aviva, an insurance company, occurred in the days of more relaxed security when official receptions could be held outside what was then City Hall, in the slick corporate pastiche of the classical amphitheatre that is in the private MoreLondon development. Johnson opens his speech with a joke about Livingstone and the GLC.[85] He praises the pioneering of causes and rights – 'ban the bomb, and, er, this and that ethnic minorities, sticking up for their rights, and lesbian and gay rights and all the rest of it' – that have become accepted, even within the Tory party and right-wing press that had opposed and ridiculed them. He goes on to commit to this 'carnival vision of London as a place of generosity', and to sticking up for LGBT rights and tackling homophobic crime and bullying. As the jokes continue, his tone becomes more mocking. Johnson teases that many of his own officials figure 'very high up in the list of pink power (or whatever it's called – what's it called?)', meaning the 'Pink List', and refers by name to some of his gay male staff. His words echo a *Spectator* column he wrote in 2000, disparaging 'Labour's appalling agenda, encouraging the teaching of homosexuality in schools, and all the rest of it'.[86]

These tongue-in-cheek performances, in which the mayor flip-flopped around serious issues of rights and discrimination, were part of the intentional cultivation of his public persona, and reflect a mayoral system that encouraged political tit-for-tat public exchanges. During the 2011 election campaign, Livingstone, as former mayor, criticized Johnson's administration as 'directionless' with 'no bold moves on LGBT equality from City Hall'.[87] It was easy to evidence this by citing material changes such as the cutting of funding for Soho Pride, which had been held since 1992, the scrapping of the annual London Pride reception at City Hall, and the GLA's withdrawal from the Stonewall Equality Index.

During the 2012 mayoral election campaign Johnson was further criticized for not mentioning LGBT communities in his manifesto.[88] In response, he repeatedly said, including at a Stonewall-hosted hustings, that he would produce a 'London gay manifesto'.[89] Questioned on this once re-elected, with no such document forthcoming, he changed tack, stating that: 'My approach unites Londoners rather than segregating communities based on their identities, as has been done in the past'.[90] His implication that other ways of governing which recognized identity-based affiliations were divisive was not accompanied by any evidence. Directly contradicting his earlier position, the statement rather underscored an ideological aversion to recognizing and responding to social difference, intersecting and forms of discrimination, or the circumstances and lived experiences of minoritized populations.

Albeit with reduced capacity and activity, LGBT engagement work did continue during Johnson's period in office. This was driven by civil servants rather than by the mayor's personal commitment or leadership. The quarterly LGBT fora which had taken place under Livingstone continued but were reduced to biannual 'LGBT Engagement Meetings'. Trans organizations also began to be more actively engaged by City Hall – an important change driven by assessment of the GLA's duties under the Equalities Act 2010.[91] Johnson's individual approach was, however, more straightforwardly aligned than Livingstone's with the new gay conservatism of the 2000s which, in the US context, Duggan named homonormativity. This was characterized by a so-called 'gay positive' vision of equality aligned with corporate agendas and the status quo – including the unquestioned centrality of wealthy white gay men.[92] Homonormative politics are can be differentiated from militant, liberationist identity politics and from anti-identarian, intersectional queer politics.

Despite the differences, Johnson's approach to equalities aligned with his predecessor in many ways. It was oriented around the perceived public benefits of regeneration, especially in relation to assumptions regarding the positive impacts of hosting the 2012 Olympics. If we look at the London Plan of 2016, however, we can see substantive change in that specific statements on LGBT communities' needs have been replaced with more generic comments on social infrastructure, with support for facilities to be 'accessible to all sections of the community'.[93] The definition of 'social infrastructure' was also tied more specifically to the need for economic growth, and a more traditional notion of physical infrastructure. This was accompanied by heavier emphasis on evidencing, in contexts of development, the need for community assets, rather than protecting them *per se*.

Governing the night

Given the close relationship between queer world-making and night-spaces, along with posturing for Pride season, night-time governance and commentaries on venues offer another gauge for understanding how LGBTQ+ populations have been addressed by the GLA and London's mayors.[94] In the UK, and in London, policy interest in the Night-Time Economy increased during the 1990s and 2000s. Under New Labour, in the early 2000s, the 'urban renaissance' agenda of regenerating cities involved analysis of the challenges and potentials of the evening and late-night economy.[95] This was part of the shift from a negative understanding of the 'inner city' to a vision of post-industrial cities as containing the seeds of their own rejuvenation through the growth of the leisure and cultural sectors. In the mid-1990s, there was already policy awareness of the potential of planning in temporally sensitive ways, and some attention to night-time leisure and the model of the 24-hour city to contribute to post-industrial urban rejuvenation, even if the UK was considered 'underdeveloped' in this regard.[96] By this time, scholars and policymakers were also cognizant of the problems associated with night-time consumption.[97] The New Labour urban renaissance agenda focused on the potential to shift from youth-centred night cultures, binge-drinking and anti-social behaviour towards a more inclusive model, which aimed to alleviate the logistical challenges of night planning and management. European cities such as Madrid and Bologna were held aloft as civilized ideals worth striving for.[98]

In 2012, when Boris Johnson was commencing his second term as mayor, the research team advising the mayor and GLA published a paper on alcohol consumption and the night-time economy.[99] This highlighted the benefits of alcohol consumption to the economy but focused largely on the associated economic and social costs, outlining ways these could be managed through policy interventions. Looking across different London boroughs' interventions, as well as at other UK and international examples, it proposed that night-time policies be developed from the basis of the harm and risks associated with alcohol consumption.

Four years later, in 2016, only as he was concluding his tenure, Johnson established a Night Time Commission as a six-month investigation into the night-time economy, remarking that

> There is no doubt that the night time economy is hugely important to our prosperity and the life of our city, but there is insufficient oversight for the way it

is managed and problems are mitigated. It is brilliantly successful, but night time activities can be seen as causes of noise and nuisance, whilst businesses complain that rising property values, the need for housing, licensing requirements and other red tape are damaging their operations, even leading to closures. If we are to compete against other world cities it is vital that we develop policies to reconcile the competing needs and concerns.[100]

This statement echoes the earlier GLA research in its focus on the leisure sector and an approach to the urban night driven primarily by its economic potential, and by attention to the problems associated with unregulated activities. Seeking to better understand the range and impact of the night-time sector, the framing of the commission underscored a tension between an ideological conviction to the reduction of regulation, and a desire to alleviate costs and maximize productivity through regulation. The establishment of the Night Commission was again driven by competition with other European cities, with Johnson referencing Amsterdam and Paris as positive models for attending to the management and economic potential of the urban night. Amsterdam had elected club promoter Mirik Milan Gelders as its first independent *Nachtburgemeester* (Night Mayor) in 2012.[101]

Saving the night

A Music Venues Taskforce which had been set up by the GLA published *London's Grassroots Music Venues Rescue Plan* in 2015.[102] This responsive document argued that a crisis of closures and threats required grassroots venues to be 'saved'. The tone of urgency, and the possibility that night-time infrastructure could be rescued, have strongly coloured subsequent discussions, including those around LGBTQ+ venues. Although the *Rescue Plan* framed the threat as a crisis, it was important in pointing to the everyday, rather than exceptional, negative impacts of London's contemporary urban dynamics: high rents, restrictive licensing, the sale of venues for conversion to residential use, and conflicts between business, leisure and residential communities. Another key argument – again relevant to LGBTQ+ premises – was that the research and development functions of these venues had been undervalued.

In his announcement of the commission, Johnson referenced the 35 per cent loss of grassroots music venues that the report highlighted had taken place since 2007.[103] Some journalistic coverage drew links to LGBTQ+ venue closures, though Johnson had not mentioned these specifically.[104] The commission was tasked to consider appointing a Night Time Economy Champion, responding to the idea for a night mayor pitched by the Music Venues Taskforce, as part of the effort to stymie music venue closures.[105] The announcement came just before the mayoral elections. Johnson was not standing for re-election, so, two months before the vote, it signaled the likely direction of travel for policy rather than his own commitment.

With Conservatives, including Johnson and the new mayoral candidate Zac Goldsmith, publicly acknowledging the detrimental effects of development on cultural venues, this was a turning point in policy.[106] Overall, the night was still framed as primarily an economic concern, with a narrowly framed analysis of costs and benefits. Goldsmith's manifesto presented London as the capital of 'booze fueled violence'.[107] He committed to use the Late Night Levy (2012), introduced by the coalition Conservative-Liberal Democrat government, to intensify policing in nightlife hotspots and stressed the need for increased policing of public transport at night.[108] This was a conventional negative caricature of the city at night, which overshadowed the more positive contributions of night venues highlighted in the *Rescue Plan*, whereby music – and by implication other – venues increase 'London's desirability as a place to live, work and visit' and 'nurture talent, create communities and ferment innovation'.[109] Goldsmith's pitch was out of sync with wider international policy and academic discussions of night-time urbanism which, as criminologist Phil Hadfield observes, were 'now emphasising the exclusionary outcomes that can result from securitisation and gentrification of the NTE'.[110]

This assessment aligns with the broader conception of interlinked social and cultural infrastructures, including night-time venues, under Sadiq Khan's administration. Khan, who was elected mayor in May 2016, had held a hustings meeting at the Royal Vauxhall Tavern (RVT), an iconic LGBTQ+ cabaret venue deemed under threat, the campaign for which Boris Johnson had supported after concerted lobbying (see Chapter 6). Khan positioned himself clearly as an advocate of LGBTQ+ communities and spaces. A month after he took up office, forty-nine people were murdered and fifty-three others were wounded in the mass shooting at LGBTQ+ nightclub Pulse in Orlando, Florida, prompting a well-attended Soho vigil to express solidarity. Just after this, Khan made his first public statement of support for the RVT Future campaign as mayor, drawing a link to Pulse in Orlando.[111] In 2016, he headed his first Pride march, using its potential to promote a message of inclusion and diversity.[112] He reinstituted the annual Pride reception that had ceased in the later years of Johnson's administration. He also connected the march with a wider diversity agenda by framing Pride as an 'antidote' to the attack on Pulse, as well as to recent terrorist attacks at London Bridge and Finsbury Park.[113] Although responsive to a tragic event, it pointed to a positive framing of night-time spaces, in which LGBTQ+ venues were highly valued.

Khan's manifesto had not specifically committed to the continuation of the Night Commission Johnson had announced, but in December 2016 Khan launched a 'revamped' version.[114] This would 'review the capital's night-time economy' in order 'to understand the challenges faced by night-time businesses, authorities and residents and develop ways to balance these as London's night-time economy grows'.[115] Philip Kolvin QC, a prominent barrister, licensing expert and industry adviser, was appointed as chair. The announcement cited Kolvin's recent *Manifesto for the Night Time Economy* (2016), in which he had argued, using the metaphor of a garden that needs to be tended, for a holistic approach to planning and managing what he interchangeably referred to as the night-time economy or the leisure economy.[116] This manifesto is framed around diversity of activities, social diversity (attractiveness to 'every sector of the population, regardless of age, race, gender, sexuality or physical or mental ability'), inclusivity regardless of wealth and income, physical accessibility and good transportation, safety and security.[117] It pointed to recent phenomena that had negatively impacted on the health of the NTE, including residential development, approved by planning permission or permitted development. It referenced the tensions between residential communities and leisure uses, with incoming residents pressuring local authorities to take stringent licensing approaches.[118] Kolvin argued convincingly that

> the key regulatory tool of the night time economy is licensing, which tends to be a reactive tool, whereas the main tool in the day time economy is planning, which works proactively. While planning is about place-making, licensing is about place-keeping. This must be resolved, for otherwise great night time economies will happen in spite of rather than because of the work of public authorities.[119]

The vision the mayor went on to publish, *From Good Night to Great Night: a Vision for London as a 24 Hour City*, in July 2017, resonates with Kolvin's manifesto. Yet Kolvin let his initial twelve-month contract as chair expire, publicly criticizing City Hall for compromising the Commission's independence and failing to resource and publicize its activities sufficiently.[120]

The Night Commission, appointed to facilitate the mayor's vision, went on to undertake a public consultation through focus groups and interviews. It published *Think Night: London's Neighbourhoods from 6pm to 6am* (2019), arguing for strategic 'diversification' of the night sector through tracking data and identifying opportunities to 'preserve segments such as LGBTQ+ and small music venues'.[121] The authors presented social diversity and diversity of activities as interconnected. The Commission also promoted a more positive and proactive use of licensing. They recommended that all policies be subject to a 'night test', to rate their impact on London's culture, sociability, well-being and economy at night; as well as a range of other measures to gather and monitor data on night activities and to guide and support local authorities in their planning and decision-making. Fully immersed in the discourse of London as a global city, the report also zoomed out to place emphasis on London as a NTE leader and tourist magnet.

As well as relaunching the Night Commission as a body to advise the mayor 'as to the sustainable development of London's night time economy', Khan fulfilled his manifesto pledge to establish the new role of night czar, 'to champion London's vibrant night-time economy'.[122] Night mayors and related structures for night governance and advocacy were first introduced in Berlin and Amsterdam in the early 2000s, proliferating in the late 2010s. By 2018 they featured in over forty cities.[123] Like directly elected mayors, appointees to night mayor roles have been charismatic individuals who are required to engage with groups across different public and professional sectors, using their profile to foster positive discourse on the night, as well as lobbying national government. In surveying the institution of night mayors internationally, governance scholar Andreina Seijas and ex-Amsterdam night mayor Mirik Milan Gelders observe a move away from a narrow framing of the night as one requiring restrictive approaches to counteract negative impacts.[124] These figures, they argue, reflect the move towards networked, partnership-based governance 'as a complex responsibility that involves a mix of agencies including the police, licensing authorities, resident groups and public health institutions'.[125] Night mayors have been distinctive for bringing embodied knowledge, personal networks and capacities for disruptive thinking and mediation between different interest groups, working either alongside or within formal city structures.

The London night czar is a special appointee of the Deputy Mayor for Communities and sits within the Greater London Authority's Culture Team, embedded within this established institutional framework. A competitive recruitment process led to around 200 applications and the appointment of Amy Lamé in November 2016.[126] Originally from New Jersey, with Irish and Italian heritage, Lamé brought grassroots knowledge of LGBTQ+ nightlife and music scenes more widely.[127] Lamé is passionate about the radical social and cultural potential of night-space. When she talks about her role and priorities she emphasizes how these have been shaped by her background and identity as a queer woman, as a night-worker and as an activist.[128] She also places emphasis on being able to 'push and explore things', drawing on a background of queer protest, performance and social practice. Lamé is a well-known LGBTQ+ community representative and this has also been important to the positioning of the night czar role, leading both to positive and negative media discourse and interactions with activists.

In London, both the night czar and Commission chairs have convening roles. For Lamé, 'whatever happens in the dark' is her brief. In practice, this cross-cuts different areas of policy and activity.[129] This framing of the role is notably broad, taking in what Seijas and Milan Gelders refer to as both 'hardware' ('improving the built environment in a way that is conducive to greater vibrancy and quality of life after dark') and 'software' ('the laws and regulations that facilitate activity and minimize nuisance at night').[130] One of the clearest aspects of this, which Lamé stresses, is to shift away from discussions of 24/7 partying and leisure, and focus attention on nightworkers and issues of equality at night.[131] This is in line with a shift in City Hall to focus NTE discussions on the welfare of nightworkers and to use licensing and other instruments to promote a more inclusive NTE.[132]

Apart from fostering productive discussion, an important question for the new designated night officials has been: what do we actually know about the city's nocturnal life and the spaces, licensed or otherwise, in which it takes place? How can these – until recently – overlooked, informal or stigmatized dimensions of urban life be quantified? Mayor Khan and the GLA's Culture Team saw the challenges to LGBTQ+ venues alongside threats to other kinds of social and cultural space, such as pubs and grassroots music venues.[133] Since a cultural infrastructure plan was one of Khan's key manifesto pledges, research within the GLA and with partners accelerated to inform this. To understand what was happening with pubs the GLA worked with CAMRA (the Campaign for Real Ale) and their data; for music venues there was the Grass Roots Music Trust; for queer venues, no established structures had existed, but new ones formed through activism and in response to threats of closure (see Chapter 4).

The question of how to evidence the profile of nocturnal social and cultural infrastructure necessitates some sensitivity as to how the elusive rhythms of the night have afforded opportunities to marginalized groups – what José Esteban Muñoz refers to as 'the cover of a protective darkness'.[134] LGBTQ+ populations, including those who are racialized or minoritized according to gender have had to avoid visibility in order to escape discrimination and criminalization. Their presence, identities and behaviour have been classified and policed, so the politics of the production of nocturnal knowledge is an area of understandable sensitivity. Access to community-based knowledge is therefore paramount, and 'having those connections that maybe, you know, others might not', to marginalized groups, is something that the night czar highlights that she brings.[135] She has continued her work as a DJ and performer, bringing knowledge and methods from these practices to the role. The serious approach and valuation of community-based knowledge, and the activation of networks to connect with hard-to-reach groups, sets Khan's administration in contrast with Johnson's flippant comments about assuming adequate LGBT representation through City Hall's gay male staff. Lamé has also influenced the membership of key advisory groups so that they are more representative.[136] As chair of the London Music Board she oversaw the enlargement of this group and instituted diversity within the membership as an explicit aim.[137]

The context in which the role of night czar was imagined and operates is not dissimilar to that in which Muñoz was writing, in New York City, given the contexts of large-scale redevelopment featuring processes of commercialization and purification (see Chapters 1; 4). Although it is not without agency, the post is constrained by these global city dynamics. Conflicting understandings of the role, and its limits – relative, for example, to the powers of local authorities to set licensing regulations – have surfaced in public debate.[138] The critiques both of Lamé and the role of night czar show that the discourse of 'saving the night', with one individual as a figurehead, offers hope but also leads to a weight of expectation.

The London night czar's work aligns with what Seijas and Milan Gelders describe as the current stage of night mayors' activities internationally, namely 'global activism to save the remains of nightlife in a context of gentrification and massive closures of music venues that have turned the night mayor into an almost necessary figure'.[139] The work that is being pursued on issues of equality and inclusion at night is not without contradiction since it attempts to alleviate the stresses caused by global city competitiveness, while being integrated within and reproducing the same logic.[140] There is pressure to resolve intractable, long-term structural challenges, without systemic change, within the limits of the strategic and external relations roles of the mayor and night czar, and subject to changes of direction with each political cycle. By 2019, Lamé had therefore understandably become careful to point out that night scenes are characterized by flux, even if some venues have special status: 'we have to recognise that London is a dynamic place. Some places will close, others will *open*. Some places will move, and that is part and parcel of, you know of, of being in London and being an operator, being a promoter [...]'.[141]

Night-time governance interventions have an opportunistic character that reflects the night-time sector's entrepreneurialism. Several of the mayor, night czar and GLA's collaborations with activists, local authorities and others are evidenced in this book. Tools such as a new LGBT Venues Charter, the *Cultural Infrastructure Toolbox* and map, and the revised London Plan (2021), have helped to give material weight to LGBT venues in planning contexts – and have filtered through to local authority plans and policies.[142] In 2023, the GLA uses the initials 'LGBTQ+' to signal broader 'queer' inclusion. This is not defined specifically, but Khan has been vocally supportive of trans and non-binary communities.[143] There has also been a collaborative approach to engagement and funding for initiatives designed to support intersectionally marginalized groups, such as Tonic Housing, a not-for-profit creating inclusive LGBT+ affirmative retirement communities; and The Outside Project, an independent LGBTQI+ community shelter, centre and refuge (see Chapter 8).[144] Although diversity is still framed through the lens of the competitive global city and Western liberationist politics, there are alignments with collectives who prioritise decolonial approaches and mutalist queer organisational models that are distinct from mainstream LGBT activism.

Over the rainbows

Since the establishment of the GLA and mayoralty, Pride has become firmly part of the apparatus of place promotion, with ever bigger rainbow stencils plastering West End facades for their power to leverage consumerism and boost corporations' diversity capital. The march and associated events have recently been run by the not-for-profit Pride in London, with City Hall contributing funding alongside numerous corporate partners. There is an annual debate about the purpose of Pride, with sharp criticism of the involvement of some of its more unlikely sponsors and participant organizations, whether global banks, major supermarkets, the military or police. Some of the generation of activists who were heavily involved in the London Lesbian and Gay Centre in the 1980s feel strongly that 'Pride in London has debased itself'.[145] Others, while sceptical, take a more pragmatic approach to Pride's compromises. One manager of a community business active from the 1980s to today, for example, points out that even in the 1980s Pride was criticized for not being political enough. He comments: 'I think, "what the hell is Barclays doing?", you know, but somebody's got to pay for it – and I've seen Pride collapse *enough* without paying their bills, many, many, *many* times over'.[146] He also emphasizes the importance of Pride's increased scale and visibility, with 'rainbows everywhere', on the streets and in the media, compared to the lack of attention in the past, and associates this with a greater degree of social acceptance and affirmation for younger generations.[147]

Political action is inherent to the tradition of the parade, as the common slogan 'pride is a protest' reminds us. The early Heritage in Pride marches in New York, commemorating the Stonewall uprisings, took place within, and drew attention to, the contradictions of the mafia-owned and controlled corporate scene.[148] Even if it was always a space of contestation – and that was fundamental to its role – Pride has increasingly, and understandably, been criticized for its institutionalization and commercialization – in London as in other cities internationally. Many perceive it as irrevocably detached from its origins as a radical expression of protest and collective remembering. Yet, radical groups still march, even while they speak out against the dilution and assimilation of Pride's political purpose, its many compromises and its reinforcement of the cisnormative, heteropatriarchal institutions of neoliberal capitalism.

Pride in London has been a contested area during Sadiq Khan's tenure (Plate 9). In 2019, Khan used the Pride reception to attack his predecessor, by then about to become prime minister, for his record of homophobic language.[149] Each year, he reminds guests that Johnson cancelled the annual reception they are attending.[150] Alongside this posturing, however, he committed funding to Pride for a more sustained period of five years from 2018. In comparing the latest phase of London government with earlier administrations, there has been renewed support for a wider range of Pride activities, above and beyond the march, including direct funding for UK Black Pride, which celebrated its fifteenth anniversary in 2020, and local prides in some boroughs.[151] This emphasizes an increased recognition of intersectional differences within LGBTQ+ communities, including uneven access to resources, and a wider perspective beyond central London's West End. Khan has also been vocal in supporting Trans Pride. In 2020, when the London Pride march had to be cancelled due to the Covid-19 pandemic, two smaller-scale marches went ahead which had more specific political aims: a Black Trans Lives Matter protest and a march led by GLF veterans. Marchers, who wore masks and practised social distancing, used the event to call for interconnected issues of racism, transphobia and economic and environmental inequality to be addressed. Trans Pride gathers larger crowds each year. These marches are a return, somewhat, to the earlier days of Pride, when the main involvement of the authorities was through policing; and when parallel marches, aligning to different but interconnected issues, were a regular feature of protest and coalitional community-building. In 2022, City Hall announced an open tender, inviting community groups to submit proposals to run Pride in London for five years, so even the main Pride events may now follow new directions shaped by grassroots initiatives.[152]

Since 2000, the timbre of discourse on LGBTQ+ issues in City Hall has reflected the politics of each executive mayor. The revolutionary drive of the feminist, lesbian and gay municipal socialism of the GLC in the 1980s had receded by the advent of the GLA, even if many of the same individuals continued to play a role. New legal and policy frontiers were now addressed within the governance and economic framework of neoliberalism, with an emphasis on London's global city status, and in a mayoral system whereby the individual politics, manifestos and reactive statements of the mayors and their interlocutors affect the reasoning behind, commitment to and speed of this work. In this period, LGBTQ+ equalities in London, a barometer of wider political changes, have been shaped by multiple external factors, including the drive to mainstream equalities thinking within the GLA and the public bodies overseen by the mayor. The definition of the role of mayor as a strategic one, with a focus on facilitating large-scale infrastructure development and property-led urban regeneration to elicit public value, has produced many contradictions that are further explored in the following chapters.

Looking at the inter-relationships between LGBTQ+ equalities and urban governance there is no straightforward linear trajectory from radical social movements to a conservative, homonormative politics. A plurality of grassroots queer activist communities, organizations and venues have continued to dialogue with the mayor and City Hall and to inform policy directions. This is clearest in the administrations of Livingstone and Khan, where methods of engagement have been more sincere, wider in scope and more flexible and strategic. Along with direct support for, and influence from, radical grassroots queer collectives and specific directives on LGBT minorities and their social infrastructures in their iterations of the London Plan,

Livingstone and Khan highlighted and acted upon the need for research on these populations' experiences to inform policy, and promoted a more expansive evidence base, integrating community knowledge and leadership. The preceding and following chapters demonstrate that this has enabled a better understanding of LGBTQ+ venues and cultures. In the Khan administration, to date, this has resulted in visualization of the most formal premises and threats to these within a more holistic set of interventions to map and protect social and cultural infrastructure.

Although LGBTQ+ equalities and attention to social infrastructure have been consistently embedded into the governance of the capital, in parallel, as will be further explored in the following chapters, through the 2000s and 2010s, outcomes of urban development for these groups, and for the venues associated with them, have often been poor. Available planning and equalities impact assessment tools, and heritage evaluation processes, have repeatedly failed to safeguard their interests and cultures. The crisis over venue closures in the mid-2010s, and the recent attention to the night-time economy and night culture in urban governance, provided new impetuses to bring LGBT communities to the table in more meaningful ways. Khan has overseen the emergence of a more proactive and joined-up approach to the identification and protection of social and cultural infrastructure. Within London's governance, the management of the city at night and engagement with LGBT communities have been approached more positively. These areas nonetheless continue to raise ethical questions and tensions with regard to, for example, the prioritization of specific groups or activities, or making these visible within formal structures in which they may sit uncomfortably. The venues crisis allowed other community space questions and issues to emerge and begin to be addressed. This emphasises the ways that night-spaces have for these communities, since the 1980s, served wider value and emblematic functions beyond consumption and leisure. This context has also influenced the re-emergence of community-centred venues. From 2020, the Covid-19 pandemic presented specific challenges, and stimulated institutional and community responses, which I reflect upon in Chapter 8.

4

Rupture and repair

From the late 2000s to the mid-2010s, a spate of closures of much-loved venues serving London's LGBTQ+ communities, and further threats of sale and redevelopment, provoked intense debate and media interest. How was the loss or decline of venues expressed and interpreted? In this chapter, I pay attention to journalists' accounts. I counterbalance these with evidence from a survey and workshops undertaken by UCL Urban Laboratory, with participants from a wide array of LGBTQ+ community members, operators of venues and freelancers working in their orbit, such as promoters, artists and DJs.[1] These sources offer a gauge to understand both the acute public concern prompted by closures and the value of venues as it has recently been understood. To add a further layer, I discuss data on the number and types of venues. This is based on a mapping exercise undertaken by Urban Laboratory, co-designed with community-based networks in 2016. This followed the media outcry and was undertaken in response to campaigners' alarm about dwindling venue numbers and as the GLA began gathering intelligence towards Mayor Sadiq Khan's *Cultural Infrastructure Plan*, map and toolbox.[2]

Across this varied evidence, I follow the language and arguments in circulation, asking: How are venues conceptualized and what values are ascribed to them? How are they understood, or are threats to them understood, in relation to practices, experiences and conceptualizations of urban change? What were the main explanatory tropes and how did these encapsulate different understandings of the past, present and future of LGBTQ+ communities and venues? In their accounts, journalists used terminology and arguments derived from urban scholarship – on gentrification, gaybourhoods and creative pioneers – to articulate the relationships between LGBTQ+ populations and urbanism. These concepts offered quick explanations for apparent patterns. Yet, detached from their specific historical, cultural and geographical roots, they can also risk oversimplification. Similarly, counting and mapping venues provides reassuring data, even though quantitative representations are necessarily partial, are reliant on crude definitions, and obscure actual complexities beneath the points in time and space that they plot. As the threats to venues became more apparent, dissatisfaction with the available evidence, and with the dominant interpretative tropes, drove a wider debate among diverse LGBTQ+ populations and campaigners in different parts of the city about both the provision and qualities of venues. This widened the scope of enquiry and understanding, as is reflected in the evidence from the survey, interviews and the workshops that I present.

Pressing headlines

In 2006, journalists began to pay increasing attention to threats posed by redevelopment to London's gay clubs and bars. They initially focused on venues around the large-scale Central London redevelopment of Tottenham Court Road Station in the preparatory phase for Crossrail, the major new trainline planned to cut across the city.[3] Some of the first articles were prompted by the announcement that a club called The Ghetto, which had been forced to move from Soho to Shoreditch in 2008 due to rising rents, would close permanently.[4] We will look closely at the Crossrail Tottenham Court Road redevelopment and its impacts in Chapter 5. In this early media coverage journalists referred to a Gay Business Association dataset that suggested an acceleration in the decline of the number of gay bars, with a 40 per cent reduction from 250 in 2004 to 150 in 2009.[5] This was substantiated by the views of another gay business, the market research agency Out Now.[6] These datasets, collated by organisations representing business interests, show how the alarm and debate were at first focused on economic factors. As well as making a specific link to the effects on gay bars of the 2008 financial crisis, the articles at this time proposed broader causal interpretations, which would reverberate in later coverage. Central themes included a shift to online dating and cruising, with the 'gay market' being an early adopter of online technology; a recession-induced reduction of disposable income for leisure and entertainment reflected in reduced footfall; and 'increasing acceptance' and integration of the 'gay community'.[7] When the GBA published its data, media reports asserted the dominance of Soho, in the West End, and Vauxhall, in the south, as the predominant scenes and those most impacted by the recession, while the coverage also flagged Shoreditch venues in East London.

Media interest in LGBTQ+ populations trends around issues and events: boosterist articles about the pink pound and specific gay villages; Pride season; public health, including HIV transmission rates; policing, homophobic attacks and homophobic crime statistics; and, more recently, trans rights and politics. Reporting on homophobic hate crime, which includes one-off high-profile homophobic attacks, and commentaries on homophobia and hate crime statistics, was high at the end of the 2000s.[8] Annually, Pride season is marked by a media fanfare. All of these preoccupations in media representations of LGBTQ+ issues are situated, in different ways, through reference to particular localities, venues and urban imaginaries, in ways that require careful decoding. Geographer Lo Marshall, for example, analyses the recent media stigmatization of trans people, elaborated through controversies over particular spaces, such as public toilets and swimming facilities.[9] Preceding the so-called 'trans debate', for a period from 2011, there was an intense media focus on the chemsex practices of men who have sex with men.[10] The surge of coverage, from 2014, featured many examples of moral panic and pathologization, as well as some more informed considerations of the phenomenon, and reports of research by public health authorities.

Media theorist Jamie Hakim has critiqued the pathologizing and moralizing tendencies of media coverage of chemsex.[11] Hakim avoids the simple cause-and-effect narratives in many media accounts. He understands the advent of chemsex as linked to novel shifts in the use of recreational drugs and the use of mobile apps to organize parties and encounters. But he takes a more nuanced view of the phenomenon than most media commentators, arguing that it represents a desire for intimate, joyful collectivity, by 'largely migrant, gay and bisexual men', 'in a wider culture in which neoliberalism has been hegemonic and that, in multiple ways, alienates them from experiencing the possibility of collectivity at all'.[12] Hakim specifically links the location of new spaces of intimacy and collectivity in the private sphere to diminished availability of other venues, due to neoliberal urban economic trends. Venues are semiprivate and semipublic spaces to different degrees at different moments. They are regulated, managed, in- or exclusive, linked to wider public infrastructures, and associated with specified communities to varied extents. They change with patterns of consumption, including the use of intoxicants, which stimulate different temporalities and forms of socialisation. Cultural producer, performer and theorist, R. Justin Hunt has argued that 'chill out' after-parties shift 'our perspective from the public club venue to the private urban residence' placing them outside of the consumerist leisure industry, even while they perform the policy aspiration of the '24-hour city'.[13] The work of Hunt, Hakim and others on such intimate spaces suggests that the opening, closure and operation of individual licensed premises, the emergence or re-emergence of distinct typologies, has to be understood and interpreted against similarly layered and long-term structural socio-economic and cultural shifts.

The chemsex debate intensified in parallel with increased coverage of venue closures. Some articles directly linked club closures and chemsex. For example, in an autobiographical comment piece in *Vice*, author and model Thomas Hibbitts presented their own and their friends' experiences of chemsex and clubbing scenes, emphasizing that these were interlinked.[14] Here, chemsex was linked to 'gay people [. . .] becoming disillusioned with the current club scene', to the unpopularity of Soho, and to the 'gentrification of east London [which] has hit the community hard'.[15] However, this piece also emphasized that many clubs were still thriving, with new scenes emerging, and concluded that 'nightlife doesn't just vanish' with new patterns of behaviour.[16] This dissatisfaction with the idea of the decline or vanishing of nightlife is useful to take forward.

Weird gentrification

The press coverage that focused on venue closures as its primary topic and which centred on the Tottenham Court Road Station redevelopment continued in the 2010s. In 2013, this featured superclub closures around London Bridge station, another big redevelopment site.[17] The mix of news coverage in the mid- to late 2010s included more specialist articles reflecting on the decline of London's nightclubs.[18] In terms of venues, more generally, Soho received the lion's share of attention, with some coverage also of Vauxhall and Shoreditch.[19] The focus on these areas as gaybourhoods, or looser constellations of LGBTQ+ spaces, overlooked the wider dispersal of venues and scenes.

As campaigners created energy around threats to specific venues, they attracted media interest too. There was increased attention to Soho in 2014 with the closure of the iconic cabaret bar Madame Jojo's, which had operated on the site under the same name from the 1960s.[20] Madame Jojo's was a cabaret, burlesque, drag and performance venue, established by Paul Raymond, venue owner and pornography publisher, with regular club nights and live music hosted by Jojo Wright. Like many venues, Madame Jojo's multiple functions are reflected in the planning designation *sui generis* (see Chapter 6). The heart of the Soho cabaret scene, it was notably mixed in its programming and clientele. The online petition launched by campaigners, which gathered more than ten thousand signatories, bears witness to the venue's strong association with LGBTQ+ populations, especially the trans community, and queer culture more broadly.[21]

Campaigners and media commentators linked the venue's closure to a broader process of state-led gentrification in Soho, accelerated through Westminster City Council's removal of its licence following a violent incident.[22] The council was perceived to be using this to fast-track a development for which the owner, Soho Estates, already had approved permission. Soho Estates oversees the property portfolio resulting from Raymond's legacy. As well as the petition, the closure sparked a 'Save Our Soho' protest in the form of a funeral procession, attracting significant press coverage. This was resonant with earlier spectacular protests, such as a cortège mourning the redevelopment of the London docklands in the 1980s.[23] Raymond Estates, which oversees a smaller part of Paul Raymond's portfolio, aligned itself with Save Soho campaigners.[24]

The controversy over Madame Jojo's marked a particular moment in public criticism of Westminster Council's enablement of what one commentator called 'weird gentrification', whereby an area with a long history of piecemeal adaptation and social heterogeneity was being negatively reconfigured towards the interests of property owners; where cultural and night-time venues were being subject to increasingly punitive regulation to facilitate redevelopment; and where the council's motivations and actions were opaque.[25] These trends are anything but weird, in that such displacements were being enacted through everyday tools of urban governance, with broad effects on a diversity of venues, and in ways that closely paralleled other examples internationally.[26] Even if these processes were not surprising, articles from this time evidence a heightened awareness of the upscaling and acceleration of gentrification, and of an intensification of threats to venues associated with alternative cultural practices and marginalized groups, including LGBTQ+ artists and communities.

Soho Estates' mixed-use Walker Court scheme involved demolition and redevelopment of multiple plots, with the construction of offices, shops, a restaurant and studio flats, as well as a theatre, live performance venue and nightclub.[27] It was the loss of the existing venue that alarmed campaigners, with the developers offering no statement of intent as to how the new venue would operate in a context of rapid commercialization that had seen an influx of chains and generic businesses. The heritage report for the scheme neglected to mention Madame Jojo's, referring vaguely to a 'number of nightclubs' on the site.[28] It instead emphasized the longer history of premises on the site, namely another of Raymond's bars, Raymond Revue Bar (opened 1958), and the restaurant Isows, opened by Jewish entrepreneur Jack Isow (opened 1938, closed 1975).[29] Like Madame Jojo's, these were both associated with social mix across different classes and marginalized groups.

The Walker Court scheme rooted itself in the earlier venues on the site while extending and upscaling these within a high-end retail and office development. Soho Estates plans to open a new incarnation of Madame Jojo's in 2023. The licensing application for the new venue was objected to by the Soho Society, representing residents concerned with negative impacts from night-time activities. This suggests a shift in tolerance which has accompanied the neighbourhood's commercialization. The application was nevertheless approved in 2019. Walker Court is framed through a narrative of return – of bringing Soho back as the heart of entertainment – and reimagination. In contrast, the campaigners' expression of grief and mourning registers displacement, erasure, amnesia, and an eradication of spaces of contact and imagination equivalent to the experiences and processes attributed to the redevelopment of New York's Times Square by queer historians and theorists (see Chapter 1).

The closure of Madame Jojo's marked a pinnacle in the sterilization of Soho, which began in the 1980s, accelerated in the 2000s, facilitated by Soho Estates and Westminster City Council, and further intensified in the 2010s.[30] With the overall shortage of affordable space in London, and the disproportionate threat to smaller-scale venues serving specific groups, some key questions emerge. To what extent are forms of queer creativity and sociality viable in the pristine, supersized venues that have resulted in redevelopments of this kind, where their earlier subcultural status has returned in commodified form, aligned with the economic status quo? Who are the creatives and audiences who will have access and under what terms?

Gaybourhood arcs

An *Evening Standard* feature published during the 2014 Pride season, the summer before Madame Jojo's closed, gave a light-hearted sketch of the dynamics between gay residential and business clusters and gentrification, celebrating 'London's prime pink pound locations', in the boosterist tone of a property developer:

> Certainly, becoming a gaybourhood hastens the gentrification of a London district, injecting energy and cash and – inevitably – raising house prices [. . .] The arc of a London gaybourhood goes like this. Either a residential community settles around a knot of businesses (i.e., clubs and bars), or vice versa. As properties are refurbished and the area becomes more desirable, more mainstream businesses move in to capitalise on footfall and spend, and rents start to rise (witness the arrival of Nando's and Dirty Burger alongside the fetish club Hoist in Vauxhall). Eventually, new arrivals attracted by the 'vibrancy' of the area start to object to late club licences [. . .] As prices skyrocket, those members of the community who can't afford to stay sell up and move on to the next 'undiscovered' 'hood.[31]

Although they do not identify themselves as LGBTQ+, the author writes autobiographically about their experience of living in gentrifying Vauxhall, alongside interview quotes from gay businesses and property organizations. The article interprets an evolutionary cycle, at the neighbourhood and city scales, with displacement of one lower income group by another as an inevitability. On balance, it suggests that gentrification is normal and venues will just come and go.

Gentrification, overall, is used positively here, as is often the case in property discourse, where it has become a commonplace to describe a wide variety of processes of urban change. Terms like 'gentrification' and 'gaybourhoods' have successfully circulated way beyond their original audiences in urban scholarship, gaining widespread popularity and often becoming detached from their original meaning. The German emigré sociologist Ruth Glass first coined the term 'gentrification' while researching London in the late 1950s, and it appeared in an essay she published in 1964.[32] Glass was writing about changes to the social character and housing markets of the Islington and Notting Hill districts. These were instigated when middle-class incomers bought up dilapidated Victorian houses and renovated them, inflating house prices and displacing 'original' working-class populations.[33] She used the term 'gentrification' with irony, referencing the 'gentry' class: historically the landed elite, below the aristocracy.[34]

Since the 1960s, the study of gentrification has developed into a lively international field of debate in urban studies and policy.[35] A wide variety of theoretical and empirical work and activism has accounted for causes and effects of gentrification in different contexts, interrogating relationships between these processes and wider socio-economic and cultural change.[36] In economic geography Neil Smith proposed the 'rent gap' – 'the disparity between the potential ground rent level and the actual ground rent capitalized under the present land use', an important contribution to a major line of debate about how capital flows towards disinvested neighbourhoods, viewed as opportunities for speculation.[37] As studies of gentrification have advanced along multiple lines, they have suggested patterns across different locations as well as highlighting the need for careful scrutiny of the particularities of different contexts, even in the same city.[38] When such terms are used to explain urban processes, we therefore have to consider how translatable they are to different periods or locations. One of the leading gentrification scholars internationally, geographer Loretta Lees, has helpfully charted different waves, from mid-twentieth century state housing schemes and individual and small-scale pioneer gentrifiers, to increased state involvement in the more highly globalized processes of financialization from the 1990s.[39] In London, Lees' term 'supergentrification', referring to the re-gentrification of already gentrified neighbourhoods by super-rich 'financial engineers', is a useful update of earlier rent gap explanations which stands out for its relevance to understanding the new scale and forms of displacement that journalists were commentating on regarding Soho and other clusters in London in the 2010s.[40]

In European and North American scholarship, there is a large body of work that looks specifically at people with minority sexualities and the relationships they have with gentrification.[41] In the UK context, Soho has been a key site for empirical work.[42] For example, economist Alan Collins has argued that Soho coheres with a typical evolutionary pattern for 'gay villages' which travels through different stages, from the liminal and illicit to the recreational, entrepreneurial and mainstream assimilation (see Chapter 1). It is questionable whether the linearity underpinning this model adequately accounts for the multiplicity and polytemporality that feature within and across London's queer scenes and venues; or for the continuing import attached to Soho by LGBTQ+ people, even in the face of what has been termed the area's 'hegemonic gentrification', amounting to the aggressive sanitization of unwanted people and cultures.[43] Amin Ghaziani, a leading sociologist of the gaybourhood, argues that – in the US context – gay enclaves and urban change have been overly studied through economic processes and the lens of gentrification at the expense of wider considerations of their functions and attractions.[44] Examples from North America cannot be simply transposed to London or other cities in terms of either the configurations of different residential, business and other uses; the data through which these phenomena can be traced; or the chronology of enclave varieties and discourses of decline recently attributed to them. Yet Ghaziani's ethnography underscores the need for substantive qualitative evidence to understand the ways that these formations have been understood and experienced; and how they have been politically, socially and culturally generative.

The gay index

Lees aligns studies of so-called 'gay gentrification' with the work of geographer David Ley, who placed emphasis on the role of a 'new cultural class' of pioneer gentrifiers.[45] In London, since the New Labour era of 'urban renaissance', policies that purport to support 'mixed communities' and sustainability have often been a cover for displacement and have worked against diversity – Lees and her collaborators have evidenced this in their research.[46] This was also the theme of my book *Remaking London*.[47] Such dubious policies have been backed up by 'creative cities' theory, an approach pioneered by urban theorist Richard Florida, and which is popular with policy makers internationally. Focusing empirically on the United States, Florida proposes a 'creative capital theory'.[48] This contends that 'creative people power regional economic growth and these people prefer places that are innovative, diverse, and tolerant'.[49] But this has been widely criticized as a discourse that has accelerated or covered up gentrification processes.[50]

Florida's narrative about pioneer gentrification linked gay and lesbian communities with canonical models for urban change, developed through the Chicago School sociologists' work on the role of bohemian and immigrant populations. He used data from a 'Gay Index', a dataset devised by Gary Gates in the 1990s, which attempted to rank cities and regions by their gay populations using census responses.[51] He correlated this with data about high-tech industries and noted strong relationships, arguing that

> There are several reasons why the Gay Index is a good measure for diversity. As a group, gays have been subject to a particularly high level of discrimination. Attempts by gays to integrate into the mainstream of society have met substantial opposition. To some extent, homosexuality represents the last frontier of diversity in our society, and thus a place that welcomes the gay community welcomes all kinds of people.[52]

Florida and economic geographer Charlotta Mellander further elaborated this naïve thinking, framing their quantitative evidence as a substantiation of a widespread assumption by journalists and developers that gays add value to housing stock.[53] They argued that, as well as adding a 'tolerance premium', 'artists, bohemians and gays

74 *Queer Premises*

affect housing values through [. . .] an aesthetic-amenity premium', leading them to propose a Bohemian-Gay index.[54] This meant that these groups add value to housing stock through raising aesthetic quality and cultural amenities. Such data, deceptive as it may be, can be exploited by investors and city authorities in ways that accelerate gentrification, as Ghaziani suggests.[55]

We should question the usefulness of such crude statistical correlations; the flawed construction and interpretation of gay identity categories as singular, fixed and stable; the reliance on one type of evidence; the assumption of general rules in diverse contexts; the treatment of homosexuality as the 'last frontier of diversity'; and the reductive ways that quantitative indices measure 'success' as growth. Such studies, as we see in the *Evening Standard* article about London gaybourhoods, discussed earlier, are reciprocated in mainstream media discourses, feeding simplistic generalizations and actively contributing to the reshaping and commodification of place in ways that are disadvantageous to minoritized groups.

In a more nuanced account of studies of gentrification and 'non-normative sexualities', urban planner Petra Doan provides a critical overview of research on the relationships between gentrification processes and diverse LGBTQ+ populations in different contexts.[56] As Doan shows, there is a large body of work, not only on gays as pioneers and bellwethers of investment opportunity, but also on cities' investments in gaybourhoods as sites of tourism, andspeculations on the recent demise of LGBTQ+ clusters. Doan emphasizes that the clusters that were formed in urban locales in the 1960s and 1970s to create safe zones were by necessity in marginal areas. She also highlights the close interrelations between the commercial and residential clusters of lesbian, gay and trans populations, and networks of activism, due to attempts to claim space within mainstream political institutions. Such reviews engage with a wealth of studies that emerged from in the 1980s which focused on gay-led processes of renovation and preservation and their influence on gentrification. These have to be understood against the context of discrimination and structural exclusions embedded in housing, employment and other areas of socio-economic life. Doan's mapping of the scholarship cautions us against generalization of 'gays' as one category, and points to how studies of gentrification lean towards analyses of areas dominated by white, wealthy, cisgendered gay men. As a prompt for the case studies in the following chapters, we can take forward Doan's insight that to understand change – in some cases the decline of LGBTQ+ clusters – we need to grasp multiple and contradictory local and global socio-economic and cultural forces and understand how these play out in specific contexts.

All a bit gay

The 2014 *Evening Standard* gaybourhood article is useful in expressing common arguments about the relationships between LGBTQ+ populations, gentrification and venues that were circulating in the mid-2010s. It flags the existence of multiple 'gay villages' in London, but oversimplifies a linear evolution from one gay village to the next, when these have overlapped and interacted. It conceives that LGBTQ+ groups contribute to place-making through their specific cultures and economies, but it only hints at how, and the effects. Presenting hearsay over evidence, it suggests that bars and clubs have become more mixed, so 'the nicest places to live in London are all a bit gay'.[57] This is an argument that has fuelled narratives about the redundancy of dedicated spaces and the inclusivity of mainstream night-time scenes, and which, as we shall see, has been challenged. The article assumes and accepts a causal relationship between an area assuming gaybourhood status and the acceleration of gentrification. It exceptionalizes the agency of gays – read wealthy white cisgendered gay male couples – within gentrification. There is light-hearted reference to there being just one lesbian venue in Soho at the time, but no serious attention given to the disparities of space or other resources across different groups. Eliding the diversity of queer people and experiences, the commentary also overlooks the distinctive histories, economies and geographies of neighbourhoods, and structural factors such as the shifting conditions for urban redevelopment set out in local and metropolitan-level plans and policies. By the time the article was published, there was already a prominent public debate and volume of studies critiquing the transnational processes of financialization accelerating displacement under the guise of regeneration in London, putting pressure on housing and all forms of cultural and social infrastructure.[58] Tied to vested interests in property and business, this is an example of journalism concealing rather than elucidating the dynamics at play.

A feature in *Estates Gazette*, written by Manchester-based property journalist David Thame, similarly gives a flavour of how debates about LGBTQ+ venues were unfolding in the mid-2010s.[59] This one pointed to some of the most distinctive and culturally influential historical and contemporary venues and estimated that at least 150 'gay venues' had 'vanished in the past 10 years'.[60] Thame tentatively laid out some of the main explanatory tropes for the decline of venues: increased regulation, such as the Licensing Act 2003, liberalization of social attitudes, straightening of gay scenes, the rise of internet and app-based dating, and commercial challenges. Although he suggested that scenes inevitably move around, he was pessimistic – more so than the *Evening Standard* article – about recent closures in East London, seeing 'no evidence of a new wave of gay venues'.[61] As with the *Evening Standard* article, this feature looks to property industry sources for its evidence: a local estate agent is quoted suggesting that there is supply but no demand for cost-effective venues from the LGBT community.

The article points to an intensifying debate among LGBTQ+ community members and industry representatives about decreasing demand for venues, as well as the suggestion that they represent an outmoded model of alcohol-centred nightlife: 'tired-looking, under-invested, wet-led gay bars of yesteryear'.[62] This perspective on Soho comes from Brian Bickell, a sixty-something, gay-identifying chief executive and co-founder of Shaftesbury, one of the dominant West End real estate companies.[63] Bickell argues that 'gay life today isn't so much about drinking and hanging around in bars', and assumes that 'younger LGBT people don't need the security of separate gay venues'.[64] He asserts that there was likely an oversupply in the 1990s, which was undergoing a market correction in the 2010s. Bickell began working in property in the 1980s as a working-class and out gay Londoner, and is a board member of Freehold LGBT+, a network for LGBT+ people working in real estate sector.[65] As someone so professionally invested in Soho's gentrification, it is unsurprising that he sees this as 'no bad thing' and has faith that the area will 'keep reinventing itself'.[66] Through their professional involvement and vested interests LGBTQ+ community members of course have varied amounts of agency in shaping the transnational real estate-led processes of urban change which the creation or sustainability of venues is subject to.

Although the mainstream media platforms on which venue decline was discussed included testimony, these were typically privileged towards certain voices while overlooking the variety of experiences among diverse, multigenerational LGBTQ+ communities. It is also notable that the emphasis on the 'gay bar', as a hedonistic and leisure space, presented only the most formal and commercial of venues, and the most visible clusters. In parallel with the ways that other small and medium size enterprises have been treated in regeneration processes, these bars were presented as anachronistic.[67] Overall, such portrayals concealed the actual diversity of venue types, and the multiplicity and continuing functions these venues have had for different groups and generations.

Ending on a note of reassurance, the piece cites historian Matt Houlbrook's scholarship on the history of queer London to support the idea that 'the geography of gay London always changes', but the 'more things change the more they stay the same'.[68] This contrasts Houlbrook's careful attention to 'accumulated historical traces of queer male networks', to the terms and forms of danger, transgression and liberation, and the specific spaces and ways of being that were available to queers at specific moments in the early twentieth century.[69] The eradication and homogenization of spaces of queer congregation and contact can be seen as one of the clearest dangers to these networks in recent times.

The ahistorical tone of the *Estates Gazette* article can be connected to parallel arguments in queer theory regarding the ephemerality and transitory qualities of queer space (see Chapter 1). It suggests why campaigners had to work hard to argue for the role of venues as repositories and generators of past, present and future heritage. The article had begun with a recognition of the damage caused by a collapse in numbers of venues, and it identified important trends such as the commercial expansion of a particular type of venues in the 1990s. Yet it concluded that the mourning of gay venues 'and the rakish gay world that went with them' was redundant and indulgent in a capital that is 'still one of the gayest cities in the world'.[70]

Razing venues

Media representations featured selective commentaries from LGBTQ+ community members, but these accounts can be illuminated through a wider scope assessment of evidence from experience. To represent views from members of these communities, I now turn to narratives gathered through a survey and workshop.[71] These were designed by Lo Marshall and myself in UCL Urban Laboratory, in collaboration with two interconnected entities – RAZE Collective and Queer Spaces Network (QSN).[72] These groups had been established in 2015 to facilitate links across individual campaigns to protect queer venues. Dissatisfied with the media narratives, they initiated their own effective media and social media campaigns. RAZE and QSN organizer Ben Walters produced regular commentaries on venue closures and threats in his blog *Not Television*.[73]

RAZE Collective was set up to support LGBTQI+ performers. Its website states that 'the organisation was established in response to queer spaces being razed, through the threats and closures of many queer performance spaces in London and elsewhere around the UK'.[74] Signalling recognition of venues' cultural and social value, and the need for collective and pragmatic action to protect them, the name presented these difficult circumstances as an opportunity for queer utopianism and futurity, and to imagine the kinds of spaces that might be needed or possible anew. QSN, a working group on venues within RAZE, was formed for members to discuss the impact of venue closures on performers whose livelihoods and creative development were so closely tethered to these resources. By 2016, it had established a separate identity, less focused on performance, with a remit to join up venue-based campaigns, respond to opportunities to influence the mayor and GLA, and link to other related campaigns such as those in support of grassroots music venues or social housing.

QSN formed following a meeting between queer space campaigners linked to RAZE, RVT Future – the campaign to protect the Royal Vauxhall Tavern (see Chapter 6) – and the GLA's Culture Team. As an unofficial means for the GLA to engage with the diverse and diffuse LGBTQ+ communities feeling pressures on space, it predated and influenced the establishment of an LGBT Venues Forum, chaired by the night czar, with its agenda set by her and the GLA. The establishment of QSN recognized that the availability and quality of venues were central to RAZE's ambition to foster queer performance.[75] QSN described itself 'as an open and inclusive forum for members of the queer community to come together and discuss issues relating to protecting, promoting and supporting queer spaces in London and feed into relevant consultations and requests for information', and 'an informal group bringing together people with an interest in preserving and supporting spaces for the LGBTQI community'.[76] The new network offered something distinctive in providing a forum for discussions across a number of independent campaigns in London – and potentially anywhere in the UK or beyond – by being open to anyone who shared its broad agenda and by amplifying campaigns and connecting with parallel ones, such as those being led by housing activists.[77]

QSN was informal in that it had a flexible, inclusive membership and an agile, responsive agenda. It was also tactical, being clued into the emerging policy discussions at an opportune moment as Boris Johnson's tenure ended, and during Sadiq Khan's mayoral campaign and first days in office. It operated through an email listing and Facebook group, and held roughly quarterly in-person meetings, with fairly small numbers, but including representation from the main campaigns, such as those related to the closures of The Black Cap and the Joiners Arms (see Chapters 6 and 7). Meetings took place in queer nightlife venues. They provided a pragmatic structure to respond to situations arising in venues, to take opportunities to influence the mayor and GLA's work, and to collaborate with other networks working on the impact of gentrification. But QSN also set out to shape a discussion about a broader and longer-term 'utopian vision for queer London'.[78] This short manifesto made the case for queer venues as community hubs vital to the welfare of the LGBTQ+ population. It flagged challenges such as poor mental health linked to social othering and social isolation. It commented on the lack of a dedicated community centre in comparison with Berlin and New

York. QSN's vision was expressed in a vocabulary and tone recognizable to City Hall, illustrating the campaigners' ability to switch modes opportunistically, which resulted in a fairly gentle and pragmatic push for a 'world class queer city'.[79]

QSN and the campaigns it brought were also intent on shaping a more informed media and policy discussion. The network lobbied the GLA, cognizant that they were working towards the mayor's manifesto promise of a cultural infrastructure plan, and that collaborative research was already underway on music venues and the NTE. They articulated a need to build an evidence base to understand how many venues had closed. In response, with QSN and RAZE Collective's Ben Walters and Tim Other, at UCL Urban Lab we co-designed a pilot research project to gather evidence on nightlife spaces, which included an online survey and a mapping of numbers of venues over time.[80]

The findings from this pilot project, presented to the night czar and GLA Culture Team in 2016, emphasized that LGBTQ+ spaces serve a variety of important functions and were facing a range of challenges that connected with other types of night venues and community spaces but also diverged from them in some important ways.[81] The pilot highlighted the importance of nightlife venues and events to community life, welfare and personal well-being, in places where other services have been lacking, and had been especially vital during the intense period of the 1980s and 1990s AIDS epidemic. When asked what they valued about LGBTQ+ night-spaces, and what concerned them about threats to and closures of venues, the survey returns overwhelmingly emphasized positive values but also included important critiques and identified aspects that were deemed problematic. Detailed responses were submitted by participants, reflecting their deep interest and concern. At the time of the research the findings had to be coded and synthesized quickly to present the principal tropes to the GLA and QSN within a short timeframe. Here, I return to these rich narratives, for their insights into LGBTQ+ individuals' views and experiences in the mid-2010s. There is, of course, an element of self-selection in terms of who responds to a survey, and the limitations of any dataset make it essential to evaluate evidence from a variety of sources, as I attempt in this book.

Safety and survival

Where individuals named closed or extant venues that they felt to be of particular value, the reasons were varied, with the top five – most important first – being diversity of clientele, relaxed atmosphere, geographical accessibility, inclusivity and conduciveness to being social. Diversity of clientele referred to gender, sexuality, age, ethnicity, class and background, though in some cases the term also expressed other variables. The survey returns emphasized common needs for nightlife space across diverse LGBTQ+ communities. This was absent from the dominant media discussion of venue closures. For survey respondents, venues were understood and celebrated as providing opportunities for social mix across the LGBTQ+ spectrum, transversing a variety of social vectors. They highlighted the ways venues were oriented towards specific groups. They understood the potential for mix as being proactively shaped by event programming. It was observed that the most highly valued spaces made positive societal contributions through affirmatively addressing and accommodating more acutely intersectionally marginalized groups, who were less well provided for in mainstream venues, including women, trans and non-binary people, and Queer, Trans and Intersex People of Colour (QTIPOC). This was evidenced through reference to examples of events. In a broader sense of socio-economic inclusion, certain venues were mentioned positively because they were deemed to cater to alternative and more affordable scenes. Impressions of exclusively expensive mainstream night-time premises provided a contrast.

Albeit that the survey was more likely to prompt responses from those for whom venues had a positive association, the responses consistently emphasized the multiplicity of ways that venues were important to individual life journeys. This included 'coming out' stories, where venues had provided opportunities for individuals to feel comfortable to explore their sexual and gender identities, and to connect with people with whom they shared common characteristics or experiences, especially on arrival in a new city. For some, the purpose of attending venues was a way of 'trying to find people like me', and of seeking likeness or like-mindedness – 'a crowd that likes the same things', although this did not exclusively mean an LGBTQ+ identifying crowd.[82] Rather than suggest a desire to be surrounded by homogeneity, these statements enforce that venues and networks of venues are vital within the apparatus of identification for minoritized populations, offering opportunities for survival, sustenance, congregation and empowerment.

The responses very strongly emphasized that dedicated LGBTQ+ venues enable positive transformation. One respondent noted, 'the diversity of women at the venues was a huge part of giving me the confidence to be who I am'.[83] Venues were perceived to provide alternatives to the dominant experience of being in spaces where cis- and heteronormativity prevailed or were implicitly assumed. This commonly facilitated feelings of confidence or comfort (a word frequently used), disinhibition and group connectivity. Respondents' observations highlighted the nuanced ways that cis- and heteronormativity are internalized and that LGBTQ+ spaces are experienced as offering distinctive and transformative opportunities for relief. In these environments respondents reported feeling able to accept themselves in ways that were healing of traumatic experiences, shame and stigma. One person articulated this as being able 'to feel comfortable in my skin', and many more commented on the positive value of feeling centred and affirmed rather than marginalized.[84] This remark evokes Sara Ahmed's argument that the 'social also has its skin, as a border that feels and is shaped by the "impressions" of others'.[85] It suggests how venues, as affectively experienced, can enable the navigation of and deviation from a dominant 'straight' social skin. The skin of the social is stretched or remade to encompass different subjectivities, embodiments, senses of collectivity and futurity.

Many respondents used the term 'safe' to express qualities of the spaces that they most valued and their concern for the consequences of the loss of these spaces for LGBTQ+ people. The practice of naming and creating 'safe(r) space' has its roots in 1970s feminism, but has since been used to define a wide range of virtual and physical spaces. Such discussions have drawn attention to the socio-cultural and institutional dynamics through which all space is produced, affording and shaping different experiences according to positionality, embodiment and privilege. A recent survey of usages by the feminist geographers known as the Roestone Collective at the University of Wisconsin-Madison states that safe spaces are constituted by the 'relational work of cultivating them' in specific and dynamic contexts.[86] This may include the articulation of binaries of safe/unsafe or inclusion/exclusion, even if it is appreciated that these boundaries are not fixed but porous and established through lived experience. Safe(r) spaces are deemed to provide refuge from forms of violence and harassment, and opportunities for marginalized groups to gather strength and resources.

LGBTQ+ venues and events are often actively exclusive because organizers are attempting to create 'safe space' relative to contrastingly 'unsafe' environments. As cases explored in *Queer Premises* show, many venues also have histories as targets for violence and discrimination. Nonetheless, some promoters and operators of venues and events proactively attempt to create conditions that will be experienced as safe by those marginalized within or entirely excluded from in mainstream venues. This is enforced through marketing, door policies, 'safe space' statements, and the negotiations around them.[87] Currently, there are debates about the implications and efficacy of such policies and the practices around them.[88] For example, what are their intentions? How do they set up certain expectations? How do these intentions and expectations align with the experiences of attendees? What are the relations between conditions of safety, risk and experimentation?

It is not surprising that within the survey returns safety was a plastic concept. It was used in reference to specific and intersecting forms of discrimination and violence that have been experienced or were felt to be a threat (e.g. transphobia, homophobia, racism, ableism). Where the term 'safe' was used, it was repeatedly qualified through association with freedom for self-expression, protection from the threat of abuse and harassment, including violence and hate crime, and respite from phobic responses and social othering, such as the feeling of being stared at, being subjected to a judgmental 'straight' gaze. Safety was expressed relatively so that (some) LGBTQ+ venues were understood as safe in comparison with other venues or against the backdrop of past experiences, whether they be of homophobia or transphobia, or of family rejection.

As with the emphasis on the active importance of night venues in empowering identity formation and expression, safety was linked with positive affirmation of diverse genders and sexualities. There was a sense of liberation from cisheteronormative relations, of opportunities to be 'safe being queer in public', as one person put it, with less need for self-censorship due to expectations of prejudice.[89] Another person phrased this as: 'safe space to express yourself and feel that you don't have to "check yourself" before you say or act freely'.[90] Feeling safe and at home varied greatly according to individuals' embodied positionality and self-presentation and a multitude of shifting factors. For one non-binary/trans-identifying respondent venues offered 'life saving experiences' to 'feel free and non-judged just for those hours'.[91]

To be experienced as safer, venues' specific designation as LGBTQ+ was an important factor for many respondents. Dedicated venues were articulated as refuges, havens or substitute homes, sometimes in neighbourhoods that were similarly perceived as (relatively) safe. They engendered feelings of security and freedom to exist, without being challenged or having to explain oneself. One example was being free to use the toilet of one's choice, without being questioned about one's gender. Others rather pointed to relief from cisheteronormative privilege: to not feel 'other' or in the minority; or to derive a sense of safety from being in a group. Safety was also noted to result from the practices of venue and event producers as they intentionally challenged the norms that shape intimate contact, such as holding hands, kissing or flirting. Outside of dedicated LGBTQ+ spaces, such acts were perceived and experienced as dangerous, and potentially attractive of unwanted attention.

Safe space was also a core issue among performers and nightlife promoters. For these groups, safety was linked to experimentation. Venues that fostered experimentation were observed to be vital launch platforms and incubators for their practices. For these freelance creative workers, there was a need for safe space to make and test out work, but their understandings of safety were also constructed relative to prejudices experienced while working in and with more mainstream, risk-averse and less supportive venues and audiences. These groups emphasized the vital research and development role of venues, alongside appropriate funding streams and mentoring programmes. This did not reflect a desire to remain cocooned in LGBTQ+ venues, since these respondents emphasized an increasing value in appropriating space outside of traditional venues, such as street performance and festivals.[92] There was a very tangible anxiety that the closure of dedicated venues left a new generation of performers with greatly diminished opportunities.

Community sense

Cultural significance was central to respondents' understanding of the value of LGBTQ+ venues. Apart from the contributions to enhancing lives and livelihoods discussed earlier, it was observed that venues facilitated a wide variety of specifically LGBTQ+ cultures, ranging from art forms such as drag, to types of music, cabaret and performance, curation and exhibition, and performative practices such as styles of protest or cruising. Threats to the heritage that venues were understood to represent and reproduce created concerns about the severance of bonds to the past, creating obstacles to the transmission or sustenance of LGBTQ+ history and culture across different generations, or a general diminishment of social and cultural infrastructure in the present which would disadvantage future generations.

One way that such themes manifested was through expressions of community. Many emphasized, for example, the active role that venues play in creating, fostering or communicating a 'sense of community'. One person asserted: 'Loss of community and the sense of shared ownership, shared experience, are devastating to marginalised individuals and groups.'[93] Observations like this suggest how venue closures, and threats of closure, have prompted a more acute awareness of LGBTQ+ heritage in its multiple dimensions, underlining future vulnerability through the reduction of already scarce and unevenly distributed resources.

Although many individual venues were cited, responses emphasized the important symbolic and practical functions of networks of venues. The network across the city as a whole was seen to express the plurality of London's LGBTQ+ communities; while micro networks – such as a string of East End venues in Shoreditch and Dalston – were also celebrated for more specific contributions. Venues and other night-spaces reassuringly signified community heterogeneity and vitality: 'I love the variety and options on my doorstep. I love the fact that they are there and it's reassuring that there is a vibrant community', one person remarked.[94] Such narratives point to how venues are understood to 'collectively create a sense of community' and belonging across a diversity of people.[95] Venues – and the discussions about threats to them – made the presence of a wider group and shared experiences visible. For some, venues were important as spaces of contact and congregation, irrespective of whether they participated directly. For others, contact included intimate kinship networks, featuring close affinities and identifications with others understood to have shared and different characteristics and affiliations.

Many respondents underscored that nightlife venues and events were materially important to LGBTQ+ heritage as significant historical artefacts. Venues were understood to actively 'demonstrate', as one respondent put it, queer culture. This demonstrative capacity was articulated by another respondent when they commented that

> all of the venues have stories to tell about how the communities developed, protected themselves, expressed themselves. Those communities have enriched London and added to its diversity, hence we should remember and respect the places where it happened.[96]

The need for respect and commemoration of venues as memory sites linked to social struggle, and as signifiers of diversity, was another repeated theme. For some of the most mentioned venues – many of which are examined in the later chapters of this book – special architectural and historical qualities were often cited. This suggests some respondents' perception of an urgent imperative to communicate the intangible heritage of LGBTQ+ populations in multiple ways. Moreover, it indicates that an increased frequency of closures precipitated reflexive evaluation of venues according to individuals' personal experiences and sense of attachment, as well as their relative significance to an imagined LGBTQ+ community or subsections within it. Of course, the limitations of a survey approach must be acknowledged, in that there was a higher likelihood that those who responded meaningfully would be those who felt that venues were important to queer heritage – whereas those who were indifferent or felt negative may not have taken the time to complete the questionnaire. Furthermore, just because respondents felt that venues were important does not mean that they were actively using them.

Importance to current and future cultural production was also accentuated. The generative capacity of venues to foster the production, experience and sharing of creative work was a strong preoccupation, with venues being places to discover and enjoy art and culture. The stress, here, was on alternative and counter-cultural forms that might otherwise be difficult to produce or access, or that have specific connections to queer lifeworlds. Yet, respondents pointed to the broader significance of venues beyond LGBTQ+ communities, given the wider role of these practices in influencing artistic production and to London's creative ecology and built fabric.

Respondents also stressed the importance of long-standing venues whose association with gender and sexual diversity spanned multiple generations. These were understood to have unique cultural significance. Although wider cultural relevance, beyond LGBTQ+ populations, was emphasized, respondents suggested that the transmission of culture and education operate differently for LGBTQ+ groups and individuals. In some cases, contrasts were drawn with dominant conventions of inheritance, whether of property or knowledge. Narratives described how venues have functioned to transmit a variety of shared resources. These support a connection between the semipublic status of these premises and their role in forging and maintaining social bonds, and as conduits within a wider queer infrastructure.

A sense of crisis due to venue closures also prompted intergenerational exchanges and empathy, including reflections on divergent and common experiences.[97] Closures and threats facilitated a macro and longer-term view in understanding LGBTQ+ nightlife as subject to broader cultural and structural changes over time. This included, for example, the sharing of knowledge about the impacts of past recessions on queer livelihoods and enterprises, the changing relationships between venues and communications technologies, the formation, composition, ideologies and trajectories of social movements, the changing availability, affordability and malleability of building stock, whether designed and authorized for night-time uses or not, at different moments.

Digital alarm

In both the media and public discussions regarding the closure of London's LGBTQ+ venues, the role of online connectivity was a recurrent theme. A 2015 article that garnered international circulation estimated that London had lost 'a quarter [of its gay bars] in recent years' and surmised that 'gay people . . . are ditching bars and clubs altogether, and with the proliferation of dating websites and mobile phone apps, are choosing to make contacts online'.[98] This article began with an odd vignette of a tattooed, leather-jacketed, recently released ex-convict, who is shocked at how the scene has changed during his thirteen years in prison. Yet, overall, the perspective this article elaborated was again that of middle-aged cisgendered gay men, focusing on how mobile apps have liberated them from cruising in bars. Familiar tropes were put forward to explain the pattern of venue closures: increased tolerance, more mixed spaces, the replacement of physical spaces with online ones and luxury flat and generic retail development have led to a quarter of spaces closing.

This account is typical in presenting an oversimplifying causal logic between the proliferation of ubiquitous technologies, with the demise of venues as forms of in-person sociality reduce or shift to more private domains. These interpretations overshadowed the continuing importance of accessing physical space and obscured the ways that venues have extended through analogue and lower-tech media and technologies in the past. As the following chapters demonstrate, such reports contradict evidence of the popularity of many venues at the time they closed and distract from more significant direct or indirect causal factors, such as urban redevelopment, or structural economic shifts, such as those triggered by the global financial crisis of 2008.[99]

As in journalists' accounts, the relationship between new technologies and LGBTQ+ spaces and communities was a preoccupation in the survey returns. Although there was a recognition of the positive aspects of apps and websites (such as the facilitation of social and sexual encounters), there were also concerns. A prominent theme was the impossibility for online spaces to substitute the need for physical ones, or their perceived inadequacy, relative to physical spaces and in-person social interactions, in building or maintaining community, or fostering a fulfilling sense of identity. One male pansexual-identifying person in their early thirties asserted: 'Whilst I understand that there are now other structures (mostly online) for LGBTQI+ individuals to meet one another, actual physical spaces allow for different types of rhythms and sociability that online spaces do not'.[100] The rise of digital spaces and proliferation of internet dating were linked to what another respondent referred to as 'the loss of good quality accessible spaces'.[101]

Some respondents also worried about the gradual disappearance of certain social practices due to technology and saw this as a generational shift. As a white British gay man in his late thirties articulated it: 'younger people are meeting via digital means, [and] the art of going to a bar and chatting is slowly dying away'.[102] One of the main issues of concern was that digital apps and platforms facilitated meeting only, or mainly, for sex. This was contrasted with a wider range of social encounters afforded by physical spaces. Features of the technology, such as the creation of interfaces and filtering akin to online shopping, were taken to exemplify commodified forms of socialization understood to be inherently superficial. However, features that were presented negatively by some respondents – such as the facilitation of easy hook-ups and other encounters – were understood positively by others. There were optimistic narratives about the role of technology to engender new venue types and socio-spatial configurations, such as the possibilities of nightlife spaces augmented through virtual reality.[103] This was prior to the Covid-19 pandemic when many venues rapidly upscaled their digital presence (see Chapter 8).

Recent studies have pointed to the nuanced relations between LGBTQ+ subjectivities technology and urban space including commercial night venues.[104] Although venues often serve multiple groups within the LGBTQ+ spectrum, and issues of uneven provision and access to space arise, studies of the impact of technology have tended to focus on specific constituents, and mostly on gay men, or men who have sex with men (even if they have considered diversity amongst these research subjects). Few studies examine the technological mediation of queer night-spaces across LGBTQ+ populations, or explicitly address the variable needs for and access to virtual or physical spaces of constituent groups.

Geographer Sam Miles's research on the use of location-based apps in London contributes to a growing evidence base. Miles comments that 'with the ongoing deconcentration and commercial redevelopment of previously queer-coded physical space in London, the idea that sociality and community can be refigured online is persuasive'.[105] The qualitative evidence he gathered suggested that, to a limited extent, apps can foster social cohesion and a sense of belonging to an area, or a network. Other findings that this research brought forward were that virtual introductions often lead to in-person meetings and that most users do not attribute a sense of community to the apps.

Sociologist Greggor Mattson, who researches the social value of provincial gay bars in the United States, also questions taken-for-granted arguments about the impact of mobile technologies as a contributor to venue closures.[106] In his interviews, gay bar professionals 'largely dismissed any negative effects of apps such as Grindr on their business, and highlighted many positive effects'.[107] Mattson cautions against simply accepting other universalizing assumptions about the perceived 'decline' of gay venues, such as the notion of increased, progressive or widespread social tolerance, because these are often made without evidence, or with bias towards certain venue types or clusters. In his work, lesbian bars and leather cruise bars, and bars in cities without established gaybourhoods, were more vulnerable to closure.

Media theorist Sharif Mowlabocus's research also suggests that relationships between digital technologies and commercial night scenes should be interpreted cautiously, revealing, for example, how the virtual spaces of the internet facilitate otherwise declining public sex subcultures.[108] To categorically think of venues and events as completely separate from online spaces is therefore unconvincing. These critiques and observations are very relevant in reading the press discussions and qualitative evidence mentioned earlier, and in observing the uneven provision of venues and impacts of closures in the London context.[109] The evidence in this book supports qualitative research in other contexts which suggests a need to challenge the argument that 'Grindr killed the gay bar'.[110] These studies prompt us to think about the ways that venues are mediated through a wider range of technologies, and call us to account for social difference, and the style and impacts of urban redevelopment in specific places.

The Urban Lab survey similarly stressed the hybridized character of digital and physical environments. It suggested a need to consider the material impacts of locative technology on embodied experience, and the filtering of a sense of belonging or community through a range of subjectivities. A more nuanced understanding of the impact of apps and websites on the sociality of LGBTQ+ communities than has been characteristic of the media coverage around venue closures is needed. These have often ascribed a simplistic, causal relationship, which disregards hybridization.[111] The digital shift, although distinctive in extending global reach and offering new material forms, is just the latest manifestation of venues' mediation and extension through communications technologies. Attention to the longer-term geography and history of these heterogeneous communities, and consideration of differential access to and uses of physical space and communications systems to forge and maintain social networks embedded in cities, will result in deeper understanding.

Claiming damages

Responses to the survey highlighted that venue closures and threats had prompted thoughtful reevaluation of the kinds of venues that are available and their accessibility to different groups. By comparison with positive statements of value, criticisms were far fewer, and this is not surprising given the anxieties prompted by the loss or potential loss of resources. However, significant numbers of respondents vocalized concerns with what they deemed to be problematic aspects of available scenes and venues and narrated how these reflected and reproduced wider social exclusion and inequality. Attention was drawn, for example, to the privilege needed to access some venues: money, youth, a certain kind of body, cisgender presentation, masculinity, whiteness, fashionable image and appearance, mobility. In some cases, such issues were articulated through comparison between contemporary and historical scenes. Other respondents documented problematic experiences in dominant commercial forms of nightlife. Critiques of the consumerist profile of LGBTQ+ nightlife were associated with decreasing social value. These centred on Soho as a cluster perceived to have been sanitized through commercialization, driven by tourism and gentrification. Drawing historical parallels, some respondents noted, from their own lived experience, negative qualitative change in the atmosphere, design, or kinds of culture accessible in venues, or their overall desirability and level of interest, due to increasing commodification and homogenization.

Strong criticism was attached to the shortage of spaces run by and for women, and especially older women, and 'lesbian friendly spaces'.[112] These remarks often drew a contrast with greater provision in the past, and with the relative abundance of gay men's venues in the present. Women's spaces were noted to have been more acutely affected by processes of gentrification, which favoured more commercial nightlife: 'There simply aren't as many spaces as there used to be, and many of the ones that survived feel more commercial, less community oriented'.[113]

Many respondents associated LGBTQ+ venues with inclusivity, and the reconfiguration of norms through which they generally felt oppressed. Venues were described idealistically as spaces to be 'without fear of prejudice or attack' or to 'feel completely free from prejudice', as 'judgement free', often based on comparison with negative personal experiences of being in other public spaces.[114] These responses must be referenced against reported experiences of intersecting forms of exclusion and discrimination in venues. One respondent observed that their initial sense of inclusivity had been over-written through experience: 'now I realise that within clubs, the same systems of oppression do just play out and if you're not a gay white cis man, you're still not a part of this community. I often have to justify why I'm there and I get inappropriate questions and harassed and it's too much effort to go out now'. This underlines how the sense of belonging (or exclusion) is made and remade through dynamic and contextual processes.

Participants criticized what one person referred to as the 'excessive whiteness' of night venues and the racism that sometimes played out in them. The following statement articulates some common sentiments:

> LGBTQIA spaces in London are far from perfect and there is a lot of racism, homo-hierarchy, whorephobia, classism, and ableism in our scene, but the solutions are in holding ourselves accountable and making better spaces? [sic] If those spaces are instead taken away from us, we will be further isolated and marginalized in this

city which obviously makes us more vulnerable to depression and other mental health problems; and, less importantly but of more social currency, it will make London a less colorful place for rich straight cis people.[115]

Even having taken to task problematic aspects of night-spaces, this respondent holds on to the historic and potential future transformative capacity of venues to address oppressions and promote positive social change and well-being. The queer utopianism of this position is dependent on the imagination of a new generation of more accountably run spaces.

In group discussions held with promoters, venue operators, artists, campaigners and venue clientele, venue closures were raised as a problem not only in London, but in other UK cities such as Manchester and Bristol.[116] In these conversations, which nevertheless largely focused on London, participants both recognized the threat of closures and were keen to highlight rich and resistant ongoing LGBTQ+ night-time scenes and events. They called attention to a decline of venues catering to specific sub-groups as well as more generally inclusive ones: both were highly valued. There was recognition of the reciprocal relations between changing expressions of identity and the production of venues and events. Some witnessed an increasing fluidity in how younger people identify and noted a lack of understanding of how this might impinge on existing types of venues and programming. As with the survey, these groups problematized the dominance of cisgendered gay men and pointed to a relative lack of venues for QTIPOC. They further observed that nightlife spaces are not typically inclusive for older people, who lack social spaces, and that they are often actively exclusive due to the sensory environments they create. Survey returns had also criticized night scenes for being too focused on younger crowds.

Many participants wrote from their own experiences of personal change, reflecting on their uses of venues in the past. Some speculated on the needs of younger individuals in the present. A small group suggested that venues were less relevant due to the 'greater acceptance of gay lifestyles', the 'accepting environment', or integration, but there was some qualification of these remarks through the recognition that they were anecdotal and based on individual experiences.[117] Integration or increased social mix with heterosexual populations was sometimes viewed negatively, as a contributor to gentrification coined, by one respondent, as 'hetrification'.[118] Where increased integration and social acceptance, or a preference for mixed spaces, were expressed, this was often offset by an understanding of a continued demand for dedicated venues, 'for the sake of folks who feel the need for spaces where they are surrounded by other queers', as one person put it.

Critiques of the ways that night-time scenes and spaces have been centred around alcohol and drugs also featured strongly. One respondent who identified as a white British cis male, early forties, gay-queer, raised issues based on his own experience of addiction:

Now sober, I see these spaces as predominantly for white affluent gay men, overtly focused on sex and hedonism, with very little in the way that one might call supportive community environments. Language can be misogynistic and racist

88   *Queer Premises*

and their populations can be hyper critical both of each other and themselves. I realise now that I used alcohol and drugs in these spaces primarily as I felt like an outsider when I was in them. I think these spaces do remain important for exploring sexuality and feeling safe from physical violence, however, I also see them as being damaging in themselves.[119]

This image of feeling like an outsider in LGBTQ+ night-spaces provides a counterpoint to more idealized expressions of community and highlights that these are environments where intra-community tensions and aggressions play out. Commentaries on such contradictions are a feature across the period upon which this book is focused. Venues which, on the one hand, may be safe spaces also consolidate traumatic experiences and can be sites of unhealthy behaviours and coping mechanisms. The dominant commercial operating model based on profit from alcohol sales, as well as other aspects of night venues' informal economies, can normalize this. It is important to note that even this respondent's quite categorical critique was balanced by their belief in a continuing role for LGBTQ+ venues as 'supportive community environments', which promote social mix, citing the Royal Vauxhall Tavern (see Chapter 6) as a positive example.[120]

Plotting change

Qualitative evidence deepens understanding of venues and the impacts of threats to them within diverse LGBTQ+ communities. Media accounts, as discussed earlier, had rather platformed a narrow range of spokespeople, often featuring views from the night-time and real estate sectors. In the late 2000s, some of these journalistic sources made reference to venue numbers. Although these were often anecdotal estimates, data from the GBA was also cited, though this was not widely available at the time or subsequently.[121] Another even more prominent source of data during these debates was an online article in *The Gay UK*, published in 2015, which used an obsolete listings magazine, *Fluid*, to catalogue 'gay/LGBT bars and clubs' by name, with a brief description and dates of opening and closure where known.[122] Although initiating this list was an important act, the resulting data was inconsistent, with gaps and errors and a lack of corroboration. For some potential users, such as urban policy-makers, this would have limited its value. Publishing the initial list, the magazine had launched a call to crowdsource 'the ultimate Lost LGBT Scene archive'.[123] The tone was melancholic and nostalgic, emphasizing loss, and an intention to 'remember and pay tribute' to closed spaces, especially those of the 'heyday' of the 1980s and 1990s. The authors speculated that 'technology and other factors have slowly become essential in connecting the LGBT+ community' and that this had caused a decline since the 2000s.[124]

It was at this time, in the mid-2010s, that QSN and the GLA Culture Team became keen to gather accurate, quantitative data to gauge numbers of venues, and dates of closures. Our research at UCL Urban Lab was therefore designed, with input from campaigners

Rupture and Repair

and policy makers, as a response to the lack of evidence. We set out to discover how many venues there were and how many had closed. Counting venues is a more complex proposition than it might at first seem. In selecting sources it is easy to overlook types of space, geographical locations or constituent groups, especially for the most acutely marginalized populations within LGBTQ+ communities. It was therefore essential to draw from a wide variety of sources, not only from a narrow set of listings magazines, and to balance the counting and mapping of venues from archives with qualitative evidence. Although the GLA were mainly interested in recent closures, it felt important to us to understand recent fluctuations against longer trajectories in venue numbers, going back to the GLC's dissolution in 1986. A definition of an 'LGBTQ+ venue' was needed for this exercise. This was agreed as licensed premises designated primarily as LGBTQ+ venues, operated by and/or for these populations, and/or with primarily LGBTQ+ programming. This of course only offers a snapshot, the most visible surface.

When in 2017 Lo Marshall and I published refined data from a second study that focused specifically on the decade from 2006, this showed that 58 per cent of London's licensed LGBTQ+ nightlife premises had closed. This headline figure received a lot of attention in the media, from other researchers, from industry representatives and from those running and campaigning for LGBTQ+ night-spaces.[125] When we presented these findings to the GLA's Culture Team and night czar, or to activists campaigning to protect or reopen venues, it was met with alarm, but not surprise.

For the GLA and campaigners, nailing a specific figure was useful because it helped to communicate the extent of closures, and enabled comparison between LGBTQ+ venues and other venues.[126] Compared with other studies it showed a drop that was deeper than the 44 per cent fall in UK nightclubs, or the 35 per cent decline in London's grassroots music venues and more than double the 25 per cent fall in UK pubs.[127] It was useful that the GLA Culture Team began gathering and comparing these datasets, given that the pressures LGBTQ+ venues were under had to be understood at a structural level alongside those faced by other forms of social and cultural infrastructure. Even so, it was vital to consider the distinctive functions, heritage and pressures LGBTQ+ venues were under.

Looking at the larger dataset Lo Marshall and I compiled and mapped, where we were recording venues from 1986, some patterns emerge (Plates 10–13). These include clusters of venues that shift over time; socially and aesthetically connected scenes that traverse different locales; and fluctuations in the number and type of venues. It is not always straightforward to match trends in the provision and closure of venues to specific phenomena, and closures must be understood through attention to particular circumstances, as the following chapters demonstrate, and by avoiding singular or simplistic cause-and-effect explanations. The changing landscape of government, mayoral and local government agendas, discussed in Chapters 2 and 3, and broader political and economic cycles in the UK and internationally, are relevant insofar as they have helped shape London's property market and the specific forms and pace of redevelopment.

The data on venue numbers for the 1980s and 1990s are inevitably more difficult to ascertain than current and recent numbers. Robert Kincaid, one of the co-founders of First Out Café, which opened in 1986, recalls: 'at the time gay venues were opening

90 *Queer Premises*

and closing within short periods of time. So there's nothing really – apart from one or two shops and one or two pubs – there was nothing terribly permanent [. . .]'.[128] Being accommodated within, or appropriating, venues that were not specifically dedicated as gay or lesbian was the typical scenario until the 1970s and 1980s, when London's scenes, having forcibly existed under cover, became more visible.

Sampling published listings, and supplementing these with mentions of venues in surveys and interviews, the number of reported venues for the decade from 1986 is quite consistent, averaging fifty-four in the Greater London area. Since we know that full-time, dedicated venues were more rare in this period, and the status of venues is harder to gauge than in more recent years, this is a very approximate number and probably an overestimation. In addition to licensed premises, we know that there were a plethora of less formal, more mobile spaces and events, which are intrinsically more difficult to identify than licensed premises, and which elude quantification (and indeed their value at the time may have been related to being hidden and clandestine). At a time of higher levels of discrimination, violence and police raids, some venues and events would by necessity operate under the radar. Nonetheless, numbers of licensed premises recorded in listings are still a useful indicator.

With the caveat that the data must be treated as incomplete it is nevertheless important to note what stands out. The number of venues remains fairly consistent from the mid-1980s to mid-1990s, rising more steeply after the 1990–1 recession. The inflation-induced downturn of 1990–91 did not precipitate a decline in the numbers of recorded venues – there was a drop of only one venue that year and the figures climbed more steeply thereafter. Between 1993 and 1994, there was a significant rise, from fifty-one to sixty-four venues, and a similar leap between 1996 and 1997, with sixty-two and seventy-four venues recorded, respectively. This is in line with contemporary broadsheet and financial media coverage which, as Johan Andersson has observed, understood the recession to have created the conditions for the new gay village in Soho.[129] The overall provision climbed steadily until 2001, which saw the biggest year-on-year rise, of 25 venues, reaching 114, before dipping slightly, and then continuing to climb until the peak, in 2006, of 119 venues. Plotting a graph of venue numbers for the city as a whole illustrates this upward curve. The trend then reversed. With the exception of 2008, numbers dropped every year until 2017, with notably sharp falls between 2007–8 and 2008–9 – the biggest drop, of twenty-two venues. Although this coincided with the global financial crisis, the case studies in *Queer Premises* show that closures have often been shaped by urban processes that have unfolded over longer periods.

After the 2008 financial crisis, the UK was in recession from 2008 to 2009. The effects of this downturn were felt long into the 2010s. In assessing the post-2008 crisis recovery of London, the UK city with the longest devolved administration, the Resolution Foundation noted that the capital was challenged by 'sluggish growth' as well as high costs of living and high levels of inequality.[130] Even so, for the UK as a whole, economic output, by some measures, grew again from 2010 and returned to pre-crisis levels in the third quarter of 2013. In London, the arts, entertainment and recreation sector grew from 80,000 jobs in 1971, to 132,000 in 1996, 159,000 in 2011 and 201,000 in 2015; the sector as a whole grew by 123 per cent, based on the measurement of GVA.[131] However, there was another sharp fall in LGBTQ+ venue numbers between 2015 and 2016. London-wide data should be viewed cautiously for the period following the 2008 crisis because although the capital may appear on average to have resumed growth and prosperity, once housing costs are factored in it can appear poorer and weaker in its recovery. Although macroeconomic cycles and sectoral data provide some context, venues cannot simply be charted against them. Many more localized factors have shaped their provision as part of the diverse urban economy, which is structured in distinct ways in different boroughs.[132]

On the digital maps we created from venue numbers, as you scroll through the years, colour-coded clusters of venues appear and disappear (Plates 10–13).[133] Although a formulaic definition of a cluster can be determined according to the presence of a certain number of venues in proximity, this is, of course, a crude method. It fails fully to capture either the scenes and spaces operating at a given moment, or the nuanced and contingent reality of how people identify with particular areas or networks of venues. Clusters are not just composed of groups of licensed night-time venues – those mapped here – but are rather constellations of commercial and service organizations and residential space, occupied, connected and extended by mobile and ad hoc nightlife events. They are not geographically bounded, even if some neighbourhoods – particularly Soho – are strongly distinguished in media representations and place-based marketing, as we have seen. They are not always confined to specific administrative boroughs, and they do not only serve people who live in an immediate catchment area. Clusters overlap in time and co-exist, although there are also examples where they entirely disappear.

In 1986, there was one dominant cluster, in Soho. At this time, there were also networks of venues in Earls Court and Kensington, in the west of inner London, and the Islington/King's Cross districts in the north. These remained important into the late 1990s. During the 1990s and 2000s, the dominant clusters shifted gradually from west to east and north to south. The number of clusters peaked between 2002 and 2005, with a strong presence of venues in Vauxhall and neighbouring Kennington in the south, Soho, in the West End, King's Cross and Islington in the north of inner London, and Shoreditch and Limehouse in the east. The Islington/King's Cross scene diminished on the Islington side by 2004. The Vauxhall/Kennington cluster, which is apparent from the mid-1990s, began to shrink on the Kennington side in 2006.[134] The King's Cross cluster disappeared in 2009. In 2012 a new cluster appeared on the Kingsland Road and Kingsland High Street branch of the A10, a major road connecting to Stoke Newington with rail stations served, from 2010, by the East London line extension of the London Overground railway. This group of venues were connected by the A10 to the Shoreditch scene, a small network which consolidated from 2002 to 2015 but which linked to an earlier generation of premises, such as the clone bar the London Apprentice, or The Alternative, a pub run by women for lesbians, bisexual women and their guests, both open in the mid-1980s. Soho is, unsurprisingly, the largest cluster throughout the study and the only one present consistently, from beginning to end, from the mid-1980s to the late 2010s. Soho, strictly speaking, is in the borough of Westminster, but the scene crosses into neighbouring Camden. There were thirty-five venues in Westminster in 2006, reduced to twenty by 2017. Camden saw a drop from fourteen to six venues, from 2006 to 2017.

Networks of venues and other related spaces and services have provided multi-layered infrastructure for LGBTQ+ communities. The city's scenes have been plural and dispersed, but they have also been concentrated in inner London. They have been further concentrated in some specific boroughs, which are important hosts over an extended period. Looking at the provision borough by borough, as well as showing the proliferation of venues in some of the inner London boroughs, highlights that the clusters are often associated with those that, working in collaboration with the GLC, were proactively supportive of gay and lesbian rights in the 1980s. These included Camden, Islington and Lambeth. In 2006, Westminster, Camden, Islington, Lambeth and Tower Hamlets all had ten or more venues, and all saw big falls in the following decade, with the biggest – significantly above average for the city as a whole – being in Islington – 80 per cent – and Tower Hamlets – 70 per cent.

What is the bigger picture, in Greater London? Nine boroughs had no venues at all throughout the period of study, and the outer boroughs had very few compared with the concentrations evident in the inner city. In 2006, twenty-three boroughs had one or more, but this reduced to just twelve by 2017. Micro-clusters and one-off spaces are important, even if these get lost in dominant accounts of the shifting geography of queer venues in Greater London. In 1986 there were single venues in Richmond in the west, Hampstead in the north, Poplar in the east and Bromley in the south. This provision was similar a decade later, and by the end of the 1990s there was a ring of venues on the outer edge of inner London. This was consistent until the steep declines in venue numbers at the end of the 2000s and in the mid-2010s.

Although there were no designated venues in the London Borough of Newham in East London in the 1980s, a *Time Out* gay and lesbian listing of 1986 recorded a weekly, unnamed disco in 1986 at The Pigeons public house. This mention of a transient event in an otherwise 'straight' pub that had been around since the early nineteenth century signals the presence of important ephemeral and mobile nightlife events serving outer London communities, which are difficult to trace.[135] That the site of The Pigeons (a host venue for gay nights) has itself been redeveloped, as a Tesco Metro supermarket, points to the wider reduction of pubs and nightclubs, and hence the loss of venues available for temporary appropriation.[136] Newham had reflected the trend of expanded provision in the 2000s, with three venues that opened between 1997 and 2006, including two cabaret spaces. By 2010 these had all closed. The continued presence of LGBTQ+ residents and of individuals and businesses that value networking opportunities and visibility are attested by the appearance of the Queer Newham events and educational programme in 2016 and Forest Gayte Pride in 2017.[137]

The sources discussed in this chapter indicate some of the ways in which venue closures and threats in the mid-2010s sparked an intense analysis of their provision and functions, as well as historical reflection, and projections of how they might decline or adapt in the future. They offer evidence to understand how venues have served as spaces of survival and utopic imagination – as scenes for integration, and sometimes conflict, across difference within heterogeneous LGBTQ+ populations. They attest to frustrations and disappointment with the ways that distinct scenes and premises reproduce wider social, economic and political norms and inequality. Even interpreted critically, as damaged or damaging, or ambivalently, due to their contradictions and entanglement within problematic institutions, venues have been invested with hope for the sustenance of future generations. As reactions to urban redevelopment, the media, community, research and policy discussions considered here demonstrate recognition of the interconnectedness of threats to these venues with the viability of other forms of social and cultural infrastructure.

The mid-2010s marked a definite rupture, with a surge in public interest and activism, imbued with a sense of alarm and loss. Narratives emphasize that the crisis precipitated by closures instigated identification with venues, as well as recognition of problems and calls for repair – for future provision to better serve collective need. This has been expressed with more nuance in qualitative evidence than in the narrower demand and supply economic explanations that have surfaced in the media and from business groups. Arguments of decline – whether due to increased social acceptance, greater assimilation of LGBTQ+ people or increased use of mobile dating apps – have often been recited with limited evidence, leading unchallenged to false or binary conclusions. The explanatory tropes in circulation can usefully be contextualized through reference to longer-running debates about changing LGBTQ+ subjectivities, and queer communities' relations with urban space and gentrification.

Looking at community members' statements, many LGBTQ+ people do still strongly identify with specific venues and clusters. A tone of critical evaluation has been counterpoised by an overwhelming recognition of the value of maintaining and improving available venues. There have been examples that have tested optimism about the possibility of repairing venues (see Chapter 7). There are also serious worries about the qualitative difference between today's proliferation of pop-up queer events and the more formal and long-term venues that have been depleted, in terms of the potentials these offer to engender community, or to facilitate interaction and integration across a diverse community in sustained ways (see Chapter 8). But in general closures have been met with an optimistic imagination of more positive futures, where existing models might transform to serve new purposes, and new spaces and typologies will emerge to become more inclusive, oriented to intersectionally marginalized groups. These critical yet optimistic statements complement a thread of commentaries on the active heritage value of venues. There is an alertness to the possibilities of even the longest-standing venues to adapt and serve new purposes, as well as recognition of the importance of commemorating sites of queer culture, history and political struggle.

The late 2010s saw the opening of political opportunities to make a case for the specific value of LGBTQ+ venues and heritage. Campaigners and policy makers sought to generate evidence, and this led to the counting of venues. Although the data and maps only show the surface – formal, licensed premises – they demonstrate the co-existence of multiple clusters, concentrated in specific boroughs, uneven provision for distinct groups, and patterns over time, including the headline 58 per cent drop in the decade to 2017, with sharp falls in the 2000s and mid-2010s. Such evidence can be read alongside other sources which illustrate the bespoke conditions that enable venues to open and thrive, or in some cases close. Following this chapter's survey of media, qualitative and quantitative evidence, next I delve more deeply into some specific cases to examine how and why venues close and the campaigns that have formed around them.

5

Seeking closure

Dramatic headlines about venue losses and the seductively simple causal explanations that accompany them conceal the multiple and interactive factors that lead to closures. Relevant knowledge is often undocumented, invisible or difficult to access in public records. Even if the impacts of closures are experienced as sudden and alarming, the processes involved typically reach back over long periods. Viewing closures solely in terms of loss to those who are disadvantaged by them risks obscuring the fact that there are often beneficiaries, too. Even where reasons for closures are given publicly, the cessation of businesses can involve multiple hidden factors, shaped by varied connections between organizations, individuals, sites, phases of redevelopment, and property exchanges, in turn influenced by changing policy and economic contexts.

The Urban Lab research conducted in 2016, discussed in the previous chapter, had pointed to some of the general trends behind venue closures.[1] Lo Marshall and I summarized these as follows: the negative impacts of large-scale infrastructure developments; a failure to effectively implement safeguarding measures in the planning system; the sale and change of use of property by landlords, whereby venue owners, operators and clients had severely limited negotiating power compared with large landowning organizations; and disproportionate rent increases, imposed in contexts of accelerating redevelopment and gentrification. These dynamics played out in a variety of ways. In this chapter, I look further into how venues and services specifically dedicated to LGBTQ+ populations, and other venues that have hosted them, have been affected by large-scale, infrastructure-led redevelopment. First, it is necessary to look at the inception of scenes and venues. Ageing transport intersections, such as the inner London King's Cross or St Giles areas, discussed in this chapter, provided affordable premises for venues prior to large-scale redevelopment. What opportunities did such transport intersections provide? How have these opportunities aligned with other forces, such as the efforts of individuals or collectives to establish new scenes, or to pitch innovative venues or operating models in response to new challenges, needs, or crises?

Once redevelopment cycles accelerate, the negative effects of blight during construction, closures of venues as sites and buildings are reconfigured, direct displacement through rent increases or changed lease terms, and indirect displacement due to rising land and rental values, all come into play. It is in some ways arbitrary to separate out LGBTQ+ venues, since all types of social and cultural space are subjected to similar pressures. There are, however, specific ways in which LGBTQ+

populations have adapted precarious and infrastructural sites, have been impacted by redevelopment and have mobilized in response.

As background to the next chapter, with its focus on highly publicized closures and the campaigns around them in the mid-2010s, here I discuss the shifting scenes of the 1980s and 1990s, before turning to a wave of closures in the mid- to late 2000s. The 1980s and 1990s scenes have recently been a focus for community archiving and remembrance, while the 2000s cases include the earliest instances of widespread public concern over the impact of large-scale redevelopment on LGBTQ+ venues. This found its voice through political lobbying, media discussion and online petitions, and prompted public responses from City Hall. This included the first tentative uses of planning procedures to safeguard venues associated with LGBTQ+ populations through provisions for protected characteristics embedded in legislation and policy. These cases orbit two large-scale redevelopment sites around the King's Cross and Tottenham Court Road stations. I draw on statements made by planners, the GLA, developers and venue owners and operators, and documents created within these redevelopment processes, to examine how and why venues have closed, and how LGBTQ+ people were recognized or overlooked.

Fallen angels

To understand venue closures in King's Cross in the 2000s, it helps to turn the clock back to the dynamic period when new forms of lesbian and gay nightlife and activism emerged in the 1980s, and to consider how those involved reflect today on the decline of those scenes in the 1990s. Until recently, there was little public acknowledgement of the significance of those scenes. Lately, however, they have been remembered in oral histories and by social media groups. Contributors have emphasized the importance of The Bell, a few minutes' walk from King's Cross station on Pentonville Road, as an epicentre of counterculture within a cluster of venues in Camden and Islington (Plate 14).[2] This Victorian pub, which had featured drag performances as early as 1972, was mentioned frequently in responses to Urban Lab's survey, too. Respondents associated its 1980s and early 1990s heyday with alternative music and pitched it against the mainstream: 'like a second home with great mates, cool music, top shags and good politics.'[3]

At the height of its popularity, The Bell hosted a packed programme of lesbian and gay nightlife seven-nights-a-week. These events were organized by collectives, with attendees paying a modest entrance fee, while the pub's licensees benefitted from the bar takings. From 1982, Women's City, a pioneering group among these collectives, used the pub for weekly, and later twice weekly, women-only disco fundraisers. This was at the invitation of the landlady, Dolores Lyons, who had moved to The Bell from The Pied Bull, in nearby Islington, a pub supplied by the same brewery, Charringtons, and which had also hosted gay and lesbian events.[4]

Women's City was an important initiative to support women prisoners and to create a 'safe building within which women can meet socially, organise, interact, teach, learn, create and trade' in a former Methodist meeting hall in Drayton Park, North London.[5]

It was initiated by the reformer Chris Ryder-Tchaikovsky (1944–2002) following her release from HM Prison Holloway, close to King's Cross, and then developed by a collective. Originally from Cornwall, Ryder-Tchaikovsky had been a regular at a lesbian club called The Gateways in West London, another definitive venue, and an equally important site of recent collective documentation and remembrance. The subculture around the club, in which Ryder-Tchaikovsky participated while running a gang of criminal forgers, was constructed around butch/femme identities and roles. The Gateways endured until the late 1960s.[6] As the historian Rebecca Jennings has shown, after the arrival of the liberation movements of the 1970s, there was a diversification and reshaping of expectations and identities in lesbian and feminist politics on this scene, and in society more generally, alongside increased provision of lesbian and gay discos elsewhere.[7] Ryder-Tchaikovsky's discos at The Bell, which aided her project to establish Women's City, reflected these shifts.[8]

The combination of nightlife and activism Women's City embodied became characteristic of The Bell and points to an important intersection between queer night scenes, venues, political consciousness-raising and fundraising for varied causes. With its youthful and politically energetic clientele of punks, students and campaigners, The Bell was 'a beacon for people with a cause and a collection bucket'.[9] Former members of the high-profile activist group Lesbians and Gays Support the Miners (LGSM), for example, highlight the importance of this 'alternative lefty gay pub' to their history.[10] Other important collaborations that orbited and attached themselves to The Bell included Movements, Icebreakers and Night Workers – names that capture the social and political spirit and momentum of the time. Movements had originated as a benefit disco linked to gay and anti-fascist organizing.[11] It moved to The Bell via other Islington pubs in 1983. Its elastic name neatly alludes to the combination of dancing, music and activism. Many of the pub's customers were unemployed and signing on for state benefits, so it was important that entry and bar prices were affordable.[12] For its members, the Night Workers collective supported livelihoods and lifeworlds at a time when other options were limited.[13]

The women-only nights run by Women's City were named 'Private Function', appropriating the prosaic door sign the pub used for private parties. Over more than a decade of popular programming, the inclusivity and exclusivity of The Bell shifted according to the night of the week and with changes to the management. The pub originally provided an alternative to the more commercial Earl's Court clone scene. DJ Ritu recalls that in the early 1980s the weekly Lesbian Discussion Group at Gay's the Word bookshop in Bloomsbury would be followed by visits to The Bell, 'which is where all "The Bell Women" hung out', who 'were kind of the equivalent of handlebar moustache women: leather jackets, studs and things'.[14] The pub was an important site for the forging of lesbian identities, and was where a diverse scene of lesbians, feminist allies, gay men, sex workers and leftist campaigners mixed.[15] The policing of different lesbian and gay identities and tense debates that permeated the atmosphere of the London Lesbian and Gay Centre (LLGC) played out in the door policy and on the dance floor of The Bell, too.[16] In his regular review column in *Capital Gay*, the important free weekly newspaper that ran in London and Brighton throughout the 1980s and early 1990s, Eric Presland reported 'roughly equal' numbers of lesbians and gay men at an event at The Bell in 1984.[17] He recounted an incident in which the DJ stopped the music to declare the venue a straight-free zone and turfed out a straight couple thought to be attending merely for the music.

By 1985, controversy engulfed The Bell when the brewery handed the pub's management to two gay men whose style was more aligned with that of the Earl's Court clone and leather scene from which The Bell's collectives had consciously distanced themselves.[18] The new operators changed the tone; they were resistant to hosting women-only nights, and even introduced a quota for the number of women allowed entry on some nights.[19] Inside the pub, the busy loos continued to offer possibilities for sex and other intimacies to men and women, with entry and behaviour policed differently according to the night. The 'separate scene' located in the women's loos has parallels with the interior compartmentalization of other queer venues discussed in this book. The women's loos became a particular site of contestation with the new management.[20] Even under their tenure, the venue continued to be a place of gender as well as sexual experimentation associated with the New Wave androgyny of the time.

Rob Pateman, a Night Workers cooperative member, has played a key role in archiving The Bell's history. He makes an interesting observation that one of the final regular events held there, from 1993, was Jo Purvis's Tea Dances, which featured 1950s and 1960s dancehall music, and was popular with an multigenerational crowd who were not all 'out'. This was quite a contrast with the punk, youth, alternative music and visibility politics of the period.[21] Jo Purvis's presence, along with the earlier influence of Ryder-Tchaikovsky, emphasizes the pioneering role of gender non-conforming women to the venue's cultural innovations. Both Ryder-Tchaikovsky and Purvis's events provided space for otherwise marginalized groups. That the throwback Tea Dances were prominent in the venue's final days emphasizes the dynamism and polytemporality of these scenes, rather than their linear evolution or rise and fall, together with their contingent, conditional inclusivity.

The scenes that appear to have spontaneously gathered around The Bell were carefully orchestrated by the individuals and collectives involved. What role was played by the pub's location, layout and interior aesthetics? The setting was vividly evoked by Jane Campbell in her memoir, *Dyke*. The Bell was, she says,

> a churning sea of skinny bodies, parted down the middle by an ornate pier of a bar and covered by blood-red leather banquette. Everything else was painted black, from the boards that covered the windows to the Victorian ceiling supports, blackest of all was the vast bar.[22]

All this served a clientele of 'druggie rent boys, lefty campaigners and wannabe performers'.[23] The large bar stands out in others' recollections, too, as do the red-curtained L-shaped interior and its pendulous, bell-like lampshades.[24] Drainage plans show how in the 1970s the venue had been opened up from its previous compartmentalisation into saloon bars, public bar, dining room and lounge.[25] The saloon bars and dining room were converted to 'Disco bars' and a designated dance floor. These interiors were captured in video footage that can be viewed on YouTube.[26]

With its 'private function' sign and closed curtains, the venue was discrete enough, and could be entered surreptitiously via a relatively hidden exit from the King's Cross underground station nearby.[27] In another of his haughty reviews, Presland comments on how the Night Workers and their collaborators had to cart in their own speakers, lights and records for a cabaret night called The Outhouse.[28] After three years of 'roaring trade' the venue was 'frayed at the edges', he complained, its walls a palimpsest of sellotape and posters, the floors a dangerous combination of cables and worn-out carpets.

A decade earlier, the actors in the 1989 film *Looking for Langston*, Isaac Julien's Gothic meditation on queer Black lives and histories, had cruised their way through the shabby nocturnal streets of post-industrial King's Cross – scenes that were interspliced with archival footage of Harlem.[29] The grand staircase of the Midland Grand Hotel fronting St Pancras Station, and which was semi-derelict at the time, is the setting for a police raid on a gay disco, which in Julien's imagining is a dreamlike 1920s speakeasy. It morphs into a pumping 1980s dance floor. A moment of high-octane adrenalin which provokes a raid by fascists and the police. The police wear rubber gloves for fear of contagion, as they had when raiding the Royal Vauxhall Tavern in 1987.[30] Set to music by Jimmy Sommerville, a Bell regular, the film's noir and electric atmosphere is embedded in the industrial infrastructure and degraded environment of King's Cross and St Pancras. Those who experienced gay and lesbian spaces in the 1980s and 1990s link the cultural richness of this ex-industrial red-light-district to its precarious condition. Richard Brunskill, a participant in the oral history project King's Cross Story Palace, evokes a heady mix of excitement, dereliction and danger.[31] It was a locus of gay and lesbian squats, as well as a contingent of National Front members.

In the mid-1980s, the affordability of the area meant that The Bell was part of a network of bars and services. In contrast with the commercial character of the established West London scene around Earl's Court and Shepherd's Bush, in the 1970s and 1980s King's Cross and neighbouring Euston and Islington became associated with more radical identity politics and a creative community.[32] The Euston Tavern, another local, had been frequented by predominantly young gay men. It featured a disco, cruising and live entertainment several nights a week from the 1970s and into the 1980s, with a residency by Tricky Dicky, the popular DJ who pioneered gay discos in London pubs from 1971.[33] In the mid-1980s, Traffic, at 126 York Way in King's Cross, was another venue popular with young gay men.[34] This tiny, low-ceilinged late-night venue offered cruise and pool bars, live acts and a disco, serving The Bell crowd into the night. The Bell was also next door to The Scala Cinema (1978–93), another iconic gay venue remembered positively for its all-night films and cruising.[35] Also nearby was The Prince Albert, where the GLF had congregated to drink and dance following the group's first demonstration, a torchlit rally against police harassment, at Highbury Fields on 27 November 1970.[36] In 1992 it would reopen as Central Station, an important, extant LGBTQ+ venue, which accommodated many of the organizations left without space when the LLGC closed (see Chapter 2). Lesbian and gay members of the unions located in the area congregated at pubs such as Mabel's Tavern after their meetings.[37] Gay's the Word bookshop, founded in 1979, and services such as Camden Lesbian Centre and Black Lesbian Group in Somers Town, were also nearby. The latter opened on 27 February 1986 in the Somers Town Estate on Phoenix Road, despite protests, verbal abuse and a local petition which claimed a danger to young school girls in the area.[38]

Presland's review of The Bell in 1984 had urged the brewery to upgrade the run-down pub to one with 'a more "gay" ambience'.[39] Out of sync with accounts that celebrated The Bell as a punk heaven, this comment indicates that at around this time more self-consciously designed gay bars had emerged, featuring a London version of what cultural theorists Christopher Castiglia and Christopher Reed refer to, in the US context, as the 'renovation aesthetic'.[40] They argue that gay pioneers' efforts to repurpose and renovate reflected an approach to the past that signaled a 'dissent from prevailing social norms' that was part of a wider 'survivalist culture'.[41] Similarly, José Esteban Muñoz speaks of 'reappropriation and refunctioning of the commonplace' in queer aesthetics.[42] In London, the repurposing of pubs and industrial spaces would see increasing demand for more modern, fresh and pastel-toned interior décors.

Nearby, and with strong overlaps in its clientele and their politics, The Fallen Angel regularly comes up in conversations about The Bell. This pub was open from 1986 to 1994 and hosted some of the same activist groups, such as LGSM. The contrast between The Fallen Angel and The Bell points to a shift in the standards of aesthetics that were happening throughout this period, where refurbishment aesthetics were bound into the politics of visibility. The Fallen Angel was a pioneer. It influenced the 'swish', 'clean' aesthetics of later bars such as First Out Café, discussed below, and the LLGC.[43] Both of these venues contrasted with the enclosed, dark and heavy interior of The Bell, which retained the lingering feel of a Victorian boozer. In a comment about The Fallen Angel on the website 'Gay in the '80s', Peter Rowlands, an Islington resident, writes:

> This pub was a Mistral of fresh thinking. Contemporary and open (light, cool, airy), dismissing the dark interiors (varnish, flock, black and bling) and camp Victoriana that had so characterised many gay watering holes. There was a sense that we no longer had to apologise at all – the secret and monitored entrances, furtive and gloomy interiors all suddenly a thing of the past.[44]

The modern looks of The Fallen Angel and the LLGC were a precursor to the glass and chrome hygiene aesthetics that would become characteristic of Soho bars in the 1990s. Geographer Johan Andersson interprets this more mannered iteration as a reaction to AIDS stigmatization.[45] When The Fallen Angel closed in 1994, the building housing it was converted into flats. Other notable features of the pub had included a ceiling mural – The Fallen Angel of the pub's name – photographs of which have not yet come to light, but the campy concept of such an image fits well with Castiglia and Reed's account of queer architectural postmodern aesthetics in the US.[46]

The Bell, which, like The Fallen Angel, survived the early 1990s recession, had closed by 1995. There were multiple factors behind the closure: the shift of focus from fringe locations to Soho's scene, which was linked to an increased visibility and social acceptance of a lesbian and gay presence; changing tastes in music and fashion, with the increasing dominance of house music and clubs; and processes of gentrification in King's Cross. The Bell was sold by the brewery, refurbished and reopened as a cocktail bar, Sahara Nights.[47] Under the ownership of the festival and venue owner and entrepreneur Vince Power, this would serve a new market.[48] Primed by central government-funded attempts to police and socially cleanse King's Cross within a programme of regeneration-as-rebranding, the forces of gentrification had escalated in scale and effect by the mid-1990s.

The queer histories of King's Cross have recently surfaced through the efforts of community archivists posting on websites and in social media, as well as in public oral history and arts projects. In *King's Cross Remixes*, a solo show performed in the nearby Camden Peoples' Theatre, multimedia artist Tom Marshman used practices of verbatim theatre, drag, lip syncing and dance to powerfully channel stories of nights at The Bell, the political dynamism of the time, and the darkest days of the AIDS crisis.[49] As part of his socially engaged practice he held a tea party, inviting those who had experienced the area in the 1980s to come and talk about it with him, and then drawing on participants' vivid recollections to make his work.

Facebook groups such as 'I Remember The Bell, King's Cross' and 'I remember the Bell', have drawn from – and in some ways have reignited – the energy and sense of community that spun around The Bell's dance floor.[50] Members post memorabilia and comment on The Bell and, more widely, on LGBTQ+ scenes and venues past and present. Questions asking why The Bell closed often come up, as do testimonies about what impact the closure had. There are speculations that closure was inevitable due to the cycle of gentrification and a geographic shift of the scene towards Soho, with its greater and more visible concentration of bars, clubs and services. Alternatively, the pub is seen as very much a product of its era, which became obsolete after serving a need that had disappeared. The Bell's clientele are also a focus. There are comments on how this politicized, creative generation went on to initiate further social change; or which point the finger at classic pioneer creative gentrifiers who became property owners in the area, and now lead homonormative lives, while younger generations are excluded from owning, renting or having a comparable sense of belonging.[51]

The Cross drops

The King's Cross scene did not end with The Bell. One pivot for its future trajectory was the decision, in 1996, to move the terminus of the Channel Tunnel Rail Link from Waterloo to St Pancras station, providing the impetus for the redevelopment of what would become known as King's Cross Central. Typically for large-scale regeneration projects, the developer's narrative flattens the complexity of social uses and displacement histories in order to naturalize their regeneration vision: 'by the late 20th Century, the area known as the railway lands had become a series of disused buildings, railway sidings, warehouses and contaminated land'.[52] Entirely omitted from this ominous spiel is any mention of the important and long-established presence of queer nightlife and queer creativity.

In the 1980s and 1990s the area's nightlife entrepreneurs had colonized the brick nineteenth-century industrial buildings on the vast railwaylands behind the King's Cross and St Pancras stations, where freight had been stored and processed, having circulated via the railways and the Regent's Canal. Bagleys Studios, later known as Canvas (1982–2008), and The Cross (1993–2008), were two large-capacity late-night venues that, although not exclusively programmed towards queer clientele, hosted long-running clubnights that were oriented towards these groups. Images posted by local *Gasholder* magazine prior to the King's Cross Central redevelopment show the vast scale of these buildings – the photographs documenting such huge empty spaces still convey a sense of the possibilities they held for congregation and experimentation. With a capacity to hold 2,500 people, Bagleys was the largest nightclub in London, and commentators estimate that about 10,000 people flocked to its clubs every weekend.[53] It was located in the Eastern Coaldrops, a coal storage warehouse built in the 1850s at this important intersection between the canal, rail and road systems. In some ways this was a fringe site, but its use as a club also constituted an appropriation of a vital strategic node in the city's circulatory systems, disrupting their intended functions through rave and house music, and the cutting-edge dance, fashion and performance cultures that featured in the queer and underground scenes.

For the first half of the 1990s, Bagleys was home to the Mud Club, which was started by Philip Salon and Malcolm McLaren after its previous home at Busby's Disco (c.1984–92) on Charing Cross Road had closed. Large venues meant large crowds. House music was associated with the power of assembly, but the Mud Club and other parties had a reputation for exclusivity. One DJ reminisces that 'Philip would scrutinise everyone entering. If you didn't meet the grade you wouldn't be let in and would be told why in no uncertain terms.'[54] However brutal the door policy of the Mud Club was, nights at Bagleys and The Cross did cater to a variety of patrons.[55] They had a close affiliation with queer club cultures, but these King's Cross warehouses were proactively 'mixed' venues – the type that some commentators argue have replaced dedicated LGBTQ+ venues (see Chapter 4). Of Bagleys, former *Time Out* nightlife journalist David Swindells writes that when it closed on new year's eve 2008, it 'had played host to twenty-five years of naughty-but-nice nightlife – illegal warehouse parties, gay superclubs, full-on fetish nights, roller discos, cutting-edge fashion shows [. . .] underground techno, UK Garage raves' as well as numerous gigs and fashion shoots.[56] He remarks on the importance of the large spaces and the location, away from residential areas, to the success of the club. Canvas and The Cross closed in 2008 as part of the King's Cross Central redevelopment. They remained unoccupied until 2015 and reopened as high-end retail in 2019. A revamped The Cross offers luxurious bars and events spaces and fine dining, in tune with the commercial vibe of the new King's Cross.

The lively, political and creative queer fabric of King's Cross in the 1980s and early 1990s – which had opportunistically taken advantage of short-lived lower rents and availability of space before sites were cleared – had largely disappeared long before the completion of the first phase of regeneration. The area did continue to have a distinctive queer presence into the 2000s, but this was curtailed by closures in the late 2000s and 2010s.[57] These were symptomatic of long-term processes. The area had been stigmatized, subjected to repeated planning proposals, intensively policed, and pump-primed with government regeneration funds, which shaped speculative land value and rent increases in parallel with active rebranding. The King's Cross regeneration was led by a private developer but was facilitated by public subsidy and publicly funded development. The scheme was framed around achieving a 'human city', a generic conception of equality, and the delivery of benefits to existing communities.[58] The redevelopment has been hailed as a success by some and criticized as state-led gentrification by others.[59] Just as venue closures cannot simply be equated with loss, so success, in such a long-term and large-scale project, must be evaluated from the different perspectives of affected groups as well as the public and private gains that are accrued. Many of the King's Cross venue closures were preceded by provisions for protecting social infrastructure, including LGBT venues, in the London Plan (2004).[60] Impacts on LGBTQ+ people do not appear to have been given any consideration. In contrast with the regeneration narratives of the 2010s that erased the area's subcultural heritage, the period of occupation by artists and ravers has more recently begun to be celebrated in the King's Cross place-marketing spiel, though this does not go so far as to point to any queer presence.[61] In a recent positive turn, Queer Britain, the UK's first dedicated LGBTQ+ museum, has rented premises in an Art Fund-owned building in Granary Square, one of the key (privately owned) public spaces in the new King's Cross. This trajectory of formalization and incorporation within the national heritage story contrasts with the experiences of other everyday queer cultural venues discussed in the next sections and chapters, although these venues, as we shall see, were also important memory sites and locations for community-driven heritage practices.

Broken glass

The Glass Bar (1995–2008) in Euston was one of the most notable venues that closed in the borough of Camden in the 2000s, not least because of its distinctive operational model and prioritization of women and the Black gay community. Established as a women-only members' club, it was housed in the Grade II-listed, TARDIS-like West Lodge of Euston Station, designed by the engineer J. B. Stansby and built with Portland stone (Plate 15).[62] As a listed and monumental neoclassical building, The Glass Bar was both the most architecturally recognized queer venue in London and one of the most discrete, hidden in plain sight within the urban fabric. As with the location of The Bell, just ten-minutes' walk away, or the warehouse clubs in edgy King's Cross, this was still a liminal site: effectively a traffic island on the historically less salubrious side of Euston Road, an administrative outbuilding on the margins of the rail and bus terminus. It is blighted by the busy and heavily polluted Euston Road, the main east-west arterial road encircling Central London.

This context is relevant to understand the area's changing affordability and how this has directed Railtrack and Network Rail's attitudes to the management of properties and their hospitability towards bespoke uses at different times. Like many of King's Cross's ex-industrial buildings, the West Lodge, as part of the Euston Station complex, had been owned by British Rail. After privatization in the mid-1990s, the site was taken over first by Railtrack, and then, in 2002, by its successor, Network Rail, which took on responsibility for coordinating rail infrastructure.[63] Network Rail is the 'arms' length' public body of the Department for Transport, which owns and manages most of the

104 *Queer Premises*

UK's rail network. It has frequently owned and managed land and buildings leased for cultural and community uses, including LGBTQ+ venues and events.

When Railtrack Property was selling off British Rail's built assets and finding tenants for the remaining buildings in the mid-1990s, Elaine McKenzie approached the company with a proposal to open a women-only club in the West Lodge, a lead-roofed building that had previously been a British Rail office but which had lain empty for many years. The proposal for a forum, 'like a gentlemen's club', was well-received by Railtrack.[64] The proposed use was suited both to the building's neo-classical form and the fact that the discrete entrance was difficult to find, even for members. The planning application, which McKenzie completed herself, was for a change of use from office 'to meeting place and networking venue', intended for 'academic and professional women'.[65] McKenzie reflects that 'if you identified as a woman, that's it you could come in [. . .] so we had cis and trans women in'.[66] In retrospect, the proposal for a dedicated women's space appears especially appropriate since the building had been used as temporary accommodation for GALS (Girls Alone in London Service), a charitable advisory for homeless girls, in the mid-1970s.[67]

Although a members-only club, the intention behind The Glass Bar was to create a welcoming, inclusive space in contrast to a scene McKenzie had experienced as 'cold and cliquey', with few spaces for women or for Black gay people.[68] McKenzie recalls having felt uncomfortable entering The Fallen Angel, in the 1980s:

> it was a *rainy* day and I was dressed in a red Kagoul and bright pink trousers with a multitude of triangles in different colours [. . .] And I walked into this night where everybody was in jeans, black leather jacket, white T-shirt, hair slicked back and short. So, I kind of stood out. And it was almost like walking into prison – well it's like these, these old-fashioned cowboy movies where the guy walks through the saloon and everybody turns, looks at them, the music stops and it's so *just* like that. And so I walked to the front, got my drink – bought a pint – walked right to the back where all the leaflets were and studied them *intensely* until I'd finished my pint, and then left. And I just thought: 'that was the most *negative* experience, really'.[69]

McKenzie views the 1980s as a time of togetherness in the face of adversity across different groups, but the 1990s as one of increasing division and racial segregation, as new and more consumerist and elitist lesbian and gay identities emerged. Alienated from white-dominant spaces, 'you had parties in odd places as a Black, gay person', she notes.[70] Of course, even a venue set up to create a safe space, and with anti-racist purpose, does not guarantee the eradication of racist behaviour. Within the conditional inclusivity of The Glass Bar, McKenzie herself experienced racism, being challenged about how she had funded the venue, or talked over, as white customers addressed her white staff members.

McKenzie, who was trained as an accountant and had previously run a restaurant, took a hands-on approach to the conversion and maintenance of the lodge: she wrote and sketched the planning application submission by hand, constructed the actual glass-brick bar, furnished and decorated the venue, managed the leaky roof and fixed the

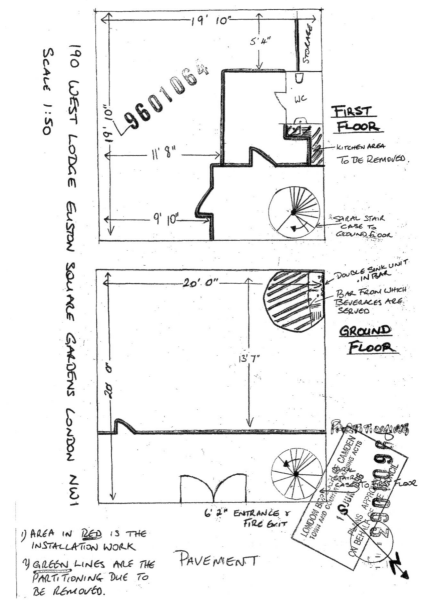

Figure 5.1 Planning application, 190 West Lodge, Euston Square, 9 April 1996, completed by Elaine McKenzie, with sketch indicating conversion from offices to a bar.

frequently defective drainage system (Figure 5.1). The idea, in this location associated with flux, transport, arrivals and departures, was to offer a homely environment, with more seating than was usual for the time, and no dress code. Members paid a nominal entry fee of £1. There were two floors, connected by a spiral stair, so the venue was only wheelchair-accessible at ground level. The contrasting stone building and glass-brick bar conveyed a material tension that reflected the status of the building and venue: a grandly appointed monumental outbuilding, a licensed members' club, but also a precarious space, which had only a temporary foothold in this central urban setting. Adapting this austere railway monument to support a network and events for women, and especially lesbian women who had historically had less access to venues, was a radical act.

Although Railtrack had originally been supportive, its managers and, once they had taken over, those of Network Rail, had a restrictive attitude to the management of the lease, which inhibited business. Today, the pub located in the West Lodge has a plentiful outside seating area.[71] But at the time of The Glass Bar, this was prohibited, as were the two sandwich boards that had pointed people to the entrance, and the air conditioning units that had been proposed to create a more comfortable interior.[72] Informed by discussions with a Railtrack employee who used the bar, McKenzie considers that once it was up and running the organization soon wanted rid of it.[73] Her experiences with the various bodies involved was varied: she experienced Railtrack as an 'old boys network', which took an unimaginative approach that favoured blue-chip franchises over bespoke venues.[74] English Heritage (now renamed Historic England) was also experienced as unsupportive; but Camden's conservation department was more helpful.[75]

In 2006, faced with the costs of maintenance works to the lead roof, and with the rent tripled and backdated, the venue closed.[76] A successful community fundraising campaign enabled it to reopen three months later. After another dramatic rent hike in 2008, McKenzie decided to close again, deciding she was in too unequal a fight. She continued The Glass Bar as a network which made temporary use of other venues. The community around the venue was disappointed in the situation, in Network Rail, and also in McKenzie, but she felt that the problem was insurmountable without further disproportionate personal and collective investment. Although unique, The Glass Bar case contains some typical elements, including the sweat equity involved in establishing the venue and the hands-on approach required; the creative response to perceived deficiencies in the existing commercial scenes; the high personal financial and emotional costs of the venture; the venue's shifting (and eventually tense) relations with the landlord and other property management and public institutions; and the repeated efforts required to protect it from multiple displacement forces.

G-A-Y power

Another major development in Central London that affected the borough of Camden's (and Westminster's) LGBTQ+ venues was Crossrail, renamed the Elizabeth Line by the time of its long-overdue opening in 2022.[77] The project comprised a major new deep-tunnel, regional express-train line connecting east-west from the capital towards Heathrow Airport and beyond. It was led by Network Rail with Transport for London – the public body for transport in Greater London overseen by the mayor. Crossrail's redevelopment of the Tottenham Court Road underground station and the multiple venues that closed as a result were a factor highlighted by respondents to Urban Lab's survey in 2016. Although the survey referenced recent venues, the back streets of Tottenham Court Road have longer histories of queer sociality, such as in the bohemian cafés and coffee stalls associated with lesbian clientele in the 1930s.[78]

The London Astoria and its interlinked sister venue LA2 were two notable premises for clubs and live music accommodated in a building that had a long history as a cultural venue. A former warehouse, The Astoria Picture Theatre and Dancehall opened in 1927, and later became a cinema and restaurant before its conversion into a nightclub.[79] It was significant as the location for London's first big gay club, Bang! (1976–c.1993) in the mid-1980s, after it moved from Busbys, another pioneering Charing Cross Road venue mentioned earlier. The Astoria was surrounded by other smaller underground venues, including the popular nightclub The Ghetto, which closed in 2008.

Promoter and DJ Jeremy Joseph had worked at Bang! and another interlinked night, Propaganda.[80] In 1993 he acquired Bang!, changing its name to G-A-Y. The Astoria hosted G-A-Y two nights a week from 1993 until closure in 2008 (Figure 5.2), at which point Joseph and his corporate investment partners (MAMA) bought Heaven nightclub. Heaven had been running in the arches beneath Charing Cross Station since 1979, but during the 2008 financial crisis, under the ownership of Pure Group, it

Figure 5.2 The Astoria, 2008, with announcement for G-A-Y. Photo by Ewan Munro. Original photograph in full colour. Creative Commons, CC-BY-SA-2.0.

had gone into administration.[81] Like Heaven in its glory days, G-A-Y exemplifies gay nightlife at its most commercially successful. G-A-Y is oriented around the celebration of mainstream pop culture, including live performances by celebrity musicians. From its roots in Bang! in the basement Sundown Club of The Astoria, to a successful, high-profile, multi-city franchise, the G-A-Y brand embodies a trajectory of expansion and assimilation from subculture to the mainstream. Such categories are crude, however, and do not capture the diversity of functions of venues, or identifications with them. Uses are not pre-determined by commercial and institutional contexts or by the intentions of entrepreneurs, even if they are strongly directed by them.

By the mid-2000s, The Astoria's ex-industrial, central location had become highly valuable, and the surrounding built environment was displaying the signs of the blight typical at sites of impending redevelopment. Prior to Crossrail, The Astoria changed owners in 2006. It was sold by Compco Holdings to developers Derwent Valley for £24 million. This was part of a plot assembly process by Derwent, which bought it along with a neighbouring building. Derwent already owned a large block between Charing Cross Road and Soho Square. Their proposal was for a mixed-use development.[82] Apart from Crossrail, Mayor Livingstone's announcement of a 'West End Policy Retail Area', incentivized retail development at Tottenham Court Road, in what was designated an 'opportunity area' in the London Plan (2004).[83]

The sale of this 2,000-person-capacity venue sparked a petition, with more than 16,000 signatories arguing that it should be retained within the proposed shopping development.[84] Although the retail scheme was taken at face value by the petitioners, the Crossrail Bill was already passing through parliament, and the developers' carefully worded statement hints at their true intention in realizing the site's longer-term value:

> The Astoria is a valuable addition and a strategic acquisition, which adjoins our existing holdings in the area and will form a potential development site for the future. We are committed to the regeneration of key areas in London and are looking forward to the opportunities afforded by such a prominent location.[85]

With a Compulsory Purchase Order on the horizon, the sale of The Astoria was part of an amassment of land holdings to maximize profit in connection with the planned Crossrail-led transformation.

Crossrail has unfolded over a long period, during which time the legislative and policy framework on sexual orientation and equality in the UK has undergone significant change. The Equality Act 2006 streamlined previously separate strands of legislation. It led to the Sexual Orientation Regulations 2006, which made discrimination on grounds of sexual orientation in the provision of goods and services illegal, with some exceptions.[86]

Like most publicly funded infrastructure projects, Crossrail was framed through reference to the public benefits of regeneration. The scheme's approach to inclusivity deferred to seven prioritized equality strands identified in Transport for London's Equality and Inclusion Policy Framework, and aimed to 'ensure the construction and operation of Crossrail with the minimum practicable negative impact on priority equality groups'.[87] Following Transport for London's equality guidance, the Crossrail project followed an initial equalities impact screening, using interviews and public consultation responses. This was to identify the groups most likely to be impacted, and the findings noted the 'potential impact' of the 'demolition of a venue used extensively by the lesbian, gay and bisexual community'.[88] A report of Crossrail's policy and assessment process, published with a period of public consultation, conceded that three nightclubs would be lost permanently, including The Astoria and another LGBTQ+ venue, Rouge.[89] The report recognized that there could be negative impacts on people prioritized under categories of both sexual orientation and young people.[90] Transport for London's equality guidance had a separate category of 'gender – women and transgender people'. While Crossrail's approach acknowledged that people may identify with more than one protected identity characteristic, in this case, impacts under the gender category were not considered in relation to sexual orientation.

At the time, in the mid-2000s, the legal framework regarding sexual orientation consisted of the Employment Equality (Sexual Orientation) Regulations (2003), underpinned by the EU's Equal Treatment Directives. Transport for London's policy can be seen as part of the wider equalities mainstreaming agenda in London's governance (see Chapter 3). The more recent Equality Act 2010 is notable for extending beyond the requirements of the EU directives, and further than the UK legislative and policy framework of the mid-2000s. Yet, Transport for London's inclusion policy, even in 2006, was proactive, emphasizing the 'seeking out [of] opportunities to promote inclusive development', and to 'ensure that no priority equality group experiences disadvantage as a result of the planning, design, construction and operation of Crossrail'.[91]

These policies prioritized decision-making based on consultation with protected minorities. When looking at who is addressed in these exchanges, however, it is the affected businesses and property owners. A statement of mitigation on the loss of the gay clubs was directed towards business owners. They would be compensated and guided by the Secretary of State in order to identify their property requirements:

> Businesses displaced by Crossrail will be compensated under the national compensation code. The Secretary of State will set up an agency service to help firms identify their property requirements and advise them on what property is available. The specific community and associated locational requirements of G.A.Y [sic] will be taken into account when the agency service provides its advice.[92]

This led to a response from the GLA, expressing concern about 'the loss of an established gay leisure venue' and seeking assurance

> that the organisers and the clientele have been consulted with regarding the developments; that a suitable and appropriate alternative venue is found, which is on a par with, if not better than the current venue and that the clientele is made aware of the change in venue so that the number of clientele remains the same, if not, increases.[93]

This statement demonstrates that the recognition of the gay clientele as a minority group, and the demand for a new venue to be provided, were framed in terms of pragmatic economics. Here, equality and inclusivity are bound into the metric of client numbers – data that was recognizable within a retail-led model of neoliberal urban governance, underpinned by an expansionist drive for growth. The designation of minority sexual orientation ('gay'), and the obligation to protect a venue associated with this minority, is constructed through the measure of commercial success and anticipated spending power. Evidence suggests that initiatives like this, which recognize LGBTQ+ minorities while being embedded in mainstream governance and economics, can have positive impacts.[94] Yet this case raises the problem of which LGBTQ+ minorities are visible and thus compensated. It highlights tensions between the radical politics and alternative economies of some queer venues, and the measures used to safeguard minority interests. The outcomes are weighted towards monetary value for individuals and small elites over social value, including for those who are intersectionally marginalized.

Crossrail's response to the GLA detailed its compliance with consultation requirements in the pre-application phase, and the methods it would use to communicate The Astoria's impending demolition.[95] It stated that the 'owners and qualifying leaseholders' of affected buildings were sent notices and that Crossrail had been in contact with the owners, the leaseholders of the venue, and the organizers of G-A-Y to explain what the proposals meant. It pointed to the project's relocation service for property owners and businesses, but it rejected any responsibility for communicating with G-A-Y's clientele, saying that this was for G-A-Y's organizers. By classifying The Astoria as a generic leisure space, business and property, the Equalities Impact Assessment (EqIA) documentation did not demonstrate an understanding of the function or social value of an LGB venue, nor why the GLA might be concerned about the loss of such an establishment, nor the context of a cluster of LGBTQ+ venues in the development's vicinity. This is even more surprising given that community objection had been rallied through an online petition. It is not clear whether G-A-Y received financial compensation.[96] What is clear is that this well-established brand was able to align with other commercial interest groups and to relocate, consolidate with Heaven, and then continue on a trajectory of expansion. The case also highlights tensions between City Hall's obligation and commitment to the protection of minorities and its incentivization, through the London Plan, of pro-business, retail- and infrastructure-led redevelopment focused on achieving economic growth according to orthodox measures.

By the time of Crossrail's Compulsory Purchase of The Astoria, G-A-Y was a well-established brand for its bars and live music. It was highly successful commercially through Joseph's commercial partnerships, and it had transitioned from radio programme, to club night, to bar, to chain, with venues in London and later Manchester. After the closure of The Astoria, G-A-Y followed the path of growth imagined by the GLA in its comments on the EqIA. In 2007, the directors of MAMA group, who were chain music venue owners and band managers, bought a 75 per cent stake in Manto Soho Limited, the holding company that operated G-A-Y bar and its sister venue G-A-Y Late, for £3.75 million, in parallel with the purchase of a number of Mean Fiddler venues.[97] In 2008 G-A-Y bought into Heaven as MAMA's recent acquisition, meaning that it could move into this similarly large-capacity venue.[98] By 2013, in its different guises, G-A-Y employed 200 people and had an annual turnover of £5.8 million and pre-tax profits of £0.8 million.[99] Joseph declared via social media that he had used personal finances and a bank loan to buy-out HMV's shares.[100]

More recently, Heaven has followed the path set by campaigners for other venues in being designated an Asset of Community Value (ACV) (see Chapter 6) by Westminster City Council.[101] That this proposal was made by the Night Time Industries Association, a trade and lobbying organization, indicates G-A-Y and Heaven's relative commercial power in the night-time industry compared with that of the smaller-scale applications by individuals and grassroots groups for other venues. The process was smooth compared with that of other venues, where ACVs were awarded, then challenged and retracted. In similarity with other venues, the ACV application is built around Heaven's importance to LGBTQ+ heritage, culture and community. It focuses heavily on the contribution to the night-time economy and on the size of the community it serves. It stresses the role of G-A-Y Group in 'saving' G-A-Y and Heaven by 'making way' for Crossrail and purchasing Heaven when the club went into administration in 2008. The case is also supported by reference to the recent establishment of the charitable arm of G-A-Y that Joseph set up – the G-A-Y Foundation – and the necessity to the venue of the foundation's future priorities of 'social inclusion and promotion of equality and diversity and community development'. Reinforcing the unusual financial scale of the venue compared with other ACV-designated venues, and the substantial personal investment of its owner-operator, the nomination states that '[redacted] is currently in the process of creating a will in which he will bequeath his interests in Heaven to the G-A-Y foundation'.[102] So while the fanfare of ACV announcements noted how this would protect the LGBTQ+ community's future interests, this was premised on an individual's future beneficence and on the anticipated work of the new charity. I will look at other ACV nominations in Chapter 6 and will return to G-A-Y and Heaven to discuss how venues reconfigured in response to the Covid-19 pandemic in Chapter 8.

Humble, First Out

Respondents to Urban Lab's 2016 survey who linked venue closures to the Crossrail redevelopment identified First Out Café as another notable venue that was impacted.[103] This was another early instance of a community mobilizing protest via an online petition in response to a threatened closure. First Out opened in the St Giles neighbourhood of Camden, on the edge of Soho, in 1986 (Plate 16). It closed in 2011.[104] The café was set up by a group of young socialists as a workers' cooperative by and for lesbians and gay men, creating a new type of venue: a continental-style, day- and night-time vegetarian café, bar and exhibition space. The idea had formed through conversations at Icebreakers, an influential telephone and in-person social group, which met at The Bell on Sundays in the early 1980s.[105] The intention was to create an antidote to the existing commercial scene: a community-focused and sociable space that was not centred around alcohol or sex.

Two years of planning began in October 1984, hosted at the London Co-operative Development Agency in Ladbrook Grove and at the LLGC. This was not an impulsive, opportunistic venture. Preparations involved an extensive business plan, careful market research, a reconnaissance trip to visit cafés in Amsterdam, and detailed liaison with existing venues, community spaces and other organizations. The group gained support from local borough representatives, from GLC Leader Ken Livingstone, and from the GLC more broadly.[106] As well as documenting these endorsements, the business plan included sketches by art graduate Mark Bullus, one of the five founding cooperative members, which he drew to help imagine the venue (Figure 5.3).[107] He recalls:

> It was 1985 and the decade had started to acquire a look. The bold shapes and colours and classical references which would become known as Post Modernism [. . .] I dreamt of film noir interiors. Black and white floors, smokey mirrors and intimate lighting. Subdued colours on the walls. A wash of stippling and sponging. Layers of tone and colour. Modern but not brash. In the end, though, the place

Figure 5.3 First Out Café, concept sketch, Mark Bullus, *First Out Coffee Shop Business Plan*, 1985.

became an expression of its function. A lively vibrant café is afterall much more inviting than any moody interior.[108]

The visual identity, palette, typography, and interior decoration of First Out resonated with the LLGC's aesthetics (see Chapter 2), which had been influenced by the look of The Fallen Angel.

Of First Out, Robert Kincaid, one of the other founders, notes:

> It was the first place we looked at really, and we just knew that this . . . we could afford . . . it was doable . . . because of the conditions of the lease, because it was always subject to this planning consent that had been delayed and delayed, then we knew that we could raise this amount of money . . . and it was in the right area.[109]

Since it was already earmarked for redevelopment, the precarity of the site – as often with small-scale cultural venues – was one of the conditions of First Out's emergence. Planning permission for a redevelopment had been sought on several occasions but had been refused by Camden Council because of insufficient provision of social housing in the proposals.[110] For First Out, the rent was relatively affordable because of the delayed planning consent. The lease included a break clause that could be activated with six months' notice, without any obligation to offer compensation. To counterbalance this insecurity, Camden agreed to act as guarantor, underwriting the necessary start-up loans and enabling the doors to open in time for Pride 1986.[111] The group envisaged repaying the loans over five years, and would count this as a success, even if the business then closed, since many gay venues at the time had shorter lifespans. The acceptance of somewhat onerous terms, and the lack of medium- or long-term security therefore have to be understood both in the context of the time (one of emergency, as discussed in Chapter 2) and in the knowledge that the venue had very active and material support by the GLC and the local authority.

As it turned out, the venue became something of an institution, particularly for the lesbian community.[112] The programming and marketing were actively oriented towards women, and the space became known as predominantly a lesbian venue, but one that was inclusive to others. Popular lesbian nights included *Company*, *Tattoo* and *Girl Friday*. The Café also provided meeting space for trans groups, for older and younger people, a Sikh group, Gay Alcoholics Anonymous, life drawing and much more, as well as being an affordable place to eat and drink.[113] Energy was expended in making the place feel inviting and less intimidating for people who were not used to entering a gay space. The group made the best of the building and the site, and in later years the café had tables and chairs outside, welcoming any passers-by.

The site was adjacent to, and therefore closely connected with, the Crossrail Tottenham Court Road station redevelopment. But it was on a separate triangular plot developed as St Giles Circus, a scheme led by ORMS architects for owners Consolidated Developments.[114] Camden refused planning permission for a large development on the site in 1991 on the basis that it was required for Crossrail. In the late 2000s, it was temporarily taken over by Crossrail for works. First Out's founders and staff emphasize that as the Crossrail development unfolded, business suffered due to construction works and closures of related venues, which had previously formed part of a circuit for their customers. Demolition and construction works directly impacted on trade and on the unique qualities of the venue as a space popular with women. Once perceived as a safer space for women due to its location adjacent to (rather than in) Soho, during construction the quality of illumination decreased and access routes were curtailed.

Consolidated Developments offered a temporary lease extension, but this was not deemed sustainable by First Out Group. Although buoyed by outpourings of public support, they were emotionally drained by the negotiations and by the losses the business had suffered as the redevelopment schemes proceeded. First Out announced its closure on 4 October 2011 and registered for insolvency a month later.[115] Consolidated Developments' offer to extend the lease was perceived as a false choice since the business was impossible to maintain in the challenging conditions of a large-scale redevelopment zone.

A petition First Out made to parliament in 2006–7, at the time the Crossrail Bill was being read, poignantly records their concerns about the impending works.[116] This 'humble petition of First Out Limited' objects to the Bill on the grounds of the injurious effect on the owners' 'rights, interests and property', the lack of adequate protection for them and the negative impacts of the works on the business. It is written in performative, floral and antiquated prose, reproducing the pomposity of parliamentary exchanges, and capturing the 'David and Goliath' power disparity between this small, community-centred business, the government and developers.

In contrast to the area's queer heritage, which was largely overlooked, other aspects of the St Giles neighbourhood's cultural history, including Denmark Street's association with music, had been noted in the planning documents, even by the early 1990s.[117] The vision for the St Giles Circus scheme that would eventually be realized, published in 2012, stated a desire to capitalize on 'the historic and current links of the area with music and other creative industries; [and] the historic built fabric' and emphasized 'social values at the heart of its ambition', with a programme that would be 'inclusive to everyone'.[118] As is typical in heritage assessments, which are authored by those in the employ of the client, the developer, or the local authority, the planning process articulated the site's history through a narrow range of techniques: morphological figure-ground drawings, photographic survey and a planning chronology. The social history manifest in the musical heritage of the area was recognized to the extent that it could lend support to the vision of a 'socially minded but commercially driven' development.[119]

This reprovision of subcultural musical heritage and the recognition of G-A-Y as a commercial entity contrast with the outcomes for First Out. The tenacity of the First Out Group, supported by the local authority, and with the backing of Livingstone as GLC Leader, had created a successful and inclusive venue on a site that was traffic-strangled and clouded by uncertainty. As a recognized women's, lesbian and trans-inclusive space it served groups that were 'protected minorities', as specified under the policy framework through which the earlier phase of the redevelopment unfolded, and which had 'protected characteristics' under the more recent Equality Act 2010, which came into force as the St Giles Circus scheme progressed. But the venue, squeezed between two development sites, and the groups it served, slipped through the cracks of the equalities impact assessment process. The result was the loss of (another) space predominantly run by and for women. The case also exemplifies the struggle of a socialist cooperative turned small-scale, multipurpose social enterprise in the context of a large urban development where only the most powerful commercial entities are visible and valued. Although First Out's final accounts suggest a business that failed, it was highly successful by many measures, and any downturn in business can be attributed to blight from Crossrail and related works. It far outlasted the future that was originally imagined for it on this precarious meanwhile site. The model it provided, of a day and night-time venue connected into the community and cultural sectors, is reflected in the aspirations of subsequent venues and has inspired recent online and in-person activism for community spaces.[120]

Over the edge

Apart from The Astoria and First Out, other LGBTQ+ venues around the Crossrail Tottenham Court Road redevelopment site closed without fanfare (Plate 17).[121] These included the Green Carnation (2001–15), The Conservatory and Vespa Lounge (1999–2006), The Ghetto (2001–8) and The Edge (1994–2015).[122] This suggests disparities in the operators' attitudes to the redevelopment impacts as well as in the resources available to these venues had they wanted to resist.

Gay entrepreneur Andy Jones, who ran The Edge and who has leased and operated a number of LGBTQ+ venues in the area, describes the effect of the works on and around Soho Square, a key public space for the LGBTQ+ community, as 'decimation'.[123] The redevelopment had a negative effect on business for The Edge, which added to the challenges of running a mainstream LGBTQ+ venue, slightly off the main drag of Soho bars. In response to the impacts of construction blight, Jones adapted the business model, adding a new restaurant. Although this helped temporarily, he surmises that ultimately 'Crossrail killed us'.[124] Jones was concurrently fighting a high-profile battle to keep open another long-running Soho venue, The Yard (1992–), located in a Victorian stableyard, which was subjected to repeated, closely similar planning applications for a proposed residential development.[125] With The Yard already feeling the effects of Crossrail, he took the decision to close and sold the lease back to the owner, the British celebrity entrepreneur Baron Alan Sugar. Like First Out, The Edge did not warrant compensation because it was outside of the line of statutory planning responsibilities for Crossrail, even if the impacts were still experienced directly.

Another impacted venue, The Ghetto (2001–08), had a long history of reinvention for different LGBTQ+ clientele – as Stallions (1982–9), Substation (1993–2001) and other iterations – each responding to and shaping new nightlife scenes and markets. The Ghetto contrasted First Out's visibility. In the recollection of one gay-identifying customer it was: 'everything a great club should be. Down a skanky back alley, small, sweaty, very rough round the edges, not part of the Gay mainstream'.[126] Ironically, The Ghetto was associated with social mix, and with gender and sexual diversity: a uniquely 'queer' Central London club, with popular 'ambisexual' nights Nag Nag Nag (2002–8) and Wig Out (1998–2008).[127] Like The Bell, First Out and Other Camden venues, The

Ghetto demonstrates the persistence of queer counter-cultural scenes in the heart of Central London. It was taken over in 2004 by promoter Simon Hobart (1964–2005) as a 'seven-nights-a-week hangout for alternative gay tribes'.[128]

Dan Beaumont, co-owner of Dalston Superstore, a bar and club he established in 2009 as part of the scene expanding northwards from Shoreditch (see Chapter 4), points to the closures of The Astoria and The Ghetto Soho as a turning point, when the acceleration of gentrification meant that an alternative scene in Central London became impossible.[129] Although it continued to thrive after Hobart's untimely death in 2005, The Ghetto, managed by Hobart's partner Tommy Moss and the company he had established, Popbarz, was faced with rising rents, and a lack of alternative venues to move to nearby, precipitating closure in 2008.[130] The club moved eastwards to Old Street, but relocation costs, and a decline in business, led to permanent closure in 2009.[131]

The Ghetto closed during the wake of the 2008 financial crisis, along with Popbarz. The Ghetto's owners reported a 'significant downturn in trade', but stated that they did not want to leave Soho.[132] At the same time, the Gay Business Association claimed that the number of gay bars in London had reduced from 250 in 2004 to 150 in 2009, arguing – oddly given The Ghetto's broad clientele and inclusive nightlife model – that the market response should be for gay venues to open up to straight audiences.[133] Apart from enforced consumer constraint during a financial downturn, there were very particular contextual factors: a background of rising land values, incentivized in the London Plan and accelerated by Crossrail, and Hobart's death.

In these cases, we see how networks of venues and the companies that they are held by are oriented around particular promoters who have different socio-economic status, and political and social aspirations that are reflected in and shaped by their relationships with property and urban processes. The outcomes of Crossrail for G-A-Y, as an event rather than a club, are more positive than they were for The Ghetto or First Out and other smaller and more independent venues. The commercial success of G-A-Y the Astoria, a twice-weekly event rather than a venue, afforded it material weight in planning.

LGBTQ+ cultural and nightlife venues are seldom operated by those who own the freehold rights to the land or property they occupy. They are therefore subject to the will and actions of powerful commercial entities and the terms of lease set by them as they transact to maximize profit and take best advantage of changing economic and policy contexts. At certain low points in the property cycle, more marginal groups have been welcome private tenants, whose presence has been incentivized by local and metropolitan government, and who contribute in direct or indirect ways to increase land and property values. At other points they can be perceived as a block to infrastructure development enacted in the wider public good and according to an agenda of economic growth; or they become aesthetically or economically incompatible with the commercial ethos of a rebranded neighbourhood. Conflict arises when venue operators or patrons have established deep-rooted and proprietorial connections with the locations, buildings and communities that premises are integrated within. These are not processes that are exclusive to LGBTQ+ venues – far from it – but evaluating the outcomes for these groups can enhance understanding of the specific forms of heritage embedded in venues, their particular, and varied historical relationships with structures of property and development; and the forms of architectural and spatial reappropriation they have contributed towards.

These were not typically pioneer gentrifiers who displaced existing businesses and were themselves later displaced. Rather, they frequently adopted and refurbished existing long-term leisure spaces in run-down and insecure stock, all of which were located at key transport intersections. Where land and property ownership is consolidated to increase revenue and pursue redevelopment, smaller and more idiosyncratic venues have not been able to maintain a foothold and have shifted to neighbourhoods with more diverse patterns of use and ownership. If the collective models of nightlife of the 1980s fizzled out, they nonetheless had enduring legacies.

Closure is not a simple concept in these cases. Looking at redevelopment outcomes in the 2000s, entrepreneurial models that have been aligned with international finance, commercial pop culture, and the growth and retail-led agenda set out in the London Plan have fared better. Venues that have been explicitly positioned against patriarchal, homonormative, cisnormative and racialized power structures have served more marginalized members of LGBTQ+ communities. Although these have been among some of the most socially and culturally innovative, such venues have been less acquisitional and have been less comfortably accommodated within property-led redevelopment in their approach. These cases raise a question of how policy and practices of property and land management can better support queer businesses and social and cultural innovation in the future.

Even with safeguarding systems in place, the negative impacts of redevelopment on groups with protected characteristics have not been easily recognized or meaningfully quantified. In some cases, they have been overlooked or purposefully disregarded, in heterosexist processes. These examples show that planning and equalities policies and legislation are implemented in crude ways that are not well equipped to account for the value of specific kinds of LGBTQ+ venue. For venues, organizations and communities the mitigation of impacts have been constrained by a lack of understanding of their needs, spaces, cultures and heritage, or because they have been ignored. In the present system, without any specific use class attributed to such premises, and with only a recent recognition of their architectural and social value within historic preservation processes, they have fallen through the gaps. With the first uses of online activism in the pursuit of more equitable outcomes from redevelopment, these cases prefigured the extensive online, direct-action and archival campaigns of the mid-2010s, discussed in the next chapter.

6

Sui generis

Closures and threats to LGBTQ+ venues in the 2010s prompted multiple campaigns to protect them. In this chapter I examine two cases around the longest-serving and highest-profile queer cabaret spots in Central London: The Royal Vauxhall Tavern and The Black Cap. These are located in purpose-built pubs. Both are sometimes claimed to be London's first gay pub. Both are categorized by their respective local authorities as *sui generis* – the planning use class meaning 'of its own kind' – due to their unique combination of bars, cabaret stage, nightclub and ancillary spaces. They have fostered distinctive and interconnected drag, performance, club and political cultures. The Royal Vauxhall Tavern (RVT) in Lambeth remains open, and campaigners have taken a series of actions to protect it. It cannot be safely said to have been saved, however. The Black Cap in Camden, which closed suddenly in 2015, remains boarded up. There are ongoing efforts to reopen it as a dedicated LGBTQ+ cabaret venue. The campaigns surrounding these venues overlap, but each has distinguishing features. I evaluate the characteristics of each situation, the proposals for change that triggered the communities of interest to act, their activities and their emphases in expressing these venues' long histories and present and future value. Both cases feature a common concern that LGBTQ+ culture and heritage are at risk of eradication, as commercial imperatives and property-led redevelopment have taken precedence.

The diverse groups participating in these campaigns have resisted the venues' closures using a variety of methods: direct-action protests and weekly vigils over many years, performance, public meetings, online petitions, media and social media, physical and digital archiving, fundraising, market research and business planning, and the sharing of proposals for planning and heritage designations. The latter – comprising applications for Asset of Community Value (ACV) registration, and, in the RVT's case, National Heritage List for England registration – have required tenacity and substantial voluntary labour. It has been necessary to lobby and engage with the institutions that govern culture and heritage, and with those who determine policy and oversee the management of venues, neighbourhoods and the built environment more widely. This has included licensees, freehold owners and their financial investors, the Mayor of London, the Greater London Authority, local authorities and Historic England. In these situations, where differing heritage value systems have been expressed and negotiated, I ask how inclusivity has been defined. What have these processes revealed about differential experiences and politics within LGBTQ+ populations and across generations? I work with the statements, actions and archives of the campaigners to

120 *Queer Premises*

understand the ways in which architectural, historical and social values have been articulated.

Queer assets

In 2013, The Black Cap in Camden (Figure 6.1) became the first LGBTQ+ venue to be registered as an ACV.[1] The nomination had been prompted by a change in the ownership of the venue. In 2010 it had been acquired with a number of other pubs by the property and investment company Kew Capital Limited. In 2012, a planning application was submitted to change the first, second and third floors from bar and restaurant use to residential.[2] In October 2014, a month after the announcement that it had been sold to property developers Immovate, The RVT would become the second LGBTQ+ venue to achieve ACV status, after its nomination by campaign group Friends of the RVT. Since then, other venues have followed suit, including Heaven and the Joiners Arms (see Chapters 5 and 7). In pursuing ACVs, The Black Cap and RVT campaigners paralleled the work of other community interest groups attempting to protect pubs and community spaces from redevelopment, changes of use and residential conversion in London and the UK more widely.[3] Yet for these *sui generis* premises, it is helpful to look closely at the circumstances. In The Black Cap's case, the campaigners were required to defend the ACV when it was challenged by the building owners. Some campaign members were involved in the establishment of another venue nearby, which also soon closed. In the RVT's case, the campaign led to the first successful application to list a building for its importance to the LGBT+ community.

Local authorities were first obliged to have a register of ACVs under the Localism Act 2011, introduced by the Conservative-led Conservative-Liberal Democrat coalition government (2010–15).[4] This use of the term 'asset' works similarly to that of 'cultural infrastructure' in articulating the material value of community resources. The term 'asset' usually refers to a thing of value that is owned, such as property and estate, which becomes the legacy (or debt payments) of the deceased.[5] ACVs are therefore attributed meaning within this normative logic of accumulation and wealth transmission. They are not designated according to market value, however, but due to a successful 'community nomination' by a parish council or 'a person that is a voluntary or community body with a local connection'.[6] The designation is used by local authorities where 'an actual or current use of the building or other land that is not an ancillary use furthers the social wellbeing or social interests of the local community', and where it is reasonable that this can continue, 'whether or not in the same way as before'.[7] Local authorities are given powers to regulate what defines an appropriate community body, as well as the conditions that must be met to be considered 'a person that is a voluntary or community body with a local connection'.[8] The RVT sits in the jurisdiction of Lambeth Council, which states that ACVs 'give communities an increased chance to save local facilities of community value'; that nominees 'need to be a constituted local community group'; and that decisions are to be made by a 'specially convened [planning] officer asset group'.[9] Camden Council, presiding over The Black Cap, determines that eligible groups 'can make a nomination where they

Figure 6.1 The Black Cap, 2011. Photo by: Rept0n1x. CC-BY-SA-3.0,2.5,2.0,1.0.

have a local connection with the area [. . .] where the group's activities are wholly or partly concerned with Camden or a neighbouring borough'.[10]

The ACV records land or property deemed to be of special importance to the nominating group for a period of five years. It places constraints on the owners, removing permitted development rights, so that if they wish to change the land use class or demolish the property, they must allow the community to comment. The status gives the Planning Inspectorate and local authority powers to refuse planning permission, or to compulsorily purchase threatened land or property. The community is given a right to bid if the land or property is put up for sale, and a moratorium allows it six months to raise funds. The vendor is not, however, obliged to favour community bids over other offers. Once the registration expires after five years, a new nomination is required.

These measures were set out in the Conservative Manifesto (2010), under the banner of the 'Big Society': the supposed empowerment of communities to counter losses 'of essential services, like post offices and pubs, because of decisions made by distant bureaucrats'.[11] Although a lack of regulation had created the conditions for the 2008 financial crisis, the coalition government's rhetoric evoked a restrictive state, and placed the blame on planners, rather than profit-oriented, property-led regeneration, for the loss of social and cultural infrastructure.[12] A tenet of the Big Society was the notion that civil liberties had to be protected against the 'database state' and 'the bureaucratic inspection regime that stops councils focusing on residents' main concerns'.[13] While offering ACVs – a monitoring and inspection tool – on the one hand, on the other, the Conservatives and their Liberal Democrat partners implemented changes to reduce planning powers – those powers designed to protect public interest, especially for minority groups with protected characteristics.[14] Although the new government continued New Labour's discourse of active, responsible citizenship, there was a shift away from state support and a stronger emphasis on the roles of the voluntary sector and philanthropy. This was undermined by fiscal austerity policies that withdrew resources and which added extra pressure on those organizations supposedly empowered. Nonetheless, the Localism Act 2011 has provided a framework that has proved effective for diverse groups of campaigners in their attempts to integrate grassroots knowledge into neighbourhood planning.[15]

The Drama Queens Drag Theatre Company, which submitted The Black Cap's original ACV nomination, described itself as a 'non-profit LGBT voluntary community-based Drag theatre company'.[16] The company had been established at the venue in 2009 and ran until 2012, when it was displaced to neighbouring Islington. The purpose of the company was to support the venue with free training and mentoring for performers who produced bespoke shows for its cabaret programme. Although the nomination was successful, the registration was challenged and the pub was delisted three months later in October 2013. The company's eligibility as a 'neighbourhood forum', under the terms of the Localism Act 2011, was disputed.[17] The Council had also failed to notify both the leaseholder and the freeholder of the property, providing further reason for the decision to be challenged. The contestation of the ACV illustrates that although Camden was initially convinced of the merit, the relatively new legislation and processes were open to interpretation and pushback. A lack of experience or precedents for evaluators to draw upon left loopholes for property owners and their agents. Neither the nomination, the registration, nor its termination were reported in the media.

The Black Cap's nomination had offered a persuasive first-person summary of the venue's history. It was written in haste, conveying the sense of urgency and anxiety created by the threatened closure. Key points included the venue's role, for more than fifty years, as 'a safe place for all members of the LGBT community to meet, [and] the entertainers of those difficult times, the Drag artists'. The venue was understood as having mobilized and amplified the gay movement: 'Drag Queens from the stage of The Black Cap encouraged us to "stand up and be seen"', 'leading us out of our English wooden closet' and to use the 'platform to encourage, support and demand as we got political'.[18] The argument to protect the venue was based on the scarcity of 'original' LGBT venues and it was asserted that The Black Cap, 'steeped in LGBT and Drag history', and 'known Worldwide as the "London Palladium of Drag" since 1969', was equally important in fostering community today.[19] Despite the bureaucratic format, the document vividly captures the unique relationship between the pub and its performance culture, not only through the production of specific shows but also in enabling the careers of celebrity drag performers, including Paul O'Grady (Lily Savage) and Reg Bundy (Her Imperial Highness, Regina Fong). Fong had been memorialized in a blue heritage plaque on the terrace – a guerrilla addition to the official English Heritage (now Historic England) scheme to commemorate the lives and associations of notable individuals on the exteriors of buildings. A photo of this commemorative marker accompanied the application, along with documentation of performances and news cuttings. This first submission for an ACV by an LGBTQ+ group demonstrates that drag and performance communities have been at the forefront of campaigns to protect venues. These have drawn from earlier LGBTQ+ activism, especially defiant drag, and have involved the rapid assembly of archives.

The withdrawal of ACV registration left the venue without protection until 2015 when Camden LGBT Forum, a charity mainly funded by Camden Council, and since renamed Forum+, re-nominated it.[20] The Forum's remit was wide. It had a track record of using history and heritage projects to activate LGBTQ+ community-building and promote LGBTQ+ well-being.[21] This included the curation of broad LGBT History Month programmes across Camden and neighbouring Islington. Led by Nigel Harris, then director of Forum, the re-nomination echoed elements of the earlier submission, but it had an expanded rationale and evidence base, and demonstrated a sophisticated, intersectional understanding of the need for a safe space in a diverse borough. There was more emphasis on the scarcity of LGBT venues in the area, linking this to property developers' actions, in a borough of approximately 25,000 LGBT residents. Issues of social isolation, stigmatization and a lack of safety at home were flagged, especially for older individuals and those minoritized according to religion and ethnicity. The application stressed the venue's role in fostering a culture of gender diversity, and its broader social role as 'the UK's oldest LGBT venue' in London, in 'the only major city in the world that has no LGBT community centre'.[22] The Forum demonstrated the strong link between commercial nightlife venues and the voluntary and community sector, documenting the use of The Black Cap as a safe space for fundraising, and for the work of charities, including the Forum's own meetings.[23]

The communal heritage significance of the venue was given added weight in the second ACV application. It brought out the value to community elders who 'remember the days of landing themselves in jail for being gay', and it documented the venue's use for funeral commemorations during the AIDS crisis.[24] Ash Kotak, an artist and dedicated campaigner for a UK AIDS memorial, began visiting the venue when he was fifteen years old to attend the Gay Teenage Group. He comments that 'everyone I knew at The Black Cap died – all the drag queens died' and notes that communities that had not previously existed formed around funerals. This traumatic past, he observes, has recently required those who survived to remember and communicate their memories as 'bridging work' to inform those who have forgotten or who are unfamiliar or too young to remember.[25]

The nomination's authors' approach to the venue, and to its heritage value, was not essentialist, conservative or aesthetic. The authors were keen to emphasize that the application was: 'very much about today', and serving the present LGBTQ+ population in the borough.[26] The ACV was duly reconfirmed.[27] Camden decided that The Black Cap 'plays the role of a community centre' and found that 'the pub's heritage contributes to its continued central role in Camden and London's gay scene and [this] means that the community value would not be easily replicable elsewhere'.[28] These processes and the outcome suggest that ACVs have provided a useful vehicle for narrating the unique qualities of some venues. Both the nomination and its evaluation went beyond aesthetic value, or a retrospective assessment of the venue as a memory site, to claim an ongoing communal value and the potential to adapt to meet present-day and future needs.

The Black Cap was re-registered as an ACV in April 2015, but this was again challenged by the owners, Kicking Horse, operating through the holding company Faucet Inn. Following a hearing three months later, convened by the borough solicitor, and providing an opportunity for the owners and nominators to speak, the status was reconfirmed.[29] The challenge had again been based on a technicality rather than on any substantive argument: that Camden LGBT Forum received funding from the local authority, so the nomination was from Camden, by proxy, rather than the Forum. The owners also contested the extent of the ACV within the building itself. They claimed that the *sui generis* planning use class should only cover the basement and ground floors, casting ambiguity on the classification – and therefore permissible uses – of the rest of the building. Both challenges were rejected, and the ACV was confirmed as applying to the entire building. Camden LGBT Forum's upbeat announcement of the success conveys how this designation gave The Black Cap campaigners renewed confidence in their determination to defend it as an LGBTQ+ venue.[30] Despite the council's enthusiastic agreement with the nominators' assessment of the venue's importance, Faucet Inn closed The Black Cap a week later.[31] The reconfirmation of the ACV, and the venue's closure, finally sparked media interest.[32]

The ACV designation would continue to be queried. In 2015, entrepreneur Jonathan Arana-Morton of restaurant group The Breakfast Club, who intended to open a restaurant in the venue, commented that 'nobody seems to fully understand the implications of the Asset of the Community Value that was granted a long time after we'd signed the contract to take the lease on part of the pub'.[33] This illustrates how ambiguities are exploited by different actors, here being used to undermine the venue's status, despite the local authority's clear decision and statement of its social value. Ambiguity worked against the campaigners in other ways too, since a lack of clarity about the process meant that they had compiled 'emotional evidence' for the hearing in the form of testimonies, which, in the event, was refused, as it was considered immaterial to the decision.[34] There was also confusion about the local authority's powers and whether it could, or would, act to reinforce the ACV if further challenges were made.

In 2014, Friends of the Royal Vauxhall Tavern submitted an ACV application on behalf of the RVT. It was assembled, according to its authors, 'in great haste in response

Sui Generis 125

to rumours of an imminent sale'.[35] The freehold of the pub had indeed been sold, to an Austrian developer, Immovate. Since neither it nor the RVT's management had made their intentions clear, there was understandable concern among performers, promoters, staff and patrons.

Vauxhall, in the borough of Lambeth, is traditionally a working-class neighbourhood, home since the 1960s to Portuguese migrants, and with a strong presence of lesbian and gay venues since the 1980s.[36] From the mid-1990s it was the location for one of the most significant clusters of queer venues. Many of the venues were large-capacity nightclubs located in railway arches owned by Network Rail, which took advantage of the big open spaces, their suitability to hosting parties with loud music through the night, and their industrial aesthetics.[37] The area underwent rapid gentrification in the 2010s, driven by the luxury residential market and by commercial development. In a high-density, mixed-use spatial development plan, it had been designated as an 'opportunity area' – often an ominous classification from the point of view of smaller-scale or bespoke organizations and minoritized groups.[38] Opportunities for some are disadvantageous for others, and the cluster of venues in the area quickly diminished, with 53 per cent of venues in Lambeth closing between 2006 and 2017.[39] The RVT is rare among remaining LGBTQ+ venues in this area because it is a purpose-built public house. It is therefore vulnerable to the form of speculative development that has seen numerous pubs close and to be converted into flats across the capital and nationally.

A campaign to protect the RVT rapidly formed. The Friends drew attention to the threat to the venue using media and social media channels. The ACV nominators expressed confidence that the evidence in support of the registration was 'overwhelming' and that their group was poised to grow quickly.[40] The intention was to use the ACV as a mechanism to instigate additional scrutiny, in the event that redevelopment proposals were announced.[41] The registration was approved in October 2014.[42] The nomination's themes overlap with those of The Black Cap. It includes a chronology of experimental performance associated with the venue, from early 'female impersonators' to more recent and notable drag acts which connect its stage performances to mainstream television, and to the anecdotal account of Princess Diana visiting the venue with rock star Freddie Mercury and comedian Kenny Everett. The history of social change was presented as being embedded in the venue, which has 'weathered changes in fashion and social attitudes'.[43]

Since The Black Cap's registration had been disputed, it was advantageous that the RVT's nominators had legal training, and that the group's eligibility, as well as the case for registration, were watertight. Two points are relevant to a wider understanding of how ACVs work and their limitations. First, the campaigners made the case not only for the general importance of the venue to LGBTQ+ communities, but to a 'strong local following' in South London, mentioning three boroughs specifically. This addressed the requirements of the legal and policy framework, which conceptualized community as associated with a specific locality or neighbourhood. Local authorities designate assets within their jurisdiction, but the catchment areas for such resources are often more dispersed. LGBTQ+ venues have networked relations with other venues and scenes, cutting across clusters, across the city, and they often have an international reach. The link between eligibility and local residence is also worth noting because in contexts of gentrification – such as in Vauxhall – conflicts often arise between night-time venues, the local and dispersed communities that use them, and residential communities, especially incomers.

Second, campaigners felt it necessary to emphasize that the venue was inclusive, with some nights that were 'very mixed'.[44] This approach differed from that of The Black Cap's original nomination, submitted by The Drama Queens Drag Theatre Company, with their greater emphasis on the venue as a hermetic 'safe space'. Forum's wider argument was for the venue's capacity to support social well-being, and the continuing need for refuge for Camden's LGBTQ+ population. The RVT nomination was distinctive in emphasizing the role of such venues in providing opportunities for encounters and integration across social difference. This laid the ground for the campaigners to carefully negotiate the media debates about whether designated LGBTQ+ venues were still needed, and about how inclusive or exclusive specific venues were, and why. This tactic was also appropriate to the RVT's history since, in the 1950s and 1960s, prior to the emergence of the dedicated 'gay pub' or 'gay bar' as typologies, the pub contained different bars, being queered only in sections, and on certain nights.[45] Queer sociality, as cases discussed earlier in this book show, has often involved the careful and temporary compartmentalization and management of interior spaces in public or semipublic venues.

Unlike The Black Cap's nominators, the RVT's stressed not only that the building was 'steeped' in history but that it was architecturally significant, noting the location – at what had been the entrance to the Vauxhall Pleasure Gardens – as well as the building's sound structure (Figure 6.2).[46] These details were important since the group saw gaining ACV status as a route to obtain the first English Heritage listing for a building of importance to the LGBTQ+ community, with the advantage that this would prohibit its demolition (Figure 6.3).[47]

Figure 6.2 The Royal Vauxhall Tavern, London, still image from a laser scan produced between Covid-19 pandemic lockdowns, 2020. UCL Urban Laboratory.

Figure 6.3 RVT Future, 'Who are RVT Future?' flyer, 2015. RVT Future.

The Friends of the RVT's nomination described the venue's long association with Duckie, the renowned arts collective founded by Amy Lamé and Simon Casson, aka Simon Strange. The membership of the Friends group included Duckie representatives, and they were central in the formation of RVT Future, chaired by Lamé, after the ACV was granted. This continues to function as the main campaign umbrella.[48] Originally a night at the RVT, Duckie was resident in the pub from 1995 to 2022, until differences with the venue's management led the group to move to other premises.[49] Duckie has expanded to many other venues in London, the UK and internationally, but it had an especially strong association with and investment in the RVT as its home.[50]

The Black Cap's campaign was substantiated by documenting the diverse Camden Council-supported LGBT history month activities run by Forum+. The RVT's nomination similarly coincided with a period of increasing attention to Vauxhall's queer histories, led by Duckie.[51] This work emanated from the RVT, taking the venue's stage, fabric, location and social history as its subject matter. Supported by Lambeth Council, the project also documented incidents of conflict with the council. Referring to an episode recounted in a tour as part of the project 'Happy Birthday RVT', Lamé recalled how 'all the drag queens we knew' protested outside of Lambeth Town Hall in 1998.[52] Lambeth owned the venue and was poised to sell it for demolition and redevelopment as a shopping centre and, of all things, a 'snow dome'. The scheme was stopped, but Lambeth sold the freehold to RVT Enterprises UK and RVT Management in 2005, making the venue less secure in the longer term.[53] The 1998 demonstration was seen as a source of empowerment in the campaign that developed to register and protect the venue in the 2010s.

ACVs have been used as a reactive, defensive tool in the face of threats to venues. They have provided a route to articulate the importance of built and place-based heritage to LGBTQ+ populations. Their content has highlighted the material impacts on LGBTQ+ populations, where some of the most highly esteemed, longest-running, multifunctional, *sui generis* establishments have been overlooked, threatened or closed. ACV nominees have demonstrated these venues' long-term use, their present-day communal and cultural standing, their relations with other venues, their functions in supporting livelihoods, professional and artistic development, specialized health services, fundraising, civic and charitable work, education, and their capacity to foster connections between grassroots and mainstream politics. Nominees have demonstrated the ways in which the cultures around these premises have been deeply rooted within and informed by the material qualities of buildings and localities in bespoke ways. Campaigners have not meant to conserve venues, or to replicate them. They have rather sought to protect them as resources through which queer culture, rooted in its histories of social struggle, creativity, alternative economies and resistance, can continue to adapt to sustain present-day and future generations. Successful registrations are simply logged, and the accounts detailed with care in nomination forms are filed away. Through the efforts of campaigners, however, the media have taken an increasing interest in ACV designations, and these reports have raised the public profile of venues, providing a channel for their histories and mythologies to be more widely expressed.[54]

The institution of ACVs demonstrated government recognition that the protection of any social and cultural infrastructure had become a struggle for local authorities and community groups alike, requiring corrective measures. Yet this planning instrument was designed within an orthodox neoliberal approach to governance which prioritizes longevity and the optimization of profit from land and property at the expense of newer, temporary and smaller-scale cultural uses for minoritized communities and social value for them. Through the ACV nomination process, the onus to identify social and cultural assets, the labour involved, and the requirements for accountability, fall disproportionately on community groups, while property owners and investors use their resources to find loopholes. Substantial investments of voluntary effort are required from community groups and local authorities who have stretched resources and who are compelled to repeat processes and renew temporary designations. Although constructed around 'community value', ACVs are not adequately set up to recognize the value that communities contribute, even within the registration process.[55]

Each time they have been required to renew ACV registrations, the nominees for the RVT and The Black Cap have refined the justification. ACVs do not offer medium or long-term protections unless the community of interest is in a position to purchase the asset, at a competitive price, in an aggressive real estate market. The legislation sets out an option for the local authority to use compulsory purchase to save an asset, but in London this is extremely unlikely to happen given the high land and property values, conditions of fiscal austerity and the pressure on councils to present as pro-development and pro-business. In 2015 the community pubs minister explicitly emphasized that communities were expected to follow ACV listings with a community purchase of the listed asset.[56] This favours communities with capital at their disposal, and it disadvantages those working to protect resources in locations with high and rapidly increasing real estate values.[57] Despite the challenges, in both The Black Cap and the RVT cases, campaigners have made efforts to organize themselves towards a community buy-out. They have established new companies and cooperative entities and led lively campaigns, some aspects of which I will now discuss.

Feeling diversity

The rapid rallying of community support for the RVT once the alarm was sounded tallies with the enthusiasm for the venue conveyed by respondents to Urban Lab's survey (see Chapter 4). When people were asked to comment on the current London LGBTQI+ nightlife events or venues they considered most valuable, the RVT was the venue most often cited, and the most cited in positive terms. It was repeatedly noted for its history as a long-standing alternative cabaret venue, for its community orientation, for its importance in enabling performers to launch and develop individual careers and artistic collectives, as a place to stage and experience experimental culture, and as distinctly inclusive, positively representing the diversity of London's LGBTQI+ population, and accommodating difference. The building was noted for its value in creating a welcoming space conducive to performance. Diversity, for some respondents, resulted from the venue's affordability and inclusive operating style:

> It's different on every night, as it caters to so many groups within the queer community. I love that feeling of queer diversity, not just a gay scene always dominated by white gay men. Beyond its historical significance and cultural value, the RVT blissfully lacks the level of pretension experienced in so many other gay bars.[58]

A trans-identifying respondent commented that it is an example of one of those 'smaller spaces' that 'are a place to feel the positive power of community [. . .] to recharge and know that you are OK and surrounded by like-minded people and loved ones'. These comments associate the venue with a politics of inclusion that is reflected in some of the specific forms of nightlife and arts activism that have emerged through relations with the venue, especially Duckie.

Duckie pitches itself as a collective offering 'arts enterprise, homo-social honky-tonk and performance clubs for extraordinary populations'.[59] It celebrates and platforms working-class and queer culture, with arts programming that explicitly addresses overlooked and disenfranchised communities. Duckie is critical, its co-founder, Casson, remarks, of 'the structural inequality that happens in the west under capitalism' and works against the reproduction of these inequalities in arts and culture.[60] The collective's organizational and financial modes are adaptive and hybrid: its commercial nightlife events have funded a wider arts and engagement programme alongside public subsidies and grants. A grassroots initiative, Duckie has been increasingly recognized by arts and heritage institutions, albeit that funding opportunities have fluctuated subject to political and policy shifts.[61] Although Duckie's programming has recently been proactively inclusive towards intersectionally marginalized groups, including Queer, Trans and Intersex People of Colour (QTIPOC), for some, its main club nights are strongly associated with white, gay, cis men.[62] As with the RVT, or any venue, the feeling of inclusion or exclusion is contextual, and dependent on one's lived experience and positionality, as well as on the pitch set by promoters.

RVT Future is a campaign rather than a political organization, and it is more politically plural than Duckie. The campaign has nevertheless reflected Duckie's queer, inclusive, grassroots, arts-activist and socially engaged approaches. RVT Future includes trusted members of the RVT community and the LGBTQ+ community more widely. The efficacy of the campaign has been reliant on an executive committee that has intimate knowledge of the venue, and that includes a wide breadth of professional experience, with all the social capital and networks individual members bring. They are patrons, artists, promoters and producers, social entrepreneurs, entertainment industry and media professionals, from mainstream journalism to independent blogging and social media, built environment professionals with knowledge of architecture, architectural history and development, and people with experience in local politics and the civil service.

In contrast with the new freehold owners' lack of communication, and at times their conflict with the RVT's management, RVT Future's communications are manifesto-like and have comprised regular updates through multiple public channels and meaningful invitations for public participation. The campaign has exposed hidden interests and alignments on the side of the developers, such as their use of planning consultants who have a track record of securing permission to demolish listed buildings in the vicinity.[63] Press interest in the RVT and Black Cap picked up because of the campaigners' concerted efforts to use social media and the media to effectively communicate the communal and heritage value of the venues.[64]

One of the leading members of RVT Future and a member of the Duckie Collective (and The Black Cap campaign), the writer, campaigner and researcher Ben Walters, describes RVT Future's politics as 'pragmatic', focused on protecting the venue, and also as utopian, being rooted in a belief in the liberatory potential of queer spaces.[65] A 2015 *Guardian* feature he wrote is an example of the campaign's consciousness-raising activities. It affirmed the value of LGBTQ+ venues and nuanced, or countered, the overly simplistic causal explanations in circulation (see Chapter 4). Of all the articles published in this period, Walters' is the one that most emphasizes a spectrum of LGBTQ+ experiences, across different generations and different socio-economic backgrounds rather than reducing the discussion to one relating to gay bars and gay men of a certain age. Precedence is given to sources from within LGBTQ+ organizations, such as the Albert Kennedy Trust, which works with vulnerable LGBT youth, and which expresses concern about a 'closure epidemic', 'because bars and clubs aren't just places to party but crucial sites of community and belonging'.[66] This contrasted the assumption underpinning other media accounts which argued or implied that all LGBTQ+ people had benefitted equally from legal gains and increased social acceptance. The article agreed with other commentators that queer scenes have always been characterized by flux and that there was a boom in the 1990s. Yet Walters recognized the intensity of the recent spate of closures and the impact on still vulnerable members of the LGBTQ+ community. In 2019, reflecting on the early days of the campaign, he comments that the article was part of a strategy of

> arguing against an implicit or explicit sense that queer spaces are less important than they used to be. [And that] these aren't just heritage sites but they're . . . [*in-breath*] you know, week-in, week-out, these engines of . . . of queerness with their complexities and problems and contradictions and all the rest of it, but still hugely vital.[67]

The central issue as presented here was not the loss of bars and clubs, per se, but rather the loss of spaces of community, and the negative impact of the rapid loss of venues on a minority population, for whom they had an important role.

Building roots

In September 2015, after the submission of two 15,000-word applications written by Walters, the RVT became the first building to be listed by Historic England for its significance to the LGBTQ+ community.[68] The listing application compiled a meticulous architectural and social history from primary and secondary sources,

132   *Queer Premises*

which must be one of the most expansive ever written for a pub. The initial application received a 'lukewarm' response, but the listing was ultimately awarded after the submission of supplementary evidence.[69] As well as the substantial voluntary labour involved, these documents attest to the necessity to comprehensively articulate the venue's unique status. Campaigners had to communicate these specificities in ways that were recognizable to the authorities and within the discourses of urban planning and heritage practice.

The listing application highlighted the fact that the RVT is much more than a pub. Yet the hybrid historic and contemporary uses of the RVT sat uncomfortably with the typological classifications of the listing guidelines. Pubs are included under the category of 'Commerce/exchange buildings'.[70] Nightclubs are not included. The guidance refers to the decline in numbers of pubs, and the consequent rise in listing applications. It offers only a superficial explanation – changes in licensing laws and the smoking ban of 2007. Nor does it consider the wider uses of pubs beyond their role as drinking establishments, or specific types of mixed-use pubs, such as cabaret venues. Although listing is intended to 'celebrate' and 'safeguard' the legacy of 'special architectural and historic interest', the criteria are weighted towards a quite traditional understanding of architectural value, whereas historic interest is determined by the building's national significance or association with 'nationally important individuals, groups or events'.[71] This is at odds with the gradual diversification of the field and methods of architectural history since the 1980s, where there has been a shift away from questions of form, style and singular authors, to processes, social significance, multiple authorship and the use and lifecycle of buildings. In overviewing the field in 2010, for example, the architectural historian Antoine Picon spoke of an '[architectural] history that includes social, political and economic dimensions at a more advanced level than before, a history that enables us to pay attention to a greater array of actors'.[72]

Although it was not reflected in their criteria, at the time of the listing application English Heritage was itself asserting a broader strategic ambition 'to understand the relationship between LGBT individuals and communities and the places that they live, work and socialise in, with the aim of increasing understanding of this poorly understood part of our heritage'.[73] As one branch of a broader diversity mainstreaming agenda, the organization commissioned research to 'possibly identify and protect [LGBT heritage] buildings at risk'.[74] The fortuitous concurrence of this initiative with the RVT application may have contributed indirectly to its ultimate success. Its eventual Grade II listing was announced alongside *Pride of Place,* as the research initiative was called.[75]

Since the building was already locally listed, but not protected, and given the general rise in listing applications for pubs, the onus was on the nominees both to prove the building's exceptional qualities and to explain its social historical importance.[76] To build a case for national significance, the application stressed the RVT's equivalence to the Stonewall Inn in New York City in being emblematic of the history of LGBTQ+ struggles. Famously the site of the police raid that sparked the Stonewall uprising (28 June to 3 July 1969), the Inn was located – like many of London's venues – in fairly unremarkable ex-transportation building stock: two mid-nineteenth-century stable buildings adjoined by a 1930s façade. Along with the adjacent park and surrounding streets it was placed on the National Register of Historic Places as early as 1999, and it was named a National Historic Landmark in 2000.[77] Stonewall was nominated by the neighbourhood-based Greenwich Village Society for Historic Preservation and the Organization of Lesbian and Gay Architects and Designers. That Stonewall was officially recognized at the turn of the century highlights the relative lack of public memorialization of LGBTQ+ civil rights in the UK's heritage story, until recently, whether through built environment designation or other means.

As symbolic and catalytic events, two police raids on the RVT – on 17 December 1983, and the 'rubber gloves raid' of 24 January 1987 – were milestones in the listing application and in the analogy with Stonewall.[78] With other raids on The Bell and Gay's the Word bookshop, 1984 was an intense period for the aggressive policing of some of London's key sites of activism and community-building.[79] For the purposes of the listing application, the rubber gloves raid served multiple purposes: it powerfully encapsulated the RVT's place within a wider history of oppression and violence against queer bodies; it communicated the venue's importance as an emblematic site during the peak of the AIDS crisis; and it conveyed an association with queer performance.

For narrative impact, it helped that drag queen Lily Savage, who launched her career at the RVT and would become its most successful graduate to mainstream entertainment, was in the venue at the time of the raid. As with the ACVs, celebrity associations and cult figures were important in both the RVT and Stonewall nominations. Stonewall could boast of visits by film stars Judy Garland and Elizabeth Taylor; while Princess Diana's reported night at the RVT featured in the case for its architectural listing.[80] These ways of articulating the significance of the venue played to the requirements of the listing authorities. They illustrate how, in the processes for safeguarding venues, what José Esteban Muñoz calls 'queer cross associations and influences' have been narrated through the fabric and histories of buildings and urban spaces.[81] Muñoz discusses how these networks of association and disidentification emerge from the negative, from a lack of queer representation in 'any heteronormative rendering of the world' (see Chapter 1).[82]

Like the Stonewall application, the RVT case emphasized that the historical significance – framed in the US criteria as the instrumental role of the site in shaping 'the broad patterns of our history' – was to be found in the connection between the building, the community and its environs.[83] In these two nominations, Vauxhall and New York's Greenwich Village are claimed to have fostered queer sociality and transgression through their spatial morphology. The Stonewall site was described as 'a favorite hangout for a diverse group of (often homeless) gay street youth'.[84] Spatially, it was an odd triangular piece of land. The application highlighted that its orientation disrupted the lines of the New York grid and facilitated, through many cross streets that connected into it, the gathering of a large crowd, and hence the 1969 uprising. The case emphasized this rebellion as a flash in time, immediately recognized by some for its historic import: a rupture that quickly prompted a change in the atmosphere of the movement for gay and lesbian civil rights, with long-lasting impacts.[85]

The RVT case instead stressed historical continuity with the Vauxhall Pleasure Gardens, which existed on the same site from 1661 to 1859, an important commercial garden which was popular for entertainment and socialising. Drawing attention to this lineage evoked the site's long history of accommodating cultural, sexual and gender experimentation in support of the RVT's continued use as an LGBTQ+ cabaret venue.[86] The application pointed out that Lambeth Council had used this association in their recent place marketing. Geographer Johan Andersson has commented on Duckie's site-specific narrativization of Vauxhall's longer histories and 'embedded hedonism'.[87] He places Duckie's performance and media work of the early 2000s within the literary history of the Pleasure Gardens, and within the wider aesthetics and branding of the area's entrepreneurial nightlife. Andersson highlights how by the turn of the millennium these performative narratives of the area's history took a romantic slant on Vauxhall's urban and pastoral conditions, stressing the link to the gardens even though the physical industrial infrastructure that appeared after their closure had arguably been more influential in setting the conditions for the area's post-industrial nightlife aesthetics in the 2000s. The association with the Pleasure Gardens was prominent in Historic England's rationale for the listing.[88] Duckie's productions continue to reveal new layers of the Gardens history, with more recent work highlighting the their associations with colonialism and the slave trade.[89]

Vauxhall Gardens were a setting for temporary public performances and ephemeral installations. Seven farewell concerts marked their eventual demolition to make way for the new development that incorporated the RVT, which, apart from the pub, was demolished in the 1970s. A watercolour from 1859 shows the neo-Gothic orchestra tower being dismantled while bits and pieces of its structure are cast about.[90] All items of furniture were sold. This dispersal means that almost nothing survives from the Gardens, and so an eminently plausible if unprovable conjecture that the twelve distinctive cast-iron columns featured in the RVT's interior were originally from the Gardens provided the perfect pivot for the listing case.[91] The application summarised that the RVT's 'community heritage grows directly out of the legacy of social and cultural transgression and innovation associated with the pleasure gardens'.[92]

Another focus of the listing application was the reconfiguration of the bar in 1980–1. During this refurbishment, the 1896 bar that had doubled up as a stage was replaced in order to optimize the space for performance.[93] This can be contextualized within the broader push in contexts of queer nightlife venues for new, more affirmative typologies and aesthetics in the 1980s, and the desire to disassociate from those that epitomized earlier atmospheres of oppression and enforced seclusion. Given the rejection of Victorian pub interiors by a young generation of lesbian and gays in the 1980s (see Chapter 5), it is ironic that – in addition to the structural, decorative columns – the RVT's listing saw the need to emphasize the presence of original interior fixtures from that era. This suggests a fissure between heritage valuation systems and queer aesthetics, temporalities and practices of historical transmission and memorialization. Recent work in the field of critical heritage studies, such as theorist Cornelius Holtorf's discussion of 'pastness', is suggestive of more nuanced ways to account for layered environments such as night-time venues, which are associated with regular incremental alteration and transitory appropriation. He observes that in lived experience, encounters with the past do not privilege 'age value' or necessitate authenticity or integrity in historic buildings; and argues that the diversity of such experiences necessitates bespoke methods of empirical research into how the past 'touches' people in different circumstances.[94] From a different perspective, planning lawyers Steven Vaughan and Brad Jessop have called for more attention to planning law in work on queer spaces, and have argued that the law should be 'better reflective of the lived history of heritage' rather than the 'material embodiment of heritage'.[95] The process of listing the RVT as a long-established and adaptive venue highlights a need for valuation systems that acknowledge the dynamic, performative, experiential, multi-sensory ways in which queer populations have engaged with the past, or activated practices of remembering or forgetting, via everyday buildings and environments.[96] As with The Black Cap, it is evident that threats to the existence of the RVT have prompted intergenerational encounters with the traumatic years of the AIDS epidemic of the 1980s and early 1990s; as well as recollection of how the venue operated as a setting for collective mourning and remembering at the time.

Ultimately, the RVT's 2015 Grade II listing acknowledged the historic interest of 'one of the best known and longstanding LGB&T [sic] venues in the capital', which is 'an enduring symbol of the confidence of the gay community in London'.[97] It noted the architectural interest of the mid-Victorian external features and interior structural and decorative cast-iron columns; the 'historic associations' with the site of the Vauxhall Pleasure Gardens; and the venue's role as a place of 'alternative culture and performance'.[98] RVT Future and the venue's management have conflicting views on the listing.[99] The management state that the decision to sell the venue's freehold was based on 'six years of heavy [financial] losses'.[100] It initiated a petition against RVT Future stating that 'If the building is listed by Historic England, it is highly likely that the RVT will be forced to close'.[101] Although the management opposed the listing based on commercial detriment, the campaigners were keen to emphasize that, on the contrary, following the listing decision 2016 saw the highest level of trading in the venue's history.[102]

Since the ACV and heritage listings did not offer sufficient protection to secure the building's use as an LGBTQ+ space into the future, RVT Future subsequently applied for, and in 2016 achieved, the *sui generis* designation. This was based on evidence submitted by hundreds of individuals who used and valued the venue.[103] Today, the fabric of the venue is protected, and the management has secured a twenty-year lease with Immovate. Yet, even with the combination of designations ascribed to it, the continuation of the RVT's use as an LGBTQ+ venue is not guaranteed. At the time of writing the freehold and leasehold are once again up for sale. Back in 2017, RVT Future began working towards a community buy-out after the building had been placed on the market at a value of £4.1 million.[104] Although the asking price was prohibitive, they committed to set up a Community Benefit Society (under the Co-operative and Community Benefit Societies Act 2014) to raise funds. This has been approached in a transparent and egalitarian way to ensure representation from across the LGBTQ+ community among shareholders, but there are no signs that the purchase is achievable. In the meantime, RVT Future's relations with the venue's management have deteriorated. Duckie also took the decision to uproot and relocate to another venue in April 2022.

Growth pipeline

The RVT's heritage of drag, alternative performance, political activism and cultural experimentation is closely entwined with that of The Black Cap. The two long-standing venues are directly linked by their patrons, by the performers and promoters who have worked their stages and DJ booths, by the campaigners who have sought to protect them, and by the processes these groups have had to follow. Their recent trajectories have also been controlled by similar commercial entities and financial arrangements.[105]

The Black Cap has two entries on the Historic England *Pride of Place* map. One is a description with online links, the other is an image of a protest vigil after its closure.[106] The former shows a blurry, low-resolution photograph of the exterior. It is accompanied by the legend of the Mother Black Cap, an apocryphal witch whose bust tops the decorative Victorian façade. Mother Black Cap's name was attributed to the pub in licensing records as early as 1751, but the building on the site today dates from 1889. The Black Cap had become well-known as a drag and cabaret venue by the mid-1960s. Between the 1970s and 2000s it was associated with numerous popular performers.[107] The contributions pinned on the map describe the pub's association with performer Rex Jameson's popular drag persona Mrs Shufflewick, a regular fixture in the 1970s. The crowdsourced map facilitates encounters with diverse ephemera from multiple periods, rather than a neat chronology. Appropriately, it links to an interview with Jameson, in which the interviewer complains about Jameson's habit of being late for performances and pontificates about how drag is old fashioned and out of date.[108] The *Pride of Place* narrative brings the story up to date, explaining how, in the 2010s, Meth Lab and the Family Fierce, hosted by drag artist Meth, oversaw the venue's revival, with popular club nights featuring stars who had appeared on *RuPaul's Drag Race*, the hugely popular TV drag competition. As a lively and intergenerational venue, and one that bridged global and local, virtual and in-person queer culture, its story contrasted with the dominant media narratives of the demise of queer spaces in the mid-2010s.

The entry concludes that the revival came to an abrupt halt: 'Owners Faucet Inn closed the pub on 12 April 2015 following controversial plans to redevelop the site.' Faucet was not the owner but rather the holding company operating the venue on behalf of the freeholder, Kicking Horse Limited. Faucet's announcement stated:

> Faucet Inn thanks its loyal customers over the time it has operated the site and regrets the impact on the LGBTQI community of the closure of the venue. This historical venue has long been recognised as an important part of the LGBTQI community and [so too has] its significant contribution to many performers on the London and international cabaret circuit.[109]

Just days before, The Black Cap had regained its ACV status following its re-nomination by Forum. It is no surprise, then, that the owners felt obliged to comment on the historical importance of the venue and concede the negative impacts of its closure, and no surprise that the closure triggered protests. That these protests would be continuing more than seven years later, as weekly vigils on the pavement outside the pub, is more remarkable (Plate 18). These 'community hub' events have maintained a presence outside The Black Cap almost every Saturday since its closure, Covid-19 lockdowns notwithstanding. They are upbeat in tone, involving the public sharing of up-to-date information on the campaign; and enabling the exchange of memories and hopes for the site and the wider neighbourhood *in situ*. For a few hours a week, the pavement outside 171 Camden High Street becomes a queer space.

The protests have cohered around #WeAreTheBlackCap, a widely reported direct-action and social media campaign. They led to the establishment of the Black Cap Foundation, a social enterprise and not-for-profit company limited by guarantee, to oversee compliance with the conditions of the ACV.[110] Other related temporary manifestations included the squatting of the venue in 2015.[111] #WeAreTheBlackCap gathered a petition of nearly 13,000 signatories in favour of reopening The Black Cap as an LGBTQ+ venue.[112] As at the RVT, the campaign has benefitted from the campaigners' wide-ranging practical skills, and their cultural and social capital.[113] The efficacy and successes of the campaign result from long-term commitment and substantial voluntary labour. Strongly supportive statements from those within the local authority, including its council leader and other elected councillors, both within and beyond the planning discussions, acknowledge the venue's historic and contemporary importance. Individual campaigners have been concurrently involved in Camden LGBT Forum, which includes a local councillor.

#WeAreTheBlackCap linked up with whistleblowers Transparency International, whose sleuth work revealed a set of financial actors and transactions as intricate as the venue's ornate façade.[114] Kicking Horse Limited, to whom the freehold had been sold in 2010, was an opaque, offshore, Jersey-based investment company whose investors were difficult to trace. These included a Russian group named Vollin Holdings, which was owned by billionaire Russian steel magnates Alexander Abramov and Alexander Frolov.[115] They resigned their share in Kicking Horse in 2013, apparently in response to a request from Moscow to return their investments to Russia. Their share was later bought out by Dragonfly Finance S.A.R.L., another difficult-to-trace company based in Luxemburg, which apparently made the acquisition in the knowledge of the campaign to reopen the venue.[116] Vollin Holdings appears to have held a mortgage in The Black Cap until January 2016.[117] The campaigners worked with Transparency International to draw investors' attention to the venue's significance and the impacts of its closure.

The RVT and The Black Cap campaigns have shown how the land and properties that accommodate LGBTQ+ venues operate within global capital flows and opaque networks of ownership and investment. Transparency International's work demonstrated how The Black Cap's case fitted into a wider pattern of speculative pub purchases. These aimed to take advantage of the premises' profitability as potential residential conversions, while, as abstract commodities, London real estate investments safeguarded investors from high corruption jurisdictions such as Russia's.[118] Within the spate of queer venue closures in London in the mid-2010s, bringing these interests to light aggravated the dissonance felt by the affected communities. Through ACVs, communities of interest gained a legally recognized but non-financial proprietary interest that conflicted with the abstract functions of land and buildings as financial instruments for owners, investors and their agents. The complex web of actors and transactions revealed how the presence and futures of venues were being shaped by the processes that geographer Loretta Lees has described as 'supergentrification': the re-gentrification of already gentrified neighbourhoods by super-rich 'financial engineers'.[119] In such cases, the old models of creative pioneer gay gentrification appear irrelevant.

For Faucet Inn, the financial model was to close each pub purchased and convert the top storeys into apartments and the pub floors into restaurant, retail or office use. To pursue this, The Black Cap was the subject of numerous closely similar planning applications between 2012 and 2014.[120] Camden rejected these applications, arguing that '[t]he pub and restaurant use at first-floor level is considered to serve the needs of a specific and local community', and that the applicants had failed to demonstrate that this was no longer required, therefore contravening a range of community-supportive policies in Camden's Local Development Framework.[121] The 2013 refusal was appealed, but the Planning Inspectorate upheld the refusal. In this process, the ACV and importance of the venue to the community were acknowledged by all parties, including the applicants.

As at the RVT, tensions arose between the generic qualities of the venue, its specific value for the LGBTQ+ community, and its inclusiveness to or exclusion of the wider public; as well as between the designated planning use class, and the actual mix of the venue's spaces and uses. The applicants and the Planning Inspector took note of the campaigners' emphasis on the venue being open and welcoming to all, both in the past and in articulations of its future. The freeholders' planning consultants were quick to use this as leverage to reopen the venue as a more general drinking establishment that would accommodate – but would not specifically be operated by and for – the LGBTQ+ community. The Inspector observed:

> Whilst the LGBT and wider community say that the premises hold a special attachment to them, the facility would not be lost. In any event, changes in the premises' target market, which could result in the loss of a meeting place for the LGBT community, could be made at any time without the need for planning permission.[122]

This is an interesting illustration of the lack of any mechanism to insist upon the protection of the continuing and specific importance of the venue to the LGBTQ+ community, even with the ACV and *sui generis* designation in place.[123] As the local authority, Camden was forced into a corner, and the venue's unique qualities did not hold material weight in the planning process. The planning application could only be evaluated against quantifiable dimensions of noise or parking provision, or generic policies on pubs and communities – which, advantageously, were relatively robust in Camden.[124]

The logic of widening inclusion was used to justify successive proposals for new restaurant and bar uses for the venue. Initially, the pitch was to open an outlet of The Breakfast Club, a business that had started with one café in Soho in 2005, and then expanded across Central London. In a blogpost, the owner, Jonathan Arana-Morton, wrote a personal petition to the public.[125] This stressed The Breakfast Club's credentials as an ethical local and community-focused business, but accepted The Black Cap's closure as an irreversible decision.[126] This situation created tension between small and community-oriented enterprises, with one choosing to participate in the aggressive eradication of a long-term, multipurpose venue, which had been acknowledged as an ACV.

Eventually, pressure from the campaigners caused freehold owner Camden Securities and their lessees, The Breakfast Club, to withdraw their interests in The Black Cap. Around the same time, the sale of the site's freehold from Kicking Horse to Camden Securities fell through. In March 2016 it was purchased by Ruth and Robinson, specialists in 'introducing new bar and restaurant concepts to the London Market', who announced they had taken a twenty-five-year lease on the property.[127] Later renamed Albion & East, the company specializes in the identification of properties with a likely high investment return for shareholders, boasting a 'very strong pipeline of potential properties which it expects will deliver significant opportunities for growth'.[128] The firm is backed by Imbiba, a venture capital company set up in 1997, which operates as an incubator for leisure businesses with potential for high returns. Imbiba was open to investors via platforms such as The Wealth Club, the 'largest investment platform for high net worth and experienced investors'.[129]

Undeterred by the recent campaign or ACV, Ruth and Robinson intended to maximize the investment value of the property through a proposal to set up a generic chain bar/restaurant, Hollenbeck's. A further four planning applications were submitted.[130] The first application by Ruth and Robinson was to confirm the use class of the vacant property as 'A4 drinking establishment, with occasional live music and entertainment'. Their intention was to 'create a unique, distinctive and vibrant drinking establishment which is welcoming to the whole community'.[131] They acknowledged the ACV status and importance to the LGBTQ+ community, but did not address the venue's specific functions for this population, offering a generic policy of inclusion instead.[132] One kind of inclusion (an idealized openness to all) was therefore pitted against another (conditional and centred on the needs of the diverse LGBTQ+ community associated with the venue over the long-term).

Heritage business

Apart from the grassroots and institutional initiatives already outlined in this chapter, conflicts over queer venues have led to multiple forms of commercial heritage work. The set of planning applications initiated by Ruth and Robinson were facilitated by CgMs, 'the largest independent archaeology and heritage consultancy in the UK'.[133] CgMs advise public sector and commercial clients in the property industry, as well as individual land and property owners. Although claiming to be independent, CgMs is in fact employed to negotiate the planning system in their clients' favour. The business is framed towards the protection of landowners' and developers' interests. Its appointment by private sector clients such as Ruth and Robinson for this expertise is understandable, in a situation, such as this, where there was a record of failed planning applications.

Ruth and Robinson's proposals prompted the chairs of Camden Town Conservation Area Advisory Committee to write to the planning committee questioning the details of its proposals.[134] They noted the pub's citation in the Camden Town Conservation Area Appraisal and Management Strategy for its 'elaborate stone decoration'. They offered a view that, although unlisted, The Black Cap is 'the best pub, in terms of architectural quality, in Camden Town', with an 'amazingly intricate Victorian elevation'.[135] The planning applications also triggered an open letter from #WeAreTheBlackCap to the investors behind Ruth and Robinson: 'we implore you to reconsider the role of your investment in the erasure of LGBTQ+ history and in the removal of a space that means so much to the LGBTQ+ community'.[136] Under pressure, Ruth and Robinson withdrew its interests in July 2016. However, the following year the owners were able to elicit a Certificate of Immunity to listing from Historic England, preventing the pub from being architecturally listed for five years.[137] It is likely that they anticipated that The Black Cap campaign would follow the path set by the RVT's successful listed building application. Awarding the certificate was a controversial decision because of the professional recognition of the building's quality and its deteriorating state since closure in 2015.

In addition to the archives of ephemera that have been produced in response to threats to venues, which have affirmed their value and multiple uses, planning applications have elicited huge databases of testimony, logged as public consultation responses in local authority portals. In The Black Cap's case, the volume of objections were a barometer of increasing indignation and anger as respondents felt forced to defend the pub repeatedly, even after the ACV status had been made and reconfirmed. These statements bear witness to fatigue with the proposals and with the barriers to engaging effectively through official public consultation channels. Whether expressed in passionate, direct language, or adopting a drier tone which mirrors the language of planning, the responses articulate the many forms of attachment people have formed with the venue. The arguments range from the technical to the moral. They expand on the ACV nominees' accounts with detailed personal narratives, and with commentaries on how the venue materializes the history of the gay movement, its unique and valuable functions in the recent past, and its place within a network of venues in the neighbourhood, London and internationally.

In contrast with the unwieldy body of evidence held in the database of public consultation responses, a twenty-one-page business plan produced by The Black Cap Foundation in March 2017 channelled arguments and information into a corporate format to which the owners and investors might be more receptive. The plan demonstrates commitment to the venue as living heritage, and as a viable business, rather than as an artefact of the past.[138] It is available online and is clear and succinct in its status, aims and authorship – contrasting with the palimpsest of planning documents and the obscure trails of ownership and investment. This document identifies the venue's unique qualities as a multi-use pub and cabaret venue and its further business potential, and it evidences the campaigners' arguments through data.[139] It details proposals for how the pub could be relaunched, presents refurbishment costings and financial projections, and includes celebrity endorsements. We can read from this that the campaigners have been prepared to engage in ways that connect with the mainstream economic logic of the investors, but that in doing so they promote a more conditional, responsible form of capitalism. In place of the competitive entrepreneurialism associated with the 1990s gay scene in media accounts (see Chapter 4), the document attests to a shift towards a mutualist approach, which prioritizes transparent flows of income, expenditure, profit and reinvestment, and which seeks to elicit maximum communal value for a cross-section of the LGBTQ+ population through nurturing queer forms of collaboration, creativity and enterprise. In this, there are parallels with the *First Out Coffee Shop Project Business Plan* (1985), discussed in Chapter 5.

Upstairs downstairs

As a long-standing venue, The Black Cap contrasts with more mobile, ephemeral and emergent queer scenes. Yet established and mixed-use venues like these do, of course, host more transient activities. Their clientele shifts over time. They gain and lose popularity. In the years just before its closure, in contrast with media reports of gay nightlife fading away, business at The Black Cap had seen a return.[140] Part of the attraction to new patrons was the strong association with Camden Town and the fact that it was the neighbourhood's only dedicated LGBTQ+ venue. The new promoters were cognizant of this in their pitch.[141] The venue's revival was also fuelled by the mainstreaming of drag and queer performance through the ascendance of *RuPaul's Drag Race*. Drag queen and promoter Meth Lab and partner Boyfriend Joe imported acts from the show, forging an interesting connection between reality television, international online queer culture and the resurgence of a long-standing London venue associated with legendary drag personas, some of whom had themselves made it to mainstream TV. The new audiences joined the campaign that formed after The Black Cap's closure, alongside older generations and local campaigners, such as Forum.

As someone who had expended substantial energy on The Black Cap's comeback, and who had helped establish the weekly protest vigils once it had closed, promoter, performer and performance theorist, Joe Parslow, offers a somewhat critical view of the campaign:

> I felt like it was moving towards lots of fairly privileged people, often whom I haven't seen in the venue for the last three years, *suddenly* being like, 'Oh, let's remember how good it was in the past'.[142]

The plural and long-running campaign associated with The Black Cap – which includes both core individuals and others more tangentially or transiently in its orbit

142   *Queer Premises*

– has inevitably featured a variety of positions on the venue's heritage value, locating this more or less in a past golden era, or the recent past, or the present or future; in the building, or its various spaces, or its social value. Parslow's point that the threat to and closure of the venue activated people who had not actually been using it highlights the sense among artists and promoters that audiences should not take their nightlife venues for granted and suggests that actual use may not align with strong feelings about threats or closures. The capacity to participate in campaigns, especially over the long-term, relies on multiple factors; just as the resources to attend venues are not even. Those who had not attended more recent events may not have identified with or felt included in the new scene that had formed around the venue; and may have attached different value to the building as a transmitter of culture or memory. Distinct sub-groups may play a vital role in a campaign at specific moments, as in the case of the Drama Queens who took an important step in submitting the first ACV for an LGBTQ+ venue, but who were less prominent afterwards.

Wayne Shires, an experienced and successful gay nightlife entrepreneur, took a view that directly contrasted with the campaign. His position was that The Black Cap's owners, Kicking Horse, had offered a workable proposal:

> The plans looked amazing. The campaigners said no. Camden Council went 'we'll go with the campaigners', and it sat there empty. And the reason is, is because of them; it would have [. . .] The Black Cap would still be open.[143]

Shires viewed the plans as an upgrading of the existing accommodation, accompanied by improvements to facilities that would have enabled the pub to keep trading. Commenting on the situation in London as a whole in 2017, he was dismissive of 'armchair activists' and the idea that there is a 'kind of *conspiracy* to wipe out the LGBT community of London. Each case has its own unique *history*. And, yes, gentrification obviously *does* come into it.'[144] It is not clear that The Black Cap or other campaigns were suggesting any such conspiracy; and indeed, the campaigners had already expended substantial energy in producing evidence and analysis of the specific histories and displacement dynamics of each context. The image of activism presented by Shires contrasts with the creative, in situ, multimedia, technical and sustained forms that were pursued around the RVT and The Black Cap.

Shires felt that Kicking Horse had a successful model since they had converted another long-standing LGBTQ+ venue in Soho, Comptons, by adapting 'underused' upper floors to residential use and reinvesting in the ground-floor venue so that it remained open and profitable. However, there is no evidence that a similar scheme would have worked at The Black Cap, in a very different location, with its distinct configuration of interior spaces and uses, and where the investors and their intermediaries repeatedly tried to downplay the specific significance of the venue to LGBTQ+ patrons. Shires is an entrepreneur who has been skilful in locating opportunities within urban change dynamics, taking over and adapting venues. This approach fits earlier models of pioneer gentrification. It contrasts the explicitly anti-gentrification stance of some of the high-profile campaigns of the 2010s, such as the Friends of the Joiners Arms (see Chapter 7), which have been framed around issues such as the uneven provision of spaces and resources across diverse LGBTQ+ populations, or the prioritisation of profit-led redevelopment in the context of a lack of affordable housing provision.

Although holding some divergent views, Shires and Parslow are both informed by their involvement in running another Camden venue that opened just three months after The Black Cap's closure, just around the corner, on Kentish Town Road. This was in a 1990s industrial shed at the back of star architect Nicholas Grimshaw's hi-tech Sainsbury's building, owned by developer Irvine Sellar's company, Sellar Properties. Shires leased the venue and opened Bloc Bar. The closure of The Black Cap, a late-licensed venue, meant that Bloc obtained a similar license when Camden would usually refuse them.[145] But it did not do well, and by the summer of 2016 it was also on the brink of closure. Shires was aware that Bloc was a risky undertaking, since previous bars on the site had been short-lived, and had passed from one operator to the next.[146]

An experienced venue operator, and aware of the challenges in making a success of this off-main-road site, Shires saw a benefit in creating an association with the Meth Lab and the group that had been responsible for The Black Cap's revival, and which had been part of the campaign to reopen it.[147] The space above Bloc Bar was let to them (Plate 19).[148] The Her Upstairs team later took over Bloc Bar from Shires when it was struggling and rebranded it as Them Downstairs. These new businesses required significant emotional and financial investment. Some of the Her Upstairs team invested personal funds, and because of this they were able to install a floor for the new bar, which they then fitted out with friends.[149] The aesthetic contrast between the industrial Bloc Bar and the bric-a-brac domesticity of Her Upstairs reflected contrasting approaches to the ethos and operation of the venues. The upstairs/downstairs arrangement and the 'camp and kitschy' furniture and fittings self-consciously echoed The Black Cap, where patrons could have a quiet drink upstairs while a club or cabaret night was taking place in the basement.[150] For those setting up Her Upstairs, the intention was to create a 'homely' atmosphere, where customers 'would walk in and feel like they have a certain ownership over the space'.[151]

Despite the popularity of its cabaret scene, Her Upstairs/Them Downstairs ceased trading in 2018. The team report that taking on the additional space had contributed additional pressure.[152] The reasons for the closure of Her Upstairs/Them Downstairs are multiple, however, including tensions with the leaseholder, and different approaches within the group. In this context, Camden, as the licensing body, only had a regulatory role. Since the venue was not problematic in terms of its licence, the council did not intervene or provide proactive support. Although the venue had fostered a popular performance scene, it did not suit an ACV registration, which is framed around longevity.

Even though the location was close, and there was a conscious effort to connect with The Black Cap's culture and clientele, these circumstances show that it is not easy simply to reopen a venue in another location – they plug into very specific conditions and resources. These cases again demonstrate the commitment required in setting up and running a venue, and the way that the relationship with the leaseholder, freeholder, the quality of the building and location, and the level and nature of risk, investment, and political contexts, produce specific financial, administrative and emotional demands. The venue combined two generations of venue operators with differing levels of security, experience and capacity to negotiate the dynamics of their tenancies. The younger queer entrepreneurs whose association was intended to buttress the failing Bloc Bar bore heavy risks.

The Black Cap, at the time of writing, remains boarded up. In August 2017 the freeholder, Kicking Horse Limited, following a meeting at which the GLA's Culture At-risk team and night czar were present, agreed to 'work together to identify a new, third-party leaseholder to reopen The Black Cap as an LGBTQ+ venue with cabaret performance at its heart as soon as possible'.[153] The venue was duly put on the market in October 2017.[154] The campaigners report that the freeholders summarily rejected an offer to purchase the site made in partnership with a local hospitality business and with appropriate financing.[155] Camden Council has expended significant energy to work with campaigners over many years, supporting the renewal of the ACV in 2020, but its representatives do not feel empowered to resolve the situation, nor do they feel that this is the council's role. 'If it were within the gift of the Council today to reopen it, they honestly would, but it's not within our gift unfortunately', one comments; while another remarks that 'it's not about the Council coming up with all the solutions'.[156] By 2021, the campaigners had set up The Black Cap Community Benefit Society as a vehicle to realize their business plan and purchase the venue. At present, there are positive signs. Ownership has been taken on by the newly formed company Kicking Horse Three, whose directors, following changes in the profile of their main investors, 'are clear that the pub should be revived as an LGBT+ venue'.[157] The Black Cap Community Benefit Society have been given access to the building to survey its condition and value. However, the building is still up for sale. Marketing materials still tout '[p]otential for residential development on the second and third floors'.[158]

The recent controversies surrounding these venues show some of the varied ways queer heritage is being understood and negotiated within LGBTQ+ communities, and in the market and governance dynamics that affect the spaces identified with them. In each case a threat to the maintenance and future existence of the venue created alarm and placed the onus on patrons, performers and promoters to articulate the venues' layered histories, multiple functions, and present-day and future value. The campaigns that formed to protect the venues and to retain or re-establish their use in the service of heterogeneous LGBTQ+ populations have been politically plural. This reflects the diverse communities of interest within their orbit, and the ways that they have provided a setting for intergenerational exchange, and cooperation and communality across difference. Nonetheless, they also reflect and reproduce biases of inclusivity in line with wider power dynamics in the ownership and management of space and other resources – and this has been raised in the discourses around campaigns. Threats to these venues and the planning procedures around them have connected with a wider public discussion about queer loss, the traumatic memory of past violence, the AIDS crisis and the mourning of those who died, the continuing legacies of past oppressions,

Plate 1 London Lesbian and Gay Centre, leaflet, 1985. Courtesy Bishopsgate Institute.

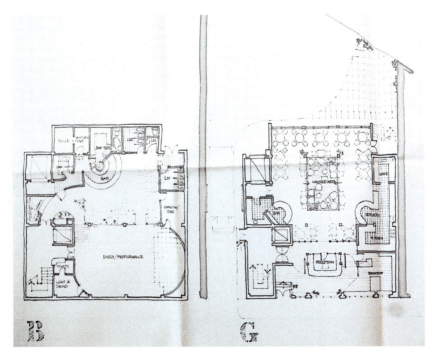

Plate 2 Sketch proposals, London Lesbian and Gay Centre, basement 1983. Courtesy Fiona McLean, McLean Quinlan.

Plate 3 Exterior of London Lesbian and Gay Centre, 1985. Photo by Robert Workman. Courtesy Bishopsgate Institute.

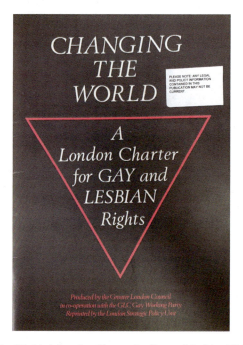

Plate 4 *Changing the World: A London Charter for Gay and Lesbian Rights*, 1985. Courtesy Bishopsgate Institute.

Plate 5 London Lesbian and Gay Centre, *Newsletter*, No. 1, November, 1988. Cover with cartoon section by NINE. Hall-Carpenter Archives, LSE Library.

Plate 6 London Lesbian and Gay Centre, 'Buy Our Centre', leaflet, 1990. Courtesy Bishopsgate Institute.

Plate 7 London Partnerships Register, first ceremony, attended by Mayor of London, Ken Livingstone, 2001. Alamy.

Plate 8 Mayor of London Boris Johnson tries on a pink cowgirl hat at London Pride, 2008. Mark Yeoman/Alamy Stock Photo.

Plate 9 Mayor of London Sadiq Khan shakes hands and takes photos with organizers before London Pride 8 July 2017. Photo by Ashley Van Haeften, Flickr. CC BY 2.0.

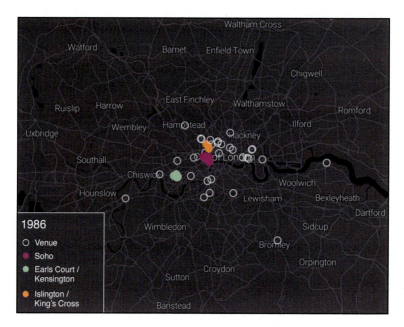

Plate 10 Map showing locations of LGBTQ+ venues and clusters of venues in London, 1986. UCL Urban Laboratory (Ben Campkin, Lo Marshall, Christopher Storey) and Drawing Office, UCL Geography, 2019.

Plate 11 Map showing locations of LGBTQ+ venues and clusters of venues in London, 1996. UCL Urban Laboratory (Ben Campkin, Lo Marshall, Christopher Storey) and Drawing Office, UCL Geography, 2019.

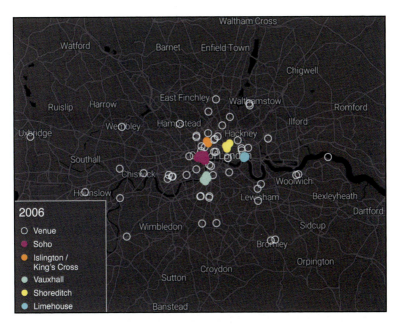

Plate 12 Map showing locations of LGBTQ+ venues and clusters of venues in London, 2006. UCL Urban Laboratory (Ben Campkin, Lo Marshall, Christopher Storey) and Drawing Office, UCL Geography, 2019.

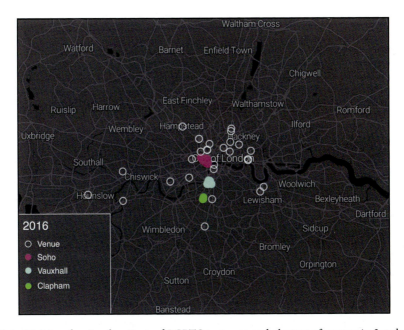

Plate 13 Map showing locations of LGBTQ+ venues and clusters of venues in London, 2016. UCL Urban Laboratory (Ben Campkin, Lo Marshall, Christopher Storey) and Drawing Office, UCL Geography, 2019.

Plate 14 The Bell, King's Cross, 1981. Photographer unknown. Courtesy London Metropolitan Archives (City of London).

Plate 15 The Glass Bar, Euston, 2007. Photo by Stephen McKay. CC BY-SA 2.0.

Plate 16 First Out Café, St Giles, London, 2005. Photo by Maria Tejada. Courtesy Maria Tejada.

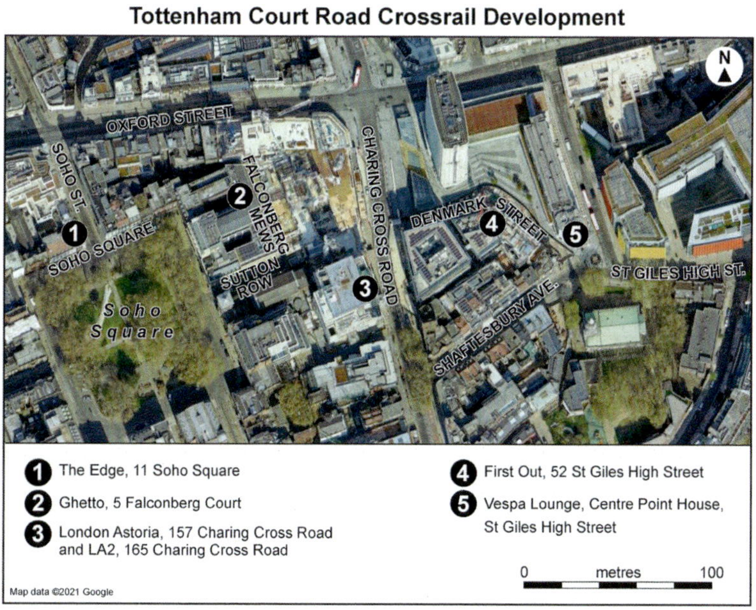

Plate 17 Map of venues affected by Crossrail 1 [Elizabeth Line] Tottenham Court Road Station redevelopment. UCL Urban Laboratory (Ben Campkin and Lo Marshall) and Drawing Office, UCL Geography, 2022.

Plate 18 Protest vigil outside The Black Cap, October 2015. Courtesy Black Cap Community Benefit Society and #WeAreTheBlackCap campaign.

Plate 19 Her Upstairs, Camden, 2017, stage. Photo by FD Photos. Courtesy FD Photos.

Plate 20 The Joiners Arms, Hackney Road, 2012. Photo by Ewan Munro CC BY-SA 2.0.

Plate 21 Mural by David Shenton, The Joiners Arms, 2012. Photo by Fran Gomez de Villaboa. Courtesy Fran Gomez de Villaboa.

Plate 22 The Joiners Arms 'completely trashed a few days after the closing night', 2015. C-Type Matt 266 x 191. Photo by Fran Gomez de Villaboa. Courtesy Fran Gomez de Villaboa.

Plate 23 Friends of The Joiners Arms, poster for public meeting, 2017. Courtesy Friends of The Joiners Arms.

Plate 24 Frame from *Will You Dance With Me?*, 2014. Directed by Derek Jarman in collaboration with Ron Peck and Mark Ayres. Shot in Benjy's, 1984. Courtesy Ron Peck.

Plate 25 Frame from *Will You Dance With Me?*, 2014. Directed by Derek Jarman in collaboration with Ron Peck and Mark Ayres. Shot in Benjy's, 1984. Courtesy Ron Peck.

Plate 26 The Backstreet, Mile End, 2018. Photo by Prem Sahib and Mark Blower. Courtesy Prem Sahib.

Plate 27 The Backstreet, Mile End, 2018. Photo by Prem Sahib and Mark Blower. Courtesy Prem Sahib.

Plate 28 The Royal Vauxhall Tavern, London. Still image from a laser scan produced between Covid-19 pandemic lockdowns, 2020. Scan produced courtesy of The Royal Vauxhall Tavern as part of the Humanities in the European Research Area-funded project NITE: Night-spaces, Migration, Culture and Integration in Europe. Scan team: Ben Campkin, Lo Marshall, Lucca Farrarese, James White, Tom Kendall. UCL Urban Laboratory, 2020.

Plate 29 The Royal Vauxhall Tavern, London. Still image from a laser scan produced between Covid-19 pandemic lockdowns, 2020. UCL Urban Laboratory, 2020.

Plate 30 The Royal Vauxhall Tavern, London. Still image from a laser scan produced between Covid-19 pandemic lockdowns, 2020. UCL Urban Laboratory, 2020.

the power of resistance and the need for queer premises to adapt to address today's forms of discrimination and intersectional inequalities.

Campaigns have necessarily shifted over time and have had multivalent agendas. They have cohered around the systematic use of legal and policy frameworks, which have required the narration of the venues' communal value through their social, architectural and urban histories. These activisms, rooted in local and international queer performance and protest traditions, have engaged with material heritage and the temporalities of neoliberal urban change in critical and agile ways, rooting today's communities within folklore and deep place-based histories, claiming and creating sites of memory and everyday creativity, while refusing to essentialize them. Each venue was already a site for the transmission of the past through multiple formal and informal modes of cultural and political practice. The crises around them channelled these efforts into the available mechanisms for designating social and architectural heritage. The import of these venues has been communicated more widely in public as a result. Echoing other contestations centred on housing and regeneration dynamics shaped by supergentrification and austerity urbanism, campaigns focused both on protecting, extending and adapting queer infrastructure.[159]

The networks that formed across London-based campaigns in the 2010s, including the RVT and The Black Cap, facilitated resource-sharing and the amplification of their actions and of marginalised voices. This was important in engaging the often-complex planning tools for community consultation, designed to protect social and cultural infrastructure, but compromised in their capacity to support diverse populations. These processes have involved grassroots engagement and collaboration with the local and municipal authorities. This included activating mechanisms established through the Localism Act 2011 and the planning processes and databases of individual boroughs, as well as actions to gain the support of the mayor of London and night czar. Although working within the normative logic of a neoliberal governance framework, dominant modes of urban development have been protested and stalled, and alternative visions of change have been articulated. Despite these efforts, the venues remain precarious and subject to changes of ownership and use.

The tensions between queer politics and neoliberal capitalism already existed in these venues, which operate as businesses but accommodate multiple queer economies and practices. The campaigns have exposed these contradictions in a variety of ways. For example, there are contrasts between the positive diversity rhetoric of the state and commercial organisations and the negative impacts of redevelopment on minoritized groups; there is a lack of will, and of tools with sufficient teeth, to protect queer cultural spaces and heritage. Within redevelopment situations there are also intentional efforts to obfuscate or to create sustained pressure on local organisations and authorities through repeated submission of closely similar proposals. In these cases, there are conflicts between management, LGBTQ+ operators, patrons and campaigners. These are drawn around different attitudes towards market economics, property and trajectories of growth and reinvestment. Asymmetrical power relations between landowners and investors and their agents, and venue operators and clients, are exposed. Campaigns have piloted new structures for community coordination and ownership. The forms of place-based activism occurring lately parallel the earlier opportunistic appropriation and re-use of ex-industrial buildings and spaces deemed dysfunctional in the 1980s. The social movements that have emerged can help us to rethink contemporary models of urbanization towards more ethical ones; they are informed by and can inform the protection of spaces elsewhere with comparable histories or functions.

7

Macho city

On 11 January 2015, The Joiners Arms closed at the peak of its extraordinary popularity. This late-night LGBTQ+ venue in Tower Hamlets, East London, had been sold by Admiral Taverns to a plastic frame manufacturer, Robobond, in 2014. The sale had anticipated approval of a planned ten-storey residential scheme, led by Regal Homes. The bar's interior was quickly dismantled in the days following its closure. Four days after The Joiners closed, Tower Hamlets approved its nomination as an Asset of Community Value (ACV). Eight years later, as this book goes to press, the building has yet to be demolished or redeveloped. Nearby, in 2016, and again in Tower Hamlets, another proposal for a mixed-use scheme required the closure and demolition of The Backstreet, a locally and internationally popular gay fetish nightclub. Public consultation responses raised the alarm, drawing the council's and the Greater London Authority's attention to the presence of the venue within the proposed redevelopment site. It had operated with a seven-days-per-week late licence in a high-density area since the 1980s, without hindrance to, or objection from, surrounding residents. In Southwark, across the river, another planning case was unfolding: Samson and Ludgate House, a large-scale mixed-use development at Bankside, which had first been proposed in 2012. The plan here was to repurpose a run of railway arches that had accommodated Pulse, a large-capacity, industrial-aesthetic gay club, for new community and leisure uses. Pulse's closure in 2019 displaced XXL, a popular club night for 'bears, cubs, chubs, muscle bears and their admirers'. Founded by Pulse's gay owner-operator, XXL was Pulse's most commercially successful and fastest-growing brand.

Planning conflicts and heated intra-LGBTQ+ community discussions have ensued in each of these situations. They involve distinctive venue types, with business and operational models oriented towards specific patrons. In this chapter I ask what we can learn from them to better understand the function and lifecycles of LGBTQ+ premises within the wider governance of social and cultural infrastructure and night-time spaces in contexts of redevelopment. How do the dynamics of localism and the global city play out through these venues and through the planning proposals? How do sexual and gender diversity and inclusion feature in the discussions about them? What is revealed by the forms (or lack) of recognition of LGBTQ+ subjectivities and heritage in the policies and practices through which each place is being reshaped? To address these questions, I look in detail at the actions and positioning of freeholders, venue operators, communities of interest, patrons, planners and other built environment

148   *Queer Premises*

professionals, local borough authorities, the mayor, GLA and the night czar. Different understandings of inclusivity emerge as decision-makers perform their duties in weighing up potential advantages and disadvantages of the schemes for LGBTQ+ populations, their likely overall public benefit, and the broader definition and value of night-time venues as social and cultural infrastructure.

These conflicts have sparked lively discussions of inclusion and exclusion within and across LGBTQ+ communities. Tensions reside in the differing perceptions of community need, relative vulnerability or privilege and in understandings of these premises' worth and potential. In the three examples, I look at the specification of LGBTQ+ subjectivities, and interdependencies between different constituent groups as these are reflected in the allocation of space for different purposes and through planning classification systems and practices.

These cases offer special potential for elucidating how gay and queer masculinities materialize in the imagination, establishment and operation of venues and in urban planning processes. The recent campaigns in response to closures have reflected the reformulation of queer subjectivities and havehighlighted changing priorities within LGBTQ+ populations. These have advocated for intersectional approaches to inclusion. This has aligned in some ways with priorities in City Hall under Sadiq Khan's mayoralty. However, the grassroots initiatives have more radically rejected norms of sexuality and gender and identarian ways of thinking that are written into and reproduced through planning policies and practices.

Life, love and liberty

Located on the ancient Hackney Road, The Joiners Arms Beerhouse was licensed for the sale of beer from as early as 1869.[1] The pub was rebuilt in its modern form in the interwar period.[2] The exterior of what had by then become a fully licensed pub included elegant decorative tiled panels depicting the name and an emblem of joiners' tools. This (previously straight) pub had closed in the aftermath of a fatal drive-by shooting in 1995.[3] Up until the murder it had been a busy venue, connected to a string of pubs and striptease bars stretching along Hackney Road. But the shooting sealed its reputation for vice and violence and it was forced to close.

On 6 May 1997, The Joiners reopened as a gay venue (Plates 20–22), licensed to David Pollard (1954–2018) (Figure 7.1). The pub's stigmatised reputation meant that the lease was affordable. The hours were restricted to start with, but informally the venue still provided after-hours entertainment and for a period 'was really only open when it was shut'.[4] At first, the target clientele were mainly gay men.[5] Pollard, a popular figure among employees and more widely, was proud of the fact that The Joiners had been the first gay pub to open after New Labour's election.[6] His liberal political leanings and broader ambition for the pub were signalled in its first months when he started 'Talking Heads', 'an early evening speakeasy', hosting Tony Banks, the high-profile New Labour minister for sport and MP for the nearby district of West Ham, for a discussion about gay rights.[7] Pollard was a working-class Prestonian who had lived nearby in Dalston in the early 1990s. He took over and rejuvenated The Joiners

Figure 7.1 David Pollard, 2010. Photo by Fran Gomez de Villaboa.

having previously worked in the pharmaceutical industry. Hampered by personal circumstances, and helped by his sister to finance the pub, he struggled to make it work in the early years.[8] Apart from the issuing of the licence, Pollard did not find Tower Hamlets to be proactively supportive in setting up the venue, although he perceived the affirmative approach of the police to have been important.[9]

Since its closure, The Joiners has become one of the most widely commented upon LGBTQ+ venues in London.[10] Long before it shut, queer geographer Johan Andersson wrote a full account of the venue's culture and aesthetics, placing it within a re-emergent East London gay scene.[11] He showed how the pub's success was partly due to its associations with a local East End heritage, rooted within tropes of working-class community, masculinity, danger and hedonism. Andersson also placed The Joiners within the wider, art-led gentrification of Shoreditch, but argued that the venue, 'more than any other bar in the area, offered a heterogeneous space that facilitated genuine interaction between the local working-class community and some of the middle-class gentrifiers'.[12] He argued convincingly that the bar and cabaret scenes of the noughties were woven into local identity in ways that countered assumptions of global homogeneity in gay culture.[13] The Joiners' story can be understood within the wider gentrification dynamics that began in the area in the 1990s, where references to working-class identity were embedded and commodified within new cultural practices in parallel with structural transformations that were taking place through property transactions and rental increases.[14] Yet Andersson's account of The Joiners suggests that there are benefits to be found in carefully evaluating any one venue's relationship with wider, long-term processes of urban change.

In the early years, The Joiners was known for its informal after-hours parties and a darkroom on the floor above.[15] Bar manager Giuliano Pistoni puts the popularity of the venue down to there being 'nothing else around', an East End attraction for outsiders.[16] Its success accelerated with the opening of another queer pub venue, The George and Dragon, nearby. Located close to the London College of Fashion, these venues became a hub for a mix of fashion and art scenes and took custom from an earlier generation of gay venues that had closed as the area gentrified.[17] Once the pub began to gain popularity, Pollard adapted the interior. The centrally placed marble-topped bar was moved to one side in 2001 to maximize a large flexible open space for a pool table, socializing and dancing (Figure 7.2). Unisex toilets, rare at the time, were installed.[18] The Hackney Road façade was adorned with a large rainbow flag and a 'Christopher Street' street sign, referencing the West Village in New York City. Customers smoked in a precariously overcrowded pen on the narrow pavement outside. The street frontage was vulnerable to homophobic attacks. As the venue became ever more popular in the noughties and early 2010s, and with tensions heightened after a man on his way to the George and Dragon was attacked in a nearby street and suffered a stab wound that left him paralysed, the smoking area shifted to a backyard.[19] By the time The Joiners closed in 2015, there were long queues to enter the pub.[20]

The Joiners was on the border of Tower Hamlets and Hackney, two traditionally working-class boroughs noted for their transition to a cosmopolitan demographic and cultural 'super-diversity' in the late twentieth and early twenty-first century.[21] During this period, as geographer Gavin Brown has observed, Tower Hamlets had transformed into something of a 'symbolic cosmopolitan zone' with varied outcomes for non-heterosexual men, shaped according to variables such as class and ethnicity.[22] In his commentary on The Joiners' qualities, Pollard stressed its social mix and multifunctionality.[23] He was keen to emphasize the venue's inclusivity to all genders and sexualities (as signalled by the unisex loos); its daytime uses for pride events, charity fundraising and HIV testing; and the international mix of its staff and customers.[24] Ten years after opening, in a somewhat idealized commentary, The Joiners was described as a nightlife venue that saw 'no line between gay and straight'.[25] The venue's business model was in many ways conventional in its structure and profit model. It brought together different currents of neoliberal entrepreneurialism central to London's global brand: new approaches to the night-time economy that saw the value of night-time venues to growth; the celebration of the creative industries, and a liberal tolerance of sexual and gender difference insofar as these were expressed in mainstream LGBT rights.

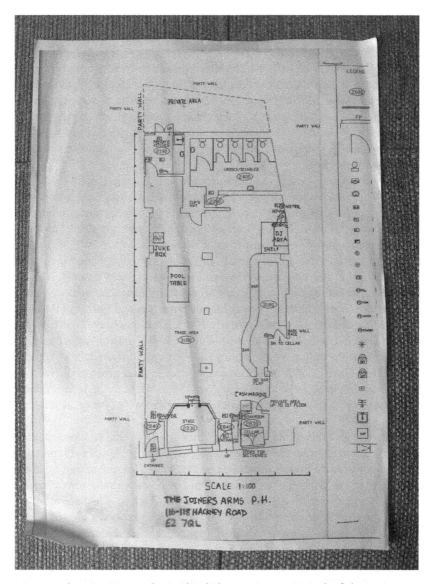

Figure 7.2 The Joiners Arms, plan, undated. The Joiners Arms/Friends of The Joiners Arms.

However, as is often the case with venues, there was an alchemy in how these general trends materialized and advanced. The venue's tone and positive, affective charge were influenced by Pollard's aspirations and charisma, as a kind, affable bar-stool philosopher who relished the social environment of the pub and nurtured the staff.[26] As a late-night business, The Joiners gained a reputation for being permissive, hedonistic and inclusive, and this was premised – at least in part – on Pollard's cultivation of a social and relaxed operational model. This included his approach to staffing. Pistoni notes that Pollard had 'a special relationship with each one of us [barstaff]', and jokes that this was 'the wrong way of running a business'.[27] Pollard's progressive values led to concrete actions such as being the first pub to pay the London Living Wage.[28] In an ethnography of the campaign that developed after The Joiners closed, one participant who spoke to social scientist Olimpia Burchiellaro used the adjective 'wonky' as a positive attribute to indicate the venue's feeling of inclusivity.[29] In his memoir of night scenes in London, LA and San Francisco, *Gay Bar* (2021), Jeremy Atherton Lin vividly evokes its 'ribald atmosphere' and 'shambolic character', and links this unruly ambience to Pollard's relaxed approach.[30] A bespoke, queer economy supported the venue's more visible commercial operation.

The Joiners' distinctiveness was intimately connected with the energy of its staff, many of whom were students or worked in the creative industries and used the venue as a platform for their work. The sense of creative community and political intent are encapsulated in the murals Pollard commissioned from a friend, the queer cartoonist David Shenton, who also worked shifts behind the bar (Plates 21 and 22). This was the last in a series of murals updated sporadically, drawn on wallpaper and then pasted onto the wall, and was documented by another barman, Fran Gomez de Villaboa, now a successful fashion photographer and art director. Shenton had asked the staff to nominate their queer icons and drew them in a formation reminiscent of the album cover for The Beatles' *Sgt. Pepper's Lonely Hearts Club Band* (1967), designed by Jann Haworth and Peter Blake. The symbol of the joiners' interlocked arms, poised to wrestle, is at the centre, along with an image of Pollard and his 'Life, Love and Liberty' motto. The rest of the mural depicts an eclectic queer genealogy of local and international, historical and contemporary icons. This last of in the series of murals for The Joiners by Shenton was produced in the knowledge that the venue was about to close.

As the creator of this spirited picture of queer genealogy, and as a former Joiners barman, Shenton celebrates the pub's social mix, but does not idealize it. He notes that the rapid growth of the business, its huge popularity and the international reputation it gained, were not planned or anticipated.[31] In reality, commercial success resulted in formalities that were the antithesis of Pollard's laid-back style and vision of 'Life, Love and Liberty'. These changes included, for example, a more regimented security and queuing system to manage the high volume of patrons, ever-increasing entrance charges and tighter management of DJ sets so that music, measured in appropriately fast beats per minute, delivered the desired vibe. Shenton observes that the experience, staffing and management of the venue were complicated by a culture of permissiveness towards drugs. He notes that Pollard's affable openness left him vulnerable to exploitation.

When Pollard's lease expired and was not offered for renewal, The Joiners had to close. Pollard, whose health was declining, accepted this. He was left financially secure enough to establish another bar in Sitges, Spain, in partnership with Pistoni, although this did not stay open long.[32] The Joiners had employed around sixteen to twenty people at any one time, as well as playing host to numerous artists. Its closure, therefore, had wider consequences for these individuals as well as well as for its patrons.

Save and evolve

Aware of threats to close the pub, a campaign formed independently of Pollard and the bar's management under the banner 'The Joiners Lives on'. Friends of The Joiners Arms (FOTJA), as the group became known, held its first public meeting in late 2014.[33] As with other campaigns (see Chapter 6) the group was buoyed by the possibility of listing the pub as an ACV with a view to a community purchase.[34] Through the nomination process, rather than reflect only on what had been lost, they began a speculative conversation about the qualities a 'queer space' should have, and what kind of venue they would like to create. The point was

> not just to save all of the features of The Joiners Arms that made it an invigorating, fun and safe space for LGBTQI+ communities to socialise, but to pursue a new vision for what a reinvigorated Joiners Arms under community control could be.[35]

As with other campaigns, FOTJA benefitted from wide-ranging expertise within the group, including legal and architectural knowledge. Its members have also had to expend substantial energy, voluntary labour and other resources, sustained over years, to engage via the planning system. They note the disparity between their own resources and those at the disposal of Regal Homes as a large residential developer.[36] Regal challenged the FOTJA's successful ACV nomination a month after the venue was registered, prompting a further submission of evidence. The FOTJA's case emphasised The Joiners' positive contribution to issues of local safety and well-being. For example, the campaigners pointed to the higher-than-average rates of homophobic hate crime and HIV infection in Tower Hamlets and provided data on LGBTQIA+ community members' perceptions of the venue as a safe space and its track record in accommodating HIV testing and promoting awareness.[37] The ACV was confirmed by Tower Hamlets.[38] The nomination had set out LGBTQ+ populations' use of the site, forcing the applicants' and local authority's attention to this important omission from the planning proposals.

As well as highly publicized street protests, the campaigners also convened large and regular public meetings (Plate 23); they conducted a detailed survey with Joiners Arms patrons and another with the wider LGBTQI+ community; they negotiated with the developer directly; worked with a heritage consultant to assess the planning application; liaised with CAMRA (the Campaign for Real Ale) to assess the developers' proposals; and composed a detailed business plan for a future LGBTQI+ venue. The vision emerged collectively as a proposition for a new LGBTQI+ Community Centre.[39] The organizational model would be non-hierarchical, cooperatively owned and managed. In many respects, this resonated with the vision for the centres and cooperatives of the 1970s and 80s, including the London Lesbian and Gay Centre (see Chapter 2) or First Out (see Chapter 5). The ambition for inclusivity was broader: to 'oppose to all forms of hate based on race, gender identity (or lack thereof), sexual identity (or lack thereof), class, age, ability, citizenship status'.[40] The vision was also framed in relation to the venue's past reputation, referencing its provision of space for political engagement, HIV awareness and testing, and affiliation with LGBTQ+ charities. FOTJA's proposals also demonstrated a shift away from the consumerist, liberal, hedonist values of The Joiners as it had existed, and towards a more intersectional queer politics. For example, it proposed an alcohol-free daytime space to address well-being challenges and drug cultures, and to support those additionally marginalized due, for example, to the intersection of their faith, gender and sexuality or to being homeless. The original venue had been cultivated around an international cosmopolitanism which was in sync with the New Labour and City Hall's branding of the creative, global city. FOTJA has consistently rooted its proposals in Tower Hamlets' status as a borough with a 'rich diversity and multicultural character', connecting this to The Joiners association with an internationalist outlook, but shifting to a more explicit anti-nationalist and pro-immigration position.[41]

Regal Homes' initial high-rise residential proposal was later adapted into a mixed-use scheme which signalled a shift towards the provision of commercial space for the creative and tech sectors.[42] A new planning application for workspace, shops and flats, submitted in 2017, involved demolition of all but the façade of The Joiners, but included a new pub on a different site within boundary of the scheme. The retention of The Joiners' distinctive facade, with its 'slightly moderne style', was justified according to local communal interest.[43] The render by architects Allford Hall Monaghan Morris showed the preserved but sanitized facade, which replaced The Joiner's colourful exterior with the beige aesthetics of a craft pottery and sandwich shop. The architects noted the building to be 'of importance due to its historic presence and the role played within the local community', using this as a rationale to include a drinking establishment in the new scheme.[44] In this reduction of the generic value of a pub to local character and community, The Joiners Arms, as a long-established and recently closed LGBTQ+ venue, widely celebrated for fostering social mix and supporting queer and creative communities, was erased.[45]

FOTJA's campaign has contrasted the developers' anodyne imagery with the DIY aesthetics of hand-drawn, colourful posters that are sprinkled with emoticons and linked to social media through QR codes. They repurposed the pub's motto of 'Life, Love and Liberty' and Shenton's drawing of the joiners' interlocked arms, signalling tradecraft and working-class solidarity. A drawing of a heart, used to decorate a protest banner, became the campaign logo. The campaign, like the venue, embedded itself in the East End, stressing that the pub was 'at the heart of the East End community for nearly twenty years'.[46] Direct-action placards demanded 'homes for homos' and asserted that #JoinersLivesOn. These slogans reflected the FOTJA alignment with a wider pushback against gentrification and its affinities with other local campaigns such as Focus E15 – a group of young mothers who had fought a high-profile battle against eviction from emergency accommodation in the London Borough of Newham, and who had resisted their planned dispersal from East London to other parts of the UK.[47]

The applicants' initial statement of community involvement referred to 'extensive consultation' with FOTJA, recording that the only outcome of this was that they would include a drinking establishment (A4 use class) in the scheme.[48] There are similarities here with the The Black Cap case (Chapter 6) in that this promise to provide a generic venue did not satisfy the campaigners' demands. In 2017, again mirroring The Black Cap, the night czar, Amy Lamé and the GLA Culture at Risk team intervened as brokers. At the request of Tower Hamlets, and prompted by the alarm raised by Queer Spaces

Network (see Chapter 4), a meeting was convened with FOTJA and Regal Homes and their representatives to try and find a resolution.

The phrase used to describe the venue in its early days – 'it was only really open when it was shut' – could be applied to the campaign that closure stimulated. Due to FOTJA's persistence and the local authority's and developers' eventual engagement, the outcomes from The Joiners conflict have been positive. The Tower Hamlets authorities recognized that, in this case, their responsibilities for planning and their Public Sector Equality Duty towards people with protected characteristics were interlinked.[49] After a protracted set of negotiations, a proposal was drawn up for the first use of a Section 106 agreement – an agreement between the local authority and developer to make an otherwise unacceptable development acceptable by imposing conditions. As first proposed, this set out legally binding obligations for the developer to actively seek, over a period of twelve months, an LGBT+ operator for the new pub. The campaigners were again dissatisfied and so they pushed for, and achieved, a more specific set of obligations. These included the following: a specification of twenty-four months for the developer to work with the GLA and Tower Hamlets to seek an LGBTQ+ operator; an increased size, to 349 square metres and added storage space to improve the venue's viability; a rent-free period of twelve months; a contribution of £130,000 to cover fit-out costs; specified late opening hours for the venue in its first year of operation; and the intention for the venue to continue as an 'LGBT+ focused venue' for twenty-five years from the date of practical completion.[50] The operator would be selected using criteria developed in consultation with the GLA and the local LGBT+ community, leading to a call for expressions of interest, and further consultation on the responses.[51] However, Burchiellaro has criticised this use of Section 106 for its instrumentalization of diversity discourse to legitimise displacement process; and building from this critique planning lawyers Steven Vaughan and Brad Jessup caution against planners well-intentioned assumptions that the application of such tools actually protect the diversity of queer venues.[52]

The conflict at The Joiners therefore led to a landmark planning decision, the emergence of a campaign for a new community-run and -oriented space, and a concrete opportunity to model queer inclusive design in the new scheme. In 2023, the venue still sits boarded up. The redevelopment scheme stalled during the pandemic and the developer – now known as Regal London – cites this as the reason they have not provided the financial contribution.[53] FOTJA continues its work to organize a community cooperative to run the venue. Throughout the lifetime of the campaign it has hosted cabaret parties at different venues under the name 'Lèse Majesté', which have centred queer women, trans and non-binary people, and has platformed queer and trans performers and DJs who identify as Black and/or QTIPOC. FOTJA have recently raised nearly £130,000 by selling shares in the community benefit society they set up as a vehicle to launch their planned community-run venue. They have attracted a capital grant from Foundation for Future London, a body set up to support local businesses in East London and to connect them with incoming institutions in the East Bank development on the Queen Elizabeth Olympic Park.[54] Despite these successes, they are circumspect. In 2018, one member of the group put it like this: 'What we've achieved is a landmark, but also it's so insignificant in the grand scheme of things. We still don't have any power.'[55]

Counterproductive

The Backstreet, another venue that was under Tower Hamlets' jurisdiction, until its closure in 2022, described itself as 'the UK's longest-running gay fetish club'.[56] Specialists Stephen Levrant Heritage Architecture Limited, a practice guided by the Society for the Protection of Ancient Buildings' (SPAB) 'principles of conservation and repair', and 'renowned for an intricate and holistic approach', wrote the 2016 Heritage Statement for the proposed development at 562 Mile End Road, the site that had accommodated The Backstreet.[57] Such reports, as discussed in the previous chapter, have an ambivalent status since they are positioned as neutral expertise while being explicitly written in support of their client's interests.[58] In this instance, the authors' definitive conclusion was that: 'This site therefore has low community value' and 'little significance is attributed to the site or immediate surrounding'.[59] The applicant, Galliard Homes, presented a proposal that was based on representation of the site as 'currently occupied by a series of run-down buildings including a disused night club'.[60] This was partially accurate in that one venue on the site, known as Boheme, had closed and was disused. The application neglected to mention the existence of The Backstreet, which had continued to be housed within the same building. Set up by solicitor John Edwards, the club had been operating since 1985 and was known for the strict dress code and etiquette Edwards instituted. Apart from its local and London following, The Backstreet became a feature on the international circuit of fetish and leather bars.[61] It was the last remaining leather bar in London when it closed.

As is typical, the applicants and heritage consultants gave a very detailed long-view history of the site, going as far back as the eighth century.[62] As described by the heritage architects, the development plot has an extended history of adaptation for cultural uses: the Electric Theatre cinema was built in 1910, with La Boheme dance hall added in 1921.[63] When these sites were bombed and cleared after the Second World War, they were purchased by London Transport and leased for storage and textile manufacturing. The heritage study notes that by the mid-1980s part of the site was taken up by 'Benji's social club [sic]'. Elsewhere in the application, there is only mention of a 'disused nightclub', of unspecified name.

The reference to 'Benji's' refers to the nightclub known as Benjy's. Benjy's (c.1984–2004) pioneered weekly gay nights in the 1980s and held regular gay events in its programme until it closed. As discussed earlier, in the 1970s and 1980s gay nights were transient, and were not typically held within dedicated venues. The club owner's son, Benjamin Arthur, happened to be gay and out and supported by his father, a factor in the initiation of Benjy's gay discos. These events had an important place in a dynamic but well-hidden and dispersed East End scene, where certain queer masculinities were able to emerge.

Experimental VHS footage shot at Benjy's by Derek Jarman on 5 September 1984 provides a rare and evocative depiction of the club (Plates 24 and 25).[64] It was made on the invitation of Jarman's friends and collaborators, the filmmaker Ron Peck and producer Mark Ayers. Jarman's improvisations contributed towards the development of Peck's feature *Empire State* (1987), which revolved around a nightclub, located in the rapidly changing London docklands, and the criminal underworld around it.[65] Peck's film displays a fascination with the de-industrialized setting of what had been the engine of empire, an area that became the focus for neoliberal experiments in urban regeneration in the 1980s. Jarman's footage was not intended for release and was only recently rediscovered, collated and edited by Peck, who titled it with the question Jarman asks as he flits and flirts around the club: *Will You Dance with Me?*

Benjy's had been hired for the occasion, with friends, regulars and some actors familiar from Jarman's films invited to be filmed enjoying a night out, served by the usual bar staff and DJs. The scenes are at once performative, naturalistic and improvised: the passage of the night unfolds as the music builds, the dance floor fills, the party-goers gossip, the DJ spins records and cracks puns, and the bar staff work. The experimental sequences depict a poignant whirligig of intense, if transitory, social interaction.[66] The Benjy's footage may be a footnote in Jarman's filmography, but it makes for the powerful viewing that is typical of his work. In painterly, impressionistic strokes he documents the layering of the scene through light, colour and sound, charming people into dancing with him.

Benjy's was a local venue, described by Peck as 'a very inclusive local club, more relaxed than many West End venues'.[67] The footage seems to confirm this: the patrons are young and old, diverse in their ethnicities and in their gender expressions. They wear the low and high fashion of early 1980s tribes and catch Hi-NRG rhythms by African-American acts freshly imported from the US.

The diverse crowd is intensely present, intimately occupying and flamboyantly expressing themselves in the compressed time-space of the club. The poignancy is made more acute in the knowledge that the film was made two years before Jarman's HIV diagnosis, and when the virus and its impacts were little understood. This was ten years before he died, aged fifty-two, in 1994. It was a decade he devoted to activism and art addressing AIDS stigmatization, and challenging Section 28 (see Chapter 3). As an archive, it attests to the ways that queer time and place are shaped by mourning and loss as well as by joy and hedonism. Even as these images give intimate access to the hermetic environment of a nightclub, they ask to be connected with the city outside, with East London, with the late twentieth-century reshaping of urban space and subjectivities through global cultural, political, technological and financial processes. A fragile capsule of intimate, micro-interactions, the footage encapsulates the tension between fragmentary evidence of the elusive queer past and the linear temporality of contemporary urban redevelopment, with its selective and reductive ways of documenting site histories.

When Benjy's shut, the venue reopened as Broke, and later as Boheme. This period had a troubled ending when, after a murder on the club's premises in 2011, Tower Hamlets withdrew the venue's licence, and Boheme closed.[68] Benjy's had by this time been split so that Boheme occupied the larger capacity nightclub at the front of the site and the licence for the smaller back part had transferred from a failing bar, Benjy's 2, to The Backstreet.[69] The Backstreet's longevity was due to the reasonable rent level, and at points the rent was even waived.[70] This was fortunate since the club's popularity, according to David Oppedisano, a customer who visited frequently during its lifetime, tended to wax and wane.[71]

In 2016, local residents noticed that The Backstreet had been omitted from the planning application submitted for the site and raised the alarm.[72] Through the public consultation process the council was alerted to the threat.[73] The Backstreet's success had in part been due to its discreet location, which meant that it could co-exist with other business and residential uses and did not attract unwanted attention – in contrast with Boheme. As the name suggests, a backstreet aesthetic and location were part of the venue's branding and its attraction to a wide customer base. Yet the discrete image of the venue – and the developers' lack of diligence or deliberate oversight in omitting it from the long historical survey of the site – had meant that the threat to it almost went unnoticed. Until the risk to The Backstreet surfaced, the GLA had supported the planning proposal. Transport for London, overseen by the mayor, was a major landowner on the site, a legacy of the development of the Central Line.

Tower Hamlets refused the application on various grounds.[74] The decision was appealed by the developer, Bestzone Limited, but was upheld by the Planning Inspector in 2019.[75] The question of whether a nightclub constitutes a 'community facility', and the likelihood that, if reprovided, a nightclub serving the LGBT+ community could be sustained for the long term in the new development, were central in this conflict. The planning consultants working on behalf of the appellant took the position that a nightclub 'is *sui generis* use, and therefore does not fall under the classification of a "social" or "community facility" as defined'.[76] They went further in arguing that understanding nightclubs as 'meeting places'

> appears counterintuitive and counter-productive. As valued a use for a night-time activity is to the fabric of society, when in the right circumstances and location, the loss of a community facility cannot reasonably be considered justification for retention of a nightclub. There are appropriate locations for such uses and Wentworth Mews is not such a location having residential uses to its south and being within the Neighbourhood Centre of Mile End [. . .][77]

Given The Backstreet's exemplary licensing record, the arguments put forward by the developer, via their planning consultant, were disingenuous. For example, that the location was not suitable for a nightclub, and that a nightclub would 'represent a bad neighbour use' because of 'the playing of loud amplified music'.[78] In contrast with the apparently unruly Boheme, The Backstreet, a venue with a seven-days-per-week late licence, and located within this dense urban neighbourhood, had not received any noise complaints.[79] The phrasing of these exchanges was thick with insinuation, presenting an unjustifiably negative image of the venue and othering those who used it. Representing the applicants, planning consultants WYG referred to 'late associated patron movements and anti-social behaviour, [which] would not be conducive to a neighbourhood environment', and they argued that 'such noisy and disturbing activities [. . .] should be located within commercial districts [. . .]'.[80] These statements evoked a purer (and implicitly heteronormative) 'neighbourhood environment' under threat. They implied a context of rigid zoning, which has not been characteristic in London.

Against the council's concerns about the loss of a facility serving a specific group, the applicant argued that nightclubs, being *sui generis* according to the Town and Country Planning (Use Classes) Order (1987):

Macho City   159

cannot be distinguished within that use separately due to their style, i.e. that it is a specialist leather and rubber club in the same way a restaurant or hot food take-away may not be distinguished by the country of origin of its cuisine, e.g. fish and chip shop compared with a Chinese.[81]

This is an interesting, if somewhat provocative, comparison. While *sui generis* implies unique qualities, the use class it covers includes a vast range of typologies (theatres, petrol stations, casinos, amusement centres, car-hire businesses and so on). If the activities associated with a site change, there is usually a requirement for planning permission.[82] However, it is correct that there is no provision to protect distinctive, specialist qualities within a specific genre.

In dismissing The Backstreet's value, the applicant's planning consultant asserted that 'the area is adequately served by alternative venues serving the LGBT community'.[83] They cited the presence of one other nearby LGBTQ+ venue; two large LGBTQ+-hosting venues that regularly programmed the popular night 'Sink the Pink'; a cocktail bar in Broadway Market with no ostensible LGBTQ+ programming; and 'various venues' in Hackney and Shoreditch.[84] Presenting The Backstreet – with its very specific scene and clientele – and these venues as interchangeable suggests a misconception of diverse LGBTQ+ communities as a singular entity, and a lack of understanding of the heterogeneity of cultures across London's large LGBTQ+ population.[85]

The original scheme would have resulted in the loss of the existing club premises, and the applicants' original position was that 'it would be inappropriate to reprovide for a nightclub use'.[86] They then acquiesced by offering to support the relocation of the venue elsewhere in the borough.[87] Later iterations provided a basement which could potentially have allowed for The Backstreet's relocation, or for another club, with a maximum of 200 patrons.[88] An amendment was submitted, this time with a letter of support attached from The Backstreet's licensee (John Edwards), stating an agreement to accept the developer's offer of proposed basement premises in the new development.[89] However, the Planning Inspector understood the risk that this would be inviable as a 'weighty concern', due to potential conflicts over noise.[90] This represented a change of position, with the developer now describing the proposal for a venue in the scheme as 'providing for a unique pre-existing community facility'.[91]

The application was rejected again, on multiple grounds, with Tower Hamlets concluding that it represented 'overdevelopment that seeks to maximise not optimise the development potential of the site' and would cause harm that outweighed its potential public benefits.[92] The nightclub issue was one of five reasons for refusal:

> The proposed measures to re-provide the nightclub would be insufficient to secure the long term retention of a facility which serves the gay community. Likely noise complaints from residents of the proposed tower would be considered to present a significant risk to eventual closure of the nightclub.[93]

In the ensuing appeal, the developer changed position again, reopening the option of relocating the venue, at the venue operator's discretion.[94] At face value this offered the operator a choice. It included an agreement to fund storage of items and to fit out a new space to the venue's instructions. The wording was unclear as to who would undertake this work.[95] The offer also provided the developer with a way of side-stepping its commitment to re-provide the venue on the site. Since the developer had expressed ambivalence in its previous statements and actions, the local authority was understandably wary.[96]

Tower Hamlets' appeal case noted the site's extended history of providing community facilities, pointing back to the original cinema and linking this to the sequence of night-time venues.[97] Statements by City Hall circulating around this time, such as the mayor's *Cultural Infrastructure Plan* (2019), clearly deemed nightclubs to be community facilities. In justifying its refusal, the council made reference to new guidance, written under Sadiq Khan's tenure to supplement the London Plan, titled 'Culture and the Night-Time Economy' (2017), 'London at night: an evidence base for a 24-hour city' (2018) and to our UCL Urban Lab research on venue closures.[98] The council reasoned that the developer's new proposal to reprovide a venue in the scheme was an add-on that had not been thought through and that the character of the primarily residential development posed a threat to the club's sustenance because noise complaints would be likely. These assumptions seem reasonable on at least two grounds. First, the planning consultant's earlier negative views of nightclubs as part of residential development suggested a lack of serious intent to re-provide the venue in any sustainable way. Second, the evidence amassed by the GLA demonstrated that the introduction of Permitted Development rights in 2013, allowing conversion from commercial to residential uses, had led to noise complaints where clubs had previously existed for long periods with no issues.[99]

Building on The Joiners Arms case, the Tower Hamlets planning team's evidence to the appeal regarding The Backstreet referred to the Equality Act 2010 and the council's duty to ensure that the development would not disadvantage a protected group under the category of 'sexual orientation', 'namely individuals from the LGBT+ community and specifically with regard to the existing users, gay men'.[100] Beyond the locally specific requirements of ACVs, here the council considered its duty to include 'the local gay community and a geographically wider client group'.[101] It concluded that the only powers it had to ensure continued use for the LGBT+ community – rather than a more generic nightclub – would be through planning conditions or a Section 106 agreement. The consultant representing the developer contested these references to the Equality Act and to policy on the 'London at night' guidance and LGBTQ+ venues, objecting to these as new matters that had not been included as grounds for refusal and therefore did not carry weight in this planning appeal.[102]

End of an era

The local authority's case to protect The Backstreet was based on its particular use and clientele, and a detailed account of the space it occupied. It had no objection to the loss of the actually disused nightclub on the same site (Boheme).[103] Counter-intuitively, to protect The Backstreet as an extant nightclub, the council had to object to the developer's proposal to re-provide a space for it. In part, this was based on expert evidence about the acoustic impact of the proposed basement venue, noting that The Backstreet had avoided causing noise disturbance.[104] Its decision also went against a proposal that had the backing of the venue operator. The letter documenting this support was taken at face value, even though it had not been signed by the licensee himself.[105] In both cases, the council had to weigh up the licensees' decisions and actions and the wider representations they received from public consultations.

The council's case against proposals for a development with a new nightclub incorporated was based upon a detailed account of the precise architecture of The Backstreet – its size, at 200 square metres, its 'unique layout', its discreet entrance and smoking area, and its décor, which had been noted for its heritage value in public consultation responses (Plates 26 and 27). In evidence to the appeal, Tower Hamlets' planning officer commented:

> The club's décor is exceptionally unique with minimal furniture, however of note is a large cage within the main area of the club. Leather boots and chains hang from the ceiling and unique posters, some by the artist Tom of Finland, line the walls of the foyer and other parts of the club. The décor reflects the dress code, values and attitudes of the club.[106]

The local authority's response to the generalizing language and tone of insuation used by those representing the developer was therefore to offer a precise and detailed account of the venue's unique qualities, including its most interior and specialized features. Ultimately, the inspector did not accept that the club comprised community infrastructure focused on local need, as defined in Tower Hamlets' policies.[107] They did recognize, however, that the venue served to meet the needs of particular groups, and that the London Plan's policies on social infrastructure, and 'ensuring life chances for all', provided an impetus to protect such spaces.[108]

Ultimately, despite the council's efforts to defend it, The Backstreet closed in July 2022. The lease had expired. Unlike The Joiners, there was no broad customer base, and no campaign that formed to protest the impending redevelopment. Regulars were invited to say farewell at a closing party: 'The End of an Era'. In a series of life drawing events held in the space in the weeks before the keys were handed over, participants documented the assemblage of masculine signifiers: posters, oil drums, cages and other paraphernalia. A series of sales provided an open invitation to the highest cash bidder to 'take home a piece of history'.[109]

Arch attitude

Across the river, in neighbouring Southwark, Pulse was a commercial event space and the home of gay club XXL, which occupied five railway arches until it closed in September 2019. At 2,000 square metres, with a capacity of nearly 1,600 people, Pulse was one of the largest London venues run by a gay-identifying operator.[110] XXL was founded in 2000 by entrepreneurs Mark Ames and David Dindol as a men-only club, and at the time of its closure it was marketed as a club for: 'bears, cubs, chubs, muscle bears and their admirers from all backgrounds'.[111] It ran on two nights a week in London, but expanded, rather like G-A-Y (see Chapter 5), with monthly nights in Birmingham, Bristol and Brighton and, like The Backstreet, a brand presence at international events.

In 2019, XXL's 'male-only' dress code stated: 'no flip flops or open toed or high healed [sic] footwear; no female shoes, clothes, wigs, overtly female hairstyles and make-up' – a confusing and possibly unpoliceable specification.[112] Some venues are actively inclusive to all who identify as LGBTQ+ for political or commercial reasons. Many large venues have been purposefully inclusive to non-LGBTQ+ individuals. But it is not unusual for venues to be implicitly or explicitly centred towards primary groups on certain nights. At XXL, the orientation, originally, was towards gay men in their thirties and above, with larger bodies.[113] Clubbers may have included trans and bi-identifying men, of course, though these groups were not actively appealed to in XXL's marketing.

In UCL Urban Lab's survey in 2016, a number of white gay men, aged twenty-six to fifty, singled out XXL in response to the question, 'which currently operating LGBTQI nightlife events are most valuable to you and why?'[114] Although just a small sample, the survey responses are revealing. When discussing their understanding of the value of XXL one respondent, in his early thirties, remarked that there are 'few dance club options for older guys'. This resonated with one of the club owner's justifications for XXL's target market. It also raises a fair and frequent criticism of LGBTQ+ venues as being centred on younger people, and those who find this alienating may feel this more intensely as the overall number and diversity of venues diminishes. Even so, the overall provision of licensed premises is oriented towards relatively affluent cisgendered white gay men, and the leasehold owners or tenants (not to mention the freehold owners and other stakeholders) are usually cisgendered, white, middle-aged or older guys.

Respondents specifically understood XXL as a gay male space. One person described it as the 'best night for gay men'. Another remarked that it is one of the venues 'I visit most often and [that] cater to my "crowd"', qualifying that it was a relaxing venue with 'attitude-free clubbing'. The strong sense of group identity expressed in the survey returns is reflective of XXL's brand, which was built around particular masc tribes that originated in 1970s gay subculture. These respondents' evaluation of positive attributes of LGBTQ+ nightlife was quite typical (see Chapter 4). They connected anxiety about diminishing venues with the possibilities that clubs such as XXL offered. One asserted that: 'all spaces are valuable to allow freedom of expression to grow'. Another emphasized that 'there is no such thing as a "universal gay venue"' and that it is 'important to have diversity since there are many different kinds of venues catering to many different people'.

What was the context, in Southwark, for XXL as part of LGBTQ+ and wider nightlife infrastructure in the borough? Southwark has traditionally been under Labour administration.[115] The borough has a long history of cabaret, drag and disco venues, such as the early gay disco scene instigated by DJ Tricky Dicky at The Father

Red Cap in Camberwell in the 1970s, or the drag nights that featured at The Ship and Whale in the 1980s and 1990s.[116] In the 1980s Southwark council supported lesbian and gay community initiatives and spaces and had a Lesbian and Gay Working Party.[117] The Black Lesbian and Gay Centre Project, established in 1985, moved from Haringey to an appropriated railway arch in Peckham, Southwark, in 1992, where it stayed until its closure in 1999.[118] This was an important example of a multipurpose Southwark lesbian and gay venue with a progressive social agenda.

Although data shows that Southwark has a large LGBTQ+ population, at the time of writing, the mayor's 'Cultural Infrastructure Map' shows just one licensed venue in Southwark: Pulse, which has closed.[119] Pulse was owned and operated by gay men, so although it was a corporate event space and hosted a range of club nights, with XXL's two dedicated nights per week for gay men it fitted the GLA's criteria for an LGBT+ venue.[120] Southwark's response to the GLA's 2018 Night-time Commission research boasted of nightlife being 'a key part of our cultural infrastructure', citing Bankside (the neighbourhood where Pulse was located).[121] Without speculating about the reasons, it conceded that 'pubs and nightclubs are generally declining', while it also celebrated new 'theme bars' that 'are pushing the envelope beyond the traditional'.[122] Working within the national and London planning frameworks, Southwark's policy emphasis was towards the restriction and regulation of venues, rather than the proactive cultivation of spaces that have been responsive to the urban fabric.

In the 1990s and 2000s, in addition to the Black Lesbian and Gay Centre, many of the nightlife venues in Southwark had been located in large-capacity clubs in converted barrel-vaulted railway arches, or, in the case of the most commercially successful, Ministry of Sound (1991–), a bus garage.[123] Nightclub uses for these venues have been encouraged by Southwark and Network Rail. They benefit the local economy and are seen as part of the borough's attraction to local and overseas visitors.[124] But leaseholders who operate these venues, and the patrons they serve, tend to be displaced at a later stage in the gentrification process, when large-scale redevelopment takes hold (see Chapter 5).[125]

Bear necessities

The railway arches that Pulse had occupied were bought in 2015 by a consortium led by a Singaporean developer, Native Land, following its acquisition of a large development site, which included the office blocks Sampson and Ludgate Houses. Situated on either side of the arches that accommodated the club, Samson and Ludgate Houses were to be demolished to make way for a new cluster of tall buildings under a scheme led by PLP Architects.[126] Samson and Ludgate House had been purchased by Carlysle Group from Minerva for £228 million in 2005.[127] With the planning permission granted in 2014, Native Land purchased the plot for £308 million the following year.[128] The approved scheme concentrated on the redevelopment of Sampson and Ludgate Houses, but the proposal stated that 'the arches below the railway viaduct will be incorporated into the Proposed Development' and that the group would have 'the option of obtaining the leasehold for the arches from Network Rail'.[129] In a scheme that includes nine new buildings, converting the late nineteenth-century arches to 'retail, gym and community uses' was a central feature of the mixed-use development.[130]

In similarity with The Joiners Arms and The Backstreet, the original Samson and Ludgate Houses development proposal omitted to name the existing nightclub, describing the arches as 'underused', in order to project future 'active retail, amenity and cultural uses'.[131] Neither the original proposal nor the subsequent applications say a word about the specific operation and use of the venue by and for LGBTQ+ minorities, or its social or other values to these or other groups. The equalities statements are instead generic, such that the proposal is set out in terms of access: '[. . .] designed to meet the needs of all potential users regardless of disability, age or gender, and has been guided by all relevant inclusive design standards'.[132]

Together with their lawyers, Pulse's co-owners, Ames and his partner James McNeill (a businessman, whose background is in architecture) actively contested the Sampson and Ludgate House scheme on multiple grounds.[133] Although they did not have access to specific data from respondents who had mentioned XXL, Pulse made use of Urban Lab's data about the value of LGBTQ+ venues, and threats to them, to defend the club.[134] They argued that the scheme was 'cleansing non-conforming uses' and alleged that the developer's actions were homophobic.[135] The inference was that the development consortium, which was international and included Singaporean and Malaysian real estate companies, was socially conservative and discriminatory on the basis that a gay club would be undesirable for investors and would negatively affect the site's value.[136]

XXL's owners argued that they were not aware of the development, and that planning permission granted to them through a 2013 appeal had reassured them of the venue's right to continue.[137] Native Land's position was that Pulse could have objected to the public consultation on the 2014 application, with its references to the redevelopment of the arches, but did not do so. In 2012, responding to an application by Ames's company A&M Leisure to enlarge the venue, Southwark had advised that the venue's consent for use as a leisure venue, including a nightclub, had expired.[138] A 2013 hearing allowed the appeal, and a subsequent planning application was invited, submitted and approved. This gave permission for retrospective works and consent for continued use of the whole of the premises as an event space and club, with enlargement beneath an additional arch.

In initially rejecting the application, Southwark had raised concerns that are indicative of the challenges that nightlife venues can pose for local authorities in managing mixed-use environments. The refusal notice commented that:

> The continued use of the property will give rise to noise and disturbance, impacting on the amenities of nearby residential occupiers and the submitted noise report has not adequately addressed or set out mitigation against the impact of the proposal on the residential amenity of existing and future occupiers of the area.[139]

The council then cited a range of policies that the club's development would contravene. It is important to note that the council had been supportive of A&M Leisure's earlier approved application, so these were new criticisms, reflecting a change of attitude with regard to the area's wider redevelopment. The case in support of A&M Leisure's successful appeal, and the reasoning behind the inspector's approval, conveyed that the venue's operation fitted within the National Planning Policy Framework, the London Plan and Southwark's local plan.[140] The multipurpose, twenty-four-hour licensed nightclub and corporate leisure space was located in London's Central Activities Zone, an area in the city's 'globally iconic core', designated as such to consolidate its role as an economic generator for the UK: a mixed-use zone with a concentration of visitor attractions, businesses and residences, where 'London's unique heritage' should be protected.[141] The use of the site and business model fitted within the London Plan's focus on reusing brownfield sites, bringing them into economically productive use, providing visitor facilities; and also with Southwark's aim to support culture, creativity, diversity and employment, and the use of railway arches as leisure spaces. It was noted that the brick-and-steel arches provided appropriate noise insulation and that the venue was evidently well managed. Part of the package submitted with A&M's application was a detailed management plan along with the license and its extensive mandatory conditions.[142]

As with other comparable venues in the area, Pulse's operators had an expectation of longer-term residency, and this was manifested through their significant investment in conversion, fit-out and planning processes, otherwise known as 'sweat equity'.[143] This was dispelled when Network Rail either changed its plans or moved into the next phase of a plan that had not been made clear to its tenants. The situation highlights the ways in which social and cultural infrastructure, and nightlife spaces, are only valued under qualified, often temporary, terms. In this extractive neoliberal supergentrification model, as redevelopment proceeds and acting within their legal prerogative, land and building owners can sidestep ethical responsibilities towards those from whose energy and labour their investments have benefitted. In Pulse's case, the owners were particularly aggrieved because they had taken out a thirty-year lease and had invested £1m to develop the space into an events centre and nightclub.[144]

The XXL saga's various stages reflect differences in the approaches to night-time governance and engagement with LGBT+ populations and heritage taken by Boris Johnson and Sadiq Khan. The dispute between Southwark and XXL, which directly involved the mayors, rested on a technicality. In 2013, Boris Johnson had delegated the planning decision on the scheme to Southwark, but with the condition that:

> An equalities impact assessment should be provided to assess the impact of the loss of the gay nightclub which currently operates in the arches [. . .]

> Subject to the equalities impact of the loss of the nightclub the principle of a mixed-use development with a cultural element is in accordance with policy 2.11 of the London Plan, and is welcomed. The mix of uses would offer a vibrant and interesting offer to the area, and the addition of retail and other commercial services to serve local residential needs is welcomed.[145]

The recommendation that a formal Equalities Impact Assessment should be undertaken, under the Equality Act 2010, was therefore clear, but this was based on the presumption that the venue would be lost, rather than as an act to prevent this or to explore alternatives or to reincorporate it. In the event, no such assessment was undertaken. This was because the proposal went to the mayor's office at the same time that Southwark had refused the nightclub's application for continued use. From the GLA's point of view, therefore, the EqIA was no longer required.[146] However, Southwark's refusal of Pulse's continuing use of the venue was overturned at appeal.[147] These processes were convoluted and are, as Vaughan and Jessup suggest, unclear in the public record.[148] The owners accused Southwark of neglecting to protect the venue because it was considered undesirable by the developer and could thereby jeopardize income from a Section 106 agreement.[149]

XXL's owners also criticized the developers for the contradiction between their scheme's provision of new community venues and the displacement of Pulse. Presenting Pulse to be an inclusive and community-centred space, they remarked:

> Yet again, London is about to lose something that is unique to its character: the idea of open arms. This is a reflection on our society. There is no room for difference; everything has to be sterilised and the same. This is being done by people who don't care about London's community. All they care about is turning a buck.[150]

Through such rhetoric, XXL's owners presented themselves in the altruistic light of socially responsible capitalists, pointing to their support for a range of LGBTQ+ community organizations.[151] This example highlights how some large-scale nightclub operators are networked into the wider economy through philanthropic and charitable work, and how in turn these associations are performatively mobilized as soft power to support private interests and to bolster individual and company reputations. Where such transactions lack transparency, or if they contradict other expressions of values, or appear to be cynical 'pinkwashing' exercises for business interests, they are understandably received sceptically.

As well as being part of the venue's appeal to the GLA for protection, Pulse's references to work with wider LGBTQ+ communities, and blue-chip clients, were an attempt to detoxify the XXL brand. This had been tainted by Ames's social media outbursts, including femmephobic and Islamophobic statements, and by the club's door policy and practices.[152] In August 2018, stating that 'we don't allow femininity', XXL's bouncers created controversy by refusing entry to Pavel Vacek, who was wearing heels.[153] This sparked a protest led by drag queen Mary Poppers.[154] Ames fanned the flames with his public Facebook posts:

> Bollox to all this PC [political correctness].
> Toxic masculinity? Why is it toxic to be masculine?[155]

Some of Ames's statements have been followed by qualified apologies, admissions of ill-judgement, references to personal circumstances, retractions and a defence of the club for its role in serving 'fat, older and masculine' gay men.[156] On the one hand, Ames dismissed 'the rest of the scene or today's so called community or society' wholesale, but on the other he used the debate regarding Vacek's refusal as an occasion to invite those offended by the club's policy to propose new nights at Pulse for different audiences.[157]

These interventions revealed XXL's desire to exclude certain groups, and in doing so the club exhibited many of the negative aspects of LGBTQ+ scenes and venues that have recently been the focus of criticism within LGBTQ+ communities (see Chapter 4).[158] The threat to close XXL, the campaigns associated with it, and a proposition (known as XXL Beacon) to Native Land to incorporate into the development an LGBTQ+ community space which XXL would lead, have understandably been met with mixed responses from within LGBTQ+ communities, including from those who have been part of campaigns to protect venues.[159] The explicit views and unconscious disclosures of XXL's owners, and the campaign that formed around the club, mean that even with the risk of losing a dedicated LGBTQ+ space many were willing to let go of XXL and Pulse, and were even pleased to see it close. Others have cautioned that the loss of any large-capacity venue should be fought. One prominent campaigner commented:

> [S]ome of these venues are just businesses and they've never really supported us. I find it absolutely appalling that XXL is now jumping on us and asking us to support them; when, you know, Mark [Ames] has been so Islamophobic online, and openly so . . . I think, you know, we're doing ourselves a disservice if we're not very clear about who has supported us.[160]

The objections have not been towards the club's 'men only' door policy *per se*, but rather with the contradictions between opportunistic engagement with the LGBTQ+ community and the venue's commercial priorities and discriminatory attitudes.

Scholarship by the cultural historian Les Wright and his collaborators has elucidated the emergence and character of bear culture within specific historical and geographical circumstances. In the US in the 1970s and 1980s, bear identities were being formulated in parallel with other figurations such as the clone and the leatherman. These were shaped by interactions across gay communities, and alongside other movements that opposed body fascism and body conformity. Beardom was an antidote to the party scenes of the 1970s and the issues of burnout, alcoholism and drug dependency that some experienced, and it was a response to the stigmatization and physical emaciation associated with HIV/AIDS. It manifested as a desire to project healthy, abundant bodies, and to foster a nurturing 'spirit of survivorship'.[161] Unlike the clone, bear culture was premised not on the reproduction of sameness, but on bodily and gender diversity, and as a challenge to hegemonic masculinity. For Wright, the bear emerged in part as a reaction to the homophobic rejection of gay men as effeminate. It was premised on being comfortable within, and being free to move within, a matrix of masculinities. He continues:

> Potentially, bears represent a new option, rather than the reverse of androgyny. Instead of a 'neutral' engenderment as devoid of either gender as possible, the bear ideal embodies positive qualities of both masculine and feminine, uniting traditional gender polarities – strong and sensitive, gruff and affectionate, independent minded and nurturing.[162]

In distinction from other gay male identities that were more polarized within a femme-butch binary, the bear therefore accommodated different expressions of masculinity.[163]

It arose, as Wright puts it, 'out of an impulse to create "safe spaces" for a wide range of homosocial identifications'.[164] The defensive framing of XXL through a reductive, singular, femme-excluding masculinity, Ames's rejection of the concept of 'toxic masculinity', and the club's commercial priorities, all combine to distance it from the origins of bear culture. As Wright contends, the intertwining of bear aesthetics with market capitalism and globalization diluted the ideal and countered its liberatory or utopian possibilities.[165] As geographer Nick McGlynn has argued, the dispersal of bear culture calls for attention to local variations, with bear spaces serving valuable functions for many gay, bisexual and queer men.[166] In XXL's case, the commercial framing of that culture mirrored the aggressive and exclusionary dynamics of urban redevelopment that Pulse itself ultimately fell victim to.

XXL's case became a wicked problem for the city authorities – it was a venue that excluded many in the LGBTQ+ spectrum, and one that did not have as wide grassroots support compared with other more inclusive venues, even if it did have many backers. In 2017, the venue's owners petitioned the mayor and the night czar for assistance and met with the night czar and GLA officers on a number of occasions, receiving support and advice via correspondence.[167] Ames's personal views and attitude made association with the venue potentially toxic for the GLA and counter to the wider attempts to protect queer venues as part of the city's cultural and social infrastructure. When asked to look into XXL's case, the night czar first requested a response to the allegations of Islamophobia, transphobia and femmephobia.[168] The GLA and night czar did then proceed to support the venue. The GLA's officers noted that the previous mayor, Boris Johnson, had decided to delegate the case to Southwark, which meant that Sadiq Khan's powers were limited.[169] What they were able to do was to broker discussions between XXL and Southwark and meet with the venue's team to discuss the proposal they had drafted for an LGBTQ+ community centre, XXL Beacon.[170] Despite the public investments made by the GLA to help the venue, in 2019 XXL publicly criticized the mayor's office for not doing enough.[171] They organized a 'Save Our Scene' Pride delegation and XXL afterparty, using posters of Lamé and Khan as part of the trio of the three wise monkeys, suggesting that they were turning a blind eye to the developers' act of 'social cleansing', and had not supported XXL.

Although XXL did not manage to avoid closure, the GLA's and night czar's intervention and collaboration with Southwark led to a Section 106 agreement with an obligation for Native Land to provide space for a new LGBTQ+ community venue. This followed the model of the agreement negotiated in Tower Hamlets in response to the loss of The Joiners Arms. A number of active community groups, including XXL and FOTJA, were invited to submit proposals. These were evaluated by a panel according to how the proposal addressed the needs of Southwark's LGBT populations. It will be a positive outcome if Southwark and the developer continue to safeguard accommodation for LGBTQ+ operators who have an inclusive community focus within the provision of cultural and performance space afforded by the railway arches on the site. XXL Beacon's proposal might have been welcomed by LGBTQ+ communities, but its credentials were undermined by the company's past statements and actions, so that it was perceived as a cynical last-ditch proposition to manipulate the planning process.

Masculinities are 'constructed in relation to other entities, including bodies, identities, institutions, ideas, social norms and categories and historical and geographical contexts', the governance of night-spaces and policies and practices of urban redevelopment.[172] Night-time premises can permit or foster critiques of hegemonic archetypes of masculinity as well as being complicit in their reproduction.[173] Gay bars have been associated with problematic and normative masculinities, but are also understood as places of men's caring, and as settings for the emergence of new or re-scripted gendered and sexual subjectivities.[174]

In the cases described in this chapter, the venue operators – typically for London's LGBTQ+ licensed premises – were all white, cisgendered, middle-aged or older gay men, and the original target clientele for the venues was in each case gay men. The Joiners Arms rooted its identity in associations with local, working-class masculinity and with the mainstream rights agendas that advanced during the New Labour administration. It also provided a permissive environment that featured a broader culture of sexual and gender diversity. The Backstreet and XXL were exclusively 'men only' and framed through strict codes rooted in gay, BDSM and bear subcultures respectively. Segregated spaces, as safer spaces, linked to genres of desire and specific subcultures and subjectivities are in general passionately defended by queer communities. But the question of which gendered subjectivities are identified or disidentified with, addressed, or overlooked, has been a continuing source of debate and stimulus for change in the history of LGBTQ+ venues.

Across the cases of The Joiners Arms, The Backstreet and Pulse/XXL, we see the bespoke ways in which the dynamics of supergentrification in the 2010s interacted with constructions of sexual and gender diversity. Their positioning in relation to historic and contemporary social movements, and the distinctive communities they engage, reveal power differentials within London's diverse LGBTQ+ population. These cases demonstrate how LGBTQ+ premises are deeply embedded in and responsive to sites and buildings with long-term cultural and leisure uses. There are common features, such as the ways in which extant venues are erased or misconstrued in planning submissions. Conflicts have arisen where the venues' social value and the clientele they serve, and the forms of sociality they have enabled, have been overlooked, and over the weight and interpretation of policies, plans and other evidence regarding the definition of community facilities and the balance of public good. It is evident that although initially overlooked in redevelopment processes, LGBTQ+ uses and heritage have surfaced in a variety of new ways. The situations display differences and tensions between the sense of attachment to these venues held by operators, customers, campaigners and developers, as well as disparities in their resources. They show the dynamic ways that LGBTQ+ populations have had to engage with sites of material heritage. The immediate disassembly of The Joiners Arms and the resistance that followed contrasts with The Backstreet's decision to accept closure and the dispersal of its of paraphernalia to customers' homes. The strong branding of XXL in bear culture demonstrates equally dense but more mobile layers of signification. The opportunities for new LGBTQ+ community centres that have arisen show how this typology has re-emerged, appropriating space in new-builds in contrast with the use of former industrial buildings in the 1980s and early 1990s.

As these processes have unfolded, some local authorities, backed by City Hall, have acquired heightened knowledge and willingness to intervene to protect LGBTQ+ venues, and to think through scenarios to establish new and more inclusive spaces within large-scale development contexts. These processes have required the GLA and campaign groups to make a case for the general value of all LGBTQ+ premises. They have also required planning authorities to articulate and address specific LGBTQ+ publics, their present and future needs and their heritage, and to experiment with available planning tools to foster new multipurpose venues. In so doing, they have had to consider evidence from lived experience, the dynamic ways individuals and groups negotiate their identities, and the complexity of multifunctional venues that adapt and have changing and dispersed constituencies. They have used equalities legislation and policy to instruct developers to address specific minorities as a condition of development. They have collaborated with campaigners dedicated to imagining better worlds that address imbalances of resources and the weight of discrimination and oppression. Far from a straightforward narrative of progress, the outcomes of each redevelopment scenario are still unfolding and are contingent upon multiple factors.

8

Pandemic premises

In 2020, the coronavirus pandemic prompted the sudden lockdown of night-time and community venues across the globe. As environments for socializing and proximity, often associated with drinking and intoxication, bars and clubs were understandably a locus of safety concerns and fears. They were also actively stigmatized as places of potential virus transmission. Some of the highest-profile and most alarmist international media stories about nightlife focused on LGBTQ+ scenes.[1] At the end of the first national lockdown in the UK, the government chose to reopen the night-time economy on a Saturday night.[2] Images of London's crowded Soho streets, a prominent 'gay village', were disseminated worldwide, accompanied by a tone of moral outrage towards irresponsible revellers.[3]

As London's night czar Amy Lamé observed, with reference to the UK government's public health slogan, 'the idea of "staying home to stay safe" is an oxymoron for so many [LGBTQ+] people [. . .] we've had to leave our homes [to stay safe], be they just up the road or be they on the other side of the world'.[4] As the pandemic took hold, evidence quickly emerged about the negative impacts of lockdowns on the mental health and well-being of LGBTQ+ populations, particularly the effects of increased isolation, and experiences of homophobia and transphobia in the home for young people.[5] Where national government support was lacking, vital community services emerged to fill the vacuum. Many of these were provided through the networks of existing venues and collectives. As one promoter put it, 'WhatsApp groups that used to just be about organising nights, and which nights people should go to, have become spaces where queer mutual aid has taken precedence'.[6]

The Outside Project, as an independent LGBTQI+ community shelter, centre and refuge, demonstrates radical and intersectional queer mutualism which works across the challenges faced by those who use its spaces and services. This grassroots project emerged as a pilot in 2017 and used a crowdfunding campaign to purchase a bus that provided an overnight shelter for people in crisis. In 2018, as a response to the reportedly high proportion of the homeless population who are queer, and with support from the mayor and GLA, the group was able to convert a former fire station in Camberwell into a community space and emergency accommodation.[7] The Outside Project exemplifies the positive ways grassroots organizations have recently worked collaboratively with City Hall and local authorities, leading the way for a new generation of LGBTQ+ community venues.[8] Prior to the pandemic, they received financial support from the Mayor of London's Rough Sleeping Innovation Fund. Beyond these interfaces with

172   *Queer Premises*

City Hall, The Outside Project suggests further potential for queer organizations to 'support new radical forms of democracy' – a call recently made by urbanist Vanesa Castán Broto in relation to participatory planning.[9]

During the pandemic, The Outside Project used its social media accounts to establish a London LGBTQI+ Covid-19 Mutual Aid network, serving those who were sick or isolating.[10] Yet the challenges the service has faced, especially during a pandemic, demonstrate how difficult it is to find and keep buildings for community uses. The service was forced to move to a hotel in spring 2021 in order to offer residents individual bathrooms to help manage quarantine requirements.[11] A plan to move the emergency shelter into longer-term accommodation fell through in March 2022. It has nonetheless succeeded in setting up a lively, multipurpose community centre in Borough, south-east London, invoking the centres of the 1970s and 1980s to garner political support. While opportunities for new premises are sought, the project continues to provide emergency housing advice and other vital services.

The demands of the pandemic exacerbated the already extreme pressures faced by venues and other forms of social and cultural infrastructure: high land and property values and rents, government prioritization of big business interests, years of austerity and cuts to public services, and the uncertainties that have followed Brexit. Lockdowns forced closures, while support packages, thought up quickly by an ill-prepared government, offered help and hope to some types of venue while entirely overlooking others.[12] Nightclubs and club events were neglected, to the dismay of industry representatives. The Night Time Industries Association made their case primarily on economic grounds, but the wider social and cultural value of these venues, especially those for minority populations, was neglected.[13]

With venues shut or curfewed, and gigs cancelled, the impacts of Covid-19 were acutely felt by night-time leisure sector workers and creative freelancers. Some businesses, including London LGBTQ+ venues, set up 'pay it forward' or other forms of fundraising for their own survival and for casual workers in their employ – those who fell between the gaps and were not eligible for the government's furlough scheme.[14] Financial aid for LGBTQ+ businesses was made available by an expanded 'Culture at Risk' team in City Hall.[15] Demand was inevitably high. Subsequent research by sociologists Mark McCormack and Fiona Measham has highlighted the negative impacts of the pandemic on queer creatives' livelihoods, health and mental health, experienced more intensely among people of colour and others with experiences of marginalization along multiple lines.[16] The research also recorded that the most formal nightlife, represented by licensed venues, was 'resilient with no queer venues closing', referencing the supportive work of City Hall and grants from the UK government's Culture Recovery Fund, distributed by Arts Council England.[17] The direct (if partial) state support offered during the pandemic would have seemed unimaginable back in 2015, when the crisis over threats to venues from redevelopment was at its peak.

After the lockdowns, continuing safety fears over Covid-19 reduced footfall to nightlife premises.[18] The virus put these venues' longer-term survival further into jeopardy. Many LGBTQ+ night-spaces are late-night trading venues, so these were hit hard by curfews on top of lockdowns and significant reductions in the numbers of customers who could safely be admitted.[19] Temporary flexibility in regulation facilitated venues' physical extension into the public realm through increased outdoor and pavement seating, alongside take-away services. Central government support to help the hospitality, entertainment and cultural sectors re-establish themselves was limited. A retail, hospitality and leisure grant, administered through local councils, was made available to businesses.[20] Yet this was only for those businesses with a ratable value under a certain threshold, meaning that few venues were eligible due to London's high property prices.[21]

So far as nightlife and the hospitality sector were concerned, as in other cultural sectors, the pandemic threw everything into a state of flux, with a need both to safeguard and adapt. It brought challenges and inequalities that were already present for queer night scenes into sharper relief, making it more urgent to address these, while also coping with decreasing resources and a reduced capacity to function beyond survival mode. Some venue operators held on to a hope that lockdowns would be a short-lived setback, or that 'something good would come out of' the dramatic shock.[22] Small changes – such as the continuation of table service or the extension into adjacent exterior space – had to be set against larger problems, such as the staffing and supply shortages created or compounded by Brexit. For others, there has been a desire for wider changes to address problems and inequalities woven deeply into venues' operational models, or for a total reset following the enforced shutdown. This has manifested in various ways – whether in terms of increasing physical accessibility and social inclusivity, shifting away from alcohol sales as a main driver of profit, or through a desire for a more strategically politicized nightlife.[23] Emerging evidence suggests that the pandemic did not reduce the demand for venues, but rather underscored their importance in sustaining the livelihoods of queer creatives, LGBTQ+ populations, and the public life of the city more broadly.[24] Those who run, work in and use the venues are still in survival mode. Even so, interesting things are happening. Workers at Dalston Superstore, a club in East London, have unionized and, connecting with UNITE which is the largest trade union in the UK, they are addressing challenges experienced by queer night-time workers in synergy with the wider trade union movement.[25] In their research, McCormack and Measham have proposed that City Hall establish a Queer Creatives Forum, expanding the model of its LGBTQ+ Venues Forum.[26] Having been set up in response to the threats to venues in the late 2010s, the LGBTQ+ Venues Forum gained importance for information sharing and collaboration during the pandemic. It seems likely that the new network will be established, although, as this book has shown, such structures of engagement are vulnerable to political shifts.

In March 2020, naming the virus 'the great mutation', trans philosopher Paul B. Preciado remarked: 'When I went to my bed, the world was close, collective, viscous, and dirty. When I got out of bed, it had become distant, individual, dry, and hygienic.'[27] This resonates with the image of venues as they tentatively reopened under social distancing rules, adapting their operational models with the new requirements. These included staff training and mask-wearing, the social distancing of tables, reduced capacity, control of movement and increased ventilation, the monitoring of customers' temperatures and any visible symptoms, and the use of mobile-phone technology to facilitate booking and transactions and to check test results and vaccination certificates.[28] Reopening therefore required careful planning, and bars and pubs took their public health responsibilities seriously. G-A-Y's Jeremy Joseph led a legal campaign to challenge a 10.00 pm curfew imposed by the government, but also offered the use of Heaven as a pop-up vaccination centre.[29] Although these actions reflect wider contradictions discussed in earlier chapters, the performative use of Heaven emphasized the role of venues as places of care linked into a wider public health infrastructure. New and changing regulations impacted on venues as small businesses that operate with small profit margins.

This book has shown that if queer venues have been associated with intimacy, proximity and serendipitous encounters, they have also been planned, produced and managed in creative tension with the limitations set by the legal, governance and economic models of the day. The pandemic regulations for licensed premises meant that these tensions were expressed more visibly through the emphatic performances of risk management with multiple aims: to protect operators and employees, to build trust and safeguard associated communities, to allay consumers' fears and to satisfy licence requirements. Queer venues, through their historical uses and association with the AIDS epidemic and HIV prevention, and because of the other health inequalities faced by these populations, could draw from experience of being directly connected with and adaptable to urban health infrastructures. The requirements for monitoring venue attendees and keeping and reporting data had different implications for different demographic groups. Within LGBTQ+ populations, these included generational differences, such as for those with lived experience of aggressive policing of bars and clubs, or for those not 'out', or only out in certain times and places. The improvised qualities of queer venues, which have often repurposed older buildings, and their locations in underground and interior spaces affected their capacity to respond to increased need for air circulation or purification.

If venues were closed and then forced to reopen in more highly regulated modes, their promoters also embraced technology to extend their activities in new ways. Online spaces quickly proliferated, expanding reach and reconfiguring the circuits that connect venues and nightlife events with activism, fundraising and creative production. Lo Marshall has documented the success of 'Queer House Party', a London-based Zoom-enabled party.[30] It created a space of joy and solidarity for a local and international audience, helping to counter the anxieties triggered by the pandemic and by isolation at home. The organizers intended to transcend some of the exclusionary dynamics associated with physical LGBTQ+ night-spaces. Since lockdowns have ended, Queer House Party – which was already a hybrid, virtual space that connected private homes – continues online, with additional events hosted in-person, in licensed premises, and still hooked up via Zoom.

Zoom events run by the Duckie collective during lockdowns further suggest how an established and locally embedded scene could experiment with hybrid formats. When regulations permitted, some of Duckie's online productions were run from otherwise empty cabaret venues. Others were more dispersed. At a time when flights were grounded, one such event, 'Duckie International', featured artists from Toronto, Johannesburg, Bytom, Goiânia and Hospet, their performances interspersed with live links to the living rooms-turned-dance floors of Duckie's loyal London regulars and its wider national and international following. Featuring inevitable online

Pandemic Premises 175

disruptions and delays, translations, miscommunications and signal drops, Duckie International showed how London's queer nightlife scenes could quickly reach new places and audiences. Given Duckie's political standpoint and experience in working internationally (see Chapter 6), this was not an expansionist, neo-colonial extension of Western identities and rights-based politics to different parts of the world. Rather, its online offer involved careful curation of a collective engagement with artists challenging normative constructions of gender and sexuality in a diversity of contexts. Like the responsive and mutualist work of The Outside Project, such events manifest the practice-based poetics of queer infrastructure imagined by Lauren Berlant, discussed in Chapter 1: emergent multimedia practices, enabling a multidirectional set of encounters, responding to crises through facilitating new counterpublics and spaces of activism and care.[31]

In August 2020, between lockdowns, at UCL Urban Lab we were given access to the Royal Vauxhall Tavern to undertake the first ever 3D-laser scan of a queer venue and its surroundings (Figure 6.2; Plates 28–30). The scan data adds to the archive of this most archived of all of the UK's queer sites. The images produced from this data show empty interiors, barstools standing in for missing punters, outside seating and temporary fencing stacked against the building, while traces of passers-by etch the contours of eerie pandemic city streets. The scan allows normally inaccessible bird's-eye views, showing the venue as both an island of a since-demolished townscape and as fully woven into the urban grain. In other glitch-ridden renders, the materiality of walls and surfaces dissolves, becoming transparent, or they superimpose multiple frames. Rendered as film, we can float through the data, which pulls baroquely towards the centre of the RVT, to what would be the dance floor, hovering between distinct but now blurred interior spaces – bar, saloon, stage, dressing room, toilets. Walls pixelate, breaking down the separation between the interior of the venue and the exterior of the Pleasure Gardens. A small tent has been pitched against the exterior wall, directly behind the stage, an emergency refuge clinging to the island that the pub forms. Might the accidental documentation of this incidental structure prompt us to recalibrate our understanding of venues' relationships with privilege, precarity, permanence or collective fragility?

The cases in this book have shown how queer scenes and venues have mutated in the recent past. They bring into focus the multiplicity of ways that diverse LGBTQ+ populations, with differing resources and access to space, connect into or are circumvented by the transactions that shape urban governance and redevelopment. They demonstrate how queer subjects have been recognized or overlooked in planning, and how changing subjectivities are formulated and continuously reinvented through interactions with venues, shaped by intra-community politics and wider socio-economic and cultural contexts and priorities. Venues associated with these populations can be understood as nodes within a wider queer infrastructure through which resources are transported, livelihoods are sustained and heterogeneous forms of sociality are enabled within and across different generations.

Licensed premises are only the most visible surface of this infrastructure. They are nonetheless an important gauge, since they reflect and actively shape processes of social and cultural reproduction within LGBTQ+ populations. Influential entrepreneurial individuals and collectives, with different access to resources, shape multiple venues in multiple neighbourhoods. Networks of venues are connected through political and cultural affinities, while they are also characterized by intra-community tensions and logics of disidentification. As new scenes appear and incubate new premises, these are facilitated through and extended by available communications and publishing technologies. The look, feel and location of specific premises, and the contours of different typologies, are shaped by interacting external drivers, including economic cycles and consumer markets, planning policy and the availability of space.

The model of a dynamic queer infrastructure highlights the variety of interconnected spaces and activities, power asymmetries in the distribution of resources, the circulation of groups between venues, and their capacity to network into structures of governance and economic circuits through interfaces that recalibrate over time. As this book evidences, the sudden withdrawal of public funds and governance structures in the late 1980s cut off resources for many innovative and intersectionally aware queer businesses, civic society and cultural initiatives. Some closed, others managed to adapt and survive. Commercial scenes expanded. The recent past, as the chapters also recount, has brought forward conversations about the extent to which different cohorts' needs have been addressed or overlooked in the commercial sector that thrived until the mid-2000s, with its profit model centred on alcohol consumption. The increased attention to night-time governance and recognition of LGBTQ+ venues as social and cultural infrastructure have provided helpful grounds to understand and compare the varied qualities of venues. At a time of decreasing resources and changing demand, it is necessary to understand the distinct models and challenges they face, and the different forms of value they produce.

In London since the late-2000s, protected characteristics specified in legislation and policy have been a tool through which minority interests have been articulated in attempts to alleviate the negative impacts of redevelopment. These inherently limited designations have been mobilized in response to, and in parallel with, online and in-person grassroots campaigns, where sexual and gender diversity are expressed in nuanced ways with reference to lived experience. The venue closures of the mid-2010s, and the pressures created in redevelopment contexts, prompted reflection on the uneven provision of space for different constituent groups and the lack of diversity among operators of licensed venues. The campaigns and resistance that emerged, in parallel with other grassroots campaigns about housing and gentrification, both defended the social value of existing queer venues and created new spaces.

Although the pandemic has necessarily increased certain forms of visibility and monitoring of the most formal venues, the scenes, collectives and spaces that are less visible and accounted for have played a vital role and will continue to do so. City authorities, planners and community organizations will need to continue to develop ways of articulating and nurturing the social value of temporary, mobile, insecure LGBTQ+ spaces. Even so, the research discussed in this book shows that there is no clear separation between venues and the scenes they accommodate, between the formal and the informal. Nor is there a proportional relationship between social value and longevity or formality. Licensed venues discreetly foster activities and services that are at once vital and transient.

For the more and less formal of venues, survival and sustenance will be based on collaboration, and the future will be enriched through conversations about forms of queer mutualism, and by learning from the most imaginative multipurpose venues and initiatives from the past. In recent years, as this book has shown, what Boris Johnson's government described as the 'outdated', 'cumbersome', 'complex' and 'slow' tools of planning have been vital as venues, campaign groups, local authorities and City Hall, have collaborated to safeguard existing venues and imagine new ones.[32] Developers have recently been prompted to make commitments to community infrastructure specifically for protected minorities, including LGBTQ+ populations. In the context of the massive profits made through transactions in land and property these returns are tiny.

Through ongoing and emerging crises – not least the impacts of the current energy crisis on struggling small businesses – the case for the overlooked cultural and heritage value of venues will need to be restated. No venue is currently secure, yet some are more so than others. At a time of decreased income, there are increased imperatives to link financial and operational models strategically to the production of social value; and to take inspiration from the ways that queer venues have always blended with emerging technologies and have accommodated a multiplicity of functions and populations.

Queer infrastructures are extendable, projective and strategic, allowing possibilities for different ways of being in the future, for the transmission of knowledge and intergenerational exchange. Positive, green shoots in London include the energetic and successful campaigns to protect long-standing venues, and even new ones opening, opportunities to purpose-design inclusive spaces, and the proliferation of events, with night-space operators facilitating more intentional and collective forms of nightlife. New multifunctional spaces can provide platforms to share and build resources and create coalitions. These could also be the places to take forward discussions about how inclusive planning, policy or architecture can help shape better outcomes for marginalized minorities within globalized processes of urban change.

Notes

Introduction

1 As a default, I use the initials 'LGBTQ+' to refer to lesbian, gay, bisexual, trans, queer, non-binary plus other people who do not conform to or are excluded by norms of sexuality, sex and gender. The terminology I use varies according to the historical context of each chapter, reflecting the precise words in circulation and the content of sources. The term 'queer' is also dependent on context. I use it in its affirmative and inclusive form, reclaimed by activists in the 1980s, to work against norms of gender and/or sexuality. I engage with queer theory and activism, where 'queer' conveys a defiant political orientation, opposed to cis-, hetero- and homonormativity, and critical of colonial, racialized, patriarchal capitalism and related structures of oppression. Where queer is used in this way, it often communicates a collective politics rather than an identity category, and it exposes the limits of such categories and troubles them. This sense can be in tension with the commonplace usage of 'queer' today as a synonym and umbrella term for 'LGBT'. Such distinctions are sometimes relevant to my case studies where there is a need to distinguish political and other qualitative differences that arise in relation to LGBTQ+ venues.

2 Although the ongoing global HIV/AIDS epidemic, which began in 1981, continues to affect millions globally, I use the phrase 'the AIDS crisis' to refer to the 1980s and 1990s as is common.

Chapter 1

1 Scholarship on sexuality, gender and urban space is extensive. The empirical evidence discussed in the following chapters is informed by insights from queer history and theory, urban geography, history and sociology, architectural history and theory and urban studies. These disciplines intersect with a wide range of practices, from activism to the built environment professions. Given the volume and scope of academic debates on sexuality and gender in geography, literature reviews have been published regularly, where the authors reflect on key themes and gaps and propose new directions. Reviews by scholars located in other disciplines have engaged a wider range of contributions on queer space, place and history, in literature and art, and the built environment. For reviews in geography, see: Jon Binnie and Gill Valentine, 'Geographies of Sexuality – A Review of Progress', *Progress in Human Geography* 23, no. 2 (1999): 175–87; Melissa W. Wright, 'Gender and Geography II: Bridging the Gap – Feminist, Queer, and the Geographical Imaginary', *Progress in Human Geography* 34, no. 1 (2010): 56–66; Michael Brown, 'Gender and Sexuality I: Intersectional Anxieties', *Progress in Human Geography* 36, no. 4 (2012): 541–50; Michael Brown, 'Gender and Sexuality II: There Goes the Gayborhood?', *Progress in Human Geography* 38, no. 3 (2014): 457–65; Gavin Brown and Kath Browne (eds.),

The Routledge Research Companion to Geographies of Sex and Sexualities (Routledge Handbooks Online, 2016); Phil Hubbard, 'Geography and Sexuality: Why Space (Still) Matters', *Sexualities* 21, no. 8 (2018): 1295–9. For wider interdisciplinary reviews see: Gordon Brent Ingram, Anne-Marie Bouthillette, and Yolanda Retter (eds.), *Queers in Space: Communities, Public Places, Sites of Resistance* (Seattle, Wash.: Bay Press, 1997); Dianne Chisholm, *Queer Constellations: Subcultural Space in the Wake of the City* (Minneapolis: University of Minnesota Press, 2004); Petra L Doan (ed.), *Planning and LGBTQ Communities: The Need for Inclusive Queer Spaces* (New York: Routledge, 2015); Petra L. Doan (ed.), *Queerying Planning: Challenging Heteronormative Assumptions and Reframing Planning Practice* (London and New York: Routledge, 2016); Brent Pilkey, Rachael M. Scicluna, Ben Campkin, and Barbara Penner (eds.), *Sexuality and Gender at Home: Experience, Politics, Transgression* (London and New York: Bloomsbury, 2017); Olivier Vallerand, 'Home Is the Place We All Share', *Journal of Architectural Education* 67, no. 1 (7 March 2013): 64–75.

2 For comparison, on the 'historical texture' and generational shifts in feminist theory, see Karen Burns, 'A Girl's Own Adventure', *Journal of Architectural Education* 65, no. 2 (2012): 125–34.

3 Doan (ed.), *Planning and LGBTQ Communities*; Doan (ed.), *Queerying Planning*; Michael Frisch, 'Planning as a Heterosexist Project', *Journal of Planning Education and Research* 21, no. 3 (2002): 254–66.

4 See, for example, Vanesa Castán Broto, 'Queering Participatory Planning', *Environment and Urbanization* 33, no. 2 (2021): 310–29; Amin Ghaziani and Matt Brim (eds.), *Imagining Queer Methods* (New York: New York University Press, 2019); Marko Jobst and Naomi Stead, *Queering Architecture: Methods, Practices, Spaces, Pedagogies* (London: Bloomsbury, 2023); Natalie Oswin, 'Planetary Urbanization: A View from Outside', *Environment and Planning D: Society and Space* 36, no. 3 (2018): 540–6; 541; Paul B. Preciado, 'Architecture as a Practice of Biopolitical Disobedience', *Log*, no. 25 (2012): 121–34.

5 José Esteban Muñoz, *Cruising Utopia: The Then and There of Queer Futurity* (New York and London: New York University Press, 2009), 3.

6 For an account of non-class-based social movements and the challenges they posed to social analysts, see: Lawrence Knopp, 'Social Theory, Social Movements and Public Policy: Recent Accomplishments of the Gay and Lesbian Movements in Minneapolis, Minnesota', *International Journal of Urban and Regional Research* 11, no. 2 (1987): 243–61.

7 For oral histories and first-hand accounts of the Gay Liberation Front, see: Lisa Power, *No Bath But Plenty of Bubbles: An Oral History of the Gay Liberation Front, 1970–73* (London: Continuum International Publishing Group, 1995); Stuart Feather, *Blowing the Lid: Gay Liberation, Sexual Revolution and Radical Queens* (Winchester: Zero Books, 2015).

8 Power, *No Bath But Plenty of Bubbles*, 12. The other pubs listed in *Time Out* were The Bell, King's Cross, The Duke of Fife, Upton Park, The City Arms, Poplar, The Great Northern Railway, Hornsey and the Windsor Castle, Maida Vale. Power details the complex infrastructure of political groups, and the coalitions that forged and then disintegrated during the life of the GLF. The book offers vivid insight into a foundational revolutionary moment in the politics of sexuality and gender.

9 The GLF first met in a basement classroom in LSE's Clare Market Building, according to Power, and in a classroom on the upper floors of the Old Building, according

to Feather. Power, *No Bath But Plenty of Bubbles*, 20; Feather, *Blowing the Lid,* 46. Historian Matt Cook also locates the meeting in a basement room at the LSE. Matt Cook, "'Gay Times": Identity, Locality, Memory, and the Brixton Squats in 1970's London', *20th Century British History* 24, no. 1 (2013): 84–109, 86.

10 Feather, *Blowing the Lid,* 107.

11 Jeffrey Weeks, *Coming out: Homosexual Politics in Britain, from the Nineteenth Century to the Present* (London: Quartet Books, 1977); Mary McIntosh, 'The Homosexual Role', *Social Problems*, no. 2 (1968): 182–92.

12 McIntosh, 'The Homosexual Role', 189.

13 McIntosh, 'The Homosexual Role', 189. For a more recent discussion of gay subculture in this period, see: Rictor Norton, *Mother Clap's Molly House: The Gay Subculture in England, 1700-1830* (Stroud, Gloucestershire: Chalford Press, 2006).

14 McIntosh, 'The Homosexual Role', 189.

15 Jeffrey Weeks, 'The "homosexual role"' after 30 Years: An Appreciation of the Work of Mary McIntosh', *Sexualities* 1, no. 2 (1998): 131–52, 137.

16 Michel Foucault, *The History of Sexuality*, translated from the French by Robert Hurley. Vol.1, An Introduction (Harmondsworth: Penguin, 1981, [1978]), 105–6. See, also: Phil Hubbard, *Cities and Sexualities* (London: Routledge, 2011), 13.

17 Other contributors to these debates included scholar-activists such as the anthropologist Gayle Rubin and the sociologist Jeffrey Weeks. These authors emphasise that various researchers working on gay and lesbian history were coming to similar conclusions regarding the construction of sexuality as a social category. Weeks has emphasised McIntosh's contribution. Weeks, 'The "homosexual role" after 30 years', 137; Gayle Rubin, 'Sexual Traffic', interview with Judith Butler, *Differences*, 6.2+3 (1994): 82.

18 Weeks, 'The "homosexual role" after 30 years', 137.

19 Bonnie Loyd and Lester Rowntree, 'Radical Feminists and Gay Men in San Francisco: Social Pace in Dispersed Communities', in *Invitation to Geography*, ed. David Lanegran and Risa Palm (New York: McGraw Hill, 1978), 78–88; Barbara Weightman, 'Bars as Private Places', *Landscape* 24, no. 1 (1980): 9–16; Barbara Weightman, 'Commentary: Towards a Geography of the Gay Community', *Journal of Cultural Geography* 1 (1981): 106–12; Manuel Castells, *The City and the Grassroots: A Cross-Cultural Theory of Urban Social Movements* (London: Edward Arnold, 1983); Martin P. Levine, 'Gay Ghetto', *Journal of Homosexuality* 4, no. 4 (1979): 363–77.

20 Carol A. B. Warren, *Identity and Community in the Gay World* (New York: Wiley-Interscience, 1974).

21 Weightman, 'Commentary: Towards a Geography of the Gay Community', 106.

22 Levine, 'Gay Ghetto', 363–77.

23 Levine, 'Gay Ghetto', 364–5.

24 Relevant work on London includes: Chisholm, *Queer Constellations*, 27; Frank Mort, 'Cityscapes: Consumption, Masculinities and the Mapping of London since 1950', *Urban Studies* 35, no. 5/6 (1998): 889–907; Matt Houlbrook, *Queer London: Perils and Pleasures in the Sexual Metropolis*, 1918–57 (Chicago and London: University of Chicago Press, 2005).

25 Weightman, 'Commentary: Towards a Geography of the Gay Community', 106; 107; 110. Weightman was influenced by the population geographer, Wilbur Zelinsky, who had advocated the study of areas where particular 'transient groups' were concentrated and had produced a 'unique cultural ambience', in order to spot avant-

garde trends. Wilbur Zelinsky, 'Personality and Self-Discovery: The Future Social Geography of the United States', in *Human Geography in a Shrinking World*, ed. Ronald Abler et al (Belmont, CA: Duxbury Press, 1975), 108–21.

26 Weightman, 'Commentary: Towards a Geography of the Gay Community', 107.

27 John Alan Lee, 'The Gay Connection', *Urban Life* 8, no. 2 (July 1979): 175–98, quoting Irving Bieber (ed.), *Homosexuality: A Psychoanalytic Study* (New York: Basic Books, 1962).

28 Weightman, 'Commentary: Towards a Geography of the Gay Community', 110.

29 Castells, 'Cultural Identity, Sexual Liberation and Urban Structure: The Gay Community in San Francisco', in *The City and the Grassroots*, 138–70.

30 Castells, *The City and the Grassroots*, 140.

31 Maxine Wolfe, 'Invisible Women in Invisible Place: Lesbians, Lesbian Bars, and the Social Production of People/Environment Relationships', *Architecture and Behavior* 8 (1992): 137–58.

32 Knopp, 'Social Theory, Social Movements and Public Policy', 242; Weightman, 'Commentary: Towards a Geography of the Gay Community', 108–9. Weightman points to an emerging strand of research which examined the role of gays as 'important agents in urban renovation and preservation programs, particularly in the restoration of decaying architecture – gentrification'.

33 Mickey Lauria and Lawrence Knopp, 'Toward an Analysis of the Role of Gay Communities in the Urban Renaissance', *Urban Geography* 6, no. 2 (1985): 152–69.

34 Knopp, 'Social Theory, Social Movements and Public Policy', 246.

35 Early uses of this term include: David Bell, Jon Binnie, Julia Cream, and Gill Valentine, 'All Hyped up and No Place to Go', *Gender, Place & Culture* 1, no. 1 (1994): 31–47; and the exhibition, *Queer Space*, 1994, Storefront for Art and Architecture in New York City.

36 Judith Butler, *Gender Trouble: Feminism and the Subversion of Identity* (Florence: Routledge, 2006); Eve Kosofsky Sedgwick, *Epistemology of the Closet* (New York and London: Harvester Wheatsheaf, 1991).

37 Susan Stryker, *Transgender History* (Berkeley, CA: Seal Press, 2008), 30.

38 'Queer theory' was used by de Lauretis in the title for a conference at the University of California, Santa Cruz. David Halperin observes that De Lauretis used it to queer the space of academic discourse, destabilise the notion of theory, and disrupt what had already become institutionalised as lesbian and gay studies. Her project was partly to critique the dominance of studies by and on white, middle-class gay men, and to promote new empirical analyses through widening the theoretical scope towards theories of multiple social difference. See: David M. Halperin, 'The Normalization of Queer Theory', *Journal of Homosexuality*, 45 (2003): 2–4, 339–43.

39 Judith Butler, 'Critically Queer', *GLQ* 1, no. 1 (1993): 17–32, 20; Stryker, *Transgender History*, 1–44

40 Halperin, 'The Normalization of Queer Theory', *Journal of Homosexuality*, 45 (2003): 2–4, 339–43.

41 Bell, Binnie, Cream, and Valentine, 'All Hyped up and No Place to Go', 31–2.

42 Bell, Binnie, Cream, and Valentine, 'All Hyped up and No Place to Go', 31–47, 32.

43 Chisholm, *Queer Constellations*, 1–62. For the wider range of literature reviews on queer space, see note 1, above.

44 Aaron Betsky, *Building Sex: Men, Women, and the Construction of Sexuality* (New York: William Morrow, 1995); Aaron Betsky, *Queer Space: Architecture and Same-Sex Desire* (New York: William Morrow & Co, 1997); Joel Sanders (ed.), *Stud:*

Architectures of Masculinity (New York: Princeton Architectural Press, 1996); Jane Rendell, Barbara Penner and Iain Borden (eds.), *Gender Space Architecture: An Interdisciplinary Introduction* (London: Routledge, 2000); Henry Urbach, 'Closets, Clothes, Disclosure', *Assemblage*, no. 30 (1996): 63–73.

45 The organisers were Beatriz Colomina, Dennis Dollens, Eve Kosofsky Sedgwick, Cindi Patton, Henry Urbach, and Mark Wigley. Vallerand, 'Home Is the Place We All Share', 64–75.

46 Chisholm, *Queer Constellations*, xi; Christopher Castiglia and Christopher Reed, *If Memory Serves: Gay Men, AIDS, and the Promise of the Queer Past* (Minneapolis: University of Minnesota Press, 2012), 74–5.

47 The closest direct comparison, in terms of specific exhibitions on queer architecture and space, in the London context is the Architecture Foundation's exhibition, 'Glory Hole' (Architecture Foundation, 7–22 July 2006). 'Glory Hole', https://www.arc hitecturefoundation.org.uk/programme/2006/renegade-city/glory-hole (accessed 13 November 2020). Ben Campkin and Johan Andersson, 'A Hole Lotta Controversy', *Building Design,* 21 July 2006, https://www.bdonline.co.uk/a-hole-lotta-controversy /3070986.article (accessed 13 November 2020).

48 Henri Lefebvre, *The Production of Space*, trans. Donald Nicholson-Smith (Oxford: Blackwell, 1991); Michel Foucault and Jay Miskowiec, 'Of Other Spaces', *Diacritics* 16, no. 1 (1986): 22–7. Chisholm quotes from Lefebvre: 'As for sex and sexuality, things here are more complicated . . . Any true appropriation of sex demands that a separation be made between the reproductive function and sexual pleasure . . . The true space of pleasure, which would be an appropriated space *par excellence*, does not yet exist. Even if a few instances in the past suggest that this goal is in principle attainable, the results to date fall far short of human desires'. Lefebvre, *The Production of Space*, 166–7. For a synthesis of Lefebvre and Foucault's impact on conceptions of urban order, see: Adrian Forty, *Words and Buildings: A Vocabulary of Modern Architecture* (London: Thames & Hudson, 2000).

49 Chisholm, *Queer Constellations*, 28.

50 Chisholm focuses on the work of Neil Bartlett, Samuel Delany, Robert Glück, Alan Hollinghurst, Gary Indiana, Eileen Myles, Sarah Schulman, Gail Scott, Edmund White and David Wojnarowicz.

51 Chisholm, *Queer Constellations*, 4. On the theme of the amneisac city, and for a comparative Benjaminian approach to urban memory, see: Mark Crinson, *Urban Memory: History and Amnesia in the Modern City* (London: Routledge, 2005); Günter Gassner, *Ruined Skylines: Aesthetics, Politics and London's Towering Cityscape* (Abingdon, Oxon and New York: Taylor and Francis, 2020).

52 Chisholm, *Queer Constellations*, 6; 33–5.

53 Chisholm, *Queer Constellations*, 34. For discussion of the usefulness of Benjamin's concept of 'constellations' in interdisciplinary urban analysis see: Matthew Gandy, 'Introduction' in Matthew Gandy (ed.), *Urban Constellations* (Berlin: Jovis Verlag, 2011), 4–9.

54 As they intervene to construct queer histories, these literary interventions refuse the deceptively linear narratives of urbanisation in London, Paris or New York: 'they glimpse utopia, dystopia, and heterotopia at once, foreseeing with hindsight the idealization and ruination of what the city could become, as well as the fetishization and fossilization of what it never really was'. Exposing the myths of progress that accompany the fast pace of late capitalist urbanization, these texts also reveal the 'multiple and contradictory character of urban sexuality', and the 'collisions between

urban gentrification and sexual emancipation'. Chisholm, *Queer Constellations*, 32–5; 46.

55 Chisholm, *Queer Constellations*, 32.

56 Samuel R. Delany, *Times Square Red, Times Square Blue* (New York: New York University Press, 1999).

57 Chisholm, *Queer Constellations*, 6; 37.

58 Chisholm, *Queer Constellations*, 11.

59 Reactivating Henri Lefebvre's notion of 'planetary urbanization', the polemic of these neo-Marxian scholars revolves around the idea that the city, in an age in which political-economic urban conditions are enmeshed worldwide, is no longer useful as a distinct unit of analysis. Instead, they prioritise understanding urbanisation *processes*, calling for new theoretical formulations to address contemporary conditions by working across conventional categories, such as the urban/rural binary. Although sympathetic to many of these aims, queer, postcolonial urban geographer, Natalie Oswin, argues that while these theorists call for new and more precise attempts to conceptualise the urban, they neglect decades of contributions from feminist, queer, postcolonial and critical race scholars. Further, their desire for a singular epistemology and 'unified voice' for urban studies is at odds with the attention to multiplicity and social difference in these bodies of work, and to the fact that 'differential embodiments yield differential life chances'. Oswin sees planetary urbanists both calling for a new turn in urban theory, while they return, problematically, to earlier accounts of postmodernism that neglected social difference. Oswin, 'Planetary Urbanization', 542; Natalie Oswin, 'Society and Space, Here and Now'. *Environment and Planning D: Society and Space* 36, no. 4 (1 August 2018): 613–16, 614. For a succinct summary of 'planetary urbanism', see: Neil Brenner and Christian Schmid, 'Planetary Urbanization', in Gandy, *Urban Constellations*, 10–13.

60 Michael Warner (ed.), *Fear of a Queer Planet: Queer Politics and Social Theory* (Minneapolis and London: University of Minnesota Press, 1993), xxi.

61 Warner, *Fear of a Queer Planet*, xxiv.

62 Warner, *Fear of a Queer Planet*, xii.

63 Warner, *Fear of a Queer Planet*, xxv.

64 Warner, *Fear of a Queer Planet*, xvi–xvii.

65 Fiona Buckland, *Impossible Dance: Club Culture and Queer World-Making* (Middletown: Wesleyan University Press: 2010), 4.

66 Rosalyn Deutsche, 'Boys Town', *Environment and Planning D: Society and Space* 9, no. 1 (1991): 5–30; Jack Halberstam, 'Queer Temporality and Postmodern Geographies', in *In a Queer Time and Place Transgender Bodies, Subcultural Lives* (New York and London: New York University Press, 2005), 1–21; David Harvey, *The Condition of Postmodernity: An Enquiry into the Origins of Cultural Change* (Oxford: Basil Blackwell, 1989); Fredric Jameson, 'Postmodernism, or the Cultural Logic of Late Capitalism', *New Left Review* 164 (1984): 53–92; Doreen Massey, 'Flexible Sexism', *Environment and Planning. D, Society & Space* 9, no. 1 (1991): 31–57; Edward W. Soja, *Postmodern Geographies: The Reassertion of Space in Critical Social Theory* (London; New York: Verso, 2011).

67 Deutsche, 'Boys Town', 5.

68 Deutsche, 'Boys Town', 7.

69 Deutsche, 'Boys Town', 6–7.

70 Halberstam, *In a Queer Time and Place*, 5.

Notes

71 Halberstam, *In a Queer Time and Place*, 7.

72 Halberstam, *In a Queer Time and Place*, 1–21. Halberstam refers to the 'queer "way of life"', which encompasses 'subcultural practices, alternative methods of alliance, forms of transgender embodiment, and all those forms of representation dedicated to capturing these willfully eccentric modes of being' (1). 'Queer subjects' frequently 'live outside the logic of capital accumulation', involve themselves in 'nonlucrative practices' and are exposed to risk while they live outside of the safety nets of normativity (10).

73 Muñoz, *Cruising Utopia*, 31; David Harvey, *A Brief History of Neoliberalism* (Oxford and New York: Oxford University Press, 2005).

74 Muñoz, *Cruising Utopia*, 31. Halberstam also builds a critique around Harvey's neglect of race. Halberstam, *In a Queer Time and Place*, 9.

75 Harvey, *A Brief History of Neoliberalism*, 57–8. The idea that identity politics weakened union solidarities is a reductive interpretation, given the lack of support for lesbian and gay groups within the heterosexist and patriarchal unions until the mid-1980s. It is put further in dispute by the alliance made between lesbian and gay activists and the miners during the miner's strike, recently represented in the historical drama, *Pride*. Recalling British politics in the 1970s and 1980s, GLF member Andrew Lumsden comments, for example, on how the left were slow to acknowledge lesbian and gay rights as worthy of attention, since homosexuality was stigmatised as a 'bourgeois deviation'. Until the mid-1980s, he argues, lesbian and gay civil rights were seen as a low priority by the unions, despite the links between these movements and socialism. Andrew Lumsden, 'Our history to inspire 50th anniversary of the GLF', Trades Union Congress, 26 February 2020. *Pride* (BBC Films, UK, 2014). Directed by Matthew Warchus.

76 Harvey's use of the word 'narcissistic' must have grated given that Muñoz aligns himself with Herbert Marcuse's queer reading of the Narcissus myth as 'The Great Refusal' of the 'repressive order of procreative sexuality'. See: Herbert Marcuse, *Eros and Civilization: A Philosophical Inquiry into Freud* (London: Routledge & Kegan Paul Ltd, 1956), 171; Muñoz, *Cruising Utopia*, 134; Halberstam, *In a Queer Time and Place*, 9.

77 Harvey, *A Brief History of Neoliberalism*, 59–60. Harvey writes: 'A noble rearguard action against neoliberal policies was mounted in many a municipality – Sheffield, the Greater London Council (which Thatcher had to abolish in order to achieve her broader goals in the 1980s), and Liverpool . . . formed active centres of resistance in which the ideals of a new municipal socialism (incorporating many of the new social movements in the London case) were both cursed and acted upon until they were finally crushed in the mid-1980s'.

78 Warner, *Fear of a Queer Planet*, xxv.

79 Leo Bersani quoted in Robert L. Caserio, Lee Edelman, Jack Halberstam, José Esteban Muñoz, and Tim Dean, 'The Antisocial Thesis in Queer Theory', *PMLA* [Publications of the Modern Language Association of America] 121, no. 3 (2006): 819–28, 819.

80 Bersani quoted in Caserio et al, 'The Antisocial Thesis in Queer Theory', 819.

81 Halberstam argues that Bersani's 'definition of sex as anticommunitarian, self-shattering, and anti-identitarian', represented an important political shift 'away from projects of redemption, reconstruction, restoration, and reclamation and toward what can only be called an antisocial, negative, and antirelational theory of sexuality'. Bersani, quoted by Caserio and Halberstam, in Caserio, et al., 'The Antisocial Thesis in Queer Theory', 819; 823.

82 Lee Edelman, *No Future: Queer Theory and the Death Drive* (Durham and London: Duke University Press, 2004), 27; 60.

83 Lisa Duggan, 'The New Homonormativity: The Sexual Politics of Neo-liberalism', in *Materializing Democracy: Toward a Revitalized Cultural Politics*, ed. Russ Castronovo and Dana D. Nelson (Durham and London: Duke University Press, 2002), 175–92.

84 This phrase is used by Muñoz in discussing Frank O'Hara's poem 'Having a Coke with You', the first example in *Cruising Utopia*. Muñoz, *Cruising Utopia*, 5.

85 Muñoz, *Cruising Utopia*, 53–4. For discussion of queer activism in response to the 'disneyfication' of Times Square, see: Gavin Brown, 'Queer Movement', in David Paternotte and Manon Tremblay (eds.) *The Ashgate Research Companion to Lesbian and Gay Activism*, (London: Routledge, 2015), 73–86, 78.

86 Delany, *Times Square Red, Times Square Blue*; Chisholm, *Queer Constellation*, 7; Halberstam, *In a Queer Time and Place*, 4.

87 Muñoz, *Cruising Utopia*, 20.

88 Muñoz, *Cruising Utopia*, 53. This phrase nods to Delany's discussion of networks. Compare this with art critic Hal Fischer's categorization of 'basic gay' in his photo project *Gay Semiotics* (1977), discussed by Jeremy Atherton Lin in *Gay Bar: Why We Went Out* (London: Granta, 2021), 169.

89 Muñoz, *Cruising Utopia*, 76.

90 He writes: 'as the clock ticks and the world of New York's culture of public sex faces extinction, I have made a point soaking up as much of it as possible'. Muñoz, *Cruising Utopia*, 57.

91 Muñoz, *Cruising Utopia*, 52–3. Muñoz frames his work in relation to Giuliani's legal and policy crackdown on public sex and the sex and nightlife industries.

92 Muñoz, *Cruising Utopia*, 15; 31. Muñoz expresses a desire to shift away from theorists, including Walter Benjamin and Michel Foucault, who have been more often used in queer studies, and who, we might note, have also been more dominant in urban studies. He chooses to engage Marxist, psychoanalytic and phenomenological theorists, including Bloch, with potential, over more obvious and well-trodden paths, to 'offer new thought images for queer critique' (15). Bloch was unorthodox in his use of Marxism, and to some extent an outsider in the Frankfurt School, as well as an exile when living in the United States, having fled Nazism. He wrote on theatre, religion and mysticism, and advocated for expressionist art. Neville Plaice, Stephen Plaice and Paul Knight, 'Translator's Introduction' in Ernst Bloch', in *The Principle of Hope*, volume 1, trans. Neville Plaice, Stephen Plaice and Paul Knight (Cambridge, MA: The MIT Press, [1959] 1986), xix–xxxiii.

93 Bloch, *The Principle of Hope*, volume 1, xx, 144–78.

94 Bloch, *The Principle of Hope*, volume 1, xxvii, xxix.

95 Muñoz, *Cruising Utopia*, 2–3.

96 Muñoz, *Cruising Utopia*, 2–3.

97 For example, he prioritises the knowledge brought forward by performance practitioners alongside 'institutionally sanctioned theorists'. Muñoz, *Disidentifications*, 32. His work has also been directly referenced by queer space makers and activists in London who feature in the research discussed in *Queer Premises*. For example, see the work of venue operator and promoter, Joe Parslow, or writer, producer, programmer and critic, Ben Walters: Joe Parslow, 'Queer Stages: LGBTQ+ Venues, Drag Performance and Hope', in Ben Campkin, Lo Marshall and Rebecca Ross (eds.), 'LGBTQ+ Nigh-time Spaces: Past, Present, Future', *Urban Pamphleteer* #7 (2018): 22–4; Ben Walters, *Queer Fun, Family and Futures in Duckie's Performance Projects*

2010–2016, doctoral thesis, Queen Mary University of London, 2019, https://qmro
.qmul.ac.uk/xmlui/handle/123456789/56817 (accessed 27 July 2021).

98 Muñoz, *Cruising Utopia*, 109; 116; 123.

99 Laurent Berlant, 'The Commons: Infrastructures for Troubling Times', *Environment and Planning D: Society and Space* 34, no. 3 (2016): 395.

100 Tim Dean, for example, critiqued the thesis for embracing homophobia, reproducing 'right-wing fantasies about how "'the homosexual agenda" undermines the social fabric'. Tim Dean, 'The Antisocial Homosexual', in Caserio, et al., 'The Antisocial Thesis in Queer Theory', 826.

101 Muñoz, *Cruising Utopia*, 34–5. This parallels the queer and feminist responses to Harvey.

102 Muñoz draws on his doctoral supervisor, Eve Kosofsky Sedgwick's notion of 'reparative reading' against 'paranoid reading'. Muñoz, *Cruising Utopia*, 11; Eve Kosofsky Sedgwick, *Touching Feeling: Affect, Pedagogy, Performativity* (Durham and London: Duke University Press, 2003).

103 Muñoz, *Cruising Utopia*, 11; Muñoz in Caserio et al., 'The Antisocial Thesis in Queer Theory', 823.

104 Muñoz, *Cruising Utopia*, 1.

105 Sara Ahmed, *Queer Phenomenology: Orientations, Objects, Others* (London and Durham: Duke University Press, 2006). Ahmed shares Edelman's critique of the homonormative politics of pragmatism. Ahmed, *Queer Phenomenology*, 85–6; 172–3

106 Ahmed, *Queer Phenomenology*, 21; Muñoz, *Cruising Utopia*, 22; 25; 73; Halberstam, 'Queer Temporality', 3.

107 Ahmed, *Queer Phenomenology*, 17.

108 Ahmed, *Queer Phenomenology*, 19.

109 Butler, *Gender Trouble*, 1–46; J. L. [John Langshaw] Austin, *How to Do Things with Words* (Cambridge, MA: Harvard University Press, 1962).

110 Muñoz, *Cruising Utopia*, 9.

111 See, for example: Sara Ahmed, *On Being Included: Racism and Diversity in Institutional Life* (Durham and London: Duke University Press, 2012).

112 Ahmed, *On Being Included*, 50.

113 See, for example: Andersson, 'Heritage Discourse and the Desexualisation of Public Space', 1081–98; 'Homonormative Aesthetics: AIDS and "de-Generational Unremembering" in 1990s London', 2993–3010; Petra L. Doan and Harrison Higgins, 'The Demise of Queer Space? Resurgent Gentrification and the Assimilation of LGBT Neighborhoods', *Journal of Planning Education and Research* 31, no. 1 (2011): 6–25; Daniel Baldwin Hess, 'Effects of Gentrification and Real-Estate Market Escalation on Gay Neighbourhoods', *Town Planning Review* 90, no. 3 (2019): 229–37; Amin Ghaziani, *There Goes the Gayborhood?* (Princeton: Princeton University Press, 2014); Sarah Schulman, *The Gentrification of the Mind: Witness to a Lost Imagination* (Berkeley: University of California Press, 2013); Vallerand, 'Home Is the Place We All Share', 64–75. In the London context, see, also: Gil M. Doron, 'The Dead Zone and the Architecture of Transgression', *City* 4, no. 2 (2010): 247–63.

114 In addition to the work cited above, see, also: Olimpia Burchiellaro, '"There's Nowhere Wonky Left to Go": Gentrification, Queerness and Class Politics of Inclusion in (East) London', *Gender, Work & Organization* (2020): 1–15; Kian Goh, 'Safe Cities and Queer Spaces: The Urban Politics of Radical LGBT Activism', *Annals of the American Association of Geographers* 108, no. 2 (4 March 2018): 463–77; Walters, *Queer Fun, Family and Futures*, 2019.

115 Castiglia and Reed, *If Memory Serves*, 1.

116 Castiglia and Reed, *If Memory Serves*, 3.

117 On the neglect of memory sites, Castiglia and Reed align with British art historian and AIDS activist Simon Watney, in seeing a disavowal of historical identities and community formations. Watney has criticised queer theory as overly theoretical and abstract, and neglectful of the subject of HIV/AIDS. He is alarmed by a rejection of earlier gay identities, and a shift to forms of queer culture that are increasingly individualist, even while they sanctimoniously reject earlier forms of gay community. This critique can seem frustratingly circular, since a monolithic understanding of 'gay identity' is rebuffed by a monolithic reading of queer theory or culture. It also reflects a tension between a tradition of British empirical lesbian and gay studies and dominant North American queer theory, informed by European poststructuralism. Castiglia and Reed, *If Memory Serves*, 162; Simon Watney, *Imagine Hope: AIDS and Gay Identity* (London; New York: Routledge, 2000), 250–1.

118 Castiglia and Reed, *If Memory Serves*, 24–6; 30; Muñoz, *Cruising Utopia*, 84; 115; 118.

119 Muñoz, *Cruising Utopia*, 119.

120 Muñoz, *Cruising Utopia*, 115.

121 Muñoz, *Cruising Utopia*, 84.

122 Muñoz, *Cruising Utopia*, 5; 123.

123 Chisholm, *Queer Constellations*, 30, note 64.

124 Chisholm, *Queer Constellations*, 10.

125 Johan Andersson, 'Homonormative Aesthetics: AIDS and "de-Generational Unremembering" in 1990s London', *Urban Studies* 56, no. 14 (2019): 2993–3010; Johan Andersson, 'Hygiene Aesthetics on London's Gay Scene: The Stigma of AIDS' in Ben Campkin and Rosie Cox (eds.), *Dirt: New Geographies of Cleanliness and Contamination*, (London: IB Tauris, 2007): 103–12; Johan Andersson, 'East End Localism and Urban Decay: Shoreditch's Re-emerging Gay Scene', *The London Journal: A Review of Metropolitan Society Past and Present* 34, no. 1 (2009): 55–71; Johan Andersson, 'Vauxhall's Postindustrial Pleasure Gardens: "Death Wish" and Hedonism in 21st Century London', *Urban Studies* 48, no. 1 (2011): 85–100; Johan Andersson, 'Heritage Discourse and the Desexualisation of Public Space: The 'Historical Restorations' of Bloomsbury's Squares', *Antipode* 44, no. 4 (2012): 1081–98.

126 Castiglia and Reed, *If Memory Serves*, 2012; Schulman, *The Gentrification of the Mind*; Duggan, 'The New Homonormativity', 175–94.

127 Caserio in Caserio et al., 'The Antisocial Thesis in Queer Theory', 820.

128 The French term 'infrastructure' is deployed in British public discourse in reference to railway construction in English as early as 1927 but is not naturalized until the 1950s, and by then had been used widely to describe a wide range of political, military, social, and linguistic systems. Urban planner and historian Justinien Tribillon is currently working on the etymology of 'infrastructure'. I am grateful to him for sharing a draft paper on this topic. Justinien Tribillon, 'Inventing "Infrastructure": Tracing the Etymological Blueprint of an Omnipresent Metaphor', 2020; *Oxford English Dictionary*, 2018.

129 Writing about Johannesburg, urbanist and ethnographer AbdouMaliq Simone says that infrastructure typically refers to 'reticulated systems of highways, pipes, wires or cables', focused on efficiency – this is the colonial project of infrastructure. AbdouMaliq Simone, 'People as Infrastructure: Intersecting Fragments in Johannesburg', *Public Culture* 16, no. 3 (1 October 2004): 407–29, 407. He offers,

instead, a 'notion of people as infrastructure' – a concept that reclaims infrastructure from below, for those who exist precariously in relation to dominant forces, and who are 'marginalised and immiserated by urban life', but develop survivalist, provisionalist solutions (407). Marginalised subjects are frequently by-passed by the benefits of infrastructural systems, even as they intimately inhabit them and are necessary to their production. Simone repurposes the notion for thinking about forms of collaboration and economy. See also: Isabel Gutiérrez Sánchez, *Infrastructures of Caring Citizenship Citizen-led Welfare Initiatives in Crisis-Ridden Athens, Greece*, doctoral thesis, UCL, 2020; Shannon Mattern, 'Infrastructural Tourism', *Places Journal*, 1 July 2013; Emma R. Power and Kathleen J. Mee. 'Housing: An Infrastructure of Care', *Housing Studies* 35, no. 3 (2002): 484–505.

130 Berlant, 'The Commons', 412.

131 They use 'queer infrastructure' to discuss the poetry of Juliana Spahr, commenting that infrastructure 'holds statements up in a tensile structure that is always making things different as they course through the material world'. Berlant, 'The Commons', 393–419, 404f.

132 Mayor of London, 'Cultural Infrastructure Map', https://www.london.gov.uk//what-we-do/arts-and-culture/cultural-infrastructure-toolbox/cultural-infrastructure-map (accessed 28 February 2019).

133 Michael Hebbert, *London: More by Fortune than Design* (Chichester: John Wiley, [1998] 2001), 164; 169.

134 Gavin Brown, 'Cosmopolitan Camouflage: (Post-)gay Space in Spitalfields, East London', in Jon Binnie, Julian Millington, and Craig Yeung (eds.), *Cosmopolitan Urbanism* (Abingdon: Routledge, 2006), 130–45, 132.

135 Alan Collins, 'Sexual Dissidence, Enterprise and Assimilation: Bedfellows in Urban Regeneration', *Urban Studies* 41, no. 9 (2004): 1789–806. See, for example: Louis Wirth, 'The Ghetto', *The American Journal of Sociology* 33, no. 1 (1927): 57–71.

136 Collins, 'Sexual Dissidence, Enterprise and Assimilation', 1789–806.

137 Johan Andersson, 'Berlin's Queer Archipelago: Landscape, Sexuality, and Nightlife', *Transactions of the Institute of British Geographers* (2022); Nadine Cattan and Alberto Vanolo, 'Gay and Lesbian Emotional Geographies of Clubbing: Reflections from Paris and Turin', *Gender, Place and Culture : A Journal of Feminist Geography* 21, no. 9 (2014): 1158–75; Petra Doan, 'Planning for LGBTQ Populations in the Global South', *Queering Urbanisms*, lecture, The Bartlett Faculty of the Built Environment, UCL, 2022; Amin Ghaziani, 'Cultural Archipelagos: New Directions in the Study of Sexuality and Space', *City & Community* 18, no. 1 (2019): 4–22. Relatedly, sites of cruising and public sex have been considered through new conceptions of complexity and extension as in Matthew Gandy's discussion of 'queer ecology'. Matthew Gandy, 'Queer Ecology: Nature, Sexuality, and Heterotopic Alliances', *Environment and Planning D: Society and Space* 30, no. 4 (2012): 569–755.

Chapter 2

1 After a period of planning from 1982, and the purchase of a building in 1983, the Centre opened in December 1984, with an official launch in spring 1985. London Lesbian and Gay Centre, *What is the London Lesbian and Gay Centre?*, pamphlet, c.1983 HCA/543.

2 Greater London Council Gay Working Party, *London Lesbian and Gay Centre*, concept note, July 1982, HCA/Ephemera/264.

3 London Lesbian and Gay Centre, *Centre News*, December to January 1989, HCA/Ephemera/621.

4 *Note of the Meeting of the GLC Gay Working Party*, 30 June 1982, HCA/Ephemera/264.

5 *Note of the Meeting of the GLC Gay Working Party*, 1982.

6 The oral history evidence was gathered through two public documented conversations: *Centre Pieces: A Public, Documented Conversation on the London Lesbian and Gay Centre*, UCL Urban Laboratory and Museum of London, 14 July 2018 and *London Lesbian and Gay Centre: A Documented Conversation*, UCL Urban Laboratory and Gays the Word, 18 October 2018. In general, I have anonymized quotes from participants. These conversations adapted the method of long-tables devised by Split Britches, http://www.split-britches.com/long-table (accessed 22 January 2023).

7 The funding amounted to £15,500. Greater London Council, 'GLC Gives More Community Grants', *Public Relations Branch News Service*, No. 395, 1982. LMA, GLC Press Releases 1982, 263–639 (July-December), GLC/DG/PRB/35/039/395.

8 London Lesbian and Gay Centre, Steering Committee, 'Open Meeting at County Hall', notes, 12 December 1983, HCA/Ephemera/264.

9 London Lesbian and Gay Centre, *What is the London Lesbian and Gay Centre?*, pamphlet, c. 1983, HCA/543.

10 'Open Meeting at County Hall', 1983. During the 1970s and early 1980s there were debates about forging coalitions between the gay rights movement and those campaigning about children's sexuality and reductions to the age of consent. For example, the Paedophile Information Exchange was affiliated to the National Council For Civil Liberties. See: Tom de Castella and Tom Heyden, 'How did the pro-paedophile group PIE exist openly for 10 years?', *BBC News*, 27 February 2014, https://www.bbc.co.uk/news/magazine-26352378

11 Greater London Council Gay Working Party, Minutes, 27 July 1983, HCA Woods Papers 2/9.

12 Greater London Council Gay Working Party, 'Note of the Meeting of Lesbian Organisations held on 24 August at 7pm', undated, c.1982, HCA Woods Papers 2/9. Women's City was an unrealized project to convert a domed building, scheduled for demolition, on the Holloway Road, into a women's centre. It was intended to be entirely realized by women. See Chapter 5. Fiona McLean, interview by Ben Campkin, London, 4 July 2018.

13 GLC Gay Working Party, 'Note of the Meeting of Lesbian Organisations', 1982.

14 GLC Gay Working Party, 'Note of the Meeting of Lesbian Organisations', 1982. The women's space was only intended for use by women who identified as lesbian. LLGC, 'Minutes of a Meeting of the Management Committee of the London Lesbian and Gay Centre Ltd', 20 April 1984, HCA/Ephemera/543.

15 Anon, 'London Centre: Gays Pack County Hall', *Capital Gay*, August 1982.

16 London Lesbian and Gay Centre, *Cowcross* 2, pamphlet, 1984, HCA/543.

17 Peter Davey, participant, 'London Lesbian and Gay Centre: A Documented Conversation', UCL Urban Laboratory/Gays the Word, 18 October 2018.

18 GLC Gay Working Party, 'LLGC', concept note, 1982.

19 'London Centre: Gays Pack County Hall', 1982.

20 Charity Commission, correspondence with Messrs Winstanley Burgess, 13 August 1984, HCA/Ephemera/955. The Commission sided with legal opinion that,

Notes 191

while homosexual acts between men over the age of 21 had been decriminalized, homosexuality was still considered immoral and corrupting, and following this logic questioned the establishment of a Centre deemed contrary to public policy.

21 LLGC, 'Notes from a Meeting with Paul Collard, Institute of Contemporary Arts', 29 May 1984, HCA/Ephemera/543.

22 When the LLGC was up and running, in 1986, the salary was £10,296 plus five weeks holiday. LLGC, 'Administrative Worker', advertisement, 14 October 1986, Bishopsgate Institute Archives LLGC_FL.C838.

23 Participant, 'London Lesbian and Gay Centre: A Documented Conversation', UCL Urban Laboratory/Gays the Word, 18 October 2018.

24 Participant, 'Centre Pieces: A Public, Documented Conversation on the London Lesbian and Gay Centre', UCL Urban Laboratory/Museum of London, 14 July 2018.

25 LLGC, Press Statement, 24 January 1984, HCA/Ephemera/543. The final date of the GLC's abolition was the 31 March 1986, under the Local Government Act 1985.

26 By 1989 the membership fee was £15 per annum, with half price concession for those on unemployment benefits, students, the disabled, and old aged pensioners. Day membership was 30 pence or 15 pence concession. 'LLGC, 'What's on?', flyer, Bishopsgate Institute Archives LLGC/LGBTM/147/10.

27 London Lesbian and Gay Centre, *First Birthday Souvenir Diary*, April 1986, LAGNA Pamphlet Collection P699, Bishopsgate Institute Archives. It would be impossible to verify these figures, which were of course intended to communicate success.

28 For example: Gay Young London Group, LLGC, *Centre News*, December to January, 1989, HCA/ Ephemera/621.

29 LLGC, poster for an Extraordinary General Meeting, 16 October 1986, Bishopsgate Institute Archives LLGC/LGBTM/147/10; Advertisement for an Administrative Worker, London Lesbian and Gay Centre, 14 October 1986, Bishopsgate Institute Archives LLGC_FL.C838; LLGC, 'Extraordinary General Meeting', poster, 16 November 1986,HCA/ Ephemera/95.

30 London Lesbian and Gay Centre, 'Centre Tackles Racism', *Centre Points*, 1986, 3, HCA/ Ephemera/174; LLGC, 'Extraordinary General Meeting', poster, 16 November 1986, HCA/ Ephemera/955.

31 Fiona McLean, interview by Ben Campkin, London, 4 July 2018.

32 The budget was £393,274. The premises were found rapidly in order to maximise the potential contribution from the GLC's capital budget. In total, for the building, conversion and repair, £751,000 was provided, with further funding for furniture and equipment.

33 Frank van Loock, interview by Ben Campkin, London, 4 July 2018.

34 Frank van Loock, interview by Ben Campkin, London, 4 July 2018.

35 Further emphasising the homophobic atmosphere, lower levels of social acceptance of lesbians and gays at the time, and the resultant stigma attached to the project, McLean also indicates that she was wary of promoting herself as the architect of the Centre after completion. Fiona McLean, interview by Ben Campkin, London, 4 July 2018.

36 Participants, 'Centre Pieces: A Public, Documented Conversation on the London Lesbian and Gay Centre', UCL Urban Laboratory/Museum of London, 14 July 2018.

37 Frank van Loock, interview by Ben Campkin, London, 4 July 2018.

38 At 274 Upper Street, Islington. The two development workers were Helen Jenkins and Brian Kennedy.

39 Fiona McLean, interview by Ben Campkin, London, 4 July 2018.

40 The Hall-Carpenter is a collection of primary sources on gay and lesbian rights, which originated in 1980 in the Gay Monitoring and Archive Project established

by the Campaign for Homosexual Equality, the leading lesbian and gay rights organization at the time.

41 Greater London Council, 'GLC Gives More Community Grants', *Public Relations Branch News Service*, No. 395, 1982. LMA, GLC/DG/PRB/35/039/395.

42 LLGC, Management Committee Meeting Minutes, 14 May 1984, HCA/Ephemera/543.

43 LLGC, correspondence, 29 February 1984, HCA/Ephemera/543.

44 LLGC, *London Lesbian and Gay Centre First Birthday Souvenir Diary*, April 1986.

45 See, for example: 'Access to LLGC', *LLGC Film Club Presents June 1989 Programme*, flyer, Hall-Carpenter Archives, HCA/ Ephemera/921; and LLGC, 'Access details for the LLGC', Memo, undated, HCA/ Ephemera/621.

46 Fiona McLean, interview by Ben Campkin, London, 4 July 2018.

47 Gay Men's Disabled Group, correspondence with Hall-Carpenter Archives, 17 July 1984, HCA/Ephemera/543.

48 Greater London Council, *Changing the World: A London Charter for Gay and Lesbian Rights'*, 1983, republished by the London Strategic Policy Unit, 1987, HCA/ CHE2/12/65. The Charter came under the public relations remit of the GLC's Public Relations Branch and Creative Unit and was printed in Peckham by Mapledon Press.

49 Greater London Council, *Changing the World: A London Charter for Gay and Lesbian Rights* (London Strategic Policy Unit, 5, 1985).

50 The Manchester Gay Centre received funding for its services under the Urban Aid Programme of Labour prime minister James Callaghan's Government in 1978. On the different iterations of the Manchester Gay and LGBT centres, see: Emily Crompton, 'We Were Born in the '80s: A History of the Joyce Layland LGBT Centre, Manchester', *Queer Beyond London*, 11 May 2017, http://queerbeyondlondon.com /manchester/we-were-born-in-the-80s-a-history-of-the-joyce-layland-lgbt-centre -manchester/ (accessed 19 April 2021).

51 On the South London Gay Centre see: Cook, '"Gay Times": Identity, Locality, Memory, and the Brixton Squats in 1970's London', 85. The Birmingham Centre was in Digbeth, and was followed by the Lesbian and Gay Community Centre, Aston. Birmingham LGBT Trust, 'Gay Birmingham Remembered', http://www.gaybirm inghamremembered.co.uk/topics/Lesbian+and+Gay+Community+Centre,+Aston (accessed 13 April 2022). Rían Kearney, is currently undertaking doctoral research that includes archival and oral history research on the Birmingham centres: *Queer Space Archive: Tracing Birmingham's LGBTQ+ Venues From Memory, 1966-1987*, UCL.

52 This and other terms are carefully defined for a reader unfamiliar with them. Greater London Council, *Changing the World: A London Charter for Gay and Lesbian Rights'*, 1983, republished 1987, 10. See also: 'Heterosexism: A Guide for Groups in the Voluntary Sector on How to Challenge Heterosexism', draft, 1985, HCA/CHE2/12/65; and Greater London Council Women's Committee, *Tackling Heterosexism: A Handbook of Lesbian Rights* (London: GLC Women's Committee, 1986).

53 *Changing the World*, 47.

54 As an attempt to safeguard the GLC's work after its abolition, multiple structures and appointments had been established within the Association of London Authorities.

55 For example, see: Joseph Massad, *Desiring Arabs* (Chicago: University of Chicago Press, 2007).

56 GLC, Inner London Education Authority, memorandum, undated, LMA GLC/DG/ PRB/08/3534.

57 LLGC, Minutes of the PR and Publicity Sub Group, 19 May 1984. HCA/ Ephemera/543.

Notes 193

58 *London Lesbian and Gay Centre: Some Useful Information* (London: London Lesbian and Gay Centre, 1985), HCA/Ephemera/955.

59 Owen Hatherley, *Red Metropolis: Socialism and the Government of London* (London: Repeater Books, 2020).

60 *Note of the Meeting of the GLC Gay Working Party*, 30 June 1982,HCA/Woods Papers 2/9.

61 Brian Kennedy, LLGC, correspondence with friends of the LLGC, undated, HCA/Ephemera/543.

62 Kate Eichhorn's analysis of the importance of Xerox copying to New York's downtown scenes from the 1970s is helpful to understand the role of these facilities. In similarity, they enabled the intensification of highly local scenes as well as their extension and migration. Kate Eichhorn, 'Copy Machines and Downtown Scenes', *Cultural Studies* 29, no. 3 (2015): 363–78.

63 See, for example, the Hall-Carpenter Archives logo or ephemera from The Bell public house (discussed in Chapter 5).

64 On the aesthetics and spatial and temporal politics of skylines in London, see: Günter Gassner, *Ruined Skylines: Aesthetics, Politics and London's Towering Cityscape* (London and New York, Routledge, 2020).

65 'Pride Success', *Centre Points*, 1986, HCA/Ephemera/955; 'Preparing for Pride', *Centre Points*, Monthly Newsletter of the LLGC, No. 2, June 1986, HCA/Ephemera/174. Leaflet, 'Lesbian and Gay Pride '87', LMA, GLC/DG/PRB/35/039/395.

66 LLGC, Fabaganza, Pride flyer, 28 September 1991. Bishopsgate Institute Archives LLGC/LGBTM/147/10. The price was £6 but there were also concessions.

67 Early in discussions about the centre, Griffith Vaughan Williams of the Campaign for Homosexual Equality had written a concept note summarising previous explorations about the potential of a gay centre. Griffith Vaughan Williams, 'Gay Centres in London', memo, 29 June 1982, HCA/Woods Papers 2/9.

68 Participant, 'London Lesbian and Gay Centre: A Documented Conversation', UCL Urban Laboratory/Gays the Word, 18 October 2018; LLGC, 'Camden Lesbian and Gay Telephone Trees', Camden Lesbian and Gay Project, leaflet, 1986, HCA/Ephemera/955.

69 It would become one of the main mental health services for LGBTQ+ people in London until its closure in 2016.

70 Participants, 'Centre Pieces: A Public, Documented Conversation on the London Lesbian and Gay Centre', UCL Urban Laboratory/Museum of London, 14 July 2018; 'London Lesbian and Gay Centre: A Documented Conversation', UCL Urban Laboratory/Gays the Word, 18 October 2018.

71 For a sample from the early years of the Centre's life, see: 'Arts Beat', *Centre Points*, 1986, 3, HCA/ Ephemera/174.

72 The Lesbian and Gay Youth Movement Conference took place there in 1984. Participant, 'Centre Pieces: A Public, Documented Conversation on the London Lesbian and Gay Centre', UCL Urban Laboratory/Museum of London, 14 July 2018.

73 Participants, 'Centre Pieces: A Public, Documented Conversation on the London Lesbian and Gay Centre', UCL Urban Laboratory/Museum of London, 14 July 2018. Outrage! had applied for office space by 1984. LLGC, 'Management Committee Meeting', minutes, 14 May 1984, HCA/Ephemera/543.

74 LLGC, 'Roll of Honour', notice, date marked 'received 5 December 1990', LSE, Hall-Carpenter Archives, HCA/ Ephemera/621. The campaign was instigated by David

194   *Notes*

Davies. I am grateful to Kell Farshéa for sharing her memories of Simon Ra-Orton via social media on World Aids Day 2020.

75 http://outrage.org.uk/ (accessed 17 August 2020).

76 Participant, 'Centre Pieces: A Public, Documented Conversation on the London Lesbian and Gay Centre', UCL Urban Laboratory/Museum of London, 14 July 2018.

77 Participant, 'Centre Pieces: A Public, Documented Conversation on the London Lesbian and Gay Centre', UCL Urban Laboratory/Museum of London, 14 July 2018.

78 Participant, 'Centre Pieces: A Public, Documented Conversation on the London Lesbian and Gay Centre', UCL Urban Laboratory/Museum of London, 14 July 2018.

79 Participants, 'Centre Pieces: A Public, Documented Conversation on the London Lesbian and Gay Centre', UCL Urban Laboratory/Museum of London, 14 July 2018.

80 There is a likely bias in that the amount of time that such individuals spent in the building, and the sense of attachment that they felt, would shape their willingness to come forward to speak about the Centre's history.

81 Once the LLGC closed Shakti, also known as 'Shakti Bhangra Disco', moved to The Dome in Tufnell Park, North London. It paved the way for Club Kali, an inclusive night for people of a South Asian background, set up by Ritu and others shortly after the Centre closed, in 1995, which continues today. Other music and social events linked to cultural and ethnic identities included Macondo, a 'Latin American party night' which supported specified charities, and Long Yang Club 'for Oriental Lesbians and Gays and "interested Westerners"'. LLGC, *Diary*, February 1990. 22 January 1990, HCA/Ephemera/621. On Club Kali, see: DJ Ritu and Lo Marshall, 'Club Kali' in Adam Nathaniel Furman and Joshua Mardell (eds.), *Queer Spaces: An Atlas of LGBTQIA+ Places and Stories* (London: RIBA Publishing, 2022): 92-93.

82 The Black Lesbian and Gay Centre Project is the subject of the excellent documentary, *Under Your Nose: The Story of the Black Lesbian and Gay Centre*, 2018, directed by Veronica McKenzie.

83 DJ Ritu, 'The only One' in Ben Campkin, Lo Marshall and Rebecca Ross (eds.), 'LGBTQ+ Night-Spaces: Past, Present, Future', *Urban Pamphleteer* #7 (July 2018), 5–7: 7.

84 Participant, 'Centre Pieces: A Public, Documented Conversation on the London Lesbian and Gay Centre', UCL Urban Laboratory/Museum of London, 14 July 2018.

85 LLGC, 'Centre Events', August 1990, HCA/ Ephemera/858.

86 Participant, 'Centre Pieces: A Public, Documented Conversation on the London Lesbian and Gay Centre', UCL Urban Laboratory/Museum of London, 14 July 2018.

87 A participant who identifies as a white gay man remembers his encounter with Shakti as a horizon-expanding experience: 'I got picked up at Shakti and when we left this guy's friends were all throwing themselves in front of his car, and I'm going "What's going on?" and he's saying, "Well, in an Indian wedding your sisters all lie down in front of the carriage [laughter] and stop you leaving". [This is] just an example of meeting different people and [. . .] it was a place, a social space which was beyond, bigger than the confines of the social spaces I had come out to as a suburban Londoner'. Participant, 'Centre Pieces: A Public, Documented Conversation on the London Lesbian and Gay Centre', UCL Urban Laboratory/Museum of London, 14 July 2018.

88 These dances later moved to The Bell in King's Cross (see Chapter 5) and then The White Swan, Limehouse, East London.

89 Participant, 'Centre Pieces: A Public, Documented Conversation on the London Lesbian and Gay Centre', UCL Urban Laboratory/Museum of London, 14 July 2018. Pink Jukebox has also been known as Jackie's Jukebox.

90 LLGC flyer, Grand Benefit Disco, 8 March, no year given. Bishopsgate Institute Archives LLGC/LGBTM/147/10.

91 Participant, Centre Pieces: A Public, Documented Conversation on the London Lesbian and Gay Centre', UCL Urban Laboratory/Museum of London, 14 July 2018.

92 Participant, Centre Pieces: A Public, Documented Conversation on the London Lesbian and Gay Centre', UCL Urban Laboratory/Museum of London, 14 July 2018.

93 Participants, 'Centre Pieces: A Public, Documented Conversation on the London Lesbian and Gay Centre', UCL Urban Laboratory/Museum of London, 14 July 2018.

94 Participants, 'Centre Pieces: A Public, Documented Conversation on the London Lesbian and Gay Centre', UCL Urban Laboratory/Museum of London, 14 July 2018.

95 Participant, 'Centre Pieces: A Public, Documented Conversation on the London Lesbian and Gay Centre', UCL Urban Laboratory/Museum of London, 14 July 2018.

96 Participant, 'Centre Pieces: A Public, Documented Conversation on the London Lesbian and Gay Centre', UCL Urban Laboratory/Museum of London, 14 July 2018.

97 Margaret Thatcher, House of Commons Prime Minister's Questions, 25 November 1982, Hansard, https://www.margaretthatcher.org/document/105059 (accessed 22 August 2018).

98 Lord (John) Boyd-Carpenter quoted in Hansard, Local Government Interim Provisions Bill debate, 16 July 1984. https://hansard.parliament.uk/Lords/1984 -07-16/debates/6570cec6-fe75-40a7-86f3-f33b6771d91a/LocalGovernment(I nterimProvisions)Bill?highlight=%22london%20lesbian%20and%20gay%20 centre%22#contribution-137b5095-0f92-4eed-9244-6f76b77ec3ae (accessed 15 January 2022).

99 'Local Government, Volume 52: debated on Monday 23 January 1984, Hansard, UK Parliament'. Accessed 4 January 2021. https://hansard.parliament.uk/Commons /1984-01-23/debates/748a97d7-0e31-483a-813c-30d50124ad06/LocalGovernment (accessed 15 January 2022).

100 'Local Government Debate in Commons Chamber', 23 January 1984, Hansard. https://hansard.parliament.uk/search/Contributions?searchTerm=%22London %20Lesbian%20and%20Gay%20Centre%22&startDate=01%2F01%2F1982%2000 %3A00%3A00&endDate=01%2F01%2F1999%2000%3A00%3A00 (accessed 15 January 2022).

101 Allan Roberts, 'Control of General Expenditure Powers Debate', Hansard, 30 July 1984. https://hansard.parliament.uk/Commons/1984-07-30/debates/2ec1859d -fb74-4adb-9f8d-13306454e8a0/ControlOfGeneralExpenditurePowers?highlight= %22london%20lesbian%20and%20gay%20centre%22#contribution-e3bf2102-788a -4321-8aa7-0bf3d5cbfd30 (accessed 15 January 2022).

102 GLC Public Relations Branch, 'GLC Abolition Threatens Gay Research', 31 July 1984, *GLC Press Releases 1984 (July-September), 469–683*, Volume 45. LMA, GLC/ DG/PRB/35.

103 'Centre Pieces: A Public, Documented Conversation on the London Lesbian and Gay Centre', UCL Urban Laboratory/Museum of London, 14 July 2018. In the early stages of planning the Centre, anxieties were raised about its liability for prosecution due to people having sex on the premises. LLGC Steering Committee, Open Meeting at County Hall, 12 December 1983, HCA Woods Papers 2/9.

104 Susan Ardill and Sue O'Sullivan, 'Upsetting and Applecart: Difference, Desire and Lesbian Sadomasochism', *Feminist Review* 23, (Summer, 1986): 31–57. See, also activst Colin Clews' account in *Gay in the '80s: From Fighting For Our Rights to Fighting For Our Lives* (Kibworth Beauchamp: Matador, 2017), 90–91.

105 Ardill and O'Sullivan, 'Upsetting and Applecart', 36.

106 Ardill and O'Sullivan, 'Upsetting and Applecart', 36.

107 They emphasise this as an historical moment of enlightenment regarding difference – where the oppressions faced by women according to class, race and other lines of identity resulted in a discourse attentive to positionality and experience. But they critique the moral timbre of articulations of identity that had become detached from the Marxist structural political analysis they understood to be necessary and lacking at the time. They also argue that although the revolutionary potential of sex was at the heart of the controversy at the Centre, sex itself was strangely suppressed in the debates that ensued. Having participated in these contestations, they point to ways that new discussions around lesbian sexuality which had previously been muted, even among sexual liberationists, were instigated. Ardill and O'Sullivan, 'Upsetting and Applecart', 40–1.

108 'each tangles with the other, feeds from or subtracts, adds to or bloats up another', Ardill and O'Sullivan, 'Upsetting and Applecart', 56.

109 'Any of us must be able to develop politics which make us sensitive and open to learning from the experience of others and provide us with the tools and a framework for critically assessing theoretical analyses and daily political life', Ardill and O'Sullivan, 'Upsetting and Applecart', 56.

110 Ardill and O'Sullivan, 'Upsetting and Applecart', 56–7.

111 Participant, 'Centre Pieces: A Public, Documented Conversation on the London Lesbian and Gay Centre', UCL Urban Laboratory/Museum of London, 14 July 2018.

112 Susan Stryker, 'Dungeon Intimacies: The Poetics of Transsexual Sadomasochism', *parallax* 14, no. 1 (2008): 36–47, 38. On San Francisco's S/M histories see also, Pat Califia, 'San Francisco: Revisiting the City of Desire', in Gordon Brent Ingram, Anne-Marie Bouthillette and Yolanda Retter (eds.), *Queers in Space: Communities, Public Places, Sites of Resistance* (Seattle: Bay Press, 1997), 177–96.

113 Stryker, 'Dungeon Intimacies', 36–47, 38. The specific term 'intersectionality' appeared during the period of the Centre's existence in the work of critical race theorists who were analysing the relationships between race with other categories of difference. It is credited to legal scholar Kimberlé Crenshaw. Kimberlé Crenshaw, 'Demarginalizing the Intersection of Race and Sex: A Black Feminist Critique of Antidiscrimination Doctrine, Feminist Theory and Antiracist Politics', *University of Chicago Legal Forum*, no. 1, Article 8 (1989): 139–67; Gill Valentine, 'Theorizing and Researching Intersectionality: A Challenge for Feminist Geography', *The Professional Geographer* 59, no. 1 (2007): 10–21.

114 Roz Kaveney, letter addressed to 'Dear sisters and brothers', undated, HCA/Ephemera/955.

115 Another Centre user recalls: 'I look back with horror at some of the anti-trans rhetoric – particularly within the women's separatist [movement].' Another user and ex-employee notes that while transvestites were eventually admitted, transexuals were not accepted. Participants, 'Centre Pieces: A Public, Documented Conversation on the London Lesbian and Gay Centre', UCL Urban Laboratory/Museum of London, 14 July 2018; London Lesbian and Gay Centre: A Documented Conversation', UCL Urban Laboratory/Gays the Word, 18 October 2018.

116 Participant, 'Centre Pieces: A Public, Documented Conversation on the London Lesbian and Gay Centre', UCL Urban Laboratory/Museum of London, 14 July 2018.

117 Participants, 'Centre Pieces: A Public, Documented Conversation on the London Lesbian and Gay Centre', UCL Urban Laboratory/Museum of London, 14 July 2018.

118 Oscar Watson, interview by Ben Campkin, Museum of London, 14 July 2018.

119 In Watson's view, when it did go ahead, Sadie Masie's did indeed put off the majority of the Centre's regular users. Although it was popular with other groups, and continued at another Islington venue, Electroworks, after the Centre closed, it was not such a success in other venues. Participants, 'Centre Pieces: A Public, Documented Conversation on the London Lesbian and Gay Centre', UCL Urban Laboratory/Museum of London, 14 July 2018.

120 Alan Travis, 'London Lesbian and Gay Centre Refused Grant – Archive, 1985', *The Guardian*, 4 May 2018, https://www.theguardian.com/world/2018/may/04/london -gay-centre-refused-grant-archive-1985 (accessed 2 September 2022).

121 Anon, 'London Lesbian and Gay Centre Refused Grant', *The Guardian*, 4 May 1985.

122 Local Government Act 1986, https://www.legislation.gov.uk/ukpga/1986/10/contents (accessed 15 January 2022).

123 LLGC, 'Buy our Centre Appeal Fund', flyer, undated, c. 1989, Bishopsgate Institute Archives LLGC/LGBTM/147/10.

124 LLGC, *Centre News*, March 1992, HCA/CHE/2/12/43.

125 Oscar Watson, interview by Ben Campkin, Museum of London, 14 July 2018.

126 The gym was refurbished and its hours extended not long before the Centre closed. LLGC, *Centre News*, March 1992, HCA/CHE/2/12/43.

127 LLGC, *Centre News*, 1989.

128 LLGC, *Centre News*, 1989.

129 LLGC, 'Letter to the members: a Statement from the Board of Directors', 25 February 1991, Bishopsgate Institute Archives LLGC/LGBTM/147/10.

130 Oscar Watson, interview by Ben Campkin, Museum of London, 14 July 2018.

131 Oscar Watson, interview by Ben Campkin, Museum of London, 14 July 2018.

132 A survey in 1989 reported a value of £1.4 million, whereas the requested sale price was £510,000. LLGC, 'Manager's Report: News from the Nose', *Centre News*, May 1989, HCA/Ephemera/921; LLGC, 'Buy Our Centre', flyer, undated, HCA/ Ephemera/921.

133 Duncan Irvine, interview by Ben Campkin and Lo Marshall, Central Station, King's Cross, 31 March 2016.

134 Participant, 'Centre Pieces: A Public, Documented Conversation on the London Lesbian and Gay Centre', UCL Urban Laboratory/Museum of London, 14 July 2018.

135 Participant, 'Centre Pieces: A Public, Documented Conversation on the London Lesbian and Gay Centre', UCL Urban Laboratory/Museum of London, 14 July 2018.

136 Christobel Hastings, 'Remembering the 1980s UK Lesbian and Gay Centre that Died Too Soon', *Vice*, 27 August 2016, https://www.vice.com/en/article/dpk7xj/london -lesbian-gay-centre-30-years (accessed 15 January 2022).

137 London Lesbian and Gay Centre, *First Birthday Souvenir Diary*, April 1986, Bishopsgate Institute Archives, LAGNA Pamphlet Collection P699.

138 Femi Otitoju, interview by Natasha Nkonde, transcribed by Sur Este, 10 July 2017, *The GLC Oral History Project*, http://glcstory.co.uk/wp-content/uploads/2017/09/ Femi-Otitoju-transcript.pdf (accessed 15 January 2022).

139 Femi Otitoju, interview by Natasha Nkonde, transcribed by Sur Este, 10 July 2017, *The GLC Oral History Project*, http://glcstory.co.uk/wp-content/uploads/2017/09/ Femi-Otitoju-transcript.pdf (accessed 15 January 2022).

140 Participant, 'Centre Pieces: A Public, Documented Conversation on the London Lesbian and Gay Centre', UCL Urban Laboratory/Museum of London, 14 July 2018.

Chapter 3

1 Leticia Sabsay, 'The Emergence of the Other Sexual Citizen: Orientalism and the Modernisation of Sexuality', *Citizenship Studies*, 16, no. 5–6 (2012): 605–23.

2 Doreen B. Massey, *World City* (Cambridge: Polity, 2007), 81. For a discussion of more recent generations' inspiration by the GLC's 'viable socialism' see: Owen Hatherley, *Red Metropolis: Socialism and the Government of London* (London: Repeater Books, 2020), 107.

3 Curran notes the contradiction that while the 'urban left's' position on lesbian and gay rights, gender and environmentalism would become mainstream, social attitudes on race have changed more slowly and inconsistently. James Curran, 'Who Won Britain's Culture Wars? The Urban Left's Mixed Success', *British Politics and Policy at LSE* (blog), 14 October 2018, https://blogs.lse.ac.uk/politicsandpolicy/culture-wars -urban-left/ (accessed 30 July 2021).

4 Ian Richard Gordon and Tony Travers, 'London: Planning the Ungovernable City', *City, Culture and Society* 1, no. 2 (2010): 49–55; Hatherley, *Red Metropolis*, 118–19.

5 Greater London Council, *The London Industrial Strategy* (London, 1985), vii.

6 GLC, *The London Industrial Strategy*, 463–4.

7 GLC, *The London Industrial Strategy*, 169. See, for example: Michel de Certeau, *The Practice of Everyday Life*, trans. Steven Rendall (Berkeley: University of California Press, 1984); Henri Lefebvre, *Critique of Everyday Life*, trans. John Moore (London: Verso, 2008).

8 GLC, *The London Industrial Strategy*, 169–70.

9 Hatherley, *Red Metropolis*, 111.

10 Curran, 'Who Won Britain's Culture Wars?'

11 For accounts of these transformations, see, for example: Nick Buck, Ian Gordon, Peter Hall, Michael Harloe, and Mark Kleinman, *Working Capital: Life and Labour in Contemporary London* (London: Taylor & Francis Group, 2002); Michael Edwards, 'Wealth Creation and Poverty Creation', *City* 6, no. 1 (2002): 25–42; Susan S. Fainstein, Ian Gordon, and Michael Harloe (eds.), *Divided Cities: New York and London in the Contemporary World* (Oxford: Blackwell, 1992); Chris Hamnett, *Unequal City: London in the Global Arena* (London; New York: Routledge, 2003); Saskia Sassen, *The Global City: New York, London, Tokyo* (Princeton and Oxford: Princeton University Press, 2001).

12 Gordon and Travers, 'London: Planning the Ungovernable City', 50; Anna Whyatt, 'London East: Gateway to Regeneration', in Tim Butler and Mike Rustin (eds.), *Rising in the East: The Regeneration of East London* (Lawrence & Wishart, London, 1996), 265–87.

13 Gordon and Travers, 'London: Planning the Ungovernable City', 55.

14 Massey, *World City*, 2007, 21; 216.

15 Carolyn Harrison, Richard Munton, and Kevin Collins. 'Experimental Discursive Spaces: Policy Processes, Public Participation and the Greater London Authority', *Urban Studies* 41, no. 4 (2004): 903–17, 904.

16 Harrison, Munton, and Collins, 'Experimental Discursive Spaces', 903–17, 914.

17 For a synthesis of sociologist Saskia Sassen's articulation of this concept see: 'The Global City: Introducing a Concept', *The Brown Journal of World Affairs* 11, no. 2 (2004): 27–43; and for wider overviews and critiques of the concepts of world and global cities see, for example: Jonathan V Beaverstock, Richard G. Smith, and Peter

J. Taylor. 'World-City Network: A New Metageography?', *Annals of the Association of American Geographers* 90, no. 1 (2000): 123–34; Peter Hall, *The World Cities* (London: Weidenfeld and Nicolson, 1977); Anthony D. King, *Writing the Global City: Globalisation, Postcolonialism and the Urban* (London and New York: Routledge, Taylor & Francis Group, 2016); Doreen B. Massey, 'Capital Delight', in *World City*, 30–53; Jennifer Robinson, *Ordinary Cities: Between Modernity and Development* (New York and London: Routledge, 2006).

18 Michele Acuto, *Global Cities, Governance and Diplomacy: The Urban Link* (Routledge New Diplomacy Studies. London: Routledge, 2013); Neil Brenner and Nikolas Theodore (eds.), *Spaces of Neoliberalism: Urban Restructuring in North America and Western Europe* (Malden, MA and Oxford: Blackwell, 2002); Ben Campkin, *Remaking London: Decline and Regeneration in Urban Culture* (London: IB Tauris, 2013); Helen Carter, Henrik Gutzon Larsen and Kristian Olesen, 'A Planning Palimpsest: Neoliberal Planning in a Welfare State Tradition', *European Journal of Spatial Development* no. 58 (June 2015): 1–20; Robert Imrie, Loretta Lees and Mike Raco (eds.), *Regenerating London: Governance, Sustainability and Community in a Global City* (London, Milton Park, Abingdon, Oxon and New York: Routledge, 2009); Massey, *World City*, 48; Anna Minton, *Big Capital: Who Is London for?* (London: Penguin Books, 2017).

19 Gordon and Travers, 'London: Planning the Ungovernable City', 49–55; Doug Yates, *The Ungovernable City: The Politics of Urban Problems and Policy Making* (Cambridge, MA: MIT Press, 1977); Joel A. Tarr, 'Review of *The Ungovernable City: The Politics of Urban Problems and Policy Making*, by Douglas Yates', *The Journal of Politics* 41, no. 1 (1979): 290–2.

20 Gordon and Travers, 'London: Planning the Ungovernable City', 49.

21 Drivers include UNESCO's definition of 'intangible heritage': 'The "intangible cultural heritage" means the practices, representations, expressions, knowledge, skills – as well as the instruments, objects, artefacts and cultural spaces associated therewith – that communities, groups and, in some cases, individuals recognize as part of their cultural heritage. This intangible cultural heritage, transmitted from generation to generation, is constantly recreated by communities and groups in response to their environment, their interaction with nature and their history, and provides them with a sense of identity and continuity, thus promoting respect for cultural diversity and human creativity. For the purposes of this Convention, consideration will be given solely to such intangible cultural heritage as is compatible with existing international human rights instruments, as well as with the requirements of mutual respect among communities, groups and individuals, and of sustainable development'. UNESCO, 'What Is Intangible Cultural Heritage?' https://ich.unesco.org/en/what-is-intangible-heritage-00003 (accessed 21 July 2020).

22 Phil Hadfield, 'The Night-Time City. Four Modes of Exclusion: Reflections on the *Urban Studies* Special Collection', *Urban Studies* 52, no. 3 (2015): 606–16; Michele Acuto, 'We Need a Science of the Night', *Nature* 576, no. 7787 (18 December 2019): 339.

23 Andreina Seijas and Mirik Milan Gelders, 'Governing the Night-Time City: The Rise of Night Mayors as a New Form of Urban Governance after Dark', *Urban Studies* 58, no. 2 (2021): 316–34.

24 See, for example: Mayor of London, *Cultural Infrastructure Plan* (March 2019), Greater London Authority.

200 *Notes*

25 'Cities can be world cities in all kinds of other ways [beyond the command functions of financial and business sectors], as dominant foci in particular spheres of activity [. . .] Sydney perhaps in lesbian and gay networks'. See: Massey, *World City*, 36.

26 Lisa Duggan, 'The New Homonormativity: The Sexual Politics of Neoliberalism', in *Materializing Democracy: Toward a Revitalized Cultural Politics*, ed. Russ Castronovo and Dana D. Nelson (Durham, NC: Duke University Press, 2002), 175–94.

27 Steve Leach and David Wilson, 'Urban Elites in England: New Models of Executive Governance', *International Journal of Urban and Regional Research* 28, no. 1 (1 March 2004): 134–49.

28 Colin Rallings and Michael Thrasher, 'Personality Politics and Protest Voting: The First Elections to the Greater London Authority', *Parliamentary Affairs* 53, no. 4 (2000): 753–64, 754.

29 Tony Travers, 'The Greater London Authority, 2000 to 2008', London School of Economics, 2 http://www.lse.ac.uk/geography-and-environment/research/lse-london /documents/Archive/HEIF-2/Tony-T.pdf. Livingstone beat Conservative candidate Stephen Norris by 58 per cent to 42 per cent when both first and second preference votes were counted.

30 Rallings and Thrasher, 'Personality Politics and Protest Voting', 763; Ben Worthy, Mark Bennister and Max W. Stafford, 'Rebels Leading London: The Mayoralties of Ken Livingstone and Boris Johnson Compared', *British Politics* 14, no. 1 (1 March 2019): 23–43.

31 For example, the age of consent for same-sex sexual relations between men was reduced from 18 to 16 in England, Wales and Scotland in 2000. From 2002, same-sex couples had the right to adopt. Other reforms included the repeal of Section 28 in England and Wales, in 2003. This infamous 1988 addition to the Local Government Act 1986, set out specifically to limit local authorities' powers to support lesbian and gay equality, stating that they could not 'intentionally promote homosexuality or publish material with the intention of promoting homosexuality' or 'promote the teaching in any maintained school of the acceptability of homosexuality as a pretended family relationship'. This legislation was both a manifestation of the moral panic engendered by the HIV/AIDS crisis and a reaction to the work that local authorities, including the GLC and London councils, were doing in support of lesbian and gay communities. Its negative impact was far-reaching and revocation was a major, hard earned accomplishment. Owen Hatherley notes that, according to Thatcher's biographer, Section 28 had been formulated in part as a direct response to the GLC's affirmative promotional approaches. The Equality Act (Sexual Orientation) Regulations 2007, introduced further measures to protect against employment legislation according to sexual orientation, adding homophobic discrimination where this had been overlooked in the Equality Act 2006. The passing of the Gender Recognition Act 2004 introduced rights for gender transition to an 'acquired gender'. This was based on a binary understanding of gender: male/female. It presented the possibility for a person to apply to a Gender Recognition Panel for a gender recognition certificate stating their acquired gender, and to marry someone of the opposite gender, but only after a diagnosis of gender dysphoria. Sexual Offences (Amendment) Act 2000, https://www.legislation.gov.uk/ukpga/2000/44/contents (accessed 16 August 2020); Adoption and Children Act 2002, https://www.legislation .gov.uk/ukpga/2002/38/contents (accessed 16 August 2020); Local Government Act *1988*, https://www.legislation.gov.uk/ukpga/1988/9/section/28/enacted (accessed 16 August 2020); Equality Act 2006, https://www.legislation.gov.uk/ukpga/2006

/3/contents (accessed 16 August 2020); The Equality Act (Sexual Orientation) Regulations 2007, https://www.netlawman.co.uk/ia/sexual-orientation-regulations (accessed 16 August 2020); Gender Recognition Act 2004, https://www.legislation .gov.uk/ukpga/2004/7/section/1/enacted (accessed 16 August 2020); Hatherley, *Red Metropolis*, 121, note 33.

32 Ben Clements and Clive D. Field, 'The Polls – Trends: Public Opinion Toward Homosexuality and Gay Rights in Great Britain', *The Public Opinion Quarterly* 78, no. 2 (2014): 523–47.

33 'Equality Mainstreaming', ILGA-Europe (2007) https://www.ilga-europe.org/ resources/ilga-europe-reports-and-other-materials/equality-mainstreaming-fact -sheet-2007 (accessed 20 July 2020).

34 Transport for London, London Development Agency, Metropolitan Policy Authority, London Fire and Emergency Planning Authority.

35 'Civil Partnership Act 2004 (c. 33)', https://www.legislation.gov.uk/ukpga/2004 /33/enacted/data.xht?view=snippet&wrap=true (accessed 14 July 2022). This was followed by the 'Marriage (Same Sex Couples) Act 2013 (c. 30)', https://www .legislation.gov.uk/ukpga/2013/30/enacted/data.xht?view=snippet&wrap=true (accessed 14 July 2022).

36 The London register followed the *Pacte Civil de Solidarité* introduced in Paris in 1999, while other European countries, including Germany and the Netherlands, had already granted full marriage rights. Ken Livingstone, *Ken Livingstone's Manifesto for London: Ken 4 London* (London: Simon Fletcher, Livingstone for London, 2000). Green Party London Assembly Member and former mayoral candidate, Darren Johnson, had also pushed for it in his first question at Mayor's Question Time. Green World, 'Darren Johnson's Legacy', https://greenworld.org.uk/article/darren-johnsons -legacy (accessed 8 August 2020). For coverage of the first ceremonies, see: '"Gay Marriage" Register Signs up 300', *BBC News*, 5 September 2002, http://news.bbc.co .uk/1/hi/england/2237949.stm (accessed 8 August 2020); CNN, 'UK Gay Couples Register Launched, CNN.Com, 7 September 2001', https://edition.cnn.com/2001/ WORLD/europe/09/05/gay.register/index.html?related (accessed 8 August 2020).

37 'Mayor Attends Gay "Marriage"', *BBC News*, 5 September 2001, http://news.bbc.co.uk /1/hi/uk/1525205.stm (accessed 30 July 2021); John Carvel, 'London Couple First to Sign Gay Register', *The Guardian*, 3 September 2001, https://www.theguardian.com/ uk/2001/sep/03/london.politics (accessed 30 July 2021).

38 Duggan, 'The New Homonormativity', 182.

39 '"Gay Marriage" Register Signs up 300', 2002.

40 Tatchell, who stood unsuccessfully as an independent candidate in the first London Assembly elections, has pressured all three of the London mayors on a variety of issues. 'Capital Move for Gay Couples', *BBC News*, 28 June 2001, http://news.bbc.co .uk/1/hi/uk/1411648.stm (accessed 30 July 2021). See, also: Peter Tatchell, 'Questions for Ken', *The Guardian*, 17 April 2008, https://www.theguardian.com/commentisfree /2008/apr/17/questionsforken (accessed 30 July 2021); Peter Tatchell Foundation, 'London Mayor Urged to Save World Pride', 26 June 2015, https://www.petertatche llfoundation.org/london-mayor-urged-to-save-world-pride/; 'Pride Parade', Mayor's Question Time, 9 July 2018, https://www.london.gov.uk/questions/2018/1979 (accessed 30 July 2021).

41 The campaign for civil partnership was championed by Lord Lester and Labour MP Jane Griffiths. Carvel, 'London Couple First to Sign Gay Register', 2001. The GLA also provided a model to other organisations in successfully applying to be listed in the

Stonewall Equality Index, a mechanism to measure and showcase good employment practices, which incentivised equalities mainstreaming. In 2007, it was ranked third place, moving up to second by 2008, with Transport for London and the London Fire Brigade, both also under the mayor's jurisdiction, ranking sixth and thirteenth respectively. Stonewall, *Workplace Equality Index 2007: The Top 100 Employers for Gay People in Britain*, 2007; MayorWatch, 'GLA Is UK's Second Most Gay Friendly Employer', 11 January 2008, https://www.mayorwatch.co.uk/gla-is-uks-second-most -gay-friendly-employer/ (accessed 30 July 2021).

42 Gavin Brown places Outrage! in the context of queer social movements and notes that it was connected to ACT UP (London) and was a response to murders of gay men in London and the policing of cruising sites. Gavin Brown, 'Queer Movement', in David Paternotte and Manon Tremblay (eds.), *The Ashgate Research Companion to Lesbian and Gay Activism* (London: Routledge, 2015), 73–86, 77.

43 After the refusal of eight couples' applications to registry offices for Civil Partnerships, an application was made to the European Court of Human Rights, on 2 February 2011. Equal = Love, http://equallove.org.uk/ (accessed 17 August 2020). Subsequently, under the Conservative-led Conservative-Liberal Democrat coalition government, the *Marriage (Same Sex Couples) Act 2013* was introduced permitting civil marriage between same-sex couples. Eventually, after a Supreme Court ruling in the UK courts, it was announced that civil partnership would be opened to heterosexual couples in October 2018. The Supreme Court, *R (on the Application of Steinfeld and Keiden) (Appellants) v Secretary of State for the Home Department (in Substitution for Secretary of State for Education (Respondent)*, https://www .supremecourt.uk/cases/uksc-2017-0060.html (accessed 17 August 2020).

44 Peter Tatchell, 'Qaradawi Not Welcome', *Labour Left Briefing*, November 2004, http:// www.whatnextjournal.org.uk/Pages/Politics/Notwelcome.html (accessed 30 July 2021).

45 Outrage!, *Mayor's Dossier on al-Qaradawi Distorts the Truth*, 2005, http://outrage .org.uk/wp-content/uploads/2008/02/mayorsdossier-thetruth.pdf (accessed 30 July 2021).

46 Tatchell, 'Qaradawi Not Welcome', 2004; 'Livingstone Embraces Visiting Muslim Cleric as "man of Tolerance"', *The Independent*, 13 July 2004, https://www.independent .co.uk/news/uk/this-britain/livingstone-embraces-visiting-muslim-cleric-as-man-of -tolerance-553002.html (accessed 30 July 2021); 'An Embrace That Shames London', *New Statesman*, 24 January 2005, https://www.newstatesman.com/node/195201 (accessed 30 July 2021); 'Qaradawi Not Welcome', http://www.whatnextjournal .org.uk/Pages/Politics/Notwelcome.html (accessed 17 August 2020). For further coverage see, for example: Bowcott, Owen and Faisal al Yafai, 'Islamic Cleric Defends Suicide Bombing Stance', *The Guardian*, 8 July 2004; Sean O'Neill, 'Livingstone Asks Controversial Cleric to Return', *The Times*, 13 July 2004; Paul Waugh, 'Fury Grows over Race Hate Cleric Who Can't Be Deported', *Evening Standard*, 8 July 2004.

47 Mayor of London, *Why the Mayor of London will Maintain Dialogues With All of London's Faiths and Communities. A Reply to the Dossier against the Mayor's meeting with Dr Yusuf al-Qaradawi*, Greater London Authority, 2005, https://www.yumpu .com/en/document/read/17782306/why-the-mayor-of-london-will-maintain -dialogue-with-all-of-londons- (accessed 18 July 2022). Livingstone writes: 'As Mayor of London, I have a responsibility to support the rights of all of London's diverse communities and to maintain a dialogue with their political and religious leaders, irrespective of the fact that there will always be different views on many issues.' The

response to the dossier was also published as a reply to Tatchell in Ken Livingstone, 'Tatchell's Islamic Conspiracy Theory', *Labour Left Briefing*, February 2005; Peter Roberts, 'Qaradawi Is Welcome', *Labour Left*, December 2004.

48 Section 28, *Local Government Act of England and Wales 1988*, https://www.legislation .gov.uk/ukpga/1988/9/section/28 (accessed 6 April 2021).

49 Massey, *World City*, 5; Peter Tatchell, 'Mayor's Dodgy Dossier on Dr. Qaradawi', http://www.petertatchell.net/religion/qaradawidossier/ (accessed 16 August 2020). The row, which included accusations of anti-Semitism, anticipated the tangle of thorny controversies that Livingstone would later become entangled in. Like his successor, Boris Johnson, he courted many controversies during his career. He was suspended from office in 2006, after comparing a Jewish *Evening Standard* reporter to a concentration camp guard. The incidents increased in his later years in public life, leading to his suspension from the Labour Party after allegations of anti-semitism and his eventual resignation from the party in 2018. Ben Worthy, Mark Bennister and Max W. Stafford, 'Rebels Leading London: The Mayoralties of Ken Livingstone and Boris Johnson Compared', *British Politics* 14, no. 1 (1 March 2019): 23–43, 32.

50 Massey, *World City*, 6.

51 Massey, *World City*, 9.

52 Michael Keith, 'Postcolonial London and the Allure of the Cosmopolitan City', *AA Files*, no. 49 (Spring 2003): 57–67, 61.

53 Keith, 'Postcolonial London', 61. In their exchanges, Livingstone accused Tatchell of submission to an Islamic conspiracy theory. Livingstone, 'Tatchell's Islamic Conspiracy Theory', *Labour Left Briefing*, 2005.

54 Michael Warner, *Fear of a Queer Planet: Queer Politics and Social Theory* (Minneapolis and London: University of Minnesota Press, 1993), xxv.

55 Warner, *Fear of a Queer Planet*, xx.

56 Jack Halberstam, *In a Queer Time and Place Transgender Bodies, Subcultural Lives* (New York and London: New York University Press, 2005), 12.

57 Livingstone states: 'it is important to support LGBT equality, challenge discrimination and celebrate diversity in this country, so that London sets a world-class benchmark that others are inspired to follow'. 'Ken Livingstone on Gay Rights', *New Statesman*, 20 July 2007, https://www.newstatesman.com/politics/2007/07/ lesbian-gay-livingstone-london (accessed 10 September 2019). The comparison with New York is made in reference to NYC's earlier commitment to marriage equality: Ken Livingstone, 'Comment: Ken Livingstone Claims Boris Johnson's City Hall Is "Passive" on Gay Rights'. *Pink News*, 30 June 2011, https://www.pinknews.co.uk/2011 /06/30/comment-ken-livingstone-claims-boris-johnsons-city-hall-is-passive-on -gay-rights/(accessed 10 September 2019). Other arguments for an internationally minded approach could of course have been made based on the history of the city as the centre of the British empire, a facilitator of the export of homophobic laws and beliefs which continue to effect violence.

58 Massey, *World City*, 36.

59 Phil Hubbard and Eleanor Wilkinson, 'Welcoming the World? Hospitality, Homonationalism, and the London 2012 Olympics', *Antipode*, 47, no. 3 (2015): 598–615; Jasbir K. Puar, *Terrorist Assemblages: Homonationalism in Queer Times* (Durham: Duke University Press, 2017).

60 Mayor of London, *The London Plan: Spatial Development Strategy for Greater* (London, February 2004), Policy 3A.14, 'Addressing the needs of London's diverse population', section 3.70.

204   *Notes*

61 Mayor of London, *The London Plan*, 2004, Policy 3A.14.

62 Mayor of London, *The London Plan*, 2004, policy 3A.14.

63 Mayor of London, *The London Plan*, 2004, 3.70, 73.

64 Mayor of London, *The London Plan*, 2004, 3.70, 73.

65 Rob Downey's present appointment is Senior Policy Officer, Equalities and Fairness Team, Greater London Authority. That he has remained in post has provided some continuity, even while modes of public engagement and priorities have changed across the Livingstone, Johnson and Khan mayoralties.

66 'Lesbian, Gay, Bisexual and Transgender Forum Terms of Reference', Mayor's Question Time, 23 February 2005, reference 2005/0472, https://www.london.gov.uk/questions/2005/0472-0 (accessed 19 September 2019).

67 The group were labelled 'Ken's Wimmin' by the right-wing press. '"Ken's Wimmin" to Be Kicked out of City Hall', *Conservative Home*, 18 June 2008, https://www.conservativehome.com/thetorydiary/2008/06/kens-wimmin-to.html (accessed 17 August 2020).

68 Peter Tatchell, 'Questions for Ken', *The Guardian*, 17 April 2008, https://www.theguardian.com/commentisfree/2008/apr/17/questionsforken (accessed 30 July 2021).

69 A request to clarify which GLA posts dealt specifically with LGBT issues identified that there was a (vacant), full-time LGBT Equality Coordinator post. 'Lesbian, Gay, Bisexual and Transgender Post', *Mayor's Question Time*, 31 March 2004, reference 2004/0473, https://www.london.gov.uk/questions/2004/0473 (accessed 19 September 2019).

70 Mayor of London, *Sexual Orientation Equality Scheme: From isolation to inclusion*, Consultation Draft (London: Greater London Authority, November 2006). This document is archived in its draft status on the GLA's current website. It states: 'The Mayor will also be working strategically with the functional bodies to ensure that LGB equality is mainstreamed across the GLA group and that service provision meets and reflects the needs of LGB Londoners' (unpaginated).

71 Mayor of London, *Sexual Orientation Equality Scheme*, 2006. Following a string of failed attempts by the GLA to be listed on the Stonewall Equality Index of employers, in 2013, London Assembly Member, Tom Copley, looked back to the extensive *Sexual Orientation Regulations* produced under Livingstone in a positive light, noting that this had 'demonstrated to both GLA staff and organisations related to the GLA how seriously LGB diversity was considered'. Tom Copley, 'City Hall Fails to Make Stonewall Equality Index for Fourth Year Running', *Tom Copley AM: Labour London Assembly Member* (blog), 17 January 2013, https://tomcopley.com/city-hall-fails-stonewall-equality-index-fourth-year-running/ (accessed 19 November 2019).

72 Outrage! and Tatchell were once again prominent in this. Tatchell, 'Questions for Ken', *The Guardian*, 17 April 2008.

73 These groups were represented by: Linda Bellos, Black Lesbians UK; Jackie Lewis, UNISON; Lynsey River, Polari; Brenda Ellis, REGARD; and Pav Akhtar, Imaan. Tatchell, 'Qaradawi Not Welcome', *Labour Left Briefing*, 2004.

74 Adam Bienkov, 'Boris Johnson Called Gay Men "Tank-Topped Bumboys" and Black People "Piccaninnies" with "Watermelon Smiles"', *Business Insider*, 9 June 2020, https://www.businessinsider.com/boris-johnson-record-sexist-homophobic-and-racist-comments-bumboys-piccaninnies-2019-6?r=US&IR=T (accessed 30 July 2021); Jasmine Anderson, 'The 18 Most Controversial Boris Johnson Quotes Unearthed This Election', *i*, 11 December 2019, https://inews.co.uk/news/politics

/boris-johnson-quotes-controversy-comments-general-election-2019-campaign-372969 (accessed 30 July 2021).

75 "'Ken's Wimmin" to Be Kicked out', *Conservative Home*, 2008.

76 Tony Grew, 'OutRage! Backs Boris over Abolition of Gay Advisory Panel', *Pink News*, 10 July 2008, https://www.pinknews.co.uk/2008/07/10/outrage-backs-boris-over-abolition-of-gay-advisory-panel/ (accessed 30 July 2021).

77 Grew, 'OutRage! Backs Boris', 2008.

78 Grew, 'OutRage! Backs Boris' 2008.

79 Gordon and Travers, 'London: Planning the Ungovernable City', 50–1.

80 Michael Keith, 'The PWC report on Tower Hamlets Highlights Fundamental Tensions in Local Democracy, Not Always Thought Through Clearly in New Mayoral Systems', *INLOGOV Blog*, 21 November 2014, https://inlogov.com/tag/michael-keith/ (accessed 8 April 2021).

81 Rob Downey, Senior Policy Officer, Equalities and Fairness Team, and Raja Moussaoui, Greater London Authority, interview by Ben Campkin, London, 30 June 2020.

82 GLF member, Mayor's Pride Reception, 27 June 2022, City Hall.

83 For example, signalling and undermining the violent associations of the Western Frontier. See, for example, its use in the work of artists such as Hal Fischer and Andy Warhol.

84 The term derives from the environmental justice movement. It was used to critique corporate uses of pink ribbons to suggest solidarity with breast cancer patients by companies who persisted to use chemicals linked to cancer. Amy Lubitow and Mia Davis, 'Pastel Injustice: The Corporate Use of Pinkwashing for Profit', *Environmental Justice* 4, no. 2 (1 June 2011): 139–44.

85 'Boris Johnson's Pre-Pride Speech', *Homovision.TV*, 2008, https://www.youtube.com/watch?v=n6h-C0p--ys (accessed 11 June 2020); 'Boris Johnson's Gay Pride Speech', *Homovision.TV*, 2009, https://www.youtube.com/watch?time_continue=2&v=trshMHpXHm8&feature=emb_logo (accessed 11 June 2020).

86 Anderson, 'The 18 Most Controversial Boris Johnson Quotes', 2019.

87 Livingstone, 'Boris Johnson's City Hall Is "Passive"', *Pink News*, 2011.

88 Joe Morgan, 'London Mayor Candidates Face Grilling from Gay Voters', *Gay Star News*, 14 April 2012 .

89 Hélène Mulholland, 'London Mayoral Candidates Campaign on Gay Issues', *The Guardian*, 14 April 2012, https://www.theguardian.com/politics/2012/apr/14/london-mayor-hustings-gay-issues (accessed 30 July 2021); Morgan, 'London Mayor Candidates Face Grilling', 2012.

90 'London Gay Manifesto', *Mayor's Question Time*, 11 November 2013, reference 2013/4148; 'London Gay Manifesto', *Mayor's Question Time*, 9 December 2013, reference 2013/5172.

91 See, for example: GLA, *Minutes of the meeting of London's Trans Organisations*, 10 September 2014; Mayor of London, *Assessment of the GLA's Impact on Trans Equality*, 2011, https://www.london.gov.uk/what-we-do/communities/assessment-glas-impact-trans-equality (accessed 30 July 2021).

92 Duggan, 'The New Homonormativity', 175–94, 183.

93 Mayor of London, *The London Plan: The Spatial Development Strategy for London Consolidated with Alterations Since 2011* (London: Mayor of London, 2016), Policy 3.16, 'Protection and Enhancement of Social Infrastructure', 128–9.

94 Warner, *Fear of a Queer Planet,* xvii.

95 House of Commons, 'Office of the Deputy Prime Minister: Housing, Planning, Local Government and the Regions Committee', *The Evening Economy and the Urban Renaissance*, Twelfth Report of Session 2002-3, HC396-1 (London: The Stationery Office, 2003).

96 Franco Bianchini, 'Night Cultures, Night Economies', *Planning Practice & Research* 10, no. 2 (1 May 1995): 121–6, 123.

97 On the different waves of urban night studies, see: Hadfield, 'The Night-Time City', 606–16; Seijas and Gelders, 'Governing the Night-Time City', 3.

98 *The Evening Economy and the Urban Renaissance*, 2003.

99 Melisa Wickham, *Alcohol Consumption in the Night-Time Economy: Policy Interventions*, GLA Economics, Working Paper 55 (London: Greater London Authority, September 2012).

100 Mayor of London, 'Mayor Announces Plan for Night Time Commission for the Capital', London, City Hall, 15 March 2016, https://www.london.gov.uk//press-releases /mayoral/night-time-commission-for-the-capital (accessed 30 July 2021); Scott Wilson, 'Boris Johnson Reveals Plan to Save London Night Time Economy', *FACT Magazine: Music News, New Music*, 15 March 2016, https://www.factmag.com/2016 /03/15/boris-johnson-night-time-commission-plans-london/ (accessed 30 July 2021).

101 Seijas and Gelders, 'Governing the Night-Time City', 6.

102 GLA, *The London's Grassroots Music Venues Rescue Plan*, 2015, http:// musicvenuetrust.com/wp-content/uploads/2016/09/londons_grassroots_music _venues_-_rescue_plan_-_october_2015.pdf (accessed 15 July 2022).

103 Mayor of London, 'Mayor Acts on Rescue Plan to Save London's Music Venues', 19 October 2015, https://www.london.gov.uk//press-releases/mayoral/mayor-helps -london-music (accessed 31 July 2021).

104 Clare Welsh, 'New Legislation Passed to Protect UK Music Venues from Developers', *FACT Magazine: Music News, New Music*, 14 March 2016, https://www.factmag.com /2016/03/14/new-legislation-passed-to-protect-uk-music-venues/ (accessed 31 July 2021).

105 The Mayor of London's Music Venues Task Force, *London's Grassroots Music Venues: Rescue Plan. A Report for the Mayor, Music Industry, Local Authorities, Government, Planners, Developers, Licensers, Police, Economists, Tourism Agencies, Musicians, Culture Funders* (London: Greater London Authority, October 2015).

106 On night policy, Conservative candidate, Zac Goldsmith followed Johnson's lead, and some of the proposals in the *Music Venues Rescue Plan*. He emphasised a desire to protect and promote the night-time economy, to deliver and extend the planned night-tube – proposed under Johnson's administration but delayed by industrial action until late 2016 – and drew attention to the detrimental effects of development on creative businesses. He promised to put the onus of noise reduction on builders and protect existing businesses. Where Goldsmith's tone changed from Johnson, and differed from Khan's manifesto, was in the strong framing of his comments under the banner of 'making London safer at night', focusing on policing and crime. Zac Goldsmith, *My Action Plan for Greater London: Manifesto Conservative Party*, 2016, 11; 54; 87–8, https://issuu.com/conservativeparty/docs/zac_manifesto (accessed 2 September 2019).

107 Goldsmith, *My Action Plan*, 88.

108 The Late Night Levy was subsequently described by City Hall as 'a discretionary power conferred on licensing authorities by the *Police Reform and Social Responsibility Act 2011* that came into effect on 31 October 2012. It enables licensing

Notes

authorities to introduce a charge for all businesses in their area that are licensed to supply alcohol between midnight and 6.00 as a means of raising a contribution towards the costs of policing the late-night economy'. Mayor of London, 'Late Night Levy', 17 March 2016, https://www.london.gov.uk/what-we-do/mayors-office -policing-and-crime-mopac/governance-and-decision-making/mopac-decisions--44 (accessed 3 September 2019).

109 Music Venues Task Force, *London's Grassroots Music Venues*, 4.

110 Hadfield, 'The Night-Time City', 606–16, 607.

111 Mayor of London, 'Mayor Backs Campaign to Save Royal Vauxhall Tavern', 24 June 2016, https://www.london.gov.uk//press-releases/mayoral/mayor-backs-campaign-to -save-royal-vauxhall-tavern-0 (accessed 31 July 2021).

112 Jamie Bullen, 'Sadiq Khan Calls on Londoners to Unite against Hatred Ahead of Pride', *Evening Standard*, 21 June 2016, http://www.standard.co.uk/news/london/ pride-in-london-sadiq-khan-says-it-is-more-important-than-ever-to-embrace-lgbt -community-a3277601.html (accessed 31 July 2021).

113 Josh Withey, '"You Are the Antidote to the Sadness": Sadiq Khan's Powerful Message to LGBT Pride in London', *The Independent*, 5 July 2017, http://www.independent.co .uk/news/uk/home-news/sadiq-khan-gay-pride-london-lgbt-mayor-peter-tatchell -parade-antidote-sadness-a7824006.html (accessed 31 July 2021).

114 Mayor of London, 'Mayor Appoints Philip Kolvin QC as Chair of the Night Time Commission', 16 December 2016, https://www.london.gov.uk//press-releases/mayoral /mayor-announces-chair-of-night-time-commission (accessed 21 July 2021).

115 Mayor of London, 'Mayor Appoints Philip Kolvin QC'.

116 Philip Kolvin QC, 'Manifesto for the Night Time Economy', 2016, https://corners tonebarristers.com/cmsAdmin/uploads/night-time-economy-final.pdf (accessed 5 September 2019).

117 Kolvin, 'Manifesto for the Night Time Economy', 3.

118 Kolvin, 'Manifesto for the Night Time Economy', pledge 4.

119 Philip Kolvin QC, 'Manifesto for the Night Time Economy', https://cornerstonebarr isters.com/cmsAdmin/uploads/night-time-economy-final.pdf (accessed 5 September 2019), 3.

120 Pippa Crerar, 'Expert Who Saved Fabric Nightclub Quits "24-Hour London" Commission', *Evening Standard*, 10 January 2018, https://www.standard.co.uk/news /london/expert-who-saved-fabric-nightclub-quits-24hour-london-commission -a3736761.html (31 July 2021).

121 London Night Time Commission, *Think Night: London's Neighbourhoods from 6pm to 6am* (London: Mayor of London, 2019), 41.

122 'Night Time Commission Opinion Research 2018 - London Datastore', https:// data.london.gov.uk/dataset/night-time-commission-consultation-2018 (accessed 29 August 2019). The manifesto also committed to deliver the Night Tube; and emphasised homelessness as a core concern. The Night Tube, along with a 24-hour bus service, had been discussed since the first mayoral election, when it had featured in Conservative candidate Stephen Norris' manifesto.

123 Seijas and Gelders, 'Governing the Night-Time City', 11. Seijas and Gelders provide a useful timeline and analysis of the role.

124 Seijas and Gelders, 'Governing the Night-Time City', 10.

125 Seijas and Gelders, 'Governing the Night-Time City', 3.

126 Following Lamé's appointment, it is notable that many other cities have established comparable offices. In September 2017, New York City Mayor Bill de Blasio

instituted an Office of Nightlife, with comparable objectives to London and Amsterdam, of both regulating and protecting night-spaces and activities. Ariel Palitz was appointed in 2018. Rallings and Thrasher, 'Personality Politics and Protest Voting', 754; Madine Toure, 'Search for New York City's First-Ever Nightlife Mayor Underway', *Observer*, 24 October 2017, https://observer.com/2017/10/new -york-city-nightlife-mayor/ (accessed 31 July 2021). As with other mayors' choices of advisers, Khan was accused of cronyism in appointing Lamé. Conservative MP and 2021 mayoral candidate, Shaun Bailey, accused Khan of cronyism when Lamé was paid a £1,000 fee, in her role as a performer and member of Duckie collective, to host an event that was part funded by the Mayor. This was reported by Conservative commentators in ways reminiscent of the coverage community events and organisations funded by the GLC under Ken Livingstone's leadership. Angharad Carrick, 'Sadiq Khan Urged to End "Culture of Cronyism"', *CityAM*, 6 February 2020, https://www.cityam.com/sadiq-khan-urged-to-end-culture-of -cronyism/ (accessed 31 July 2021); 'Sadiq's £75,000 Night Czar Trousered £1000 From Community Event', Amy Lamé Archives', *Guido Fawkes*, https://order-order .com/people/amy-lame/ (accessed 18 August 2020).

127 Lamé had worked in London's LGBTQ+ night venues, including at First Out Café (see Chapter 5), since 1992, co-founded and compered the award-winning artistic and activist club night, Duckie, and chaired RVT Future. She also brought experience of engagement in mainstream Labour party and city politics, having served as Mayoress of Camden, one of the London local boroughs, between 2010 and 2011. In 2017 she published a children's book on LGBTQ+ rights: Amy Lamé, *From Prejudice to Pride: A History of the LGBTQ+ Movement* (London: Wayland, 2017).

128 'I am a woman who has worked my entire life at night; I know what it's like to come off a shift at 3 in the morning . . . I knew that there was this hidden workforce of people that are making our city tick, that are just not being recognised, nor do they have the access to the same services and equality that people do during the day'. Amy Lamé, interview by Ben Campkin, 4 September 2019, City Hall, London. Lamé's appointment was criticised at the time. Her links to the Labour party and forthright tweets about Tory politicians surfaced as controversies after her appointment. This led to additional scrutiny of the recruitment process. Mayor of London, 'Scrutinising the Night Czar Appointment', 22 November 2016, https://www.london.gov.uk//press -releases/assembly/scrutinising-the-night-czar-appointment (accessed 6 July 2020). Pippa Crerar, 'Night Czar Ordered to Delete Offensive Tweets - Including Osborne "c***" Comment', *Evening Standard*, 24 November 2016, http://www.standard.co.uk /news/london/night-czar-amy-lam-ordered-to-delete-all-of-her-offensive-tweets -about-the-tories-including-one-a3403456.html (accessed 6 July 2020).

129 Amy Lamé, interview by Ben Campkin, 4 September 2019, City Hall, London.

130 Seijas and Gelders, 'Governing the Night-Time City', 4.

131 Amy Lamé, interview by Ben Campkin, 4 September 2019, City Hall, London.

132 London Assembly Economy Committee, *Rewrite the Night: The Future of London's Night-Time Economy*, 2018.

133 Mayor of London, *Cultural Infrastructure Plan* (London: Mayor of London, March 2019).

134 José Esteban Muñoz, *Cruising Utopia: The Then and There of Queer Futurity* (New York and London: New York University Press', 2009, 52.

135 Amy Lamé, interview by Ben Campkin, London, 21 May 2020.

136 The original Music Venues Task Force, under Johnson, comprised seven white middle-aged men, including two club owners, three other industry reps, and two civil servants. Music Venues Task Force, *London's Grassroots Music Venues,* 2015, 5.

137 London Music Board, Terms of Reference, April 2017, https://www.london.gov.uk/ sites/default/files/terms_of_reference_-_london_music_board_-_april_2017_-_final .pdf (accessed 14 July 2020).

138 Mattha Busby, 'London's Night Czar Criticised Following Strict New Hackney Nightlife Rules', *The Independent,* 20 July 2018, https://www.independent.co.uk/news /uk/home-news/london-hackney-nightlife-curfew-rules-amy-lame-criticism-sadiq -khan-a8456666.html (accessed 31 July 2021); Resident Advisor, 'Opinion: Hackney Council's Decision Is a Huge Setback for London Nightlife', *Resident Advisor,* 20 July 2018, https://www.residentadvisor.net/features/3306 (accessed 19 August 2020); Marissa Cetin, 'London Night Czar Amy Lamé Responds to Criticism around Controversial New Hackney Licensing Policy', *Resident Advisor,* 26 July 2018, https:// www.residentadvisor.net/news/42204 (accessed 19 August 2020).

139 Seijas and Gelders, 'Governing the Night-Time City', 8.

140 Mayor of London, '7 Things the Mayor's Night Czar Has Done in Her First Year', 3 November 2017, https://www.london.gov.uk//city-hall-blog/7-things-mayors-night -czar-has-done-her-first-year (accessed 31 July 2021). This article is an example of the competitive framing of London as a 24/7 city, referring to 'Mayor Sadiq Khan's vision for London to become a trailblazing night-time city, competing with the likes of Berlin, Tokyo and New York'.

141 Amy Lamé, interview by Ben Campkin, 4 September 2019, City Hall, London.

142 For example, see: Westminster City Council, *City Plan 2019–2040,* publication draft (London: Westminster City Council, 2019).

143 He has made unequivocal statements in support of the rights of trans people and those who identify as non-binary. He supported the expansion of binary gender classifications in official data collection, with the introduction of non-binary, intersex and transgender categories. In 2018, he submitted an official response to the UK government's consultation on the reform of the Gender Recognition Act 2004, strongly supporting the call for recognition of self-identification and de-medicalisation of this process. 'Trans women are women. Trans men are men. Non-binary people are non-binary. All gender identities are valid'. Twitter account, @ MayorofLondon, 16 February 2020; Nick Duffy, 'Mayor of London Sadiq Khan Makes Emphatic Statement about Transgender Rights That's Impossible to Argue with', *Pink News,* 17 February 2020, https://www.pinknews.co.uk/2020/02/17/mayor-london -sadiq-khan-transgender-rights-labour-party-twitter-muslim/ (accessed 31 July 2021); Nick Duffy, 'Mayor of London Reforms Gender Options to Recognise People Who Aren't "Male" or "Female"', *Pink News,* 26 September 2016, https://www.pinknews.co .uk/2016/09/26/mayor-of-london-reforms-gender-options-to-recognise-people-who -arent-male-or-female/ (accessed 8 August 2020); Mayor of London, 'Consultation response on the reform of the *Gender Recognition Act 2004,* 2018', https://www.london .gov.uk/sites/default/files/mayor_of_london_consultation_response_-_reform_of_the _gra_2004.pdf (accessed 31 July 2021). For examples of the use of 'LGBTQ', see Mayor of London, 'LGBTQ+ Nightlife Venues', 5 July 2017, https://www.london.gov.uk//what -we-do/arts-and-culture/lgbtq-nightlife-venues (accessed 20 July 2020); Mayor of London, 'Figures Reveal LGBTQ+ Venue Numbers Remain Stable for a Second Year', 5 July 2019, https://www.london.gov.uk//press-releases/mayoral/londons-lgbtq-venue -numbers-remain-stable (accessed 20 July 2020).

144 The Outside Project, https://lgbtiqoutside.org/ (accessed 31 July 2021); Tonic Housing, https://www.tonichousing.org.uk/ (accessed 31 July 2021). See, also: Michael Cowan, "'LGBT Shelter Means I Can Be Myself'", *BBC News*, 2 May 2019, https://www .bbc.com/news/uk-48122185 (accessed 8 May 2020); Yas Necati, 'London to Get First Permanent LGBT+ Homeless Shelter', *The Independent*, 23 August 2018, https://www .independent.co.uk/news/uk/home-news/gay-homeless-shelter-lgbt-london-stonewall -housing-carla-ecola-sadiq-khan-pride-a8435256.html (accessed 8 May 2020); "'UK's First" LGBT Retirement Community to Open in London', *BBC News*, 2 March 2021, https://www.bbc.com/news/uk-england-london-56252018 (accessed 8 May 2020).

145 Participant, 'London Lesbian and Gay Centre: A Documented Conversation', UCL Urban Laboratory/Gays the Word, 18 October 2018.

146 Participant, 'London Lesbian and Gay Centre: A Documented Conversation', UCL Urban Laboratory/Gays the Word, 18 October 2018.

147 Participant, 'London Lesbian and Gay Centre: A Documented Conversation', UCL Urban Laboratory/Gays the Word, 18 October 2018.

148 *The Death and Life of Marsha P. Johnson* (Netflix, 2017). Directed by David France. See discussion of Stonewall in Chapter 6.

149 Adam Forrest, 'Sadiq Khan Attacks Boris Johnson for Using "homophobic Language" at Pride in London Launch', *The Independent*, 6 July 2019, https://www.independent .co.uk/news/uk/politics/pride-london-2019-sadiq-khan-boris-johnson-latest -homophobic-language-abuse-lgbt-a8991471.html (accessed 8 May 2020). In response, Johnson tweeted good wishes to Pride-goers and recalled 'fond memories of my pink stetson march as Mayor!'; George Bowden, 'Sadiq Khan Uses London Pride Launch To Blast Boris Over "Homophobic" Language', *HuffPost UK*, 6 July 2019, https://www .huffingtonpost.co.uk/entry/london-pride-2019-sadiq-khan-blasts-boris-johnson-over -homophobic-language_uk_5d209a12e4b0f3125684b918 (accessed 8 May 2020).

150 For example, Khan referred to Johnson's cancellation of the City Hall Pride reception during his speech at the 2022 event.

151 Mayor of London, 'MD2251 Pride in London 2018-2022', 4 April 2019, https://www .london.gov.uk//decisions/md2251-pride-london-2018-2022 (accessed 16 January 2023).

152 GLA, 'Mayor Invites Community Groups to Bid to Run London's Pride Events', 20 May 2022, https://www.london.gov.uk/press-releases/mayoral/tender-open-for -londons-pride-events (accessed 18 July 2022).

Chapter 4

1 The survey and workshops were conducted in 2016. The methods are described in: Ben Campkin and Lo Marshall, *LGBTQI Nightlife in London, 1986 to the Present: Interim Findings* (London: UCL Urban Laboratory, November 2016), https://www.ucl .ac.uk/urban-lab/sites/urban-lab/files/LGBTQI_nightlife_in_London_from_1986_to _the_present_-_interim_findings.pdf (accessed 15 July 2019). See also: Ben Campkin and Lo Marshall, 'Fabulous Façades', in Marko Jobst and Naomi Stead (eds.), *Queering Architecture: Methods, Practices, Spaces, Pedagogies* (London: Bloomsbury, 2023): 120–40.

2 Mayor of London, *Cultural Infrastructure Plan: A Call to Action* (London: Greater London Authority, 2019), https://www.london.gov.uk/what-we-do/arts-and-culture/ culture-and-good-growth/cultural-infrastructure-plan (accessed 17 May 2021).

3 Marc Shoffman, 'Petition Launched to Save Gay Club', *Pink News*, 24 August 2006, https://www.pinknews.co.uk/2006/08/24/petition-launched-to-save-gay -club/ (accessed 26 August 2020); Marc Shoffman, 'Thousands Oppose Gay Venue Closure', *Pink News*, 29 August 2006, https://www.pinknews.co.uk/2006/08/29/ thousands-oppose-gay-venue-closure/ (accessed 26 August 2020); Daniel Thomas, 'Derwent Valley Buys West End's Astoria', *Property Week*, 23 June 2006, https://www .propertyweek.com/news/derwent-valley-buys-west-ends-astoria/3069151.article (accessed 26 August 2020); Tony Grew, 'Music Group Buys into G-A-Y Bars', *Pink News*, 13 August 2007, https://www.pinknews.co.uk/2007/08/13/music-group-buys -into-g-a-y-bars/ (accessed 26 August 2020); Joseph McCormick, 'Jeremy Joseph Buys G-A-Y from HMV Administrators', *Pink News*, 24 January 2013, https://www .pinknews.co.uk/2013/01/24/jeremy-joseph-buys-g-a-y-from-hmv-administrators/ (accessed 26 August 2020).

4 'Gay Club Owner Goes into Administration', *Pink News*, 18 December 2009, https:// www.pinknews.co.uk/2009/12/18/gay-club-owner-goes-into-administration/ (accessed 26 August 2020); 'Popbarz, the Owner of Gay Clubs Such as Ghetto and Popstarz in London, Has Gone into Administration', *Pink News*, 18 December 2009, https://www.pinknews.co.uk/2009/12/18/gay-club-owners-hope-to-relaunch-ghetto -in-2010/ (accessed 26 August 2020).

5 'Pink Pound Dries up as Recession Begins to Bite', *Evening Standard*, 18 December 2009, http://www.standard.co.uk/business/pink-pound-dries-up-as-recession-begins -to-bite-6704807.html (accessed 4 August 2021); David Thame, 'Urban Regeneration: Everything Rosy?', *EG News*, https://www.egi.co.uk/news/822813/ (accessed 18 May 2021). I requested the GBA's data but the organisation do not have it unfortunately. Thame cites the GBA's Director, Stephen Coote, as reporting a decline from 259 to 100 venues.

6 'Pink Pound Dries up', *Evening Standard*, 18 December 2009.

7 The recession ran from quarter two, 2008, to quarter two, 2009. 'Pink Pound Dries up', 2009; 'Pink Pound Wobbles in the Recession', *Management Today*, 18 December 2009, http://www.managementtoday.co.uk/pink-pound-wobbles-recession/article /974759?utm_source=website&utm_medium=social (accessed 26 August 2020).

8 For example, early in this period, in 2009, see the coverage around the murder of Gerry Edwards, in which his partner was also stabbed, on 3 March 2009; or the murder of Ian Baynham in Trafalgar Square in September 2009. This coverage often extends over years as investigations move forward and cases progress through the courts. Rebecca Camber, 'Gay Civil Servant Kicked to Death for Standing up to Homophobic Abuse', *Mail Online*, 15 October 2009, https://www.dailymail.co .uk/news/article-1220311/Homophobic-assault-Ian-Baynham-Police-hunt-girls -kicked-gay-man-death.html (accessed 27 August 2020); Peter Jackson, 'Gay Hate "Alive and, Sometimes, Kicking"', *BBC News*, 16 December 2010, https://www.bbc .com/news/uk-11831556 (accessed 27 August 2020); Adam Fresco, 'Man Stabbed to Death in Possible Homophobic Attack in Bromley', *The Times*, 5 March 2009, https://www.thetimes.co.uk/article/man-stabbed-to-death-in-possible-homophobic -attack-in-bromley-tk6thcrs7q2 (accessed 27 August 2020); Matthew Taylor, 'Two Held over Suspected Homophobic Murder', *The Guardian*, 6 March 2009, http:// www.theguardian.com/uk/2009/mar/06/fatal-stabbing-bromley-arrests (accessed 27 August 2020); Chris Greenwood, 'Murder Hunt as Man Dies after Homophobic Assault', *The Independent*, 14 October 2009, http://www.independent.co.uk/news/uk/ crime/murder-hunt-as-man-dies-after-homophobic-assault-1802467.html (accessed

27 August 2020). For an example of an article grouping crimes and responding to crime data, see: Sam Jones, 'Reports of Homophobic Crimes Rise in London', *The Guardian,* 16 October 2009, http://www.theguardian.com/world/2009/oct/16/ homophobic-crime-rise-london (accessed 27 August 2020).

9 Lo Marshall, 'Negotiating Gender Diverse Realities Built on Binary Expectations: Public Toilets, in Britain', in Jess Berry, Timothy Moore, Nicole Kalms and Gene Bawden (eds.), *Contentious Cities: Design and the Gendered Production of Space,* (Abingdon: Taylor and Francis, 2020), 216–33; *Making Sense of Gender: Exploring Gender Diversity through the Experiences of People with Trans Identities and Histories,* doctoral thesis, 2021, UCL.

10 Chemsex is defined by media theorist Jamie Hakim as 'group sexual encounters between gay and bisexual men in which the recreational drugs GHB/GBL, mephedrone and crystallized methamphetamine are consumed'. Jamie Hakim, 'The Rise of Chemsex: Queering Collective Intimacy in Neoliberal London', *Cultural Studies* 33, no. 2 (4 March 2019): 249–75, 1. For examples of coverage, see: Denis Campbell, 'Gay Men Warned on Risks of "chemsex"', *The Guardian*, 8 April 2014, https://www.theguardian.com/society/2014/apr/08/chemsex-gay-men-drugs-health -risk-hiv-aids (accessed 27 August 2020); Paul Flynn, 'Addicted to Chemsex: "It's a Horror Story"', *The Observer,* 22 November 2015, https://www.theguardian.com /world/2015/nov/22/addicted-to-chemsex-gay-drugs-film (accessed 27 August 2020); Jamie Hakim, 'Having a Moral Panic About Chemsex? It's Not as Bad as You Think', *The Independent,* 25 November 2015, http://www.independent.co.uk/voices /having-a-moral-panic-about-chemsex-here-s-why-it-s-not-as-bad-as-you-think -a6748136.html (accessed 27 August 2020); Sessi Kuwabara, 'Moral Panic Around "Chemsex Crimewave" Predictably Lacks Coherent Analysis', *Filter,* 5 November 2018, https://filtermag.org/moral-panic-around-chemsex-crimewave-predictably -lacks-coherent-analysis/ (accessed 27 August 2020); Denio Lourenco, 'Sex and Drugs: Popular Gay Dating App Allows Users to Find More than a Date', *NBC News,* 1 August 2018, https://www.nbcnews.com/feature/nbc-out/sex-drugs-popular-gay -dating-app-allows-users-find-more-n896081 (accessed 27 August 2020); Hannah McCall, Naomi Adams, David Mason, and Jamie Willis, 'What Is Chemsex and Why Does It Matter?', *BMJ* 351 (3 November 2015); James Meikle, 'Chemsex Rise Prompts Public Health Warning', *The Guardian,* 3 November 2015, https://www.theguardian .com/society/2015/nov/03/chemsex-rise-public-health-warning-drugs (accessed 17 January 2023); Omar Oakes, 'Chemsex' Warning: Sex on Drugs Blamed for Rise in HIV Among Gay Men', *Your Local Guardian,* 31 March 2014; Marco Scalvini, 'Gay Men Need Clear Information about "Chemsex", Not Messages about Morality', *The Guardian,* 10 November 2015, https://www.theguardian.com/commentisfree/2015/ nov/10/gay-men-chemsex-moral-panic (accessed 27 August 2020); Richard Smith, 'The Media's Moral Panic Over Chemsex Demonises Gay Men', *Vice,* 4 December 2015, https://www.vice.com/en_uk/article/gqmkj3/media-moral-panic-chemsex -demonises-gay-men (accessed 27 August 2020); Patrick Strudwick, 'This Is What Chemsex Is Doing To Young Men', *BuzzFeed,* 3 December 2016, https://www .buzzfeed.com/patrickstrudwick/inside-the-dark-dangerous-world-of-chemsex (accessed 27 August 2020).

11 Hakim, 'The Rise of Chemsex', 249–75; 270–1; 253.

12 Hakim, 'The Rise of Chemsex', 249–75, 253, 271–2. See also, R. Justin Hunt, 'After the After-Party', in Ben Campkin, Lo Marshall and Rebecca Ross (eds.), *Urban*

Pamphleteer #7 (2018), 29–30; and Javier Guzmán, 'Notes on the Comedown', *Social Text* 32, no. 4 (2014): 59–68.

13 R. Justin Hunt, 'After the After-Party', in Ben Campkin, Lo Marshall and Rebecca Ross (eds.), *Urban Pamphleteer* #7 (2018): 29–30.

14 Thomas Hibbitts, 'Is Chemsex Killing Gay Clubbing?', *Thump*, 30 November 2015, https://www.vice.com/en_uk/article/kb5b8e/is-chemsex-killing-gay-clubbing (accessed 27 August 2020).

15 Hibbitts, 'Is Chemsex Killing Gay Clubbing?'.

16 Hibbitts, 'Is Chemsex Killing Gay Clubbing?'.

17 'Southwark's Cable Nightclub Shut by Landlord Network Rail', *BBC News*, 4 May 2013, https://www.bbc.com/news/uk-england-london-22408279 (accessed 3 August 2021); Andy Malt, 'Cable Founder Says Network Rail Gave Assurances Club Would Not Be Closed', *Complete Music Update*, 3 May 2013, https://completemusicupdate .com/article/cable-founder-says-network-rail-gave-assurances-club-would-not-be -closed/ (accessed 3 August 2021); Joseph McCormick, 'Jeremy Joseph Buys G-A-Y from HMV Administrators', *Pink News*, 24 January 2013, https://www.pinknews .co.uk/2013/01/24/jeremy-joseph-buys-g-a-y-from-hmv-administrators/ (accessed 3 August 2021).

18 Faith Fanzine, 'Luke Howard's Brief History of London's Gay Clubs: From Bang to Heaven', *Sabotage Times*, 2014, https://sabotagetimes.com/music/luke-howards -brief-history-of-londons-gay-clubs-pt-1-from-bang-to-heaven (accessed 29 May 2019); Will Coldwell, 'What Happened to the Great London Nightclubs?', *The Guardian*, 13 August 2015, https://www.theguardian.com/music/2015/aug/13/what -happened-to-the-great-london-nightclubs (accessed 29 May 2019); Rahul Verma, 'My London . . . Sister Bliss; The Faithless DJ Mourns King's Cross's Lost Nightclubs', *Metro*, 4 December 2015; 'From Bagley's to Spiritland', *KX Quarterly*, Autumn 2018, 19 October 2018, https://www.kingscross.co.uk/newspaper/2018/10/19/from-bagleys -to-spiritland (accessed 29 May 2019).

19 For a representative selection of Soho coverage, see: Hannah Ellis-Petersen, 'Madame Jojo's, Legendary Soho Nightclub, Forced to Close', *The Guardian*, 24 November 2014, https://www.theguardian.com/uk-news/2014/nov/24/madame-jojos-legendary -soho-nightclub-forced-close (accessed 29 May 2019); 'In-Depth: Is Soho Over?' *Attitude*, 22 April 2015, http://attitude.co.uk/article/in-depth-is-soho-over/6278/ (accessed 29 May 2019); Eleanor Margolis, 'Closing Time: The Loss of Iconic Gay Venues Is a Nasty Side-Effect of London's Sanitisation', *New Statesman*, 11 March 2015, https://www.newstatesman.com/culture/2015/03/closing-time-loss-iconic -gay-venues-nasty-side-effect-londons-sanitisation (accessed 29 May 2019); Alex Proud, 'A Gentrified Soho Is Terrible News for London', *The Telegraph*, 1 December 2014, https://www.telegraph.co.uk/men/thinking-man/11260969/A-gentrified -Soho-is-terrible-news-for-London.html (accessed 29 May 2019); 'So Long, Soho: London's Seediest District Hints at Some of the Ways the Capital Is Changing', *The Economist*, 30 December 2014, https://www.economist.com/britain/2014/12/30/so -long-soho (accessed 29 May 2019); Laurie Tuffrey, 'London Club Madame Jojo's Closes', *The Quietus*, 24 November 2014, https://thequietus.com/articles/16766 -madame-jojos-to-close (accessed 29 May 2019). Some local newspapers still picked up singular closures in outer London. For example, see: Ben Weich, 'Richmond LGBT Community in Mourning after Gay Bar The Richmond Arms Announces Closure after 30 Years', *Richmond & Twickenham Times*, 4 April 2016, https://www

.richmondandtwickenhamtimes.co.uk/news/14402654.richmond-lgbt-community-in-mourning-after-gay-bar-the-richmond-arms-announces-closure-after-30-years/ (accessed 29 May 2019).

20 Ellis-Petersen, 'Madame Jojo's, Legendary Soho Nightclub, Forced to Close', *The Guardian*, 24 November 2014; Gander Kashmira, 'Soho's Madame Jojo's forced to close "in attempt to gentrify area"', *The Independent*, 25 November 2014; Alex Proud, 'A Gentrified Soho Is Terrible News for London', *The Telegraph*, 1 December 2014, https://www.telegraph.co.uk/men/thinking-man/11260969/A-gentrified-Soho-is-terrible-news-for-London.html (accessed 3 August 2021).

21 Change.org. 'Save Madame Jojo's', https://www.change.org/p/cllr-tim-mitchell-save-madame-jojo-s (accessed 2 August 2022).

22 Change.org. 'Save Madame Jojo's', https://www.change.org/p/cllr-tim-mitchell-save-madame-jojo-s (accessed 2 August 2022).

23 Franco Milazzo, 'In Pictures: Madame Jojo's Protest March', *Londonist,* 30 November 2014, https://londonist.com/2014/11/in-pictures-madame-jojos-protest-march (accessed 3 August 2021). For coverage of the Madam Jojo's procession independent of mainstream media outlets see: Ben Walters, 'Death by Luxury: The Threat to Culture and the Power of Coffins in the Street', *Not Television*, https://www.nottelevision.net/death-luxury-threat-culture-power-coffins-street/ (accessed 7 December 2022). The funeral procession had been used in earlier protests against corporate-led redevelopment in London's Docklands in the 1980s. See: Loraine Leeson, 'Our Land: Creative Approaches to the Redevelopment of London's Docklands', *International Journal of Heritage Studies* 25, no. 4 (3 April 2019): 365–79.

24 David Thame, 'Welcome to Shoho', *Estates Gazette,* 27 June 2015.

25 Hannah llis-Petersen, 'Madame Jojo's, Legendary Soho Nightclub, Forced to Close', *The Guardian*, 24 November 2014, https://www.theguardian.com/uk-news/2014/nov/24/madame-jojos-legendary-soho-nightclub-forced-close (accessed 3 August 2021).

26 For a discussion of the perceived decline of gaybourhoods in the US context, for example, see, for example: Petra L. Doan and Harrison Higgins, 'The Demise of Queer Space? Resurgent Gentrification and the Assimilation of LGBT Neighborhoods', *Journal of Planning Education and Research* 31, no. 1 (2011): 6–25; Amin Ghaziani, *There Goes the Gayborhood* (Princeton, NJ: Princeton University Press, 2014).

27 Westminster Council, 13/09185/FULL, permission date, 20 May 2014; Soho Estates, 'Walker's Court', https://sohoestates.co.uk/projects/walkers-court/ (accessed 28 August 2020).

28 Heritage Collective, *Heritage Statement: Walker's Court, Soho, Westminster, on behalf of Soho Estates Limited*, September 2013, reference 12/054, 14.

29 Heritage Collective, *Heritage Statement: Walker's Court, Soho, Westminster, on behalf of Soho Estates Limited*, September 2013, reference 12/0540, 12; 16;21; 27. The report concludes that 'the present character and appearance of Walker's Court and the associated properties affected by the proposal are not considered to be of particular interest or key to the understanding of the area as a whole'. In this way the report takes a very limited view of what English Heritage at the time referred to as 'communal value', defined, as the report mentions, as: value 'deriving from the meanings of a place for the people who relate to it, or for whom it figures in their collective experience or memory. English Heritage, *Conservation Principles, Policies and Guidance for the Sustainable Management of the Historic Environment* (2008), https://historicengland.org.uk/images-books/publications/conservation-principles-sustainable-management

-historic-environment/ (accessed 28 August 2020). Now that Soho Estates have refurbished the building, there are plans to reopen the venue in spring 2023. However, the licensing application for the new venue, approved in 2019, was objected to by the Soho Society, representing local residents' concerns with negative impacts from night-time activities. Tom Foot, '"Crime Hotspot" Row as Madame Jojo's Gets Go-Ahead to Reopen', *Islington Tribune*, 6 December 2019, http://islingtontribune.com/article/crime -hotspot-row-as-madame-jojos-gets-go-ahead-to-reopen (accessed 28 August 2020).

30 Durmaz-Drinkwater, Bahar, Stephen Platt, and Işın Can-Traunmüller. 'Do Perceptions of Neighbourhood Change Match Objective Reality?' *Journal of Urban Design* 25, no. 6 (1 November 2020): 718–37; Erin Sanders-Mcdonagh, Magali Peyrefitte, and Matt Ryalls. 'Sanitising the City: Exploring Hegemonic Gentrification in London's Soho', *Sociological Research Online* 21, no. 3 (1 August 2016): 128–33; Phil Hubbard, 'Cleansing the Metropolis: Sex Work and the Politics of Zero Tolerance', *Urban Studies* (Routledge) 41, no. 9 (August 2004): 1687–702.

31 Nick Curtis, 'Welcome to the Gaybourhood; A Guide to London's Prime Pink Pound Locations', *Evening Standard,* 12 June 2014, https://www.standard.co.uk/ lifestyle/london-life/welcome-to-the-gaybourhood-a-guide-to-london-s-prime-pink -pound-locations-9531398.html (accessed 28 August 2020). The article continues: '"LGBTQ+ culture" creates an environment where things can happen, and a "gayborhood" forms. It soon attracts new middle-class incomers who then use their social capital to enforce stricter regulation. Once the arc reaches its pinnacle, the prestige environment is "de-gayed"'. For a sociologist's definition of the concept of gayborhoods see: Ghaziani, *There Goes the Gayborhood*, 2.

32 Ruth Glass (ed.), *London: Aspects of Change*, Centre for Urban Studies Report; No. 3 (London: Macgibbon and Kee, 1964), xviii; Loretta Lees, 'Gentrification', chapter 10, in *International Encyclopedia of the Social & Behavioral Sciences*, ed. James D. Wright (Amsterdam and New York: Elsevier, 2015), 46–52.

33 Glass, *London: Aspects of Change,* xviii-xix.

34 Chris Hamnett, 'Gentrification and the Middle-Class Remaking of Inner London, 1961–2001', *Urban Studies* 40, no. 12 (2016): 2401–26, 2401.

35 Loretta Lees, 'A Reappraisal of Gentrification: Towards a "Geography of Gentrification"', *Progress in Human Geography* 24, no. 3 (1 September 2000): 389–408; Loretta Lees and Martin Phillips (eds.), *Handbook of Gentrification Studies* (Cheltenham, Gloucestershire: Edward Elgar Publishing, 2018); Loretta Lees, Hyun Bang Shin, and Ernesto López Morales, *Global Gentrifications: Uneven Development and Displacement* (Bristol and Chicago: Policy Press, 2015).

36 Hamnett, 'Gentrification and the Middle-Class Remaking of Inner London', 2401.

37 Neil Smith, 'Toward a Theory of Gentrification: A Back to the City Movement by Capital, not People', *Journal of the American Planning Association* 45, no. 4 (1979): 538–48, 545.

38 Lees and Phillips, *Handbook of Gentrification Studies*, 1–12.

39 For a summary, see: Lees, 'Gentrification', in *International Encyclopedia of the Social & Behavioral Sciences*, 46–52.

40 Lees, 'Gentrification', in *International Encyclopedia of the Social & Behavioral Sciences*, 48.

41 Petra Doan, 'Non-normative Sexualities and Gentrification', in Lees and Phillips, *Handbook of Gentrification Studies*, 155–69; Andrew Gorman-Murray, 'Gay gentrification', in Abbie E. Goldberg (ed.), *The SAGE Encyclopedia of LGBTQ Studies*, Clark University (Los Angeles: SAGE reference, 2016), 433–5.

42 For a recent summary see: Marco Venturi, *Out of Soho, Back into the Closet: Rethinking the London Gay Community,* doctoral thesis, UCL, 2018.

43 Sanders-Mcdonagh, Peyrefitte and Ryalls, 'Sanitising the City', 128.

44 Ghaziani, *There Goes the Gayborhood,* 7.

45 David Ley, *The New Middle Class and the Remaking of the Central City* (Oxford: Oxford University Press, 1996).

46 Gary Bridge, Tim Butler, and Loretta Lees (eds.), *Mixed Communities: Gentrification by Stealth?* (Bristol: Policy, 2012); Damaris Rose, 'Discourses and Experiences of Social Mix in Gentrifying Neighbourhoods: A Montréal Case Study', *Canadian Journal of Urban Research* 13, no. 2 (2004): 278–316.

47 Ben Campkin, *Remaking London: Decline and Regeneration in Urban Culture* (London: IB Tauris, 2013).

48 Richard L. Florida, *The Rise of the Creative Class: And How it's Transforming Work, Leisure, Community and Everyday Life* (New York: Basic Books, 2002); 'Cities and the Creative Class', *City & Community* 2, no. 1 (2003): 3–19; *The Rise of the Creative Class, Revisited* (New York: Basic Books, 2012); Richard Florida and Charlotta Mellander, 'There Goes the Metro: How and Why Bohemians, Artists and Gays Affect Regional Housing Values', *Journal of Economic Geography* 10, no. 2 (1 March 2010): 167–88.

49 Florida, 'Cities and the Creative Class', 8.

50 On the controversies over Florida's work, see: Andrew Harris and Louis Moreno, *Creative City Limits: Urban Cultural Economy in a New Era of* Austerity (London: UCL Urban Laboratory, 2011); and Oliver Wainwright, '"Everything Is Gentrification Now": But Richard Florida Isn't Sorry', *The Guardian.* 26 October 2017, http://www .theguardian.com/cities/2017/oct/26/gentrification-richard-florida-interview-creative -class-new-urban-crisis (accessed 20 August 2020). Lees comments: 'Florida's work on the 'creative class' allowed policy makers to promote gentrification while describing their strategies in a new, popular language summarized in the three T's of technology, talent, and tolerance. The creative class that Florida discusses is none other than Ley's (1996) cultural new class described earlier, even if they seem more interested in technology now!' Lees, 'Gentrification', in *International Encyclopedia of the Social & Behavioral Sciences,* 49.

51 Florida, 'Cities and the Creative Class', 12–13.

52 Florida, 'Cities and the Creative Class', 13.

53 Florida and Mellander, 'There Goes the Metro', 168.

54 Florida and Mellander, 'There Goes the Metro', 168.

55 Ghaziani, *There Goes the Gayborhood,* 25.

56 Doan, 'Non-Normative Sexualities and Gentrification', 155–69. See, also: Petra L. Doan (ed.), *Planning and LGBTQ Communities: The Need for Inclusive Queer Spaces* (New York: Routledge, 2015); Petra L. Doan (ed.), *Queerying Planning: Challenging Heteronormative Assumptions and Reframing Planning Practice* (Abingdon: Taylor and Francis, 2016); Petra L. Doan and Harrison Higgins, 'The Demise of Queer Space? Resurgent Gentrification and the Assimilation of LGBT Neighborhoods', *Journal of Planning Education and Research* 31, no. 1 (2011): 6–25.

57 Curtis, 'Welcome to the Gaybourhood'.

58 See, for example: Ben Campkin, David Roberts, and Rebecca Ross (eds.), 'Regeneration Realities', *Urban Pampleteer* #2, 2013; Owen Hatherley, *A Guide to the New Ruins of Great Britain* (London: Verso, 2010); Robert Imrie and Loretta Lees

(eds.), *Sustainable London?: The Future of a Global City* (Bristol: Policy Press, 2014); Anna Minton, *Ground Control: Fear and Happiness in the Twenty-First-Century City* (London: Penguin, 2009).

59 Thame, 'Welcome to Shoho', 27 June 2015.

60 I highlight the term because often the press coverage has referred to 'gay venues' or 'gay bars', but has not attended to the representation of specific LGBTQ+ constituent groups in the operation or use of the spaces.

61 Thame, 'Welcome to Shoho', 27 June 2015.

62 Brian Bickell quoted in Thame, 'Welcome to Shoho', 27 June 2015.

63 It was described in 2017 as a '£3.5 billion empire' with over '600 properties from China Town to Carnaby Street'. Joanna Bourke, 'Brian Bickell: Meet the Boss of London Property Giant Shaftesbury', *Evening Standard*, 27 October 2017, https://www.standard.co.uk/business/brian-bickell-meet-the-shaftesbury-boss-at-the-helm-of-a-35bn-london-property-empire-a3669866.html (accessed 29 May 2019).

64 Thame, 'Welcome to Shoho', 27 June 2015.

65 'Shaftesbury Boss Brian Bickell: You'll Change Your Mind as I Lead You through the Streets of London', *The Times*, 12 December 2021.

66 Thame, 'Welcome to Shoho', 27 June 2015.

67 Mike Raco and Emma Tunney, 'Visibilities and Invisibilities in Urban Development: Small Business Communities and the London Olympics 2012', *Urban Studies*, 47, no. 10 (2010): 2069–91; Myfanwy Taylor, 'The Role of Traders and Small Businesses in Urban Social Movements: The Case of London's Workspace Struggles', *International Journal of Urban and Regional Research*, 44, no. 6 (2020): 1041–56.

68 Thame, 'Welcome to Shoho', 27 June 2015. Matt Houlbrook, *Queer London: Perils and Pleasures in the Sexual Metropolis, 1918–1957* (Chicago and London: University of Chicago Press, 2005), 4.

69 Houlbrook, *Queer London*, 4–5.

70 Thame, 'Welcome to Shoho', 27 June 2015.

71 Campkin and Marshall, *LGBTQ+ Cultural Infrastructure in London, 1986–Present*, 2016.

72 RAZE Collective is led by a board of volunteers and QSN was led by RAZE organizers Ben Walters and Tim Other. The RAZE Collective board are listed at http://www.razecollective.com (accessed 26 August 2020). QSN was disbanded in 2018.

73 *Not Television*, blog, http://www.nottelevision.net (accessed 8 December 2022). For Walters' direct critical engagement with the dominant media narratives, see: Ben Walters, 'How the Economist got it Wrong on Queer Venue Closures', *Not Television*, 2 January 2017, https://www.nottelevision.net/economist-got-wrong-queer-venue-closures/ (accessed 8 December 2022).

74 This was later formalised as a charity http://www.razecollective.com (accessed 24 August 2019).

75 Ben Walters, interview by Ben Campkin, UCL Urban Laboratory, 16 July 2019.

76 Just Space, *Draft London Plan: LGBTQI+ Community Response*, submission to the Greater London Authority, 2 March 2018, https://justspacelondon.files.wordpress.com/2018/02/lgbtq-community-response.pdf (accessed 10 August 2019).

77 Robin Brown, Michael Edwards and Richard Lee, 'Just Space: Towards a Just, Sustainable London', chapter 3 in *Sustainable London? The Future of a Global City* (London: Policy Press, 2014): 43–64.

78 Queer Spaces Network Agenda, Monday 6 June 2016, The Queen Adelaide, Hackney Road. The vision is summarised in Queer Spaces Network, 'A Vision for Queer Cultural Spaces in London', in Ben Campkin, Lo Marshall and Rebecca Ross (eds.), 'LGBTQ+ Night-time Spaces: Past, Present, Future', *Urban Pamphleteer* #7, July 2018, 35.

79 Switching is a term used by Sara Ahmed in *On Being Included: Racism and Diversity in Institutional Life* (Durham and London: Duke University Press, 2012), 75.

80 Summaries of the method and findings were first published in Campkin and Marshall, *LGBTQI Nightlife in London, 1986 to the Present*. At the time of the research, in 2016, due to practical constraints, the findings had to be coded and synthesised to present the principal tropes to the GLA and QSN within a short timeframe. Here I analyse a wider range of responses, in more detail. The survey of course only brought forward the views of those who were interested and had the resources to respond. However, we proactively elicited involvement from a diverse cross-section of LGBTQ+ individuals and organisations. For the workshops, we reached out widely to community members, venue operators, promoters and performers, and asked them to reflect on the profile and value of LGBTQ+ venues and events, venue closures and future trajectories. We did this by inviting provocations from producer, performer and academic, R. Justin Hunt (aka Dr Sharon Husbands), venue operators Lyall Hakaraia and Dan Beaumont, DJ Ritu, an experienced promoter who is a recognised champion of musical and cultural diversity, and academic Chryssy Hunter. These individuals facilitated charrettes where small groups had the opportunity to discuss and think about the issues from a particular perspective: either performers, local authorities, venues or the LGBTQ+ community more widely. For a report of an associated public event convened as part of the research, held at Peckham Festival, see: Lo Marshall, 'What's Happening to London's LGBTQI Nightlife Spaces?', *UCL Events Blog*, https://blogs.ucl.ac.uk/events/2016/09/15/whats-happening-to-londons-lgbtqi-nightlife-spaces/ (accessed 4 September 2020).

81 Campkin and Marshall, *LGBTQI Nightlife in London*; Ben Campkin and Laura [Lo] Marshall, *LGBTQ+ Cultural Infrastructure in London: Night Venues 2006-Present* (London: UCL Urban Laboratory, July 2017); Campkin, Marshall, and Ross (eds.), 'LGBTQ+ Night-time Spaces'; Ben Campkin and Lo Marshall, 'London's Nocturnal Queer Geographies', *Soundings* 20 (Autumn 2018): 82–96. These publications can all be downloaded at: https://www.ucl.ac.uk/urban-lab/research/research-projects/lgbtq-nightlife-spaces-london (accessed 17 January 2023)

82 UCL Urban Laboratory survey, 2016.

83 UCL Urban Laboratory survey, 2016.

84 UCL Urban Laboratory survey, 2016.

85 Sara Ahmed, *Queer Phenomenology: Orientations, Objects, Others* (London and Durham: Duke University Press, 2006), 9, 20.

86 The Roestone Collective, 'Safe Space: Towards a Reconceptualization', *Antipode* 46, no. 5 (2014): 1346–65.

87 For example, see Pxssy Palace Policy, undated, which at the time of writing is available on the Pxssy Palace Facebook page. Pxssy Palace is defined on this page as 'a space that prioritises women and femmes of colour and other queer, intersex and trans people of colour (QTIPOC)' and is an example of numerous London-based queer collectives that run events with explicit safe space policies.

88 Diana Raiselis, 'The A-Team: Awareness Teams in Berlin Club Culture as Practice for 'Safe(r) Space', unpublished manuscript, 2022.

89 UCL Urban Laboratory survey, 2016.

90 UCL Urban Laboratory survey, 2016.

91 UCL Urban Laboratory survey, 2016.

92 Campkin and Marshall, *LGBTQI Nightlife in London, from 1986 to the Present*, 24.

93 UCL Urban Laboratory survey, 2016.

94 UCL Urban Laboratory survey, 2016.

95 UCL Urban Laboratory survey, 2016.

96 UCL Urban Laboratory survey, 2016.

97 Including during events convened through Urban Lab's research.

98 Mohammed Abbas, 'London Gay Bars Wilt as Tolerance Blooms, Property Booms', *Yahoo! News*, 10 August 2015, https://news.yahoo.com/london-gay-bars-wilt-tolerance-blooms-property-booms-043233690.html (accessed 4 August 2021). The article, by Agence France Presse, was printed in *Daily Nation* (Kenya), *Global English* (Middle East and North Africa Financial Network) and *Naharnet* (Lebanon). The piece also highlighted the multiple functions of LGBTQ+ spaces, and hinted at a relationship with rising homophobic crime and cuts to services.

99 Hakim, 'The Rise of Chemsex', 249–75.

100 UCL Urban Laboratory survey, 2016.

101 UCL Urban Laboratory survey, 2016.

102 UCL Urban Laboratory survey, 2016.

103 Campkin and Marshall, *LGBTQI Nightlife in London, 1986 to the Present*, 25.

104 Hakim, 'The Rise of Chemsex', 249–75; Greggor Mattson, 'Centering Provincial Gay Bars', *Greggor Mattson (blog)*, 1 September 2017, https://greggormattson.com/2017/09/01/centering-provincial-gay-bars/ (accessed 4 August 2021); Sam Miles, 'Sex in the Digital City: Location-Based Dating Apps and Queer Urban Life', *Gender, Place & Culture* 24, no. 11 (2 November 2017): 1595–610; Sharif Mowlabocus, 'Revisiting Old Haunts Through New Technologies: Public (Homo)Sexual Cultures in Cyberspace', *International Journal of Cultural Studies* 11, no. 4 (2008): 419–39; Regner Amaury Ramos Ramirez, *Spatial Practices / Digital Traces: Embodiment and Reconfigurations of Urban Spaces through GPS Mobile Applications*, doctoral thesis, UCL, 2016.

105 Miles, 'Sex in the digital city', 1602.

106 Greggor Mattson, 'Centering Provincial Gay Bars', Royal Geographical Society Annual Conference, 1 September 2017.

107 Mattson, 'Centering Provincial Gay Bars'.

108 Mowlabocus, 'Revisiting Old Haunts through New Technologies', 420; Sharif Mowlabocus, *Gaydar Culture: Gay Men, Technology and Embodiment in the Digital Age* (Farnham: Ashgate, 2010).

109 Campkin and Marshall, *LGBTQI Nightlife in London*, 4-5;. Campkin and Marshall, 'Nocturnal Queer Infrastructures', *Soundings* (2018): 90.

110 Bryce J. Renninger, 'Grindr Killed the Gay Bar, and Other Attempts to Blame Social Technologies for Urban Development: A Democratic Approach to Popular Technologies and Queer Sociality', *Journal of Homosexuality* 66, no. 12 (15 October 2019): 1736–55.

111 For an early example, put forward by a representative of the Gay Business Association, see: 'Pink Pound Dries up', *Evening Standard*, 18 December 2009.

112 UCL Urban Laboratory survey, 2016.

113 UCL Urban Laboratory survey, 2016.
114 UCL Urban Laboratory survey, 2016.
115 UCL Urban Laboratory survey, 2016.
116 Campkin and Marshall, *LGBTQI Nightlife in London, 1986 to the Present*, 25.
117 UCL Urban Laboratory survey, 2016.
118 UCL Urban Laboratory survey, 2016.
119 UCL Urban Laboratory survey, 2016.
120 UCL Urban Laboratory survey, 2016.
121 The GBA dataset had suggested an acceleration in the decline of numbers of gay bars, with a 40% reduction from 250 in 2004 to 150 in 2009.
122 'Gay Bars That Have Closed In London Since The Turn of the Century', *The Gay UK*, 5 November 2015, https://www.thegayuk.com/gay-bars-that-have-closed-in-london -since-the-turn-of-the-century/ (accessed 23 May 2019).
123 'Gay Bars That Have Closed In London', *The Gay UK*.
124 Although it had ambitions to expand beyond London, the archive does not seem to have been updated, or contributions published after the initial launch.
125 The figure of 58% only refers to licensed premises, excluding saunas, and as discussed above excludes events that occupy multiple venues, which may or may not be primarily designated for LGBTQ+ use. Campkin and Marshall, *LGBTQ+ Cultural Infrastructure in London*, 2017.
126 Amy Lamé, interview by Ben Campkin, 4 September 2019, City Hall, Greater London Authority.
127 According to Inter-Departmental Business Register data, the number of pubs in the UK fell by 25% from 2001 to 2016. GLA/CAMRA data showed a fall of 25% in the number of pubs in London between 2001 and 2016. According to GLA/Nordicity data, there was a 35% drop in London's grassroots music venues from 2007 to 2016, with 94 venues extant in 2016. According to data from the Association of Licensed Multiple Retailers, nearly 50% of the UK's nightclubs closed from 2005 (3,114) to 2015 (1,733). Greater London Authority, 'Shocking Data Reveals Number of Pubs in London Fell by 25% since 2001', London City Hall, 19 April 2017, https://www .london.gov.uk//press-releases/mayoral/number-of-pubs-in-london-fell-by-25 -since-2001 (accessed 17 July 2019); Mayor of London, 'Rescue Plan for London's Grassroots Music Venues: Making Progress', GLA, 2017, https://www.london.gov.uk /sites/default/files/rescue_plan_for_londons_grassroots_music_venues_-_progress _update_-_jan_2017.pdf (accessed 17 July 2019); Jim Connolly, 'UK Nightclubs Closing at "Alarming Rate", Industry Figures Suggest', *BBC Newsbeat*, 10 August 2015, http://www.bbc.co.uk/newsbeat/article/33713015/uk-nightclubs-closing-at-alarming -rate-industry-figures-suggest (accessed 17 July 2019).
128 Malcolm Comely, Robert Kincaid, Maria Tejada, interview by Ben Campkin and Lo Marshall, London, 11 April 2017.
129 Johan Andersson, 'Homonormative Aesthetics: AIDS and "de-generational Unremembering" in 1990s London', *Urban Studies*, 56, no. 14 (2019): 2993–3010, 3001.
130 Resolution Foundation, *London Stalling: Half a Century of Living Standards in London* (Trust for London, 2018).
131 There was a drop of more than 4% real terms median net income in London households after housing costs between 2007–8 and 2013–14. 'Trends in the UK Economy - Office for National Statistics', https://www.ons.gov.uk/economy/economi

coutputandproductivity/productivitymeasures/articles/trendsintheukeconomy/2015
-02-27 (accessed 18 June 2019).

132 GLA, 'London's Economy, Trade and Specialisation', *Economic Evidence Base for London* (London: Greater London Authority, 2016), https://www.london.gov.uk/sites/default/files/chapter1-economic-evidence-base-2016.pdf (accessed 18 June 2019).

133 Clusters of venues were defined here as a group of three or more within 500 metres of each other. The clustering and map design were conducted by Christopher Storey for UCL Urban Lab, in collaboration with Ben Campkin and Lo Marshall.

134 UCL Urban Lab data, 2016. The data records more than 20 venues in Vauxhall from the 1980s to 2017. Artist Nina Wakeford's recentoral history project and book tells the interesting story of Covent Garden's Market's move to the area at Nine Elms, which lead to the establishment of a late license pub, the Market Tavern, appropriated by queer communities in the early 1980s. Nina Wakeford, *Our Pink Depot: The Gay London Underground. FLO-N202-236000000-TRK-MST-00002-SAY-HELLO-WA VE-GOODBYE-KEN-NIE-BPS* (London: Bookworks, 2019).

135 DJ Luke Howard, in his 2014 brief history of London's gay clubs comments on how in the 1970s innovative promoter, Tricky Dicky, innovatively began hiring out pubs and bars for gay nights, such as Dick's Inn Gay Disco, which 'operated out of straight venues as far afield as Croydon, Ilford, Bishopsgate and Euston, for a few hundred gay boys and girls at a time'. Faith Fanzine, 'Luke Howard's Brief History of London's Gay Clubs', *Sabotage Times*, 2014.

136 Next to Newham, the borough of Waltham Forest had four dedicated venues that opened in the 1990s and closed in 2005/6. In this borough, in 2016, there were an additional two venues that are pitched as inclusive of LGBTQ+ people with weekend or regular programming. This is not simply a recent replacement of 'gay' with 'mixed' though – one of the dominant media explanations for venue closures – since one of these had been running specific programming for these communities since at least the mid-1980s.

137 This is paralleled by other local prides which signal disaffection with the main London Pride events and its financial underpinnings (see Chapter 3). Queer Newham, https://queernewham.weebly.com/ (accessed 17 January 2023).

Chapter 5

1 Ben Campkin and Lo Marshall, *LGBTQ+ Cultural Infrastructure in London, 2006–present*, UCL Urban Laboratory, 2017, https://www.ucl.ac.uk/urban-lab/sites/urban-lab/files/LGBTQ_cultural_infrastructure_in_London_nightlife_venues_2006_to_the_present.pdf (accessed 17 July 2019).

2 King's Cross Story Palace, 'The Bell: Ghosts on the Dancefloor', History Pin and The Building Exploratory, https://storypalace.org/stories/the-bell-ghosts-on-the-dancefloor/ (accessed 28 June 2019); Richard Brunskill, 'Dark, Unlit Places' and 'Love Girls, Kiss Boys', https://storypalace.org/stories/love-girls-and-kiss-boys/ (accessed 28 June 2019).

3 Survey, UCL Urban Laboratory survey, 2016. The mention of drag performance in 1972 is featured in Islington's Pride, 'Heritage Map', 14 May 2021, https://islingtonspride.com/humap/ (accessed 4 August 2021).

4 'Breaking The Fourth Wall: *The Other Tchaikovsky*, BBC Radio 4 Play – Review', 30 August 2020, https://breaking-the-fourth-wall.com/2020/08/30/the-other-tchaikovsky-bbc-radio-4-play-review/ (accessed 4 August 2021). Rebecca Jennings, 'The Gateways Club and the Emergence of a Post-Second World War Lesbian Subculture', *Social History* 31, no. 2 (2006): 206–25.

5 'Women's City', Progress Women's City, 29 October 1982, typed memorandum. Local History Centre, Islington.

6 Jennings, 'The Gateways Club', 206–25

7 Jennings, 'The Gateways Club', 222–3.

8 Women's City wound down, but with a group of women Ryder-Tchaikovsky also founded Women in Prison in 1983 – a research, support and campaigning organisation extant today. Yvonne Roberts, 'Chris Tchaikovsky', *The Guardian*, 24 May 2002, http://www.theguardian.com/news/2002/may/24/guardianobituaries (accessed 4 August 2021); 'Breaking The Fourth Wall'; Women in Prison, *The Women in Prison Manifesto*, https://www.womeninprison.org.uk/media/downloads/the-original-women-in-prison-manifesto.pdf (accessed 28 June 2021); Women in Prison, https://www.womeninprison.org.uk/about/our-story (accessed 28 June 2021); 'Women in Prison: A Conversation between Chris Ryder-Tchaikovsky and Jill Box-Grainger', undated, https://www.womeninprison.org.uk/media/downloads/conversation-with-Chris-Tchaikovsky.pdf (accessed 28 June 2021); Fiona McLean, architect of the LLGC, was one of Tchaikovsky's close collaborators, with Women in Prison being fostered under the auspices of the GLC's Women's Committee, on which McLean was General Services Officer.

9 Rob Pateman, 'Pub: The Bell, Kings Cross, London – Gay in the 80s', https://www.gayinthe80s.com/2017/09/pub-bell-kings-cross-london/ (accessed 29 June 2021).

10 LGSM, 'Yes, Gay Is Indeed The Word', http://lgsm.org/news/273-yes-gay-is-indeed-the-word (accessed 3 July 2019).

11 Bernard Hodson, 'Movements at the Bell 1980–1990', *Medium*, 1 October 2017, https://medium.com/@babesnhorny/movements-at-the-bell-1980-1990-337f8d7a8461 (accessed 13 July 2021).

12 Eric Presland, 'Cruising: 158: The Outhouse', *Capital Gay*, 24 August 1984, 17.

13 Rob Pateman, interview by Ben Campkin, UCL Urban Laboratory, 2 August 2019.

14 DJ Ritu, 'The Only One', in Ben Campkin, Lo Marshall and Rebecca Ross (eds.), 'LGBTQ+ Night-Time Spaces: Past, Present, Future', *Urban Pamphleteer* #7 (November 2018): 5–8, 5. The discussion group continues at Gays the Word today.

15 Jane Campbell, 'The Bell: 1980–1990', extract from the memoir *Dyke*, unpaginated manuscript, collection of Rob Pateman; Rob Pateman, interview by Ben Campkin, UCL Urban Laboratory, 2 August 2019; Pateman, 'Pub: The Bell, Kings Cross, London – Gay in the 80s'.

16 For example, in dress codes, and debates about them, such as the banning of leather jackets or other items associated with fascist uniforms. Participant, 'Centre Pieces: A Public, Documented Conversation on the London Lesbian and Gay Centre', UCL Urban Laboratory/Museum of London, 14 July 2018.

17 Presland, 'Cruising: 158: The Outhouse'17. Eric Presland, now known as Peter Scott-Presland, is a gay community theatre activist and director, and author of *Amiable Warriors: A History of the Campaign for Homosexual Equality and Its Times* (London: Paradise Press, 2015).

18 Rob Pateman, interview by Ben Campkin, UCL Urban Laboratory, 2 August 2019.

19 After Dolores Lyons (1984), the licensees were Kevin Bolt (1984/5); Robert Driver and Chris Youlten (1985). 'Breaking The Fourth Wall: *The Other Tchaikovsky*, BBC Radio 4 Play – Review'; Presland, 'Cruising: 158: The Outhouse', 17. The licencees names are taken from gay media and the electoral register. On the impact of the change in management in the mid-1980s on the treatment of women, see: Rob Pateman, interview by Michael Hall, 'The Bell: Women Quota', 18 January 2018, https://soundcloud.com/michael-hall-964148813/the-bell-women-quota (accessed 30 June 2021).

20 Campbell, 'The Bell: 1980–1990'; Rob Pateman, interview by Michael Hall, 'The Bell: Women Quota', 18 January 2018, https://soundcloud.com/michael-hall-964148813/the-bell-women-quota (accessed 30 June 2021).

21 Purvis's Tea Dances also occupied Paradise, Islington, and The White Swan and Joiners Arms in East London. Q.X. Team, 'The reluctant DJ – Part 2', 13 July 2011, https://www.qxmagazine.com/2011/07/the-reluctant-dj-part-2/ (accessed 30 June 2021).

22 Campbell, 'The Bell: 1980–1990'.

23 Campbell, 'The Bell: 1980–1990'.

24 Rob Pateman, interview by Ben Campkin, UCL Urban Laboratory, 2 August 2019.

25 This is based on a comparison between two sets of plans: 'The Bell Public House, Pentonville Road, N1, Proposed Alterations', November 1964; and John V. Sharp, 'The Bell Public House, King's Cross. Ground Floor Plan', May 1972. Camden Local Studies and Archives Centre.

26 Mamba 2105, *The Bell - Kings Cross, c. 1991–1992*, https://www.youtube.com/watch?v=D9_2jeYb3Vo (accessed 10 July 2021) and the LWT documentary footage of The Bell in the mid-1980s, archived on the Facebook group 'I Remember the Bell at King's Cross', https://www.facebook.com/stephen.blight/videos/10159536758211388 (accessed 10 July 2021).

27 Rob Pateman, interview by Ben Campkin, UCL Urban Laboratory, 2 August 2019.

28 Presland, 'Cruising: 158: The Outhouse', 17.

29 For a discussion of this film, and the regeneration of King's Cross, see Ben Campkin, *Remaking London: Decline and Regeneration in Urban Culture* (London: IB Tauris, 2013), 105–26.

30 Ben Walters, 'The Police Wore Rubber Gloves (Part 1 of 3)', *Not Television*, 16 January 2017, https://www.nottelevision.net/police-wore-rubber-gloves-part-1-of-3/ (accessed 15 August 2022). Walters reports that the raid resulted in eleven arrests for the offence of being drunk in a pub and that the RVT's landlord Pat McConnon was charged for permitting the drunkenness.

31 Richard Brunskill, *King's Cross Story Palace*, https://storypalace.org/stories/love-girls-and-kiss-boys/ (accessed 28 June 2019).

32 Stuart Feather, *Blowing the Lid: Gay Liberation, Sexual Revolution and Radical Queens* (Winchester; Zero Books, 2016), 108–9.

33 DJ Tricky Dicky, Richard Scanes, persuaded a number of publicans to run gay discos, starting with the Father Redcap in Camberwell. He ran what Keith Howes describes as the first dedicated gay club night, Fangs. 'Cruising: The Euston Tavern', *Capital Gay*, 25 September 1981; Euston Tavern, advert, *Capital Gay*, 24 August 1984. Rob Pateman, private collection; Howes, Keith, *Remembering Tricky Dicky/Richard Scanes*, 2016, https://www.youtube.com/watch?v=SMhe-OVRx4Y (15/8/22); 'Nightclubbing: Gay Clubbing in '70s London', https://daily.redbullmusicacademy.com/2013/05/coming-out-ball-70s-gay-clubbing-in-london (accessed 15 August 2022).

224   *Notes*

34   In 1984, Traffic was run by Jamie Baker. Advert, *Capital Gay*, 24 August 1984.

35   Rob Pateman, interview by Ben Campkin, UCL Urban Laboratory, 2 August 2019. Jane Giles, *Scala Cinema 1978–1993* (Godalming: FAB Press, 2018).

36   For an account of the demonstration, which mentions that demonstrators went to the pub afterwards, but does not name The Prince Albert specifically, see: Lisa Power, *No Bath But Plenty of Bubbles: Stories from the London Gay Liberation Front, 1970–1973* (London: Continuum International Publishing Group, 1995), 30–4; Feather, *Blowing the Lid*, 7.

37   Anton Johnson, 'Witnessing London's Queer Nightlife', in Campkin, Marshall and Ross (eds.), 'LGBTQ+ Night-time Spaces: Past, Present, Future', *Urban Pamphleteer* #7, 2018: 12–14.

38   Historic England, 'Camden Lesbian Centre', https://historicengland.org.uk/research/inclusive-heritage/lgbtq-heritage-project/activism-and-community-building/camden-lesbian-centre/ (accessed 1 July 2019); Ben Campkin and Lo Marshall, *LGBTQ+ Spaces in Camden* (London: UCL Urban Laboratory, 2020).

39   'Cruising: The Euston Tavern', *Capital Gay*, 1981.

40   Christopher Castiglia and Christopher Reed, *If Memory Serves: Gay Men, AIDS, and the Promise of the Queer Past* (Minneapolis: University of Minnesota Press, 2012), 99.

41   Castiglia and Reed, *If Memory Serves*, 99–100.

42   José Esteban Muñoz, *Cruising Utopia: The Then and There of Queer Futurity* (New York and London: New York University Press, 2009), 135.

43   '[The LLGC] reminded me of The Fallen Angel – the *clean* colours, the way chairs had been chosen; I mean, *money* had been spent: this was not run-down and shabby or clinical or social work, you know, it was like *wow*, "look at this space we've got!" And you'd go – and drinks at the bar were cheap enough, the food was cheap and cheerful. It reminded me too of First Out . . . pinks and greys and very subtle. But it was swish. You thought oh *ye-ah*, no blacked-out windows'. Participant, 'London Lesbian and Gay Centre: A Documented Conversation', UCL Urban Laboratory/Gays the Word, 18 October 2018.

44   He continues: 'There was good, simple vegetarian food – now unremarkable but then exceptional and innovative. The two men who ran the place were of a different order too: activists, articulate, reflective and involved with gay publishing'. '1984. Pub: The Fallen Angel, Islington, London', *Gay in the 80s*, https://www.gayinthe80s.com/2012/09/1984-pub-the-fallen-angel-islington-london/ (accessed 29 June 2021).

45   Johan Andersson, 'Homonormative Aesthetics: AIDS and "De-Generational Unremembering" in 1990s London', *Urban Studies* 56, no. 14 (2019): 2993–3010.

46   Islington's Pride, 'Heritage Map', 14 May 2021, https://islingtonspride.com/humap/ (accessed 29 June 2021); Castiglia and Reed, *If Memory Serves*, 91–100.

47   The Bell reopened briefly as a gay venue under a different name, in 2002, and in its current form, as Big Chill, a non-LGBTQ+-specific venue, in 2006.

48   Rob Pateman, interview by Ben Campkin, UCL Urban Laboratory, 2 August 2019; Michael Hall, 'The Bell: Ghosts on the Dance Floor', *King's Cross Story Palace*, https://soundcloud.com/michael-hall-964148813/the-bell-ghosts-on-the-dance-floor (accessed 30 June 2021).

49   Ryan Gilbey, 'Kink, Drink and Liberty: A Queer History of King's Cross in the 80s', *The Guardian*, 16 May 2017, http://www.theguardian.com/stage/2017/may/16/queer-history-kings-cross-lgbt-80s-london (accessed 1 July 2021).

50   The 'I Remember The Bell, King's Cross' Facebook group, which describes itself as 'a refuge for lesbians and gay men who spent more time drinking and dancing at The

Bell than they care to remember - and now wish they could remember a little more than they do' succeeded the earlier, defunct, 'I remember the Bell Kings X' group, initiated by Sam Wingard. This had been similarly active but closed due to a conflict within the user community, highlighting the fragility of these groups as archives administered by individuals or small groups. 'Lost gay London' is another highly active Facebook group.

51 Pateman comments: 'it's striking to see how many of The Bell crowd have gone on to work in the creative industries or as agents or advocates for social, political, sexual and environmental change, impacting people's lives across the world'. As the administrator of 'I Remember the Bell' and a former employee of the free weekly newspaper, *Capital Gay*, Pateman provides a link between the gay print media of the 1980s and 1990s and social media platforms. Alternatively, respondents to 'The Bell: Ghosts on the Dance Floor', make a link between the creative, politicized generation of The Bell and well-heeled Islington property owners today: participant, 'The Bell: Ghosts on the Dancefloor', https://soundcloud.com/michael-hall-964148813/the-bell -ghosts-on-the-dance-floor (accessed 30 June 2021).

52 King's Cross, 'The Story So Far', https://www.kingscross.co.uk/the-story-so-far (accessed 8 July 2019).

53 David Swindells, 'From Bagleys to Spiritland', 2018, https://www.kingscross.co.uk/ newspaper/2018/10/19/from-bagleys-to-spiritland (accessed 29 June 2019).

54 Anon, 'You're too young to remember the eighties', *Datacide*, undated, c. 2009, https://datacide-magazine.com/you're-too-young-to-remember-the-eighties---danc ing-in-a-different-time/ (accessed 29 June 2019).

55 Bagleys' popularity led Billy Reilly to open The Cross, as an Ibiza-styled club, in the arches of the adjacent King's Cross Freight Depot in 1993. This became known for nights such as Fiction, produced by Blue Cube Promotions, who also ran events at Fabric next to Smithfields market, another large-capacity superclub. Fiction was marketed as 'polysexual', hosted by drag queens, but reviewed as 'a huge, sweaty and mainly boyzy Friday night session'. Rob Humphreys, *The Mini Rough Guide to London* (London: Rough Guides, 2003), 267. For a detailed write-up of Fiction see @ gergi108, 'HF / Features - Fiction 6th Birthday @ The Cross, Friday 4 March', https:// www.harderfaster.net?section=features&action=showfeature&featureid=11320 (accessed 27 August).

56 Swindells, 'From Bagleys to Spiritland', 2018.

57 UCL Urban Lab data records the provision of LGBTQ+ night venues, day spaces and services and host venues in Camden peaking in 2005, at eighteen. The numbers rose sharply in the late 1980s and then stayed fairly constant in the early 1990s before rising again and remaining at between fourteen and eighteen until 2008. In 2006 there were ten dedicated LGBTQ+ venues, but by 2018 this had decreased to six, with two of those no longer overtly marketing as LGBTQ+ venues, and including two men-only venues: a sauna and a cruise bar. For discussion of Camden's LGBTQ+ venues see: Campkin and Marshall, *LGBTQ+ Spaces in Camden*.

58 Argent St George, *Principles for a Human City*, 2001, https://www.kingscross.co.uk/ media/Principles_for_a_Human_City.pdf (accessed 28 June 2019).

59 Peter Bishop and Lesley Williams, *Planning, Politics and City Making: A Case Study of King's Cross* (London: RIBA Publishing, 2016); Campkin, *Remaking London*, 105–26; Michael Edwards, 'King's Cross: Renaissance for Whom' in John Punter (ed.), *Urban Design and the British Urban Renaissance* (London: Taylor and Francis, 2009), 189–205.

60 On the provisions for social infrastructure in the London Plan (2004), see Chapter 3.

61 'About us', Coal Drops Yard, https://www.coaldropsyard.com/history-of-coal-drops-yard/ (accessed 6 August 2019).

62 Although not an international hub like St Pancras, Euston is another key node in the city's transportation network, and because of that a site of repeated large-scale redevelopment. Modernised in the mid-1960s, it is currently being reconfigured in association with the High-Speed 2 rail-link from London to the midlands.

63 Euston was also Network Rail's Headquarters until 2008. Since 2014, Network Rail has been classified as a public sector body.

64 Elaine McKenzie, interview by Ben Campkin and Lo Marshall, UCL Urban Laboratory, 15 February 2019.

65 Elaine McKenzie, Application for listed building consent, London Borough of Camden, 9 April 1996; Elaine McKenzie, Planning Application, West Lodge, 190 Euston Road, London NW1, London Borough of Camden, 9 April 1996.

66 Elaine McKenzie, interview by Ben Campkin and Lo Marshall, UCL Urban Laboratory, 15 February 2019.

67 Contributors to debates in the House of Lords in the mid-1970s recognised the centrality of the location but also emphasised its role as a gateway to London for newly arrived and vulnerable people. There was an unrealised proposal to set up an information kiosk on the East Lodge, which was in a 'miserable condition'. GALS did receive some central government funding, however, and would later move to King's Cross as demand for its service increased there. Hansard, 20 December 1976, vol. 378, cc 1072-7.

68 Elaine McKenzie, interview by Ben Campkin and Lo Marshall, UCL Urban Laboratory, 15 February 2019.

69 Elaine McKenzie, interview by Ben Campkin and Lo Marshall, UCL Urban Laboratory, 15 February 2019.

70 Elaine McKenzie, interview by Ben Campkin and Lo Marshall, UCL Urban Laboratory, 15 February 2019.

71 The building reopened as The Euston Tap in 2011. The venue is currently leased and operated by a free house, Bloomsbury Leisure Group, who also run various other local and regional venues. In contrast with McKenzie's experience, they managed to negotiate use of the outside space, as well as having external signage and aircon units that she had been forbidden to use. Since the Covid-19 pandemic, with further relaxation of licenses for outdoor seating, the pub's outdoor area has increased.

72 McKenzie asserts that: 'all these things that were . . . that could help me grow, or you know, just be more efficient in my operation, I couldn't do; I just couldn't do; I was not given the permission to do it'. Elaine McKenzie, interview by Ben Campkin and Lo Marshall, UCL Urban Laboratory, 15 February 2019.

73 Elaine McKenzie, interview by Ben Campkin and Lo Marshall, UCL Urban Laboratory, 15 February 2019.

74 McKenzie comments: 'it was a case of not just being queer but being female as well, they just wanted to keep you hidden'. Elaine McKenzie, interview by Ben Campkin and Lo Marshall, UCL Urban Laboratory, 15 February 2019.

75 Elaine McKenzie, interview by Ben Campkin and Lo Marshall, UCL Urban Laboratory, 15 February 2019.

76 Elaine McKenzie, interview by Ben Campkin and Lo Marshall, UCL Urban Laboratory, 15 February 2019.

Notes 227

77 The project for a cross London railway has its origins in schemes as far back as the 1940s and was iterated through the 1970s to 1990s. The Cross London Rail Links initiative that led to Crossrail was instigated by the Department for Transport and Transport for London in 2001. Crossrail was approved in 2007, with the Crossrail Act given royal assent in 2008. Construction began in 2009.

78 Jennings, 'The Gateways Club', 209–11.

79 The Arthur Lloyd Music Hall history website tells the story of the conversion of the theatre from a late nineteenth-century Cross and Blackwell pickle warehouse and stables, and of the building's operation into the 1980s as a cinema, theatre and theatre restaurant, and finally a nightclub and music venue. In this last phase it became significant as a gay venue. Bang! (1976–c.1993), the city's first big gay club night, was hosted at the venue in the mid-1980s, after moving from Busbys, another Charing Cross Road venue. At the time of its closure, The Astoria was surrounded by other smaller underground venues, including The Ghetto, which closed concurrently. 'The Astoria Theatre, 157, Charing Cross Road, London, WC2', http://www.arthurlloyd.co .uk/AstoriaTheatreCharingCrossRoad.htm (accessed 11 July 2019).

80 The history of G-A-Y is given on the company's Facebook page and has been articulated by Joseph via his social media accounts, including Facebook and Twitter. For example, see the announcement that he had bought out HMV's G-A-Y shares, 24 January 2013.

81 Heaven was established by the entrepreneur Jeremy Norman in 1979 in a former roller disco in what had been part of the wine cellars for the Charing Cross Station Hotel. The club's interior was designed by Norman's partner, Derek Frost. In 1982 it was purchased by Richard Branson's Virgin Group. For a recent account of the opening of Heaven, and its sale to Virgin Group, see: Derek Frost, *Living and Loving in the Age of AIDS: A Memoir* (London: Watkins, 2021). Heaven's successful 2020 Asset of Community Value Nomination also summarises the club's history: Night-time Industries Association, Heaven, Westminster City Council, Asset of Community Value Nomination Form, redacted, 2020.

82 At the time Derwent bought the property it was let by Mean Fiddler Group, a subsidiary of American media company Clear Channel, for £1 million per year, under a lease to owners Compco, until 2008. The large capacity was matched with a high turnover of '£6.2 million excluding an annual payment of £5.75 million to Jeremy Joseph', founder and manager of G-A-Y. Marc Shoffmann, 'Petition Launched to Save Gay Club', *Pink News*, 24 August 2006, https://www.pinknews.co.uk/2006/08 /24/petition-launched-to-save-gay-club/ (accessed 11 July 2019).

83 Mayor of London, *The London Plan: Spatial Development Strategy for Greater London* (London: Greater London Authority, February 2004). See, also: 'Ken Revises London Plan . . ', *Property Week*, 9 June 2006, https://www.propertyweek.com/news/ken-revises -london-plan-/3068639.article (accessed 11 July 2019); Daniel Thomas, 'Derwent Valley Buys West End's Astoria', *Property Week*, 23 June 2006, https://www.propertyweek.com/ news/derwent-valley-buys-west-ends-astoria/3069151.article (accessed 11 July 2019).

84 Marc Shoffman, 'Thousands Oppose Gay Venue Closure', *Pink News*, 29 August 2006 https://www.thepinknews.com/2006/08/29/thousands-oppose-gay-venue-closure/ (accessed 11 July 2019). The petition has since been taken down.

85 John Burns quoted in Marc Shoffmann, 'Petition Launched to Save Gay Club', *Pink News*, 24 August 2006a, https://www.pinknews.co.uk/2006/08/24/petition-launched -to-save-gay-club/ (accessed 11 July 2019).

86 The most recent legislation, the Equality Act 2010, incorporates the Public Sector Equality Duty, requiring public bodies to evaluate policies and consider impacts on equality. This means they must have due regard to eliminate discrimination, harassment and victimization related to protected characteristics: age; disability; gender reassignment; marriage and civil partnership; pregnancy and maternity; race; religion or belief; sex; sexual orientation. They are required to have 'due regard to the need to advance equality of opportunity and foster good relations between persons who share a "relevant protected characteristic" and persons who do not' (this refers to the above protected characteristics, except marriage and civil partnership). To achieve this, Equality Impact Assessments are a system used to assess how a policy will impact on equality. Equality Act 2010, http://www.legislation.gov.uk/ukpga/2010/15/contents (accessed 27 April 2020).

87 Department for Transport, *Race Equality Impact Assessment: First Report of the Full Assessment* (London: Department for Transport, 2006). Priority equality groups are specified under point 3.2 as: 'i) gender – women and transgender people; ii) race – black and minority ethnic people; iii) disability – people with physical and sensory impairments, learning difficulties and mental health requirements; iv) sexual orientation – lesbians, gay men, and bisexual people; v) religion – faith groups; vi) age – older people, children and young people; vii) economically deprived – people with limited access to employment opportunities'. Crossrail, *Crossrail Information Paper F1 Inclusivity* (London: Crossrail, 2007).

88 Department for Transport, *Crossrail Equality Impact Assessment, Project and Policy Assessment Report* (London: Department for Transport, 2006), Table 1.2; 9.

89 Rouge was active from 2004 to 2008.

90 Department for Transport, *Crossrail Equality Impact Assessment*, 4.3 Impacts by Location, 53.

91 Crossrail, *Crossrail Information Paper*, 'F1 – Inclusivity', 2007, 2.

92 Department for Transport, *Crossrail Equality Impact Assessment*, 4.3 Impacts by Location', 53. Three clubs are referred to by name. I understand this to mean The Astoria, LA2 and Rouge.

93 Department for Transport, *Crossrail Equality Impact Assessment: Public Consultation Comments and Crossrail's Response* (London: Department for Transport, January 2008), Table 3.1, 9.

94 Maurizio Curtarelli, Charlotte Ruitanga, and Maryam Shater Jannati, *The Business Case of Diversity for Enterprises, Cities and Regions with Focus on Sexual Orientation and Gender Identity* (European Commission, 2016), https://op.europa.eu/en/publication-detail/-/publication/8132dd9f-3e2f-11e9-8d04-01aa75ed71a1/language-en/format-PDF/source-93873476 (accessed 8 August 2021).

95 Department for Transport, *Crossrail Equality Impact Assessment: Public Consultation*, Table 3.1.

96 I tried to ascertain this through a request to interview Jeremy Joseph, which was unsuccessful; through a Freedom of Information request to Crossrail which was refused due to the costs that this might accrue (FOI-3722-1920, April 2020), and through raising the query with GLA representatives who did not recall the outcome.

97 Tony Grew, 'Music Group Buys into G-A-Y Bars', *Pink News*, 13 August 2007, http://www.pinknews.co.uk/2007/08/13/music-group-buys-into-g-a-y-bars/ (accessed 8 August 2021).

98 Heaven had been consistently used as a gay nightclub since the late 1970s. It is currently owned by The Arch Company Properties, part of US private equity

company Blackstone who bought up many of the UK's railway arches when they were controversially sold off by Network Rail. On Blackstone and The Arch Company see: Anna Minton, 'Ruthless Private Equity Firms Gobble up Property and Wreak Havoc on Tenants' Lives', *The Guardian*, 20 September 2019, http://www.theguardian.com/society/2019/sep/20/ruthless-private-equity-firms-gobble-up-property-wreak-havoc-on-tenants-lives (accessed 8 August 2021); Rob Davies, 'Network Rail Sells Railway Arches to Investors for £1.5bn', *The Guardian*, 10 September 2018, http://www.theguardian.com/business/2018/sep/10/network-rail-sells-railway-arches-real-estate-investors-telereal-trillium-blackstone-property-partners (accessed 8 August 2021).

99 Joseph McCormick, 'Jeremy Joseph Buys G-A-Y from HMV Administrators', *Pink News*, 24 January 2013, https://www.pinknews.co.uk/2013/01/24/jeremy-joseph-buys-g-a-y-from-hmv-administrators/ (accessed 15 July 2019).

100 Jeremy Joseph, 'G-A-Y Statement', *Canal St Online*, 24 January 2013, http://www.canal-st.co.uk/news/g-a-y-statement?Win (accessed 22 June 2021).

101 Night-time Industries Association, Heaven, Asset of Community Value Nomination Form, redacted and undated, c. 2020, Westminster City Council.

102 Night-time Industries Association, Heaven, Asset of Community Value Nomination Form, redacted and undated, c. 2020, Westminster City Council; Nick Duffy, 'London's Iconic Heaven Nightclub Granted Protected Status from Property Developers', *Pink News*, 29 January 2020, https://www.pinknews.co.uk/2020/01/29/london-heaven-nightclub-granted-asset-community-value-status-amy-lame-jeremy-joseph/ (accessed 17 August 2022).

103 Overall, this was the third most cited venue when people were asked which closed venues they valued most. UCL Urban Lab survey, 2016.

104 A fire in September 1986 forced a brief closure, but the venue reopened and remained open until 2011, gaining a bar license in 1991. For recent accounts of the history of queer venues in Soho and surrounds, including commentary of the impacts of recent development, see: Marco Venturi, *Out of Soho, Back into the Closet: Rethinking the London Gay Community,* doctoral thesis, University College London, 2018; Johan Andersson, 'Homonormative Aesthetics: AIDS and "de-Generational Unremembering" in 1990s London', *Urban Studies* 56, no. 14 (2019): 2993–3010.

105 Malcolm Comely, Robert Kincaid, Maria Tejada, interview by Ben Campkin and Lo Marshall, UCL Urban Laboratory, London, 11 April 2017.

106 First Out, *First Out Coffee Shop Project Business Plan* (London: First Out, 20 March 1985), private collection; *Prospectus for First Out Coffee Shop Project Ltd* (London: First Out, 1985), private collection.

107 The cooperative members in 1985 were: Mark Bullus, Malcolm Comley, Robert Kincaid, Andrew Stephens and Bruce Wood, five gay-identifying men, aged 23 to 36 years old. First Out, *First Out Coffee Shop Project Business Plan*, 39.

108 Correspondence with Mark Bullus, 11 August 2020.

109 Malcolm Comely, Robert Kincaid, Maria Tejada, interview by Ben Campkin and Lo Marshall, UCL Urban Laboratory, London, 11 April 2017.

110 Malcolm Comely, Robert Kincaid, Maria Tejada, interview by Ben Campkin and Lo Marshall, UCL Urban Laboratory, London, 11 April 2017.

111 Through a 'Local Economic Unit' scheme Camden awarded a loan of £25,000 and a marketing grant of £2,000. The group were also awarded a loan from the London Cooperative Enterprise Group. Malcolm Comely, Robert Kincaid, Maria Tejada,

interview by Ben Campkin and Lo Marshall, UCL Urban Laboratory, London, 11 April 2017; First Out, *First Out Coffee Shop Project Business Plan*, 45.

112 As well as in UCL Urban Laboratory's 2016 survey, the venue's success and high esteem within the community are attested by reviews associated with its tenth birthday, and more poignantly by the outpouring of positive memories and support in cards, guestbook entries, newspaper articles and social media comments when the venue's closure was announced in 2011.

113 Malcolm Comely, Robert Kincaid, Maria Tejada, interview by Ben Campkin and Lo Marshall, UCL Urban Laboratory, London, 11 April 2017.

114 Consolidated Developments owned the land from c.1997. Consolidated Developments Ltd., *St Giles Circus Design and Access Statement* (London: Consolidated Developments, December 2012), 25.

115 The premises were temporarily taken over as a Korean restaurant, which was served with a demolition notice at the start of 2013. The plan was to retain only the façade. This is an increasingly common heritage practice known as façadism. London Borough of Camden, Development Control and Building Services, correspondence, 23 January 2013, application reference 2012/6860C; Clemency Gibbs, *Façadism in London: Exploring the Gap Between Critical Heritage Theory and Conservation Practice*, doctoral thesis, UCL (forthcoming, 2023).

116 Maria Tejada and Malcolm Comley, 'The Humble Petition of First Out Ltd', House of Commons, session 2006–7, Crossrail Bill, Additional Provision.

117 There was a 1990 plan for a mixed-use development by Consolidated Developments, including music studios and a basement museum for contemporary music. One of the justifications for refusal was that the 'proposals could harm the music industry'. Consolidated Developments, *St Giles Circus Design and Access Statement*, 25.

118 Consolidated Developments, *St Giles Circus Design and Access Statement*, 3, 5.

119 Consolidated Developments, *St Giles Circus Design and Access Statement*, 6. In these documents, neighbouring Oxford Street East is boasted as a 'Prime Zone A Rent' area which saw a 75% rise in retail rental values from 2012 to 2016. The character of the St Giles Circus redevelopment is modelled on this, with 'large modern boxes' of 3,300 square feet aimed to attract national brands and an expansion of tech and media businesses. Colliers International, *St Giles: A Renewed Quarter Emerges* (2016). The scheme included a new gallery and a 280-person capacity basement music venue, recognizing the area's subcultural music heritage as the site of Tin Pan Alley, a location associated with the development of numerous superstar musicians' careers. This was intended to replace 12 Bar, a venue previously on the site; The Astoria, closed in 2009 prior to demolition; and another local venue, The Old Marquee, demolished in the Crossrail preparations.

120 It is cited, for example, by the Friends of the Joiners Arms campaign(see Chapter 7).

121 Marco Venturi comments on some of these in Venturi, *Out of Soho, Back into the Closet*, 121.

122 Vespa Lounge was a lesbian bar cocooned in a gay and lesbian pub called The Conservatory. 'The Intrepid Conservatory', *Londonist*, 12 December 2006, https://londonist.com/2006/12/the_intrepid_co (accessed 14 July 2019); Robert Andrews and Matthew Teller, *The Rough Guide to England* (London: Penguin, 2004), 170. Vespa Lounge hosted the London Biwomen's Group, a network for whom some other Camden venues that closed between the late 1990s and 2011, including The Glass Bar, were important. The website, Lost Womyn's Space comments: 'The group behind The Glass Bar, the London BiWomen's Group, formerly met at Vespa Lounge

(1999–2001), Drill Hall (1998–1999), and the London Women's Centre (1991–1998).' Lost Womyn's Space, 'The Glass Bar', 2011, http://lostwomynsspace.blogspot.com /2011/11 (accessed 14 July 2019).

123 Andy Jones, interview by Ben Campkin, The Yard, 26 April 2017.

124 Andy Jones, interview by Ben Campkin, The Yard, 26 April 2017.

125 Westminster City Council planning applications: 10/01213/FULL (2010); 14/04624/ FULL (2014); 14/12447/FULL (2014); 15/06867/FULL. The Yard, Soho, is another venue in a transport-related building: a Victorian carriage house and stable yard, close to a horse hospital. It was opened as a gay venue (The Loft and The Yard) by entrepreneur Gordon Lewis in 1993. The threat posed by The Yard's proposed redevelopment prompted a highly publicised campaign, supported by high-profile actors, Save Soho, Historic England, and an online petition. The campaign, using the hashtag #savetheyard, mobilised petitioners to record their opposition to the development on the Historic England 'Pride of Place' map. In a homonationalist gesture, #SaveTheYard repurposed British wartime military recruitment imagery – the famous poster, designed by Alfred Leete, of Field-Marshall Lord Kitchener pointing his finger with the phrase 'Your country needs you!' (1914), and of Winston Churchill, replicating this gesture, during World War II. 'The Yard: Lift Off', *Boyztown* 104, 10 July 1993, 3; Jamie Bullen, 'The Yard: Soho Gay Bar Saved after Two-Year Battle with Developers', *London Evening Standard*, https://www.standard.co .uk/news/london/the-yard-soho-gay-bar-saved-after-twoyear-battle-with-developers -a3321036.html (accessed 13 July 2021); John Harris, 'A Lament for the Death of Bohemian London', *The Guardian*, 6 February 2015, http://www.theguardian .com/commentisfree/2015/feb/06/death-bohemian-london-12-bar-club-squatters (accessed 8 August 2021).

126 UCL Urban Laboratory survey, 2016.

127 Ambisexual, meaning bisexual or androgynous. Nag Nag Nag was founded by Johnny Slut and featured post-electroclash music, growing from the electroclash wave, which fused 1980s electro music with 1990s techno. For a listing entry for the final Nag Nag Nag see: 'The Death of Nag Nag Nag', *Londonist*, 28 May 2008, https:// londonist.com/2008/05/the_death_of_na (accessed 8 August 2019).

128 In 1995, Hobart had established Popstarz, a popular and long-running indie gay and lesbian night, at the subsequently demolished 900-capacity Paradise Club in Angel, crafting its identity against the more homogenous commercial spaces and pop and house music scenes of the day. Popstarz continued until 2014, occupying various large-capacity venues including The Scala, King's Cross, and Sin, opposite The Astoria. Popstarz, 'Our history', https://popstarz.org (accessed 15 July 2019); David Hudson, 'Obituary: Simon Hobart', *The Guardian*, 2 November 2005, https://www .theguardian.com/news/2005/nov/02/guardianobituaries.artsobituaries (accessed 17 July 2019).

129 'In-Depth: Is Soho Over?', *Attitude*, 22 April 2015, http://attitude.co.uk/article/in -depth-is-soho-over/6278/ (accessed 15 July 2019).

130 'Pink Pound Dries up as Recession Begins to Bite', *Evening Standard*, 18 December 2009, http://www.standard.co.uk/business/pink-pound-dries-up-as-recession-begins -to-bite-6704807.html (accessed 15 July 2019).

131 Popbarz Limited went into administration in 2009 and was dissolved in 2015. 'Gay Club Owners Hope to Relaunch Ghetto in 2010', *Pink News*, 18 December 2009, https://www.pinknews.co.uk/2009/12/18/gay-club-owners-hope-to-relaunch -ghetto-in-2010/ (accessed 15 July 2019). The Old Street venue that accommodated

232 *Notes*

The Ghetto was viable when The Ghetto closed since it then reopened and was successful for a time, as East Bloc (2011–18), operated by another influential nightlife entrepreneur on the London scene, Wayne Shires, who had run Substation in the club that became The Ghetto in Soho.

132 'Pink Pound Dries up as Recession Begins to Bite'.

133 'Pink Pound Dries up as Recession Begins to Bite'.

Chapter 6

1 The Drama Queens Drag Theatre Company, 'The Black Cap', Assets of Community Value Nomination, London Borough of Camden, undated, 2013. The individual writing on behalf of the Company was named in the nomination but this information has been redacted by Camden for data protection reasons. The ACV was awarded in July 2013.

2 The Black Cap's ACV was subsequently challenged by the owners, removed, and then reinstated after a new application by Camden LGBT Forum, in 2015. The Forum is a registered charity, who had used the venue for their meetings. It has subsequently been renamed as Forum+.

3 By 2015, over 600 pubs had been nominated, encouraged by the government alongside a raft of other measures headed-up by a new Community Pubs Minister. The Campaign for Real Ale (CAMRA) actively encouraged communities to protect pubs through applying for ACV designation. Kris Hopkins MP, 'Community Pubs', Statement by Community Pubs Minister, 26 January 2015. Minister for Housing, Communities and Local Government, https://www.gov.uk/government/speeches/community-pubs (accessed 11 April 2019).

4 Localism Act 2011, https://www.legislation.gov.uk/ukpga/2011/20/contents/enacted (accessed 18 July 2021); The Assets of Community Value (England) Listings Regulations 2012, http://www.legislation.gov.uk/uksi/2012/2421/contents/made (accessed 29 September 2018).

5 'Asset', *Oxford English Dictionary*, https://www.oed.com/view/Entry/11866?redirectedFrom=asset (accessed 27 July 2021).

6 Localism Act 2011, 89(2).

7 Localism Act 2011, 88 (1) (a) and (b).

8 Localism Act 2011, 89(4).

9 Lambeth Council, 'Assets of Community Value', https://beta.lambeth.gov.uk/about-council/transparency-open-data/assets-community-value (accessed 20 July 2021).

10 Eligible groups are defined as: an unincorporated body with a membership including at least 21 people registered to vote in Camden, or a neighbouring borough; neighbourhood forums; a charity, industrial and provident society or company limited by guarantee which does not distribute any surplus to its members; or a community interest company. Camden Council, 'Assets of Community Value', https://www.camden.gov.uk/assets-of-community-value#zzok (accessed 18 July 2021).

11 'Nothing underlines the powerlessness that many communities feel more than the loss of essential services, like post offices and pubs, because of decisions made by distant bureaucrats'. Conservative Party', *Invitation to Join the Government of Britain: The Conservative Manifesto 2010* (Conservative Party, 2010), 75, https://

conservativehome.blogs.com/files/conservative-manifesto-2010.pdf (accessed 19 July 2021).

12 Ben Kisby, 'The Big Society: Power to the People?', *The Political Quarterly* 81, no. 4 (2010): 484–91.

13 *The Conservative Manifesto 2010*, 76.

14 This imperative to reduce planning powers continues. See, for example: Ministry of Housing, Communities and Local Government, *Planning for the Future,* White Paper (London, August 2020), https://www.gov.uk/government/consultations/planning-for -the-future (accessed 29 September 2020).

15 Barbara Lipietz, Richard Lee, and Sharon Hayward, 'Just Space: Building a Community-Based Voice for London Planning', *City* 18, no. 2 (2014): 214–25.

16 The Drama Queens Drag Theatre Company, 'The Black Cap', 2013.

17 Correspondence with London Borough of Camden, Planning, 22 July 2021.

18 The Drama Queens Drag Theatre Company, 'The Black Cap', 2013.

19 The Drama Queens Drag Theatre Company, 'The Black Cap', 2013.

20 Camden LGBT Forum, 'The Black Cap', London Borough of Camden Assets of Community Value Nomination Form, undated, c. 2015. Forum+ is: 'an independent charity working to promote equality for LGBTQ+ people in Camden and Islington, by hosting social groups and events which celebrate LGBTQ+ life in the boroughs and working to reduce social isolation and loneliness.' Forum+ https://www .consortium.lgbt/member-directory/forum/ (accessed 18 August 2022).

21 'LGBT History Month Events in Camden', *Scene Magazine*, 17 January 2014, https://www.gscene.com/arts/books/lgbt-history-month-events-in-camden/ (accessed 20 July 2021). LGBT History Month in the UK is coordinated by Schools OUT, a charity that evolved from The Gay Teachers' Group, established in 1974. The programme was established in 2005 and takes place every February in commemoration of the abolition of Section 28.

22 Camden LGBT Forum, 'The Black Cap', c. 2015.

23 Camden LGBT Forum, 'Black Cap Gets Community Asset Status', 8 April 2015, http://camdenlgbtforum.org.uk/2015/04/08/black-cap-gets-community-asset-status/ (accessed 13 July 2021). The Act legalised homosexual acts between two consenting adults over the age of twenty-one, in private. It applied only to England and Wales. Loulla-Mae Eleftheriou-Smith, 'London's Historic Gay Pub The Black Cap in Camden Closed by Owners a Week after Being Awarded "asset of Community Value" Status', *Independent*, 14 April 2015, https://www.independent.co.uk/news/uk/home -news/londons-historic-gay-pub-the-black-cap-in-camden-closed-by-owners-a-week -after-being-awarded-asset-10176344.html (accessed 31 July 2021).

24 Camden LGBT Forum, 'The Black Cap', c. 2015.

25 'LGBTQ+ Venues in Camden', UCL Urban Lab and Camden Council, roundtable on LGBTQ+ Venues in Camden, July 2019, transcript.

26 Camden LGBT Forum, 'The Black Cap', c. 2015.

27 London Borough of Camden, letter to Nigel Harris, Camden LGBT Forum, 8 April 2015.

28 London Borough of Camden, letter to Nigel Harris, Camden LGBT Forum, 8 April 2015.

29 Anon, 'Protected Status of Black Cap is upheld after Owners Launch Legal Challenge', *Camden New Journal*, 13 July 2015, http://camdennewjournal.com/article/blackcap -acv-review?sp=14&sq=when%2520is%2520a%2520basement%2520not%2520a %2520basement (accessed 6 August 2021); Ben Walters, 'Exclusive: Black Cap

Regains Protective Community-Asset Status', *Not Television*, 8 April 2015, http://www
.nottelevision.net/black-cap-regains-acv-status-camden-council/ (accessed 31 July
2021).

30 We Are The Black Cap, http://www.weareblackcap.com/ (accessed 26 July 2021);
Anon, 'Protected status of Black Cap is upheld', 2015.

31 Eleftheriou-Smith, 'London's Historic Gay Pub'; Ben Walters, 'Black Cap's Council
Protection Hangs in the Balance', *Not Television*, 7 July 2015, http://www.nottelevision
.net/black-cap-council-protection-hangs-in-balance/

32 Eleftheriou-Smith, 'London's Historic Gay Pub'; Godfrey, Chris. 'The Black Cap
Protest: Drag Queens and LGBT Activists Gather to Save Iconic London Gay Bar
from Developers', *Independent*, 18 April 2015, https://www.independent.co.uk/news
/uk/home-news/the-black-cap-protest-drag-queens-and-lgbt-activists-gather-to
-save-iconic-london-gay-bar-from-10186891.html (accessed 25 August 2022); Tom
Marshall, 'Natalie Bennett Leads Protest at Pub Company Faucet Inn's Headquarters
after Black Cap Closure', *Evening Standard*, 1 May 2015, https://www.standard
.co.uk/news/london/natalie-bennett-leads-protest-at-pub-company-faucet-inns
-headquarters-after-black-cap-closure-10220094.html (accessed 25 August 2022);
Alexandra Rucki, 'Drag Queens Don Flamboyant Costumes to Protest against Closure
of North London Gay Pub', *Evening Standard*, 18 April 2015, https://www.standard.co
.uk/news/london/drag-queens-don-flamboyant-costumes-to-protest-against-closure
-of-north-london-gay-pub-10186748.html (accessed 22 August 2022).

33 Jonathan Arana-Morton, 'Breakfast Club set to open in former Black Cap', *Kentish
Town News*, 24 June 2015, https://www.kentishtowner.co.uk/2015/06/24/breakfast
-club-open-former-black-cap/ (accessed 26 April 2019).

34 Joe Parslow and Meth, interview by Ben Campkin and Lo Marshall, UCL Urban
Laboratory, 30 August 2019.

35 Alarm at the sale of the RVT was first raised via a Facebook group, with campaigners
organising themselves as the Friends of the RVT. The original Facebook group was
initiated by performer Thom Shaw. The ACV nomination was submitted by Richard
Heaton. Friends of the Royal Vauxhall Tavern, 'Royal Vauxhall Tavern', Community
Right to Bid for Assets of Community Value Nomination Form', London Borough of
Lambeth, 18 September 2014; Ben Walters, interview by Ben Campkin, UCL Urban
Laboratory, 19 July 2019.

36 UCL Urban Lab's dataset (see Chapter 4) shows a cluster appearing in 1996; however,
in the 1980s, earlier than the period covered within the cluster analysis, there was
a vibrant scene, with 'six or seven pubs within walking distance'. Rob Pateman,
interview by Ben Campkin, UCL Urban Laboratory, 2 August 2019.

37 Johan Andersson, 'Vauxhall's Post-Industrial Pleasure Gardens: "Death Wish" and
Hedonism in 21st-Century London', *Urban Studies* 48, no. 1 (2011): 85–100.

38 Mayor of London, *Vauxhall Nine Elms Battersea: Opportunity Area Planning
Framework*, Greater London Authority, 2012.

39 UCL Urban Lab dataset.

40 Friends of the Royal Vauxhall Tavern, 'Royal Vauxhall Tavern'.

41 RVT Future, 'The RVT Gets Asset of Community Value Status', 29 October 2014,
http://www.rvt.community/the-rvt-as-an-asset-of-community-value/ (accessed
20 July 2021).

42 Lambeth Council, 'Iconic Gay Venue's Listing to Help Ensure the Party Goes on',
Lambeth News, 15 October 2014, https://lambethnews.wordpress.com/2014/10/15/
iconic-gay-venues-listing-to-help-ensure-the-party-goes-on/ (accessed 25 July 2021).

Notes

43 Friends of the Royal Vauxhall Tavern, 'Royal Vauxhall Tavern'.

44 Friends of the Royal Vauxhall Tavern, 'Royal Vauxhall Tavern'; Reverend Alison Kennedy, St Peter's Vauxhall, letter to Lambeth Borough Council, 7 June 2015.

45 'The building itself as an iconic venue goes back to 1860. Around the 1950s, '60s, it started to get into the LGBT side of it, where we had two sides to the bar – we had the little snug at one side, where you had the people, the old ladies in there drinking their port and lemon; and then you'd have the drag queens on the bar ... going mental on the bar'. James Lindsay, CEO, The Royal Vauxhall Tavern, interview by Ben Campkin, London, 10 November 2020. See, also: RVT Future, 'Tales of the Tavern: 1956 – Drag on the Bar-Top', RVT Future, 6 April 2016, http://www.rvt.community/tales-of-the-tavern-the-true-story-behind-1956/ (accessed 19 January 2023)

46 Friends of the Royal Vauxhall Tavern, 'Royal Vauxhall Tavern'. The exterior of the RVT had recorded by Lambeth on its Local List for its quality on 26 March 2012. London Borough of Lambeth, *List of Buildings of Architectural or Historic Interest (Local List)*, 24 April 2013, http://lambeth.gov.uk/sites/default/files/pl-buildings-local -list.pdf (accessed 28 July 2021).

47 RVT Future, 'The RVT Gets Asset of Community Value Status'.

48 http://www.rvt.community/ (accessed 19 August 2022).

49 At the time of writing, Duckie has a residency at The Eagle, Vauxhall, and operates as a daytime tea dance.

50 Ben Walters, interview by Ben Campkin, UCL Urban Laboratory, 16 July 2019.

51 The RVT was the subject of a successful Heritage Lottery Fund bid (£100,000), led by Duckie and backed by Lambeth Council in 2014, http://happybirthdayrvt.com/ (accessed 13 July 2021); 'Iconic Gay Venue's Listing to Help Ensure the Party Goes on', *European Union News*, 17 October 2014. For a summary of some of Duckie's engagements with queer history in and around the RVT see: Laura Gowing, 'LGBT Histories and the Politics of Identity' in Adam Sutcliffe, Anna Maerker, and Simon Sleight, *History, Memory and Public Life: The Past in the Present* (London: Routledge, 2018), 294-316.

52 Amy Lamé, interview by Ben Campkin, City Hall, 4 September 2019; *Save The Tavern*, 25 April 2015. Directed by Tim Brunsden; Ben Walters, 'Supporting Statement for an Application to have the Royal Vauxhall Tavern Added to the National Heritage List for England', January 2015, 28, http://www.rvt.community /wp-content/uploads/2015/09/Initial-RVT-listing-application-January-2015.pdf (accessed 25 Nov 2018); David Northmore, 'Inn with a Sporting Chance?', *Pink Paper*, 2 October 1998, http://www.rvt.community/wp-content/uploads/2015/03/Fig-44. -Pink-Paper-report-on-90s-threat1.jpg (accessed 5 August 2021).

53 Royal Vauxhall Tavern, '1 July 2021 Updated – The Royal Vauxhall Tavern – The Story So Far', London, https://www.vauxhalltavern.com/royal-vauxhall-tavern-the -story-so-far-20-february-2021/ (accessed 30 July 2021).

54 Lambeth Council, 'Iconic Gay Venue's Listing'; 'The Black Cap Protest: Drag Queens and LGBT Activists Gather to Save iconic London gay bar from developers', *The Independent*. 18 April 2015, https://www.independent.co.uk/news/uk/home-news/ the-black-cap-protest-drag-queens-and-lgbt-activists-gather-to-save-iconic-london -gay-bar-from-developers-10186891.html (accessed 19 August 2022).

55 'LGBTQ+ Venues in Camden', UCL Urban Lab and Camden Council, roundtable on LGBTQ+ Venues in Camden, July 2019, unpublished transcript.

56 Hopkins, 'Community Pubs', 2015.

57 By 2019, only one pub in London had been bought and operated by a community after its registration as an ACV. This was Ivy House, Nunhead, which was the first pub to be registered. Centre for London, *Act Local: Empowering London's Neighbourhoods* (London: Centre for London, 2019), 17.

58 UCL Urban Lab survey, 2016.

59 Michela Chirgwin, 'Queer Cabaret Is a Hit with "lonely" and "Marginalised" Older People', *Homecare*, 9 July 2018, https://www.homecare.co.uk/news/article.cfm/id /1597656/queer-caberet-is-a-hit-with-vulnerable-and-marginalised-older-people (accessed 26 August 2022).

60 Simon Casson quoted in 'Duckie', *Inquiry into the Civic Role of Arts Organisations*, Calouste Gulbenkian Foundation, undated, https://civicroleartsinquiry.gulbenkian .org.uk/resources/duckie (accessed 12 April 2019).

61 Casson quoted in 'Duckie', *Inquiry into the Civic Role of Arts Organisations*.

62 Participant, 'Who Cares?', Online Long Table, Night-spaces, Culture and Integration in Europe (NITE), UCL Urban Laboratory, 22 July 2021.

63 http://www.rvt.community/the-story-so-far/ (accessed 1 September 2021).

64 Eleanor Margolis, 'Closing Time: The Loss of Iconic Gay Venues Is a Nasty Side-Effect of London's Sanitisation', *New Statesman*, 11 March 2015, https://www .newstatesman.com/culture/2015/03/closing-time-loss-iconic-gay-venues-nasty -side-effect-londons-sanitisation (accessed 29 May 2019); Lambeth Council, 'Iconic Gay Venue's Listing'; Walters, 'Exclusive: Black Cap Regains Protective Community-Asset Status'; Chris Godfrey, 'The Black Cap Protest: Drag Queens and LGBT Activists Gather to Save Iconic London Gay Bar from Developers', *Independent*, 18 April 2015, https://www.independent.co.uk/news/uk/home-news/the-black -cap-protest-drag-queens-and-lgbt-activists-gather-to-save-iconic-london-gay -bar-from-10186891.html (accessed 31 July 2021); Alexandra Rucki, 'Drag Queens Don Flamboyant Costumes to Protest against Closure of North London Gay Pub', *Evening Standard*, 18 April 2015, https://www.standard.co.uk/news/london/drag -queens-don-flamboyant-costumes-to-protest-against-closure-of-north-london-gay -pub-10186748.html (accessed 31 July 2021); Future of the Royal Vauxhall Tavern, 'The RVT Gets Asset of Community Value Status', 29 October 2014, http://www.rvt .community/the-rvt-as-an-asset-of-community-value/ (accessed 31 July 2021); Ben Walters, 'Closing Time for Gay Pubs – a New Victim of London's Soaring Property Prices', *The Guardian*, 4 February 2015, https://www.theguardian.com/society/2015/ feb/04/closing-time-gay-pubs-lgbt-venues-property-prices (accessed 31 July 2021).

65 Ben Walters, interview by Ben Campkin, UCL Urban Laboratory, 16 July 2019.

66 The Albert Kennedy Trust's Tony Butchart-Kelly links the closures to high incidence of depression, suicide and self-harm among LGBT communities. Walters, 'Closing Time for Gay Pubs'.

67 Ben Walters, interview by Ben Campkin, UCL Urban Laboratory, 16 July 2019.

68 Walters, 'Supporting Statement'. Historic England was formerly known as English Heritage. Royal Vauxhall Tavern, Historic England, Listed Building 1426984.

69 RVT Future, 'The Story So Far', June 2015, http://www.rvt.community/the-story-so -far/ (accessed 31 July 2021).

70 Historic England, *Commerce and Exchange Buildings: Listing Selection Guide* (English Heritage, 2011). See: 'Public Houses': 'The number of pubs was in decline in the later twentieth century, and the rate of loss increased in the early twenty-first century with 50 pubs a week closing in 2009. Whatever the reason (changes in licensing laws and the smoking ban of 2007 are both held to have played a part) the result was the same:

The conversion of some premises to other uses, demolitions and an increase in listing requests' (15).

71 Department for Digital, Culture, Media and Sport, *Principles for Selection for Listed Buildings* (November 2018). Although updated in 2018, the criteria are consistent with those in place at the time of the RVT's listing. Section 22 includes a provision for buildings deemed nationally significant by representing a local industry.

72 Antoine Picon, *Some Concluding Remarks. First International Meeting of the European Architectural History Network* (Portugal: Guimarães, 2010), 11.

73 English Heritage, *National Heritage Protection Plan: Project Brief for LGBT Heritage Project*, December 2014.

74 English Heritage, *National Heritage Protection Plan: Project Brief for LGBT Heritage Project*, December 2014. The main focus of the brief was on public engagement and the crowd sourcing of an interactive map. The selected project, 'Pride of Place', led by the social and historical historians Alison Oram and Justin Bengry, led to valuable online resources on LGBTQ+ heritage across England. Historic England, *Pride of Place*, https://historicengland.org.uk/research/inclusive-heritage/lgbtq-heritage -project/ (accessed 4 August 2021). For the map, see: https://www.historypin.org/ en/prideofplace/ (accessed 5 August 2021). The crowdsourced map uses a standard crowdsourcing platform, *History Pin*. It offers a repository for descriptions, links, media and ephemera; and the possibility to see concentrations of spaces across England.

75 Couch MP, Tracey and Department for Culture, Media and Sport, 'Royal Vauxhall Tavern Receives Listed Status', https://www.gov.uk/government/news/royal-vauxhall -tavern-receives-listed-status (accessed 26 August 2022).

76 Lambeth Council, *Local Heritage List: Buildings and Structures*, 26 March 2012, https://beta.lambeth.gov.uk/sites/default/files/2022-01/local_heritage_list_19.01.22 .pdf (accessed 26 August 2022).

77 'Stonewall Gains Federal Recognition on its 30th Anniversary', 26 June 1999, https://vparchive.gvshp.org/stonewall.htm (accessed 2 August 2021); United States Department of the Interior, National Park Service, National Register of Historic Places, 'Stonewall', http://media.villagepreservation.org/wp-content/uploads/2020 /03/15122950/Stonewall-National-Resgister-Districts-State-and-National-Register -Report.pdf (accessed 16 April 2019). Christopher Park was also re-landscaped by a gay landscape designer, Philip Winslow, in 1992, and included a memorial 'Gay Liberation', by George Segal. Christopher Castiglia and Christopher Reed, *If Memory Serves: Gay Men, AIDS, and the Promise of the Queer Past* (Minneapolis: University of Minnesota Press, 2012), 78–80.

78 The listing application describes how the latter saw a reported thirty-five officers raid the pub, some wearing rubber gloves, and arresting eleven men, including drag queen Lily Savage: 'The raid instantly entered the city's LGBT lore. The rubber gloves stood out for their combination of symbolic marginalisation – they were assumed to be an attempt on officers' part to defend themselves against potential exposure to HIV-infected blood, intimating both the threat of violence and abhorrence at queer bodies – and their sheer camp value'. It draws on evidence from GALOP, *Gay London Policing Group 3rd Annual Report 1986–1987*, 1987 and interview materials from the artist-led Heritage Lottery-funded oral history and archiving project 'Happy Birthday RVT', http://happybirthdayrvt.com/ (accessed 13 July 2021). Walters, 'Supporting Statement', 19. See also, Ben Walters, 'The Police Wore Rubber Gloves', *Not Television*, 16 January 2017, https://www.nottelevision.net/police-wore-rubber-gloves-part-1-of -3/ (accessed 30 November 2022).

79 Movements disco at The Bell was raided in March 1984 and Gays the Word was raided on 10 April 1984. Graham McKerrow, 'Saving Gays the Word: The Campaign to Protect a Bookshop and the Right to Import Queer Literature', in Leila Kassir and Richard Espley (eds.), *Queer Between the Covers: Histories of Queer Publishing and Publishing Queer Voices* (London: University of London Press, 2021), 91–122. The Gay Liberation Front's Highbury demonstration in 1970 could claim to be a more direct parallel with Stonewall, and between the US and British movement (see note 32, Chapter 5). This was commemorated with a triangular plaque organised by activist group Outrage! with funding by GLF member Andrew Lumsden in 2000. Outrage!, 'GLF Memorial Plaque to be Unveiled', 10 November 2000.

80 United States Department of the Interior, 'Stonewall', 10; Walters, 'Supporting Statement', 16.

81 José Esteban Muñoz, *Cruising Utopia: The Then and There of Queer Futurity* (New York and London: New York University Press, 2009), 121–4.

82 Muñoz, *Cruising Utopia*, 118.

83 United States Department of the Interior, 'Stonewall', 5.

84 United States Department of the Interior, 'Stonewall'. Barack Obama, 'Presidential Proclamation – Establishment of the Stonewall National Monument', 24 June 2016, https://obamawhitehouse.archives.gov/the-press-office/2016/06/24/presidential -proclamation-establishment-stonewall-national-monument (accessed 26 August 2022).

85 United States Department of the Interior, 'Stonewall', 14–15.

86 The listing application stated that the RVT 'is the country's oldest continually operating site of lesbian, gay, bisexual and transgender socialising, and the last vestige of a culture of experimental recreation that stretches back four centuries'. Walters, 'Supporting Statement', 1. See, also the work of David Coke, historian of Vauxhall Pleasure Gardens, who links the RVT to the extended history of artistic expression, entertainment and experimental socialisation, with its particular association with cross-dressing and sexual permissiveness. He comments that the RVT is 'the only direct continuation and development on-site of the entertainments that formed such an integral part of the Vauxhall Gardens experience'. David Coke, 'Vauxhall Gardens: 1661–1859: Brief History', http://www.vauxhallgardens .com/vauxhall_gardens_briefhistory_page.html (accessed 25 November 2018). The long-term association between Vauxhall, hedonism and gender and sexual experimentation has been commented on by historian Chris Roberts; by queer geographer Johan Andersson in his discussion of the Vauxhall gay clubbing scene of the 2000s, of the use of historical references to the Pleasure Gardens in place marketing, and of Duckie's narration of these histories; by social historian, Peter Ackroyd; by humanities scholar Simon Avery in his account of queer space; and by architectural historian Joe Crowdy's account of the gardens and queer desire. Simon Avery, 'Structuring and Interpreting Queer Spaces of London', in *Sex, Time and Place: Queer Histories of London, c.1850 to the Present*, ed. Simon Avery and Katherine M. Graham (London: Bloomsbury Academic, 2016). Chris Roberts, *Cross River Traffic – A History of London's Bridges* (Granta, 2005), 15; Andersson, 'Vauxhall's Post-Industrial Pleasure Gardens', 91; Joe Crowdy, 'Queer Undergrowth: Weeds and Sexuality in the Architecture of the Garden', *Architecture and Culture*, 5 (2017): 423–33; Peter Ackroyd, *Queer City: Gay London from the Romans to the Present Day* (London: Chatto and Windus, 2017), 230.

87 Andersson, 'Vauxhall's Post-Industrial Pleasure Gardens', 91.

88 Historic England, 'Royal Vauxhall Tavern Listed', 9 September 2015, https://historicengland.org.uk/whats-new/news/royal-vauxhall-tavern-listed/ (accessed 25 November 2018).

89 Duckie, 'Princess', September 2021, http://www.duckie.co.uk/events/princess (accessed 26 August 2022).

90 *Vauxhall Gardens* (1859). Watercolour, Museum of London, A6983/4, https://collections.museumoflondon.org.uk/online/object/94028.html (accessed 4 August 2021).

91 The listing application refers to the columns and speculates that the RVT's name was a self-conscious nod to the gardens, playing on nostalgia for them. It states that there may have been a tavern of this name prior to the 1860s building of today. Walters, 'Supporting Statement', 3, 6. The theory about the columns was made on the basis of a rare item of ephemera, an 1859 auction catalogue from the sale at the time the Gardens closed. Historian David Coke has since noted that: 'One thing this catalogue does do is to show that there was a real market for all the old fixtures and fittings, probably largely among those people who had been regular visitors to the pleasure garden, and who wanted something to remind them of the gardens after they had disappeared. Londoners felt very nostalgic for the place where, in some cases, they had first met their first love, or, in their younger days, marvelled at some of the spectacular displays'. Coke, 'Vauxhall Gardens 1661–1859: The 1859 Auction Catalogue', Object of the Month Archive, Number 1, April 2016, http://www.vauxhallgardens.com/vauxhall_gardens_object_archive_april2016_page.html (accessed 22 November 2018).

92 Walters, 'Supporting Statement', 3.

93 Walters, Royal Vauxhall Tavern, 372 Kennington Lane, London SE11 5HY (ref: 1424488). Response to Patience Trevor's consultation report of 19 May 2015, 8 June 2015, section 6.

94 Cornelius Holtorf, 'Perceiving the Past: From Age Value to Pastness', *International Journal of Cultural Property*, Oxford 24, no. 4 (November 2017): 498.

95 Steven Vaughan and Brad Jessup, 'Backstreet's Back Alright: London's LGBT+ Nightlife Spaces and a Queering of Planning Law and Planning Practices' in Maria Lee and Carolyn Abbot (eds.), *Taking Planning Law Seriously: New Research in English Planning Law* (UCL Press, London, 2022), 35–63.

96 Holtorf, 'Perceiving the Past', 497–515, 500f.

97 Royal Vauxhall Tavern, Grade II listing, Historic England, 8 September 2015, https://historicengland.org.uk/listing/the-list/list-entry/1426984 (accessed 16 April 2019).

98 Royal Vauxhall Tavern, Grade II listing, Historic England, 8 September 2015, https://historicengland.org.uk/listing/the-list/list-entry/1426984 (accessed 16 April 2019).

99 James Lindsay, interview by Ben Campkin, London, 10 November 2020.

100 James Lindsay, interview by Ben Campkin, London, 10 November 2020.

101 RVT, 'Love the RVT: Stop the Listing', petition, undated.

102 James Lindsay, 'RVT Year End Trading Statement', Royal Vauxhall Tavern, 30 June 2016, http://www.vauxhalltavern.com/james-lindsay-chief-executive-royal-vauxhall-tavern-rvt-year-end-trading-statement-30-june-2016/ (accessed 18 April 2019).

103 http://www.rvt.community/the-story-so-far/ (accessed 31 July 2021).

104 David Hudson, 'London's Royal Vauxhall Tavern is being Sold to New Owner', *Gaystar News*, 2 February 2017, https://www.gaystarnews.com/article/londons-royal-vauxhall-tavern-sold/#gs.4kzn3w (accessed 11 April 2019).

105 For example, Faucet Inn, the London-based pub company that has attempted to convert The Black Cap, and closed it in 2015, were in negotiations to buy the RVT in 2017. Rashid Razaq, 'Vauxhall Tavern "set to be Sold to Chain that Closed Cabaret Bar"', *Evening Standard*, 17 February 2017.

106 *Pride of Place*, https://www.historypin.org/en/prideofplace/geo/51.538227,-0.142042 ,18/bounds/51.537036,-0.146363,51.539418,-0.137721/paging/1/pin/1037621 (accessed 5 August 2021) and https://www.historypin.org/en/prideofplace/geo/51 .538227,-0.142042,18/bounds/51.537036,-0.146363,51.539418,-0.137721/paging/1/ pin/1037621 (accessed 5 August 2021).

107 For example, Mrs Shufflewick, Hinge and Bracket, Danny la Rue, Lily Savage, HIH Regina Fong, Sandra, Adrella, Julian Clary, Titti la Camp, Graham Norton and Dave Lynn.

108 'Rex Jameson (Mrs Shufflewick) Rare Interview [by Keith Howe] (*Gay News*, 1977)', https://www.youtube.com/watch?v=tn9JW-E17MI (accessed 5 August 2021).

109 'Unknown Future for Black Cap as Doors Close and Customers Celebrate "Last Night"', *Camden New Journal*, 13 April 2015, http://camdennewjournal.com/article /black-cap-closes-uncertain-future?sp=9&sq=Black%2520Cap%2520Pub (accessed 5 August 2021).

110 The Black Cap Foundation was a registered company from 25 May 2016 to 22 December 2020. Thereafter The Black Cap Community Benefit Society was established.

111 The pub was squatted by Camden Queer Punx 4eva. 'Camden: Queer Punx Squat Black Cap', *Squat!Net*, 11 June 2015, https://en.squat.net/2015/06/11/camden-queer -punx-squat-black-cap/ (accessed 9 December 2022); Ben Walters, 'Inside the Squatted Black Cap', *Not Television*, 6 June 2015, https://www.nottelevision.net/inside -the-squatted-black-cap/ (accessed 9 December 2022).

112 Black Cap Foundation, correspondence with London Borough of Camden, 2019, http://camdocs.camden.gov.uk/HPRMWebDrawer/Record/7444032/file/document ?inline (accessed 13 July 2021).

113 Within the core membership, as well as first-hand knowledge of the venue and political experience in LGBT campaigns, including those around other London venues, there are artists, journalists/critics, experts in social enterprise, media and hospitality, and a magistrate. Black Cap Foundation, *The Black Cap Business Plan*, March 2017, 8, http://www.weareblackcap.com/ (accessed 13 July 2021).

114 My summary of these transactions is based on the following sources: Transparency International UK, *Faulty Towers: Understanding the Impact of Overseas Corruption on the London Property Market* (March 2017), 52; Make Public, 'Re-open the Black Cap Pub', timeline, http://www.makepublic.uk/campaign-timeline/8#2 (accessed 26 September 2018); Danny Beales, 'Petition Update: Black Cap Pub. As No-Longer-Secret Financiers Vollin Left the Scene, Dragonfly S.A.R.L. stepped in', *Reopen the Black Cap*, Change.org, 20 March 2017; Emma Youle, 'Calls to Re-open Iconic Black Cap Pub as Links to Russian Billionaires' Offshore Cash Revealed', *Ham and High*, 9 March 2017, https://www.hamhigh.co.uk/news/calls-to-reopen-iconic-black-cap -pub-as-links-to-3550302 (accessed 5 August 2021).

115 In April 2022 they were reported to own a £100m portfolio of property in Britain and were seeking to purchase Shepherd's Bush Market. Miranda Bryant, 'Unsanctioned Abramovich Partners "Have £100m in British Assets"', *The Times*, 7 April 2022, https://www.thetimes.co.uk/article/unsanctioned-abramovich-partners-have-100m -in-british-assets-78ngkhs7b (accessed 24 August 2022).

116 Transparency International, *Faulty Towers*, 52.

117 Youle, 'Calls to Reopen Iconic Black Cap Pub', *Ham and High*, 2017.

118 Transparency International, *Faulty* Towers, 52.

119 Loretta Lees, 'Gentrification', chapter 10, in James D. Wright (ed.), *International Encyclopedia of the Social & Behavioral Sciences* (Amsterdam and New York: Elsevier, 2015), 46–52.

120 For relevant planning history, see: London Borough of Camden 2012/1444/P; 2013/0262/P; 2013/2301/P; 2013/0191/NEW; 2014/2176/P. The proposals were submitted via planning consultants such as Surrey-based Grainger Associates Limited.

121 London Borough of Camden, Decision notice, 2012/1444/P, 16 May 2012.

122 Elizabeth Hill, Appeal Decision, APP/X5210/A/12/2184317, The Planning Inspectorate, 4 March 2013, 2.

123 At an appeal in 2013, the Planning Inspector noted that the Council's view was that the ground floor should be considered distinct within the venue as *sui generis* use, but that there had been 'no formal Council determinations' on this. Elizabeth Hill, Appeal Decision, The Planning Inspectorate, 4 March 2013, 2. Camden later clarified their view that the entire venue fell under this designation, but this continued to be a point of contention with the freehold owners, who appealed in 2020. Correspondence with London Borough of Camden Policy Team, 16 March 2020.

124 London Borough of Camden, *Local Plan* (2017), policies C2, 3 and 4; *Camden Planning Guidance: Community Uses, Leisure Facilities and Pubs* (London: Camden, 2018).

125 Jonathan Arana-Morton, 'Breakfast Club set to open in former Black Cap', *Kentish Town News*, 24 June 2015, https://www.kentishtowner.co.uk/2015/06/24/breakfast -club-open-former-black-cap/ (accessed 26 April 2019). There are thirteen outlets at the time of writing, with tongue-in-cheek names such as 'The King of Ladies Man' and 'Call me Mr Lucky'.

126 'The decision to close the venue was made a long time before ourselves or Camden Securities got involved. You can form your own opinions on whether this closure was done in the right way. We have ours.' Arana-Morton, 'Breakfast Club', 2015.

127 Albion & East [Ruth and Robinson], https://www.enterprise-ip.com/investment/ albion-east-ltd-ruth-robinson-ltd/ (accessed 26 April 2019).

128 Albion & East [Ruth and Robinson], https://www.enterprise-ip.com/investment/ albion-east-ltd-ruth-robinson-ltd/ (accessed 26 April 2019).

129 The Wealth Club, https://www.wealthclub.co.uk/about/ (accessed 26 April 2019).

130 London Borough of Camden, 2016/0350/P; 2016/1307/P; 2016/0347/P; 2016/0528/A.

131 London Borough of Camden 2016/0347P, 20 January 2016.

132 This was followed by three related applications for associated work, such as installing a new shopfront, displaying advertising and minor works. London Borough of Camden 20 January 2016; 1 February 2016; 9 March 2016.

133 In 2018, CgMs' website stated that they aid clients 'from development companies, to construction companies, to individual homeowners', CgMs, http://www.cgms.co.uk/ page/About_51/1.html (accessed 20 April 2018). CgMs has since been rebranded as RPS Group.

134 For a proposed shopfront redesign. Gordon Macqueen and Margaret Richardson, email correspondence addressed to David Peres Da Costa, 29 February 2016.

135 Gordon Macqueen and Margaret Richardson, email correspondence addressed to David Peres Da Costa, 29 February 2016.

136 #WeAreTheBlackCap, 'An Open Letter to the Investors of Ruth and Robinson Limited', 8 April 2016, https://weareblackcap.wordpress.com (accessed 27 April 2019).

137 Historic England, 'The Black Cap', 21 September 2017, https://historicengland.org.uk/listing/the-list/list-entry/1449431 (accessed 6 October 2018).

138 The Black Cap Business Plan, March 2017, http://www.weareblackcap.com/ (accessed 13 July 2021).

139 The document cites 11,000 supporters, and a social media group of 2,500 members and growing. Black Cap Foundation, 'Black Cap Pub Business Finance Forecasts', 24 January 2017.

140 Black Cap Foundation, 'Black Cap Pub Business Finance Forecasts'; *The Black Cap Business Plan*, March 2017. The campaigners project a £2.075m annual turnover which they state is an increase on the turnover in the year the venue closed - a figure known to them but confidential. Business reportedly stagnated in the early 2000s before the latest revival.

141 Joe Parslow, interview by Ben Campkin and Lo Marshall, UCL Urban Laboratory, 7 April 2017.

142 Joe Parslow, interview by Ben Campkin and Lo Marshall, UCL Urban Laboratory, 2016.

143 Wayne Shires, interview by Ben Campkin, Bloc South, 2017.

144 Wayne Shires, interview by Ben Campkin, Bloc South, 2017.

145 Wayne Shires, interview by Ben Campkin, Bloc South, 2017; Joe Parslow and Meth, interview by Ben Campkin and Lo Marshall, UCL Urban Laboratory, 2019. This was supported by local Councillor, Danny Beales.

146 Venues included WKD in the early 1990s, then Camden Rock, members club, The Record Club, directed by local nightlife entrepreneur Lee Bennett, and bar and late-night members' club The Stillery.

147 Wayne Shires, interview by Ben Campkin, Bloc South, 2017.

148 The bar was leased from Camden Town Bars.

149 Joe Parslow, interview by Ben Campkin and Lo Marshall, UCL Urban Laboratory, 2016.

150 Joe Parslow, interview by Ben Campkin and Lo Marshall, UCL Urban Laboratory, 2016.

151 Joe Parslow, interview by Ben Campkin and Lo Marshall, UCL Urban Laboratory, 2016.

152 Joe Parslow and Meth, interview by Ben Campkin and Lo Marshall, UCL Urban Laboratory, 30 August 2019.

153 Ben Walters, 'New Hopes for Black Cap as Campaigners and Owner Reach Agreement', *Not Television*, 25 August 2017.

154 http://www.daviscofferlyons.co.uk/property/detail/black-cap-171-camden-high-street-camden-nw1-7jy/15061 (accessed 13 July 2021). #WeAreTheBlackCap have drawn attention to the pub as an investment opportunity for an LGBT operator, widely advertising the sale.

155 Email correspondence with #WeAreTheBlackCap Campaign, 10 September 2022.

156 'LGBTQ+ Venues in Camden', UCL Urban Lab and Camden Council, roundtable on LGBTQ+ Venues in Camden, July 2019, unpublished transcript.

157 Emma Powys Maurice, 'Beloved London Gay Bar Could Soon Reopen after Sitting Shuttered for Six Long Years', *Pink News*, 10 June 2021, https://www.pinknews.co.uk

/2021/06/10/london-gay-bar-black-cap-camden-high-street-reopen-historic-pub/
(accessed 25 August 2022).

158 Davis' Coffer Lyons, *Project Defender: Rare Opportunity to Acquire Four Public Houses Located Across Central England and the South of England*, undated PDF.

159 See, for example: David Roberts, 'Make Public: Performing Public Housing in Ernő Goldfinger's Balfron Tower', *Journal of Architecture* 22, no. 1 (2017): 123–50; Tom Gillespie, Kate Hardy, and Paul Watt, 'Austerity Urbanism and Olympic Counter-Legacies: Gendering, Defending and Expanding the Urban Commons in East London', *Environment and Planning D, Society and Space* 36, no. 5 (2018): 812–30.

Chapter 7

1 *Post Office Directory*, cited in 'Joiners Arms, 118 Hackney Road, Bethnal Green E2', https://pubwiki.co.uk/LondonPubs/BethnalGreen/JoinersArms.shtml (accessed 26 August 2021).

2 KM Heritage, *114-150 Hackney Road London, Heritage & Townscape Appraisal*, January 2017.

3 Peter Corke, a 20-year old doorman, trainee police mechanic, and the son of a police officer, was gunned down in a case which has not been solved. John Sweeney, 'Hit Men are Back and the Price is Right', *The Observer*, 24 September 1995; Press Association, 'Pub bouncer shot dead in retribution killing', 4 November 1996; 'Peter Corke - Unsolved Murder 1995 - Joiners Arm, Hackney Road, Hoxton', *Unsolved Murders*, 23 September 1995 http://www.unsolved-murders.co.uk/murder-content .php?key=1937&termRef=Peter Corke (accessed 22 July 2020).

4 David Pollard and Giuliano Pistoni, interview by Ben Campkin, London, 14 June 2016.

5 David Pollard and Giuliano Pistoni, interview by Ben Campkin, London, 14 June 2016.

6 David Pollard and Giuliano Pistoni, interview by Ben Campkin, London, 14 June 2016.

7 Jasper Gerard, 'In the Pink', *The Times*, 4 November 1997; Paul Flynn, 'Remembering The Joiners Arms', *i-D*, 6 November 2014 https://i-d.vice.com/en_uk/article/7xv8pq/ remembering-the-joiners-arms (accessed 8 August 2021). The event with Banks took place in November 1997.

8 David Pollard and Giuliano Pistoni, interview by Ben Campkin, London, 14 June 2016.

9 David Pollard and Giuliano Pistoni, interview by Ben Campkin, London, 14 June 2016.

10 For extended and poignant commentaries, see: Amelia Abraham, *Queer Intentions: A (Personal) Journey through LGBTQ+ Culture* (London: Picador, 2019); Dan Glass, *United Queerdom: From the Legends of the Gay Liberation Front to the Queers of Tomorrow* (London: Zed Books, 2020), 146–57; Jeremy Atherton Lin, *Gay Bar: Why We Went Out* (London: Granta Books, 2021).

11 The Joiners and Shoreditch scene, flourishing at the time Andersson was conducting the research, provided a counter to Soho's sanitized aesthetics, which he has analysed in detail. Johan Andersson, 'East End Localism and Urban Decay: Shoreditch's Re-Emerging Gay Scene', *The London Journal* 34, no. 1 (1 March 2009): 55–71,

63–6; Johan Andersson, 'Homonormative Aesthetics: AIDS and "de-Generational Unremembering" in 1990s London', *Urban Studies* 56, no. 14 (1 November 2019): 2993–3010.

12 Andersson, 'East End Localism and Urban Decay', 66.

13 Andersson, 'East End Localism and Urban Decay', 69.

14 Ben Campkin, 'Ornament from Grime: David Adjaye's Dirty House, the Architectural "aesthetic of Recycling" and the Gritty Brits', *Journal of Architecture* 12, no. 4 (2007): 367–92; Andrew Harris, 'Art and Gentrification: Pursuing the Urban Pastoral in Hoxton, London', *Transactions of the Institute of British Geographers* 37, no. 2 (1 April 2012): 226–41.

15 Flynn, 'Remembering The Joiners Arms'.

16 David Pollard and Giuliano Pistoni, interview by Ben Campkin, London, 14 June 2016.

17 Jonny Woo, quoted in Andersson, 'East End Localism and Urban Decay', 62. The Joiners Arms is in Tower Hamlets on the border with Hackney. Looking at the longer-term picture, across Hackney and Tower Hamlets, UCL Urban Lab data shows that the total number of dedicated LGBTQ+ venues was fairly consistent from the mid-1980s to the mid-1990s, at 10 venues. By 2009 this had nearly doubled, to 20 venues, dropping to 13 by 2016. Breaking down the figures for more recent years, Tower Hamlets had 10 LGBTQ+ venues in 2006, but only 3 by 2017. The borough saw a gradual decline from 2006 to 2009, and then a sharp drop between 2015/16. Hackney had 4 in 2006, and a series of closures, but there were still 4 venues open by 2017.

18 Flynn, 'Remembering The Joiners Arms'; David Shenton, interview by Ben Campkin, London/Norwich, 27 July 2021.

19 'Gay Fears Rise after Street Gang's Murderous Attack', *East London Advertiser*, 3 September 2008 https://www.eastlondonadvertiser.co.uk/news/gay-fears-rise -after-street-gang-s-murderous-attack-7652020 (accessed 31 August 20220); 'Police Update on East End Homophobia at Joiners Arms', *East London Advertiser*, 16 February 2010 https://www.eastlondonadvertiser.co.uk/news/police-update-on -east-end-homophobia-at-joiners-arms-3406602 (accessed 31 August 2022); Lin, *Gay Bar* (2021), 208.

20 Martyn Fitzgerald, 'LGBT No Queue', *Medium*, 2 June 2020 https://medium.com/an -injustice/lgbt-no-queue-456909ba0f56 (accessed 6 August 2020).

21 For commentaries on these processes relevant to the locations of case studies in Queer Premises see, for example: Suzanne Hall, *City, Street and Citizen: A Measure of the* Ordinary (London: Routledge, 2012); Michael Keith, 'Postcolonial London and the Allure of the Cosmopolitan City', *AA Files* 49 (2003): 57–67; Garry Robson, 'Class, Criminality and Embodied Consciousness: Charlie Richardson and a South East London Habitus', Working Paper, Goldsmiths College, University of London, New Cross, London; Steven Vertovec, 'Super-diversity and its Implications', *Ethnic and Racial Studies*, 30, no. 6 (2007): 1024–54.

22 Gavin Brown, 'Cosmopolitan Camouflage: (Post-)gay space in Spitalfields, East London', in Jon Binnie, Julian Millington and Craig Yeung (eds.), *Cosmopolitan Urbanism* (Abingdon: Routledge, 2006), 130–45, 131.

23 David Pollard and Giuliano Pistoni, interview by Ben Campkin, London, 14 June 2016.

24 David Pollard and Giuliano Pistoni, interview by Ben Campkin, London, 14 June 2016.

25 Flynn, 'Remembering The Joiners Arms'.
26 David Shenton, interview by Ben Campkin, Norwich, 27 July 2021.
27 David Pollard and Giuliano Pistoni, interview by Ben Campkin, London, 14 June 2016.
28 FOTJA, correspondence with Tower Hamlets, PA/17/00250/A1, 114150, Hackney Road, 20 July 2017.
29 Olimpia Burchiellaro, '"There's Nowhere Wonky Left to go": Gentrification, Queerness and Class Politics of Inclusion in (East) London', *Gender Work Organization* 28 (2021): 24–38.
30 Lin, *Gay Bar* (2021), 203
31 David Shenton, interview by Ben Campkin, London/Norwich, 27 July 2021.
32 David Shenton, interview by Ben Campkin, London/Norwich, 27 July 2021.
33 Friends of The Joiners Arms, https://thejoinersliveson.wordpress.com/about-us/ (accessed 25 August 2021).
34 Jon Ward, Amy Roberts and Peter Cragg, interview by Andy Garraway, 'Friends of The Joiners Arms: a Sort of Victory', *The London Salon: Queer Night Scenes*, curated by Ben Campkin and Lo Marshall, UCL Urban Laboratory, Museum of London, *City Now, City Future*, 13 February 2018.
35 FOTJA, correspondence with Tower Hamlets, PA/17/00250/A1, 114150 Hackney Road, 20 July 2017.
36 FOTJA, correspondence with Tower Hamlets, PA/17/00250/A1, 114150 Hackney Road, 20 July 2017.
37 FOTJA, 'Submission to Tower Hamlets Council: Response to Review of Asset of Community Value Status', 17 February 2017.
38 FOTJA, correspondence with Tower Hamlets, PA/17/00250/A1, 114150 Hackney Road, 20 July 2017.
39 The vision is summarized in FOTJA, correspondence with Tower Hamlets, PA/17/00250/A1, 114150 Hackney Road, 20 July 2017.
40 FOTJA, correspondence with Tower Hamlets, PA/17/00250/A1, 114150 Hackney Road, 20 July 2017.
41 FOJA, correspondence with Tower Hamlets, PA/17/00250/A1, 114150 Hackney Road, 20 July 2017.
42 Gareth Gwynne, 'Idea Exchange: We're the First Council to Use Planning Powers to Save an LGBT Venue', *Local Government Chronicle*, 24 November 2017.
43 KM Heritage, *114-150 Hackney Road, London, Heritage & Townscape Appraisal*, January 2017.
44 Allford, Hall, Monaghan Morris, *114-150 Hackney Road, Design and Access Statement*, 2017, 72.
45 Flynn, 'Remembering The Joiners Arms'; Aric Chen, 'Where the Club Boys Are', *The New York Times*, 20 May 2007 https://www.nytimes.com/2007/05/20/travel /20surfacing.html (accessed 8 August 2021).
46 Friends of The Joiners Arms, *What is The Joiners Arms?*, campaign leaflet, 2015.
47 Focus E15 https://focuse15.org/about/ (accessed 26 August 2021); Glass, *United Queerdom*, 150.
48 Statement of Community Involvement, 116–18 Hackney Road, PA/17/00250/A1, 114150 Hackney Road.
49 Gwynne, 'Idea Exchange'.
50 The Mayor and Burgesses of the London Borough of Tower Hamlets, Planning Obligation by Deed Under Section 106 of the Town and Country Planning Act,

11 June 2018, schedule 7. This agreement has been documented and celebrated by LGBT+ planning network, Planning Out, in Planning Out, *LGBT+ Placemaking Toolkit*, July 2019 https://res.cloudinary.com/fieldfisher/image/upload/v1574347193 /PDF-Files/PDFs%20from%20old%20website/planning-out-placemaking-toolkit -2019_vxjryp.pdf (accessed 3 August 2020).

51 The Mayor and Burgesses of the London Borough of Tower Hamlets, Planning Obligation by Deed Under Section 106 of the Town and Country Planning Act, 11 June 2018, schedule 7, 25. The specifications also included detailed considerations and requirements for noise control and management, especially to account for the late opening hours. If the selected LGBT+ operator ends their lease within the 25-year period, there is an obligation to repeat the call and selection processes.

52 Burchiellaro, "'There's Nowhere Wonky Left to go'", 24–38; Steven Vaughan and Brad Jessup, 'Backstreet's Back Alright: London's LGBT+ Nightlife Spaces and a Queering of Planning Law and Planning Practices' in Maria Lee and Carolyn Abbot (eds.), *Taking Planning Law Seriously: New Research in English Planning Law* (UCL Press, London, 2022), 35–63, 52.

53 Jane Clinton, 'Fundraiser for East London Gay Bar Hits £100,000 Target after Surge in Donations', *The Guardian*, 1 August 2022 https://www.theguardian.com/world /2022/aug/01/fundraiser-for-east-london-gay-bar-hits-100000-target-just-before -deadline (accessed 2 September 2022).

54 Queen Elizabeth Olympic Park, 'East Bank', https://www.queenelizabetholympicpark .co.uk/east-bank (accessed 2 September 2022).

55 Jon Ward, Amy Roberts and Peter Cragg, interview by Andy Garraway, 'Friends of The Joiners Arms: A Sort of Victory', *The London Salon: Queer Night Scenes*, curated by Ben Campkin and Lo Marshall, UCL Urban Laboratory, Museum of London, *City Now, City Future*, 13 February 2018.

56 The Backstreet, https://www.facebook.com/TheBackstreet/about/?ref=page_internal (accessed 24 July 2020).

57 Heritage Architecture, https://www.heritagearchitecture.co.uk/about (accessed 24 July 2020).

58 Stephen Levrant Heritage Architecture Limited, *562 Mile End Road: Heritage Statement, Townscape and Visual Impact Assessment*, March 2017, 4.

59 Stephen Levrant Heritage Architecture Limited, *562 Mile End Road: Heritage Statement, Townscape and Visual Impact Assessment*, March 2017, 34.

60 BUJ Architects, *562 Mile End Road, London E3: Design and Access Statement*, March 2016, 1.1, 2.4.

61 For example, The Backstreet participated in international 'Manfest' events in Amsterdam in 1989 and New York in 1990.

62 BUJ Architects, *562 Mile End Road, London E3: Design and Access Statement*, March 2016, 3, 16.

63 Stephen Levrant Heritage Architecture Limited, *562 Mile End Road: Heritage Statement, Townscape and Visual Impact Assessment*, March 2017, 2.4.2, 12.

64 *Will You Dance With Me?* (UK: Team Pictures, and RLP Projects, 2014). Directed by Derek Jarman in collaboration with Ron Peck and Mark Ayres, filmed on Olympus VHS camera. For commentaries, see: RLP Projects, '*Will You Dance with Me?* Notes from RLP Projects Limited', unpublished screening notes; and Ron Peck quoted in Alice Newell-Hanson, 'Derek Jarman's Rediscovered 80s Gay Nightclub Film Comes to NYC', *i-D*, 4 August 2016 https://i-d.vice.com/en_us/article/59b74b/derek-jarmans -rediscovered-80s-gay-nightclub-film-comes-to-nyc (accessed 27 July 2020).

Notes

65 *Empire State* (UK: Team Pictures, 1987). Directed by Ron Peck.

66 Jarman would later produce footage for the Pet Shop Boys song *Heart* for their 1989 tour. This was also shot at Benjy's and echoes the earlier experiments but is more polished in execution. Pet Shop Boys, *'Heart': Projections* (1989 tour footage). Directed by Derek Jarman.

67 Personal email correspondence with Ron Peck, 3 March 2022.

68 'Kelvin Easton - Unsolved Murder 2011 - Boheme Nightclub, 562a Mile End Road, Bow', *Unsolved Murders,* 27 March 2011. Metropolitan Police, http://www.unsolved -murders.co.uk/murder-content.php?key=345&termRef=Kelvin Easton (accessed 27 July 2020). The club had also been fined for posting illegal posters and had been the subject of noise complaints and criticized for poor security.

69 Christina Gawne, Tower Hamlets, interview by Ben Campkin, Tower Hamlets Town Hall, 1 October 2019; David Oppedisano, 'Ode to The Backstreet: London's Last Leather Bar Closes Permanently', *Gay Cities,* 15 July 2022 https://www.gaycities.com /articles/62786/ode-to-the-backstreet-londons-den-of-iniquity-was-last-of-a-leather -kind/ (accessed 31 August 2022).

70 Christina Gawne, Tower Hamlets, interview by Ben Campkin, Tower Hamlets Town Hall, 1 October 2019.

71 David Oppedisano, 'Ode to The Backstreet: London's Last Leather Bar Closes Permanently', *Gay Cities,* 15 July 2022 https://www.gaycities.com/articles/62786/ode -to-the-backstreet-londons-den-of-iniquity-was-last-of-a-leather-kind/ (accessed 31 August 2022).

72 'Tower @ 562 Mile End Road – Back Again . . . No . . . and It's Gone Away Again! – Mile End Residents', http://www.mile-end-residents.co.uk/local-news/562-mile-end -road/ (accessed 25 July 2020).

73 Christina Gawne, Tower Hamlets, interview by Ben Campkin, Tower Hamlets Town Hall, 1 October 2019.

74 Tower Hamlets Application Reference PA/16/00943, refusal notice 14 December 2017.

75 Julia Gregory, *Appeal Decision,* The Planning Inspectorate, 9 August 2019. Appeal Reference: APP/E5900/W/18/3204874, 562 Mile End Road and 1a, 1b and 1c Burdett Road, Tower Hamlets, London E3 4PH.

76 Correspondence, Richard Evans, WYG Planning Limited, and Brett McAllister, London Borough of Tower Hamlets, 22 December 2016.

77 Correspondence, Richard Evans, WYG and Brett McAllister, London Borough of Tower Hamlets, 22 December 2016. The term 'meeting places' refers to the London Borough of Tower Hamlets Development Management Policy on 'Community Infrastructure', DM8.

78 Correspondence, Richard Evans, WYG and Brett McAllister, London Borough of Tower Hamlets, 22 December 2016.

79 The Backstreet, License, 15 December 2005, amended 2 November 2010. The venue was licensed for sale of alcohol and regulated entertainment, to 3am or 5am every night except Sundays, which are licensed to 2am. Christina Gawne, Principal Planner, Tower Hamlets, interview by Ben Campkin, Tower Hamlets Town Hall, 1 October 2019.

80 Correspondence, Richard Evans, WYG and Brett McAllister, London Borough of Tower Hamlets, 22 December 2016.

81 Correspondence, Richard Evans, WYG and Brett McAllister, London Borough of Tower Hamlets, 22 December 2016.

82 '*Sui Generis* and Planning Permission', https://www.designingbuildings.co.uk/wiki/ Sui_generis_and_planning_permission (accessed 1 September 2022).

83 Correspondence, Richard Evans, WYG and Brett McAllister, London Borough of Tower Hamlets, 22 December 2016.

84 'The White Swan Nightclub, 556 Commercial Road (1 mile away) to the south at Limehouse is local being situated within the Borough and serving the LGBT community within the area. The Troxy, also on Commercial Road, Limehouse and Bethnal Green Working Men's Club, 42 Pollard Row (2 miles away) both regularly hold LGBT nights including Sink the Pink, both within LB Tower Hamlets and serving the local community. Furthermore, there are alternative LGBT venues at Off Broadway, 63-65 Broadway Markets, London Fields (2.5 miles to the north) and various venues in Shoreditch and Kingsland, Dalston'. Correspondence, Richard Evans and Brett McAllister, 22 December 2016.

85 Their branding and visual identities emphasise the contrast: 'East London's most ridiculous gay, drag, gender-fuck, queer, FUN party for all! Come join our SINK THE PINK family!', in comparison with The Backstreet as: 'London's Leather Club, and "the UK's longest running fetish club"'.

86 Richard Evans, WYG, correspondence with London Borough of Tower Hamlets, 22 December 2016.

87 Richard Evans, WYG, correspondence with London Borough of Tower Hamlets, 20 March 2017.

88 Julia Gregory, *Appeal Decision,* The Planning Inspectorate, 9 August 2019. Appeal Reference: APP/E5900/W/18/3204874, 562 Mile End Road and 1a, 1b and 1c Burdett Road, Tower Hamlets, London E3 4PH.

89 John C. Edwards, correspondence with London Borough of Tower Hamlets, 15 June 2017.

90 Gregory, *Appeal Decision*, 2019

91 Richard Evans, WYG, correspondence with London Borough of Tower Hamlets, 7 July 2017.

92 London Borough of Tower Hamlets, decision notice, PA/16/00943, 14 December 2017.

93 'As such, the proposal fails to accord with policy 3.1 of the London Plan, policy DM8 of the Managing Development Document (2013) and Culture and Night-Time Economy SPG (2017)'. London Borough of Tower Hamlets, decision notice, PA/16/00943, 14 December 2017.

94 Richard Evans, WYG, correspondence with London Borough of Tower Hamlets, 17 December 2018.

95 'A further sum of £22,500 would be provided to fit out the Club space to specifications requested by the operator of the Existing Nightclub'. Richard Evans, WYG, correspondence with London Borough of Tower Hamlets, 17 December 2018.

96 Christina Gawne, interview by Ben Campkin, Tower Hamlets Town Hall, 1 October 2019.

97 *Proof of Evidence of Ms Christina Gawne on Town Planning Issues,* Public Inquiry, 15 January 2019, 5.1.1, 14.

98 Mayor of London, *Culture and the Night-Time Economy.* Supplementary Planning Guidance (London: GLA, November 2017); GLA Economics, *London at Night: An Evidence Base for a 24-hour City* (London: GLA, 2018); Ben Campkin and Lo Marshall, *LGBTQI Nightlife in London, from 1986 to the Present* (London: UCL Urban Laboratory, 2016).

99 Mayor of London, *Culture and the Night-Time Economy* (2017), 3.4.

100 'The Council was and remain particularly concerned by the threat to an operational nightclub that serves the LGBT+ community, and is properly pursuing the

retention of a nightclub that serves the LGBT+ community on the appeal site. Sexual orientation is a protected characteristic under the Equality Act 2010 and the "Culture and the Night-time Economy SPG" [paragraphs 3.9 and 4.15] also specifically seeks to retain LGBT+ facilities. In land use terms, a nightclub use is *sui generis* whether it serves the LGBT+ community or not. Without planning conditions or a s106 agreement, the LPA [Local Planning Authority] could not prevent the change from an LGBT+ nightclub to a mainstream nightclub. However, the Equality Act is a material consideration and the Council wants to ensure that any decision made has demonstrated due regard to the Equality Act and ensures the development does not disadvantage a protected characteristic group, namely individuals from the LGBT+ community and specifically with regard to the existing users, gay men. The Council is clear there is duty both in respect of the Equality Act and planning policy to retain this valuable facility which serves both the local gay community and a geographically wider client group'. *Proof of Evidence of Ms Christina Gawne*, 15 January 2019, 9.72.

101 *Proof of Evidence of Ms Christina Gawne*, 15 January 2019, 9.72.

102 Richard Evans, WYG, correspondence with Helen Skinner, The Planning Inspectorate, 20 December 2018.

103 *Proof of Evidence of Ms Christina Gawne*, 15 January 2019, 9.72.

104 Paul Buckenham, Development Manager, correspondence with Richard Evans, WYG Planning Limited, 24 December 2018.

105 Christina Gawne, Principal Planner, Tower Hamlets, interview by Ben Campkin, Tower Hamlets Town Hall, 1 October 2019.

106 *Proof of Evidence of Ms Christina Gawne*, 15 January 2019, 9.67. The Tom of Finland artwork had also attracted the attention of local artists Prem Sahib and Mark Blower who undertook a photograhic survey of the venue in response to the threat to it (Plates 25–26). Tom of Finland artwork is currently attracting interest among heritage scholars, such as Tom Cubbin at the University of Gothenburg.

107 Julia Gregory, *Appeal Decision,* The Planning Inspectorate, 9 August 2019. Appeal Reference: APP/E5900/W/18/3204874, 562 Mile End Road and 1a, 1b and 1c Burdett Road, Tower Hamlets, London E3 4PH, points 52-54. The specific policy referred to was *Tower Hamlets Managing Development Document and Adopted Policies Plan* (London: Tower Hamlets, 2013), DM8.

108 Mayor of London, *The London Plan: the Spatial Development Strategy for London, Consolidated With Alternations Since 2011* (London: Mayor of London, 2016). Policy 3.1, 'Ensuring Equal Life Chances for All', states: 'Development proposals should protect and enhance facilities and services that meet the needs of particular groups and communities. Proposals involving loss of these facilities without adequate justification or provision for replacement should be resisted'.

109 David Oppedisano, 'Ode to The Backstreet: London's Last Leather Bar Closes Permanently', *Gay Cities,* 15 July 2022, https://www.gaycities.com/articles/62786/ode -to-the-backstreet-londons-den-of-iniquity-was-last-of-a-leather-kind/ (accessed 31 August 2022); The Backstreet, Sale poster, 18 July 2022.

110 Prior to the opening of Pulse, XXL had been resident at The Arches (2001–2010), which then became Arcadia, before closing in 2012. This site, near to The Shard, then became a street food market, Flat Iron Square, with bars, and a venue mainly used for live music, Omeara (2016-). The owners of XXL took the opportunity to open Pulse and move XXL to this new venue. Omeara continued to host one LGBTQ+ event, 'Little Gay Brother'. This is an intentionally mobile series of events that emerged from

the events series Secret Garden Party in 2012, pitched as bi-monthly 'queer raves' featuring drag and performance. Little Gay Brother, https://www.littlegaybrother.com /about (accessed 29 July 2019).

111 XXL London, https://www.xxl-london.com/xxl-london/ (accessed 22 July 2019).

112 XXL London, https://www.xxl-london.com/xxl-london/ (accessed 22 July 2019).

113 Mark Ames and James McNeill, interview in *Attitude*, Summer, 21 June 2019, 60.

114 The number who mentioned the venue was 8/239, a relatively high number considering this is a twice weekly event and given the overall diversity of respondents. It is difficult to draw conclusions from a small sample, and the responses do not necessarily provide an accurate indicator of the club's demographic profile. We asked people to self-describe their gender, sexual orientation and ethnicity. Those who mentioned XXL identified their gender as either 'male' or 'gay man'; seven identified their sexual orientation as 'gay', one as 'gay/queer'. Four identified their ethnicity as 'white' and four as 'white British'. UCL Urban Lab survey, 2016.

115 Southwark has been under Labour control since the 1960s, except 2002–10 when it was governed by the Liberal Democrats (2002–6) with no overall controlling party, and by a Liberal Democrat/Conservative coalition (2006–10). From 1986 to the present, Southwark has had fourteen venues that have either been operated by and for LGBTQ+ groups (9/14) or have regularly hosted LGBTQ+ programming (5/14). UCL Urban Lab data, 2016.

116 Some intriguing smaller spaces, such as Attitude, a mid-1990s men-only drag club, or Bam-Bs, a women-only space in Surrey Quays in 1994, only appear fleetingly in the listings.

117 For information on archives of Southwark's gay and lesbian rights and services see, for example: Southwark Council. 'LGBTQ+ Communities Collections Guide', Southwark Council. UK, London, Europe. https://www.southwark.gov.uk/libraries /southwark-archives/lgbtq-communities-collections-guide (accessed 2 September 2022).

118 The Black Lesbian and Gay Project first had temporary space in the borough of Haringey, but later occupied a roughly converted arch in Peckham. *Under Your Nose: the Story of the Black Lesbian and Gay Centre (BLGC)* (UK, 2018). Directed by Veronica McKenzie.

119 Office for National Statistics data 'suggests that the borough is the local authority area with the second highest LGBTQ+ population in the UK, after Lambeth, at around 5% of the population', Southwark LGBTQ+ Network, *Southwark LGBTQ+ Community Consultation 2018-19: Key Background, Findings and Draft Recommendations* (London: Soutwark LGBTQ+ Network, 2019). Mayor of London, Cultural Infrastructure Map, https://apps.london.gov.uk/cim/index.html?_gl=1*4tfk72*_ga*M jAzMTExOTYwLjE2NjE3NjMzMzU.*_ga_PY4SWZN1RJ*MTY2MTc2MzMzNS4xLj AuMTY2MTc2MzMzNS42MC4wLjA (accessed 29 August 2022).

120 GLA, *LGBT+ Venues Charter* (London: GLA, 2017), https://www.london.gov.uk/sites /default/files/lgbt_venues_charter_2017.pdf (accessed 7 August 2020).

121 Southwark Council, *Night Time Commission Consultation – Southwark Council Response* (London: Southwark Council, 2018), http://moderngov.southwark.gov.uk /documents/s74197/Appendix%201%20Consultation%20Response.pdf (accessed 25 July 2019).

122 '[. . .] theme bars, i.e. microbreweries with tap rooms, and multi-use spaces such as Peckham Levels, Flat Iron Square and Mercato Metropolitano, are pushing the

envelop [sic] beyond the traditional'. Southwark Council, *Night Time Commission consultation – Southwark Council Response*, 2018.

123 5/14 venues have been in railway arches. UCL Urban Lab data, 2016.

124 Southwark Council, *Night Time Commission Consultation – Southwark Council Response* (London: Southwark Council, 2018), http://moderngov.southwark.gov.uk /documents/s74197/Appendix%201%20Consultation%20Response.pdf (accessed 25 July 2019).

125 Entrepreneur Euan Johnston established two of Southwark's other railway arch venues, SeOne (2002–10) and Cable (2009–13), which were both demolished in the redevelopment of London Bridge station. Although SeOne, a 3,000-capacity venue, appears to have struggled financially, Cable, a 1,300-capacity space, closed while performing well. Johnston says Network Rail approached him with a proposal to redevelop the space as a nightclub in 2008 and was assured that the redevelopment would not affect them. Network Rail countered that the development was public knowledge for a long period prior to eviction. Contemporary newspaper reports detail how Cable were notified of the intention to redevelop the site in 2011, and then, after a two-year legal battle, bailiffs cut their way into the club to take possession, with Johnston claiming to have been 'brushed aside'. A short film on the club's TV channel documents the moment bailiffs saw through the metal shutters and presents the views of some of the seventy-two employees as they try to interview Network Rail staff. The eviction took place under a high court ruling, but as in other cases a conflict arose here regarding the venue operators' expectations and understanding of the owner's proposals, between ownership and tenants' sense of possession and their rights in relation to their labour and other investments. Network Rail and Southwark accommodated nightclub use as a meanwhile solution and income generator, but only temporarily. The operators, who had invested their own funds and built globally recognizable brands were uprooted, uncompensated. 'Top London Nightclub Forced to Close', *BBC News*, 4 May 2013 https://www.bbc .com/news/uk-england-london-22408279 (accessed 25 July 2019); Andy Malt, 'Cable Founder Says Network Rail Gave Assurances Club Would Not Be Closed', *Complete Music Update*, 3 May 2013 https://completemusicupdate.com/article/cable -founder-says-network-rail-gave-assurances-club-would-not-be-closed/ (accessed 25 July 2019); Will Coldwell, 'What Happened to the Great London Nightclubs?', *The Guardian*, 13 August 2015 https://www.theguardian.com/music/2015/aug/13/what -happened-to-the-great-london-nightclubs (accessed 25 July 2019); 'Smashing up the Dancefloor - Network Rail Take Possession of Cable', https://www.youtube.com/ watch?v=Zbac-_-VKWA&t=328s (accessed 25 July 2019).

126 PLP, had been associated with another densification and tower scheme, at Bishopsgate, slated by architecture critic Oliver Wainright as 'steroidal' in its scale and ambition. Oliver Wainwright, '22 Bishopsgate – and the Steroidal Towers Set to Ruin London's Skyline', *The Guardian*, 30 June 2015 https://www.theguardian .com/artanddesign/2015/jun/30/22-bishopgate-skyscraper-london-skyline -development (accessed 9 August 2021). The broader development context of this huge mixed-use development is Bankside Quarter, close to the River Thames. Designated as an opportunity area in the London Plan, these schemes aim to densify and join up the Bankside district, between Tate Modern and Blackfriars Station. Associated developments include a tower by CIT developers; and the completed redevelopment of London Bridge station and construction of The Shard nearby.

127 The Samson and Ludgate House scheme was awarded planning permission under a previous owner, The Carlyle Group. 'Minerva Sells Sampson House and Ludgate House', *SE14* August 2005 http://www.london-se1.co.uk/news/view/1688 (accessed 30 July 2020).

128 The Carlyle Group, 'International Consortium To Buy London South Bank Regeneration Project From The Carlyle Group For £308 Million', https://www.carlyle.com/media-room/news-release-archive/international-consortium-buy-london-south-bank-regeneration-project (accessed 30 July 2020).

129 The Carlyle Group, *Sampson House and Ludgate House Design and Access Statement*, October 2012, 1.2.3.

130 London Borough of Southwark, planning application, 'Sampson House, Ludgate House and Railway Arches', 12/AP/3940, 10 December 2012. The 2012 proposal was updated in 2018, with the removal of one building and some changes to heights and further details added.

131 'The existing railway arches are currently underused, with car parking, storage areas and a night club that is located within the southern arches. The northern part of the arches, adjacent to the station development currently provides vehicular and service access to Ludgate House'. The Carlyle Group, *Sampson House and Ludgate House Design and Access Statement*, October 2012, Executive Summary, ES10; ES29.

132 The Carlyle Group, *Sampson House and Ludgate House Design and Access Statement*, October 2012, Executive Summary, ES33.

133 McNeill specializes in the design of large volume spaces such as nightclubs and airports. James McNeill, LinkedIn Profile, 2020.

134 XXL London, 'Save Our Scene', https://www.xxl-london.com/saveourscene/ (accessed 29 July 2020).

135 'What is actually taking place is a social cleansing of the neighbourhood so they can maximise their price on each unit by not having a Gay nightclub there'. James McNeill and Mark Ames, correspondence with James Murray, Deputy Mayor, 15 May 2017; XXL London, General Notice to XXL members and guest customers', undated, https://twitter.com/XXLLondon/status/1144584614608064514; XXL London, 'Save Our Scene', https://www.xxl-london.com/saveourscene/ (accessed 30 July 2020).

136 The consortium is described at: 'Native Land', 19 June 2015 https://www.native-land.com/news/international-consortium-to-buy-london-south-bank-site-for-308m (accessed 9 August 2021).

137 Alliance Planning for A&M Leisure Limited, *Statement in Support of Planning Application*, April 2012. London Borough of Southwark, 12/AP/1213.

138 A letter from a Southwark Enforcement Officer dated 24 January 2012 advised that Southwark considered the club's use unauthorized as 2008 consent had expired without discharge of pre-commencement conditions.

139 Southwark Council, Refusal of Planning Permission, 12/AP/1213, 11 January 2013.

140 Joanna Reid, The Planning Inspectorate, Appeal Decision, 13 November 2013, APP/A5840/.

141 Mayor of London, Greater Central Activities Zone, https://www.london.gov.uk/what-we-do/planning/implementing-london-plan/planning-guidance-and-practice-notes/central-activities-zone (accessed 24 July 2019).

142 *Pulse, Blackfriars Events Limited, 1-4 Invicta Plaza, London SE1 9UF, Management Plan*, updated 4 May 2012; Southwark Council, *Licensing Act 2003 Premises License 834962, Pulse.*

143 On 'sweat equity', see: Phil Hubbard, *The Battle for the High Street* (London: Palgrave Macmillan UK, 2017), 1.

144 James McNeill and Mark Ames, correspondence with GLA, undated, GLA FOI response mgla180719-7961, redacted.

145 GLA, Ludgate and Samson House, Bankside, Planning Report PDU/2942/01, 27 February 2013, 'Principle of Land Use', 21 and 22, 4. This condition was recorded at London Borough of Southwark, Planning Committee, 8 October 2013, item 6.1, 12/AP/3940, 64 http://moderngov.southwarksites.com/documents/s41084/Report.pdf (accessed 30 July 2020): 'An equalities impact assessment should be provided to assess the impact of the loss of the gay nightclub that operates within the arches. Subject to this assessment, the mix of uses, including the cultural uses, is welcomed'.

146 GLA, *Planning report D&P/2942/02 27, November 2013, Ludgate and Sampson House, Bankside in the London Borough of Southwark*, planning application no. 12/AP/3940, point 32, 5 https://www.london.gov.uk/sites/default/files/public%3A//public%3A//PAWS/media_id_342178///sampson_house_report.pdf (accessed 31 July 2020).

147 Joanna Reid, The Planning Inspectorate, Appeal Decision, 13 November 2013, APP/A5840/A/13/2201540.

148 Vaughan and Jessup, 'Backstreet's Back Alright' (2022), 52.

149 James McNeill and Mark Ames, correspondence with GLA, undated, FOI response mgla180719-7961, redacted.

150 Robert Booth, 'London Gay Nightclub XXL Faces Closure to Make Way for Flats', *The Guardian*, 28 June 2019, https://www.theguardian.com/uk-news/2019/jun/28/london-gay-nightclub-xxl-faces-closure-to-make-way-for-flats (accessed 24 July 2019); Vic Parsons, 'London Gay Nightclub XXL Could Close to Make Room for Luxury Flats', *Pink News* 28 June 2019 https://www.pinknews.co.uk/2019/06/28/london-gay-nightclub-xxl-closing-luxury-flats/ (accessed 24 July 2019).

151 See correspondence between Ames, McNeill and the GLA documented at: https://www.london.gov.uk/sites/default/files/mgla180719-7961_-_foi_response_redacted.pdf (accessed 1 August 2020). This charitable work is set out in general terms rather than pointing to specific contributions or the level of donations. Nonetheless, the organizations mentioned are all certainly reliant upon donations from successful LGBTQ+ owned businesses. The XXL website lists Albert Kennedy Trust (AKT) as its current partner and lists other familiar LGBTQ+ charities, https://www.xxl-london.com/support/ (accessed 25 July 2019). There are no mentions of relevant company names within the list of extensive donors in AKT's annual reports (2015, 2016, 2017, 2018 or 2019), https://beta.charitycommission.gov.uk/charity-details/?subid=0&regid=1093815 (accessed 1 August 2019).

152 'Gay Muslim Groups Angry at Club Owner's "Boycott Muslims" Remarks', *Pink News*, 30 June 2010. https://www.pinknews.co.uk/2010/06/30/gay-muslim-groups-angry-at-club-owners-boycott-muslims-remarks/ (accessed 9 August 2021). Mark Ames, Facebook post quoted in 'XXL Owner's Shocking Femme-Phobic Rant Provokes "Queer" Protest', *Gay Star News*, 11 September 2018.

153 Peter Dunne, 'Owner of London Club XXL Posts Toxic Masculinity Rant about Man in Heels', *GCN* [*Gay Community News*], 12 September 2018, https://gcn.ie/owner-london-club-xxl-toxic-masculinity-rant-man-heels/ (accessed 29 August 2022).

154 Dunne, 'Owner of London Club XXL Posts Toxic Masculinity Rant', *GCN*, 2018.

155 Dunne, 'Owner of London Club XXL Posts Toxic Masculinity Rant', *GCN*, 2018.

156 Dunne, 'Owner of London Club XXL Posts Toxic Masculinity Rant', *GCN*, 2018 .

157 Mark Ames', Facebook post quoted in 'XXL Owner's Shocking Femme-Phobic Rant Provokes "Queer" Protest', *Gay Star News*, 11 September 2018.

158 Ben Campkin and Lo Marshall, *LGBTQ+ Cultural Infrastructure in London: Night Venues, 2006 to the Present* (London: UCL Urban Laboratory, 2017), 19.

159 Robert Booth, 'London Gay Nightclub XXL Faces Closure', 2019; XXL, *XXL Beacon: Celebrating, Showcasing and Supporting the LGBTQ Community*, July 2019.

160 UCL Urban Laboratory, roundtable on LGBTQ+ Venues in Camden, July 2019, unpublished transcript.

161 Les Wright (ed.), *The Bear Book: Readings in the History and Evolution of a Gay Male Subculture* (New York and London: Harrington Park Press, 1997),28; 14–16.

162 Wright, *The Bear Book*, 38.

163 One of the foundational texts to define the bear, was George Mazzei's glossary of gay animals in *The Advocate* in 1979. In this text, the bear is described as one category in a taxonomy parodying 1970s urban US gay culture. Bears are hairy and generally but not always big men. Their characteristics include good humour, loyal companionship, generosity, sociability, self-deprecation, a domestic inclination and an endearing insecurity. Alongside the other gay animals Mazzei describes bears appear less pretentious and less fashion and body image conscious. Mazzei's bear was a queer type of man, an attitude rather than a pre-determined or essential form. George Mazzei, 'Who's Who in the Zoo? A Glossary of Gay Animals', *The Advocate* (26 July 1979): 42–3.

164 Wright, *The Bear Book*, 4.

165 'In reality, bears collectively harbor all the same problems as before. To what extent are bears caught up in a utopian romantic impulse to reinvent themselves, to what extent are bears merely exploited customers in a highly fragmented niche market system [. . .] In microcosm we find in the bear phenomenon an expression of the contemporary dialectically opposed forces of globalism (instant communication and a homogeneity in style of thought and behavior) and tribalism (the banding together, for any given reason, of smallish, overseeable numbers of people into an identifiable group)'. Wright, *The Bear Book*, 38.

166 Nick McGlynn, 'Bears in Space: Geographies of a Global Community of Big and Hairy Gay/bi/queer Men', *Geography Compass*, 15, no. 2 (2020): 1–13, 2.

167 Mark Ames and Amy Lamé, correspondence, June 2019 https://www.london.gov.uk/ sites/default/files/mgla180719-7961_-_foi_response_redacted.pdf (accessed 1 August 2020).

168 Mark Ames and Amy Lamé, correspondence, June 2019 https://www.london.gov.uk/ sites/default/files/mgla180719-7961_-_foi_response_redacted.pdf (accessed 1 August 2020).

169 GLA Public Liaison Officer, correspondence with James McNeill and Mark Ames, undated, https://www.london.gov.uk/sites/default/files/mgla180719-7961_-_foi _response_redacted.pdf (accessed 7 December 2022).

170 XXL, *XXL Beacon: Celebrating, Showcasing and Supporting the LGBTQ Community*, July 2019.

171 Parsons, 'London Gay Nightclub XXL Could Close', 2019.

172 Andrew Gorman-Murray and Peter Hopkins, 'Introduction', in *Masculinities and Place*, ed. Andrew Gorman-Murray and Peter Hopkins (London and New York: Routledge, 2016), 1–24, 6.

173 Gorman-Murray and Hopkins, 'Introduction', 1–24, 6.

174 Michael Brown, Stefano Bettani, Larry Knopp, and Andrew Childs, 'The Gay Bar as a Place of Men's Caring', in *Masculinities and Place*, ed. Andrew Gorman-Murray and Peter Hopkins (London and New York: Routledge, 2016), 300–15.

Chapter 8

1 For example, an outbreak associated with a cluster of venues in Itaewon, Singapore, stirred homophobic responses in a context already characterized by intense discrimination. Allan C Simpson and Sini-Petriina Klasto, 'Gay Korea: Homophobia Sparked by Seoul Coronavirus Cluster Driven by Protestant Right', *The Conversation*, http://theconversation.com/gay-korea-homophobia-sparked-by-seoul-coronavirus-cluster-driven-by-protestant-right-138491 (accessed 5 August 2020).

2 The first national UK lockdown ran from 23 March 2020. In England, pubs and restaurants were allowed to reopen on 4 July 2020, except where local lockdowns were in place. During the national lockdown, large gatherings continued, highlighting that the closure of formal premises instigated an upsurge in unregulated parties. Media attention focused controversially on areas with long historical associations with Black communities in South London, such as Brixton. Emily Goddard, 'More than 500 Illegal Raves in London in Last Month, Police Say', *The Independent*, 24 July 2020, https://www.independent.co.uk/news/uk/home-news/illegal-raves-lockdown-coronavirus-london-met-police-violence-a9636651.html.

3 '"Absolute Madness": This Is What England's First Night out in Three Months Looks Like', *Sky News*, https://news.sky.com/story/coronavirus-lockdown-pubs-and-hairdressers-throw-open-their-doors-as-super-saturday-arrives-12020798 (accessed 5 August 2020); 'People Rush to Town Centres as Pubs Reopen', *BBC News*, 5 July 2020, https://www.bbc.com/news/business-53297652 (accessed 5 August 2020).

4 'Amy Lamé, interviewed by Ben Campkin, 21 May 2020, 'Reimagining the Night', *Urban Pamphleteer* #9, December 2021, 6–7. This refers to UK government public health slogans such as #Stayathome and 'Stay home, save lives'.

5 Dylan Kneale and Laia Becares, 'The Mental Health and Experiences of Discrimination of LGBTQ+ People during the Covid-19 Pandemic: Initial Findings from the Queerantine Study', *MedRxiv*, 4 August 2020, https://doi.org/10.1101/2020.08.03.20167403 (accessed 31 August 2021).

6 Participant, 'Who Cares?', Long Table, UCL Urban Laboratory, 21 July 2021.

7 Finbar Toesland, 'Following Successful Pilot Project, UK Will Get Permanent LGBTQ Crisis Shelter', *NBC News*, 29 August 2018, https://www.nbcnews.com/feature/nbc-out/following-successful-pilot-project-u-k-will-get-permanent-lgbtq-n904526 (accessed 21 July 2022).

8 Mayor of London, 'What the Mayor is Doing to Tackle Rough Sleeping', https://www.london.gov.uk/what-we-do/housing-and-land/homelessness/mayors-rough-sleeping-services#acc-i-59988 (accessed 19 July 2022). During the pandemic, the GLA commissioned 14 hotels to accommodate 1,400 people who previously been sleeping rough.

9 Vanesa Castán Broto, 'Queering Participatory Planning', *Environment and Urbanization*, 33, no. 2 (2021): 310–29.

10 https://www.facebook.com/groups/646616226125829 (accessed 5 August 2020).

11 The Outside Project, 'Outside Project LGBTIQ+ Shelter Closed – Looking For New Home', 12 March 2022, press release, https://lgbtiqoutside.org/press/ (accessed 19 July 2022).

12 Georgina Hutton, 'Eat Out to Help Out Scheme', 15 June 2022, https://commonslibrary.parliament.uk/research-briefings/cbp-8978/ (accessed 16 June 2022).

13 'London's Nightclubs and Casinos Slam "Suicidal" New Coronavirus Guidelines', *CityAM*, 24 June 2020. https://www.cityam.com/londons-nightclubs-and-casinos-slam-suicidal-new-coronavirus-guidelines/ (accessed 16 June 2022); Stuart Wood,

"'Uncertainty and Concern" around Lockdown Strategy, Says NTIA', Access All Areas (blog), 11 May 2020. https://accessaa.co.uk/uncertainty-and-concern-around-lockdown-strategy-says-ntia/ (accessed 16 June 2020).

14 *Coronavirus Job Retention Scheme*, in operation 1 March 2020 to 30 September 2021. See, for example: 'Dalston Superstore Hardship Fund', Crowdfunder, https://www.crowdfunder.co.uk/p/dalston-superstore-hardship-fund (accessed 1 September 2022).

15 Safer Sounds Partnership, 'Covid-19 Support Service', https://www.safersounds.org.uk/lgbtqvenuessupportservice (accessed 5 August 2020).

16 Mark McCormack and Fiona Measham, *Building a Sustainable Queer Nightlife in London: Queer Creatives, COVID-19 and Community in the Capital* (London: Arts Council England, 2022), 9.

17 Arts Council England, 'Culture Recovery Fund: Grants', https://www.artscouncil.org.uk/funding/culture-recovery-fund-grants#section-1 (accessed 1 September 2022).

18 Bloomberg,Marc Daniel Davies, 'Why Nightclubs in Britain Will Never Be the Same', 11 July 2021, https://www.bloomberg.com/news/articles/2021-07-11/britian-s-nightlife-prepares-for-reopening-wounded-by-pandemic (accessed 19 July 2022).

19 James Lindsay, interview by Ben Campkin, London, 10 November 2020.

20 UK Government, 'Retail, Hospitality and Leisure Grant', 1 April 2020, https://www.gov.uk/guidance/check-if-youre-eligible-for-the-coronavirus-retail-hospitality-and-leisure-grant-fund (accessed 19 July 2022).

21 The grants were £25,000, administered through local councils, made available to businesses with a ratable value of £51,000 or under, https://www.gov.uk/guidance/check-if-youre-eligible-for-the-coronavirus-retail-hospitality-and-leisure-grant-fund (accessed 15 June 2022).

22 James Lindsay, interview by Ben Campkin, London, 10 November 2020.

23 R. Justin Hunt, interview by Lo Marshall, London, 27 August 2021; Jo Alloway, interview by Ben Campkin, London, 26 November 2021; James Lindsay, interview by Ben Campkin, London, 10 November 2020.

24 McCormack and Measham, *Building a Sustainable Queer Nightlife in London* (2022), 10.

25 Owen Jones, 'An East London Nightclub Has Shown How to Unionise the Nightlife Sector – and Win', *The Guardian*, 17 August 2022, https://www.theguardian.com/commentisfree/2022/aug/17/london-nightclub-unionise-nightlife-sector-britain (accessed 1 September 2022).

26 McCormack and Measham, *Building a Sustainable Queer Nightlife in London* (2022), 10.

27 Paul B. Preciado, 'On Life after Covid-19', https://www.artforum.com/slant/the-losers-conspiracy-82586 (accessed 4 August 2020).

28 For example, see Dalston Superstore, The Glory, VFD, The Karaoke Hole, *Jjoint CovidOVID-19 policy*, 15 July 2022, https://twitter.com/dsuperstore/status/1415728420613468162/photo/1 (accessed 1 September 2022).

29 Night Time Industries Association, 'Owner of G-A-Y Jeremy Joseph Instructs Kings Chambers & Simpson Miller to Challenge the Government's 10pm Hospitality Curfew', https://ntia.co.uk/owner-of-g-a-y-jeremy-joseph-instructs-kings-chambers-simpson-miller-to-challenge-the-governments-10pm-hospitality-curfew/ (accessed 16 August 2022); Josh Milton, 'London's Famous Heaven Nightclub to Give out Covid Vaccines', *Pink News*, 30 July 2021, https://www.pinknews.co.uk/2021/07/30/heaven-coronavirus-vaccine/ (accessed 1 September 2022).

30 Lo Marshall, 'Queer House Party' in Adam Nathaniel Furman and Joshua Mardell (eds.), *Queer Spaces: An Atlas of LGBTQIA+ Places and Stories* (London: RIBA Publishing, 2022), 166–7.

31 Laurent Berlant, 'The Commons: Infrastructures for Troubling Times', *Environment and Planning D: Society and Space* 34, no. 3 (2016): 393–419, 404f.

32 Robert Jenrick, 'Radical and Necessary Reforms to Our Planning System Will Get Britain Building', *The Telegraph*, 1 August 2020, https://www.telegraph.co.uk/politics/2020/08/01/radical-necessary-reforms-planning-system-will-get-britain-building/ (accessed 5 August 2020).

Select bibliography

Abraham, Amelia, *Queer Intentions: A (Personal) Journey through LGBTQ+ Culture*, London: Picador, 2019.

Ackroyd, Peter, *Queer City: Gay London from the Romans to the Present Day*, 230, London: Chatto and Windus, 2017.

Acuto, Michele, *Global Cities, Governance and Diplomacy: The Urban Link*, Routledge New Diplomacy Studies, London: Routledge, 2013.

Acuto, Michele, 'We Need a Science of the Night', *Nature* 576, no. 7787 (18 December 2019): 339.

Ahmed, Sara, *Queer Phenomenology: Orientations, Objects, Others*, London and Durham: Duke University Press, 2006.

Ahmed, Sara, *On Being Included: Racism and Diversity in Institutional Life*, Durham and London: Duke University Press, 2012.

Andersson, Johan, 'Hygiene Aesthetics on London's Gay Scene: The Stigma of AIDS', in Ben Campkin and Rosie Cox (eds.), *Dirt: New Geographies of Cleanliness and Contamination*, 103–12, London: IB Tauris, 2007.

Andersson, Johan, 'East End Localism and Urban Decay: Shoreditch's Re-emerging Gay Scene', *The London Journal: A Review of Metropolitan Society Past and Present* 34, no. 1 (2009): 55–71.

Andersson, Johan, 'Vauxhall's Post-Industrial Pleasure Gardens: "Death Wish" and Hedonism in 21st-Century London', *Urban Studies* 48, no. 1 (2011): 85–100.

Andersson, Johan, 'Heritage Discourse and the Desexualisation of Public Space: The "Historical Restorations" of Bloomsbury's Squares', *Antipode* 44, no. 4 (2012): 1081–98.

Andersson, Johan, 'Homonormative Aesthetics: AIDS and "de-Generational Unremembering" in 1990s London', *Urban Studies* 56, no. 14 (2019): 2993–3010.

Ardill, Susan and Sue O'Sullivan, 'Upsetting and Applecart: Difference, Desire and Lesbian Sadomasochism', *Feminist Review*, 23, (Summer, 1986): 31–57.

Austin, J. L. [John Langshaw], *How to Do Things With Words*, Cambridge, MA: Harvard University Press, 1962.

Avery, Simon and Katherine M. Graham (eds.), *Sex, Time and Place: Queer Histories of London, c.1850 to the Present*, London: Bloomsbury Academic, 2016.

Baldwin Hess, Daniel, 'Effects of Gentrification and Real-Estate Market Escalation on Gay Neighbourhoods', *Town Planning Review* 90, no. 3 (2019): 229–37.

Beaverstock, Jonathan V., Richard G. Smith, and Peter J. Taylor, 'World-City Network: A New Metageography?', *Annals of the Association of American Geographers* 90, no. 1 (2000): 123–34.

Bell, David, Jon Binnie, Julia Cream, and Gill Valentine, 'All Hyped up and No Place to Go', *Gender, Place & Culture* 1, no. 1 (1994): 31–47.

Berlant, Laurent, 'The Commons: Infrastructures for Troubling Times', *Environment and Planning D: Society and Space* 34, no. 3 (2016): 393–419.

Bersani, Leo, *Homos*, Cambridge, MA: Harvard University Press, 1995.

Betsky, Aaron, *Building Sex: Men, Women, and the Construction of Sexuality*, New York: William Morrow, 1995.

Betsky, Aaron, *Queer Space: Architecture and Same-Sex Desire*, New York: William Morrow & Co, 1997.

Bianchini, Franco, 'Night Cultures, Night Economies', *Planning Practice & Research* 10, no. 2 (1 May 1995): 121–6, 123.

Binnie, Jon and Gill Valentine, 'Geographies of Sexuality – a Review of Progress', *Progress in Human Geography* 23, no. 2 (1999): 175–87.

Bishop, Peter and Lesley Williams, *Planning, Politics and City Making: A Case Study of King's Cross*, London: RIBA Publishing, 2016.

Bloch, Ernst, *The Principle of Hope*, Volume 1, translated by, Neville Plaice, Stephen Plaice and Paul Knight, Cambridge, MA: The MIT Press, 1986 [1959].

Brenner, Neil and Christian Schmid, 'Planetary Urbanization', in Matthew Gandy (ed.), *Urban Constellations*, 10–13.

Brenner, Neil and Nikolas Theodore (eds.), *Spaces of Neoliberalism: Urban Restructuring in North America and Western Europe*, Malden and Oxford: Blackwell, 2002.

Bridge, Gary, Tim Butler, and Loretta Lees (eds.), *Mixed Communities: Gentrification by Stealth?* Bristol: Policy, 2012.

Broto, Vanesa Castán, 'Queering Participatory Planning', *Environment and Urbanization* 33, no. 2 (2021): 310–29.

Brown, Gavin, 'Cosmopolitan Camouflage: (post-)gay Space in Spitalfields, East London', in Jon Binnie, Julian Millington, and Craig Yeung (eds.), *Cosmopolitan Urbanism*, 130–45, Abingdon: Routledge, 2006.

Brown, Gavin, 'Queer Movement', in David Paternotte and Manon Tremblay (eds.), *The Ashgate Research Companion to Lesbian and Gay Activism*, 73–86, London: Routledge, 2015.

Brown, Gavin and Kath Browne (eds.), *The Routledge Research Companion to Geographies of Sex and Sexualities*, Routledge Handbooks Online, 2016.

Brown, Michael, 'Gender and Sexuality I: Intersectional Anxieties', *Progress in Human Geography* 36, no. 4 (2012): 541–50.

Brown, Michael, 'Gender and Sexuality II: There Goes the Gayborhood?', *Progress in Human Geography* 38, no. 3 (2014): 457–65.

Brown, Michael, Stefano Bettani, Larry Knopp, and Andrew Childs, 'The Gay Bar as a Place of Men's Caring', in Andrew Gorman-Murray and Peter Hopkins (eds.), *Masculinities and Place*, London and New York: Routledge, 2016, 300–15.

Brown, Robin, Michael Edwards, and Richard Lee, 'Just Space: Towards a Just, Sustainable London', in Robert Imrie and Loretta Lees (eds.), *Sustainable London? The Future of a Global City*, 43–64, London: Policy Press, 2014.

Buck, Nick, Ian Gordon, Peter Hall, Michael Harloe, and Mark Kleinman, *Working Capital: Life and Labour in Contemporary London*, London: Taylor & Francis Group, 2002.

Buckland, Fiona, *Impossible Dance: Club Culture and Queer World-Making*, Middletown: Wesleyan University Press, 2010.

Burchiellaro, Olimpia, '"There's Nowhere Wonky Left to Go": Gentrification, Queerness and Class Politics of Inclusion in (East) London', *Gender, Work & Organization* 28, no. 1 (2021): 24–38.

Burns, Karen, 'A Girl's Own Adventure', *Journal of Architectural Education* 65, no. 2 (2012): 125–34.

Butler, Judith, 'Critically Queer', *GLQ* 1, no. 1 (1993): 17–32.

Butler, Judith, *Gender Trouble: Feminism and the Subversion of Identity*, London and New York: Routledge, 2006.

Califia, Pat, 'San Francisco: Revisiting the City of Desire', in Gordon Brent Ingram, Anne-Marie Bouthillette, and Yolanda Retter (eds.), *Queers in Space: Communities, Public Places, Sites of Resistance*, 177–96. Seattle: Bay Press, 1997.

Campkin, Ben, 'Ornament from Grime: David Adjaye's Dirty House, the Architectural 'aesthetic of Recycling' and the Gritty Brits', *Journal of Architecture* 12, no. 4 (2007): 367–92.

Campkin, Ben, *Remaking London: Decline and Regeneration in Urban Culture*, London: IB Tauris, 2013.

Campkin, Ben and Lo Marshall, *LGBTQI Nightlife in London, 1986 to the Present: Interim Findings*, London: UCL Urban Laboratory, November 2016.

Campkin, Ben and R. Justin Hunt, 'Letters Home' in Brent Pilkey, Rachael M. Scicluna, Ben Campkin and Barbara Penner (eds.), *Sexuality and Gender at Home: Experience, Politics, Transgression*, 232–51, London: Bloomsbury, 2017.

Campkin, Ben and Lo Marshall, *LGBTQ+ Cultural Infrastructure in London: Night Venues 2006-Present*, London: UCL Urban Laboratory, July 2017.

Campkin, Ben and Lo Marshall, 'London's Nocturnal Queer Geographies', *Soundings* 20 (Autumn 2018): 82–96.

Campkin, Ben and Lo Marshall, 'Fabulous Façades', in Marko Jobst and Naomi Stead (eds.), *Queering Architecture*, 120–40, London: Bloomsbury, 2023.

Campkin, Ben, David Roberts, and Rebecca Ross (eds.), 'Regeneration Realities', *Urban Pampleteer* #2, 2013.

Campkin, Ben, Lo Marshall, and Rebecca Ross (eds.), 'LGBTQ+ Night-time Spaces: Past, Present, Future', *Urban Pamphleteer* #7, 2018.

Carter, Helen, Henrik Gutzon Larsen, and Kristian Olesen, 'A Planning Palimpsest: Neoliberal Planning in a Welfare State Tradition', *European Journal of Spatial Development* no. 58 (June 2015): 1–20.

Caserio, Robert L, Lee Edelman, Jack Halberstam, José Esteban Muñoz and Tim Dean, 'The Antisocial Thesis in Queer Theory', *PMLA* [Publications of the Modern Language Association of America] 121, no. 3 (2006): 819–28.

Castells, Manuel, *The City and the Grassroots: A Cross-Cultural Theory of Urban Social Movements*, London: Edward Arnold, 1983.

Castiglia, Christopher and Christopher Reed, *If Memory Serves: Gay Men, AIDS, and the Promise of the Queer Past*, 74–5, Minneapolis: University of Minnesota Press, 2012.

Chisholm, Dianne, *Queer Constellations: Subcultural Space in the Wake of the City*, Minneapolis: University of Minnesota Press, 2004.

Clements, Ben and Clive D. Field, 'The Polls – Trends: Public Opinion Toward Homosexuality and Gay Rights in Great Britain', *The Public Opinion Quarterly* 78, no. 2 (2014): 523–47.

Clews, Colin, *Gay in the '80s: From Fighting For Our Rights to Fighting For Our Lives*, Kibworth Beauchamp: Matador, 2017.

Collins, Allan, 'Sexual Dissidence, Enterprise and Assimilation: Bedfellows in Urban Regeneration', *Urban Studies* 41, no. 9 (2004): 1789–806.

Cook, Matt, '"Gay Times": Identity, Locality, Memory, and the Brixton Squats in 1970's London', *20th Century British History* 24, no. 1 (2013): 84–109.

Crenshaw, Kimberlé, 'Demarginalizing the Intersection of Race and Sex: A Black Feminist Critique of Antidiscrimination Doctrine, Feminist Theory and Antiracist Politics', *University of Chicago Legal Forum*, no. 1, Article 8 (1989): 139–67.

Crinson, Mark, *Urban Memory: History and Amnesia in the Modern City*, London: Routledge, 2005.

Curtarelli, Maurizio, Charlotte Ruitanga, and Maryam Shater Jannati, *The Business Case of Diversity for Enterprises, Cities and Regions with Focus on Sexual Orientation and Gender Identity*, European Commission, 2016.

de Certeau, Michel, *The Practice of Everyday Life*, translated by Steven Rendall, Berkeley: University of California Press, 1984.

Delany, Samuel R., *Times Square Red, Times Square Blue*, New York: New York University Press, 1999.

Deutsche, Rosalyn, 'Boys Town', *Environment and Planning D: Society and Space* 9, no. 1 (1991): 5–30.

Doan, Petra L. (ed.), *Planning and LGBTQ Communities: The Need for Inclusive Queer Spaces*, 1st edn, New York: Routledge, 2015.

Doan, Petra L. (ed.), *Queerying Planning: Challenging Heteronormative Assumptions and Reframing Planning Practice*, Milton: Routledge, 2016.

Doan, Petra L., 'Non-normative Sexualities and Gentrification', in Loretta Lees and Martin Phillips (eds.), *Handbook of Gentrification Studies*, 155–69, Cheltenham, Gloucestershire: Edward Elgar Publishing, 2018.

Doan, Petra L. and Harrison Higgins, 'The Demise of Queer Space? Resurgent Gentrification and the Assimilation of LGBT Neighborhoods', *Journal of Planning Education and Research* 31, no. 1 (2011): 6–25.

Doron, Gil M., 'The Dead Zone and the Architecture of Transgression', *City* 4, no. 2 (2010): 247–63.

Duggan, Lisa, 'The New Homonormativity: The Sexual Politics of Neo-liberalism', in Russ Castronovo and Dana D. Nelson (eds.), *Materializing Democracy: Toward a Revitalized Cultural Politics*, 175–94, Durham and London: Duke University Press, 2002.

Durmaz-Drinkwater, Bahar, Stephen Platt, and Işın Can-Traunmüller. 'Do Perceptions of Neighbourhood Change Match Objective Reality?', *Journal of Urban Design* 25, no. 6 (1 November 2020): 718–37.

Edelman, Lee, *No Future: Queer Theory and the Death Drive*, Durham and London: Duke University Press, 2004.

Edwards, Michael, 'Wealth Creation and Poverty Creation', *City* 6, no. 1 (2002): 25–42.

Edwards, Michael, 'King's Cross: Renaissance for Whom', in John Punter (ed.) *Urban Design and the British Urban Renaissance*, 189–205, London: Taylor and Francis, 2009.

Eichhorn, Kate, 'Copy Machines and Downtown Scenes', *Cultural Studies* 29, no. 3 (2015): 363–78.

Fainstein, Susan S., Ian Gordon, and Michael Harloe (eds.), *Divided Cities: New York and London in the Contemporary World*, Oxford: Blackwell, 1992.

Feather, Stuart, *Blowing the Lid: Gay Liberation, Sexual Revolution and Radical Queens*, Winchester: Zero Books, 2015.

Florida, Richard L., *The Rise of the Creative Class: and How it's Transforming Work, Leisure, Community and Everyday Life*, New York: Basic Books, 2002.

Florida, Richard L., 'Cities and the Creative Class', *City & Community* 2, no. 1 (2003): 3–19.

Florida, Richard L., *The Rise of the Creative Class, Revisited*, New York: Basic Books, 2012.

Florida, Richard L. and Charlotta Mellander, 'There Goes the Metro: How and Why Bohemians, Artists and Gays Affect Regional Housing Values', *Journal of Economic Geography* 10, no. 2 (1 March 2010): 167–88.

Forty, Adrian, *Words and Buildings: A Vocabulary of Modern Architecture*, London: Thames & Hudson, 2000.

Foucault, Michel, *The History of Sexuality*, Volume 1, translated from the French by Robert Hurley. An Introduction, Harmondsworth: Penguin, 1981 [1978].

Foucault, Michel and Jay Miskowiec, 'Of Other Spaces', *Diacritics* 16, no. 1 (1986): 22–7.

Frisch, Michael, 'Planning as a Heterosexist Project', *Journal of Planning Education and Research* 21, no. 3 (2002): 254–66.

Frost, Derek, *Living and Loving in the Age of AIDS: A Memoir*, London: Watkins, 2021.

Gandy, Matthew, 'Queer Ecology: Nature, Sexuality, and Heterotopic Alliances', *Environment and Planning D: Society and Space* 30, Issue 4 (2012): 569–755.

Gandy, Matthew (ed.), *Urban Constellations*, Berlin: Jovis Verlag, 2011.

Gassner, Günter, *Ruined Skylines: Aesthetics, Politics and London's Towering Cityscape*, London and New York: Routledge, 2020.

Ghaziani, Amin, *There Goes the Gayborhood?* Princeton: Princeton University Press, 2014.

Ghaziani, Amin and Matt Brim (eds.), *Imagining Queer Methods*, New York: New York University Press, 2019.

Gillespie, Tom, Kate Hardy, and Paul Watt, 'Austerity Urbanism and Olympic Counter-Legacies: Gendering, Defending and Expanding the Urban Commons in East London', *Environment and Planning D, Society and Space* 36, no. 5 (2018): 812–30.

Glass, Dan, *United Queerdom: From the Legends of the Gay Liberation Front to the Queers of Tomorrow*, London: Zed Books, 2020.

Glass, Ruth (ed.), *London: Aspects of Change, Centre for Urban Studies Report; no. 3*, London: Macgibbon and Kee, 1964.

Goh, Kian, 'Safe Cities and Queer Spaces: The Urban Politics of Radical LGBT Activism', *Annals of the American Association of Geographers* 108, no. 2 (4 March 2018): 463–77.

Gordon, Ian Richard and Tony Travers, 'London: Planning the Ungovernable City', *City, Culture and Society* 1, no. 2 (2010): 49–55.

Gorman-Murray, Andrew, 'Gay Gentrification', in Abbie E. Goldberg (ed.), *The SAGE Encyclopedia of LGBTQ Studies, Clark University*, 433–5, Los Angeles: SAGE Reference, 2016.

Gorman-Murray, Andrew and Peter Hopkins (eds.), *Masculinities and Place*, London and New York: Routledge, 2016.

Gutiérrez Sánchez, Isabel, *Infrastructures of Caring Citizenship Citizen-led Welfare Initiatives in Crisis-Ridden Athens, Greece*, doctoral thesis, UCL, 2020.

Guzmán, Javier, 'Notes on the Comedown', *Social Text* 32 no. 4 (2014): 59–68.

Hadfield, Phil, 'The Night-Time City. Four Modes of Exclusion: Reflections on the *Urban Studies* Special Collection', *Urban Studies* 52, no. 3 (2015): 606–16.

Hakim, Jamie, 'The Rise of Chemsex: Queering Collective Intimacy in Neoliberal London', *Cultural Studies* 33, no. 2 (4 March 2019): 249–75.

Halberstam, Jack, *In a Queer Time and Place Transgender Bodies, Subcultural Lives*, New York and London: New York University Press, 2005.

Hall, Peter, *The World Cities*, London: Weidenfeld and Nicolson, 1977.

Hall, Suzanne, *City, Street and Citizen: A Measure of the Ordinary*, London: Routledge, 2012.

Halperin, David M., 'The Normalization of Queer Theory', *Journal of Homosexuality* 45: 2–4 (2003): 339–43.

Hamnett, Chris, *Unequal City: London in the Global Arena*, London and New York: Routledge, 2003.

Hamnett, Chris, 'Gentrification and the Middle-Class Remaking of Inner London, 1961–2001', *Urban Studies* 40, no. 12 (2016): 2401–26.

Harris, Andrew, 'Art and Gentrification: Pursuing the Urban Pastoral in Hoxton, London', *Transactions of the Institute of British Geographers* 37, no. 2 (1 April 2012): 226–41.

Harris, Andrew and Louis Moreno, *Creative City Limits: Urban Cultural Economy in a New Era of Austerity*, London: UCL Urban Laboratory, 2011.

Harrison, Carolyn, Richard Munton, and Kevin Collins. 'Experimental Discursive Spaces: Policy Processes, Public Participation and the Greater London Authority', *Urban Studies* 41, no. 4 (2004): 903–17, 904.

Harvey, David, *The Condition of Postmodernity: An Enquiry into the Origins of Cultural Change*, Oxford: Basil Blackwell, 1989.

Harvey, David, *A Brief History of Neoliberalism*, Oxford and New York: Oxford University Press, 2005.

Hastings, Christobel, 'Remembering the 1980s UK Lesbian and Gay Centre that Died Too Soon', *Vice*, 27 August 2016. .

Hatherley, Owen, *A Guide to the New Ruins of Great Britain*, London: Verso, 2010.

Hatherley, Owen, *Red Metropolis: Socialism and the Government of London*, London: Repeater Books, 2020.

Hebbert, Michael, *London: More by Fortune Than Design*, Chichester: John Wiley, 2001 [1998].

Holtorf, Cornelius, 'Perceiving the Past: From Age Value to Pastness', *International Journal of Cultural Property*, Oxford 24, no. 4 (November 2017): 497–515.

Houlbrook, Matt, *Queer London: Perils and Pleasures in the Sexual Metropolis, 1918–1957*, Chicago and London: University of Chicago Press 2005.

Hubbard, Phil, 'Cleansing the Metropolis: Sex Work and the Politics of Zero Tolerance', *Urban Studies* 41, no. 9 (August 2004): 1687–702.

Hubbard, Phil, *Cities and Sexualities*, London: Routledge, 2011.

Hubbard, Phil, 'Geography and Sexuality: Why Space (Still) Matters', *Sexualities* 21, no. 8 (2018): 1295–9.

Hubbard, Phil and Eleanor Wilkinson, 'Welcoming the World? Hospitality, Homonationalism, and the London 2012 Olympics', *Antipode* 47, no. 3 (2015): 598–615.

Hunt, R. Justin, 'After the After-Party', in Ben Campkin, Lo Marshall, and Rebecca Ross (eds.), 'LGBTQ+ Night-spaces: Past, Present, Future' *Urban Pamphleteer* #7 (2018): 29–30.

Imrie, Robert and Loretta Lees (eds.), *Sustainable London?: The Future of a Global City*, Bristol: Policy Press, 2014.

Imrie, Robert, Loretta Lees, and Mike Raco (eds.), *Regenerating London: Governance, Sustainability and Community in a Global City*, London, Milton Park, Abingdon, Oxon and New York: Routledge, 2009.

Ingram, Gordon Brent, Anne-Marie Bouthillette, and Yolanda Retter (eds.), *Queers in Space: Communities, Public Places, Sites of Resistance*, Seattle: Bay Press, 1997.

Jameson, Fredric, 'Postmodernism, or the Cultural Logic of Late Capitalism', *New Left Review*, no. 164 (1984): 53–92.

Jennings, Rebecca, 'The Gateways Club and the Emergence of a Post-Second World War Lesbian Subculture', *Social History* 31, no. 2 (2006): 206–25.

Jobst, Marko and Naomi Stead, *Queering Architecture: Methods, Practices, Spaces, Pedagogies*, London: Bloomsbury, 2023.

Keith, Michael, 'Postcolonial London and the Allure of the Cosmopolitan City', *AA Files*, no. 49 (Spring 2003): 57–67.

King, Anthony D., *Writing the Global City: Globalisation, Postcolonialism and the Urban*, London and New York: Routledge, Taylor & Francis Group, 2016.

Kisby, Ben, 'The Big Society: Power to the People?', *The Political Quarterly* 81, no. 4 (2010): 484–91.

Knopp, Lawrence, 'Social Theory, Social Movements and Public Policy: Recent Accomplishments of the Gay and Lesbian Movements in Minneapolis, Minnesota', *International Journal of Urban and Regional Research* 11, no. 2 (1987): 243–61.

Kosofsky Sedgwick, Eve, *Epistemology of the Closet*, New York and London: Harvester Wheatsheaf, 1991.

Kosofsky Sedgwick, Eve, *Touching Feeling: Affect, Pedagogy, Performativity*, Durham and London: Duke University Press, 2003.

Lamé, Amy, *From Prejudice to Pride: A History of the LGBTQ+ Movement*, London: Wayland, 2017.

Lauria, Mickey and Lawrence Knopp, 'Toward an Analysis of the Role of Gay Communities in the Urban Renaissance', *Urban Geography* 6, no. 2 (1985): 152–69.

Leach, Steve and David Wilson, 'Urban Elites in England: New Models of Executive Governance', *International Journal of Urban and Regional Research* 28, no. 1 (1 March 2004): 134–49.

Lee, John Alan, 'The Gay Connection', *Urban Life* 8, no. 2 (July 1979): 175–98.*Homosexuality: A Psychoanalytic Study*

Lees, Loretta, 'A Reappraisal of Gentrification: Towards a "Geography of Gentrification"', *Progress in Human Geography* 24, no. 3 (1 September 2000): 389–408.

Lees, Loretta, 'Gentrification', in James D. Wright (ed.), *International Encyclopedia of the Social & Behavioral Sciences*, 46–52, Amsterdam and New York: Elsevier, 2015.

Lees, Loretta and Martin Phillips (eds.), *Handbook of Gentrification Studies*, Cheltenham, Gloucestershire: Edward Elgar Publishing, 2018.

Lees, Loretta, Hyun Bang Shin, and Ernesto López Morales, *Global Gentrifications: Uneven Development and Displacement*, Bristol and Chicago: Policy Press, 2015.

Lefebvre, Henri, *The Production of Space*, translated by Donald Nicholson-Smith, Oxford: Blackwell, 1991.

Lefebvre, Henri, *Critique of Everyday Life*, translated by John Moore; with a Preface by Michel Trebitsch, London: Verso, 2008.

Levine, Martin P., 'Gay Ghetto', *Journal of Homosexuality* 4, no. 4 (1979): 363–77.

Ley, David, *The New Middle Class and the Remaking of the Central City*, Oxford: Oxford University Press, 1996.

Lin, Jeremy Atherton, *Gay Bar: Why We Went Out*, London: Granta Books, 2021.

Lipietz, Barbara, Richard Lee, and Sharon Hayward, 'Just Space: Building a Community-Based Voice for London Planning', *City* 18, no. 2 (2014): 214–25.

Loyd, Bonnie and Lester Rowntree, 'Radical Feminists and Gay Men in San Francisco: Social Pace in Dispersed Communities', in David Lanegran and Risa Palm (ed.), *Invitation to Geography*, 78–88, New York: McGraw Hill, 1978.

Lubitow, Amy and Mia Davis, 'Pastel Injustice: The Corporate Use of Pinkwashing for Profit', *Environmental Justice* 4, no. 2 (1 June 2011): 139–44.

Marcuse, Herbert, *Eros and Civilization: A Philosophical Inquiry into Freud*, London: Routledge & Kegan Paul Ltd, 1956.

Marshall, Lo, 'Negotiating Gender Diverse Realities Built on Binary Expectations: Public Toilets, in Britain', in Jess Berry, Timothy Moore, Nicole Kalms and Gene Bawden (eds.), *Contentious Cities: Design and the Gendered Production of Space*, Abingdon: Taylor and Francis, 2020, 216–33.

Marshall, Lo, *Making Sense of Gender: Exploring Gender Diversity Through the Experiences of People with Trans Identities and Histories*, doctoral, 2021, UCL.

Marshall, Lo, 'Queer House Party', in Adam Nathaniel Furman and Joshua Mardell (eds.), *Queer Spaces: An Atlas of LGBTQIA+ Places and Stories*, 166–7, London: RIBA Publishing, 2022.

Massad, Joseph, *Desiring Arabs*, Chicago: University of Chicago Press, 2007.

Massey, Doreen, 'Flexible Sexism', *Environment and Planning. D, Society & Space* 9, no. 1 (1991): 31–57.

Massey, Doreen, *World City*, Cambridge: Polity, 2007.

Mattern, Shannon, 'Infrastructural Tourism', *Places Journal*, 1 July 2013.

Mattson, Greggor, 'Small–City Gay Bars, Big–City Urbanism', *City & Community* 19, no. 1 (2020): 76–97.

McCormack, Mark and Fiona Measham, *Building a Sustainable Queer Nightlife in London: Queer Creatives, Covid-19 and Community in the Capital*, London: Arts Council England, 2022.

McIntosh, Mary, 'The Homosexual Role', *Social Problems*, no. 2 (1969 1968): 182–92.

McKerrow, Graham, 'Saving Gays the Word: The Campaign to Protect a Bookshop and the Right to Import Queer Literature', in Leila Kassir and Richard Espley (ed.), *Queer Between the Covers: Histories of Queer Publishing and Publishing Queer Voices*, 91–122, London: University of London Press, 2021.

Miles, Sam, 'Sex in the Digital City: Location-Based Dating Apps and Queer Urban Life', *Gender, Place & Culture* 24, no. 11 (2 November 2017): 1595–610.

Minton, Anna. *Ground Control: Fear and Happiness in the Twenty-First-Century City*, London: Penguin, 2009.

Minton, Anna, *Big Capital: Who Is London for?* London: Penguin Books, 2017.

Mort, Frank, 'Cityscapes: Consumption, Masculinities and the Mapping of London since 1950', *Urban Studies* 35, no. 5/6 (1998): 889–907.

Mowlabocus, Sharif, 'Revisiting Old Haunts Through New Technologies: Public (Homo) Sexual Cultures in Cyberspace', *International Journal of Cultural Studies* 11, no. 4 (2008): 419–39.

Mowlabocus, Sharif, *Gaydar Culture: Gay Men, Technology and Embodiment in the Digital Age*, Farnham: Ashgate, 2010.

Muñoz, José Esteban, *Cruising Utopia: The Then and There of Queer Futurity*, New York and London: New York University Press, 2009.

Muñoz, José Esteban, *Disidentifications: Queers of Color and the Performance of Politics* (Minneapolis and London: University of Minnesota Press, 1999).

Oswin, Natalie, 'Planetary Urbanization: A View from Outside', *Environment and Planning D: Society and Space* 36, no. 3 (2018): 540–6.

Parslow, Joe, 'Queer Stages: LGBTQ+ Venues, Drag Performance and Hope', in Ben Campkin, Lo Marshall, and Rebecca Ross (eds.), *Urban Pamphleteer* #7 (2018): 22–4.

Pilkey, Brent, Rachael M. Scicluna, Ben Campkin, and Barbara Penner (eds.), *Sexuality and Gender at Home: Experience, Politics, Transgression*, London and New York: Bloomsbury, 2017.

Power, Emma R. and Kathleen J. Mee. 'Housing: An Infrastructure of Care', *Housing Studies* 35, no. 3 (2002): 484–505.

Power, Lisa, *No Bath But Plenty of Bubbles: Stories from the London Gay Liberation Front, 1970–1973*, London: Continuum International Publishing Group, 1995.

Preciado, Paul B., *An Apartment on Uranus*, London: Fitzcarraldo Editions, 2020.

Preciado, Paul B., 'Architecture as a Practice of Biopolitical Disobedience', *Log*, no. 25 (2012): 121–34.

Puar, Jasbir K., *Terrorist Assemblages: Homonationalism in Queer Times*, Durham: Duke University Press, 2017.

Raco, Mike and Emma Tunney, 'Visibilities and Invisibilities in Urban Development: Small Business Communities and the London Olympics 2012', *Urban Studies* 47, no. 10: 2069–91.

Rallings, Colin and Michael Thrasher, 'Personality Politics and Protest Voting: The First Elections to the Greater London Authority', *Parliamentary Affairs* 53, no. 4 (2000): 753–64, 763.

Ramos Ramirez, Regner Amaury, *Spatial Practices/Digital Traces: Embodiment and Reconfigurations of Urban Spaces through GPS Mobile Applications*, doctoral thesis, UCL, 2016.

Ramos, Regner and Sharif Mowlabocus, *Queer Sites in Global Contexts: Technologies, Spaces, and Otherness* (Milton: Taylor and Francis, 2020).

Rendell, Jane, Barbara Penner, and Iain Borden (eds.), *Gender Space Architecture: An Interdisciplinary Introduction*, London: Routledge, 2000.

Renninger, Bryce J. 'Grindr Killed the Gay Bar, and Other Attempts to Blame Social Technologies for Urban Development: A Democratic Approach to Popular Technologies and Queer Sociality', *Journal of Homosexuality* 66, no. 12 (15 October 2019): 1736–55.

Ritu, DJ, 'The Only One', in Ben Campkin, Lo Marshall, and Rebecca Ross (eds.). 'LGBTQ+ Night-spaces: Past, Present, Future', *Urban Pamphleteer*, no. 7 (July 2018): 5–7; 7.

Roberts, David, 'Make Public: Performing Public Housing in Ernő Goldfinger's Balfron Tower', *Journal of Architecture* 22, no. 1 (2017): 123–50.

Robinson, Jennifer, *Ordinary Cities: Between Modernity and Development*, London and New York: Routledge, 2006.

Robson, Garry, 'Class, Criminality and Embodied Consciousness: Charlie Richardson and a South East London Habitus', Working Paper, Goldsmiths College, University of London, New Cross, London, 1997.

Roestone Collective, The, 'Safe Space: Towards a Reconceptualization', *Antipode* 46, no. 5 (2014): 1346–65.

Rose, Damaris, 'Discourses and Experiences of Social Mix in Gentrifying Neighbourhoods: A Montréal Case Study', *Canadian Journal of Urban Research* 13, no. 2 (2004): 278–316.

Rubin, Gayle, 'Sexual Traffic', interview with Judith Butler, *Differences* 6.2+3 (1994): 62–99.

Sabsay, Leticia, 'The Emergence of the Other Sexual Citizen: Orientalism and the Modernisation of Sexuality', *Citizenship Studies* 16, no. 5–6 (2012): 605–23.

Sanders, Joel (ed.), *Stud: Architectures of Masculinity*, New York: Princeton Architectural Press, 1996.

Sanders-Mcdonagh, Erin, Magali Peyrefitte, and Matt Ryalls, 'Sanitising the City: Exploring Hegemonic Gentrification in London's Soho', *Sociological Research Online* 21, no. 3 (1 August 2016): 128–33.

Sassen, Saskia, *The Global City: New York, London, Tokyo*, Princeton and Oxford: Princeton University Press, 2001.

Sassen, Saskia, 'The Global City: Introducing a Concept', *The Brown Journal of World Affairs* 11, no. 2 (2004): 27–43.

Schulman, Sarah, *The Gentrification of the Mind: Witness to a Lost Imagination*, Berkeley: University of California Press, 2013.

Seijas, Andreina and Mirik Milan Gelders, 'Governing the Night-Time City: The Rise of Night Mayors as a New Form of Urban Governance After Dark', *Urban Studies* 58, no. 2 (2021): 316–34.

Simone, AbdouMaliq, 'People as Infrastructure: Intersecting Fragments in Johannesburg', *Public Culture* 16, no. 3 (1 October 2004): 407–29.

Smith, Neil, 'Toward a Theory of Gentrification: A Back to the City Movement by Capital, Not People', *Journal of the American Planning Association* 45, no. 4 (1979): 538–48.

Soja, Edward W., *Postmodern Geographies: The Reassertion of Space in Critical Social Theory*, London and New York: Verso, 2011.

Stryker, Susan, *Transgender History: The Roots of Today's Revolution*, Berkeley: Seal Press, 2008.

Stryker, Susan, 'Dungeon Intimacies: The Poetics of Transsexual Sadomasochism', *Parallax* 14, no. 1 (2008): 36–47; 38.

Taylor, Myfanwy, 'The Role of Traders and Small Businesses in Urban Social Movements: The Case of London's Workspace Struggles', *International Journal of Urban and Regional Research* 44, no. 6 (2020): 1041–56.

Tribillon, Justinien, 'Inventing "Infrastructure": Tracing the Etymological Blueprint of an Omnipresent Metaphor', 2020, manuscript, in preparation.

Urbach, Henry, 'Closets, Clothes, Disclosure', *Assemblage*, no. 30 (1996): 63–73.

Valentine, Gill, 'Theorizing and Researching Intersectionality: A Challenge For Feminist Geography', *The Professional Geographer*, 59, no. 1 (2007): 10–21.

Vallerand, Olivier, 'Home Is the Place We All Share', *Journal of Architectural Education* 67, no. 1 (7 March 2013): 64–75.

Venturi, Marco, *Out of Soho, Back into the Closet: Rethinking the London Gay Community*, doctoral thesis, UCL, 2018.

Vertovec, Steven, 'Super-Diversity and its Implications', *Ethnic and Racial Studies* 30, no. 6 (2007): 1024–54.

Walters, Ben, *Queer Fun, Family and Futures in Duckie's Performance Projects 2010–2016*, doctoral thesis, Queen Mary University of London, 2019.

Warner, Michael (ed.), *Fear of a Queer Planet: Queer Politics and Social Theory*, Minneapolis and London: University of Minnesota Press, 1993.

Warren, Carol A. B., *Identity and Community in the Gay World*, New York: Wiley-Interscience, 1974.

Watney, Simon, *Imagine Hope: AIDS and Gay Identity*, London and New York: Routledge, 2000, 250–1.

Weeks, Jeffrey, *Coming Out: Homosexual Politics in Britain, from the Nineteenth Century to the Present*, London: Quartet Books, 1977.

Weeks, Jeffrey, 'The "homosexual role" after 30 years: An Appreciation of the Work of Mary McIntosh', *Sexualities* 1, no. 2 (1998): 131–52.

Weightman, Barbara, 'Bars As Private Places', *Landscape* 24, no. 1 (1980): 9–16.

Weightman, Barbara, 'Commentary: Towards a Geography of the Gay Community', *Journal of Cultural Geography* 1 (1981): 106–12.

Whyatt, Anna, 'London East: Gateway to Regeneration', in Tim Butler and Mike Rustin (eds.), *Rising in the East: The Regeneration of East London*, 265–87, London: Lawrence & Wishart, 1996.

Wirth, Louis, 'The Ghetto', *The American Journal of Sociology* 33, no. 1 (1927): 57–71.

Wolfe, Maxine, 'Invisible Women in Invisible Place: Lesbians, Lesbian Bars, and the Social Production of People/Environment Relationship', *Architecture and Behavior* 8 (1992): 137–58.

Worthy, Ben, Mark Bennister, and Max W. Stafford, 'Rebels Leading London: The Mayoralties of Ken Livingstone and Boris Johnson Compared', *British Politics* 14, no. 1 (1 March 2019): 23–43.

Wright, Les (ed.), *The Bear Book: Readings in the History and Evolution of a Gay Male Subculture*, New York and London: Harrington Park Press, 1997.

Wright, Melissa W., 'Gender and Geography II: Bridging the Gap – Feminist, Queer, and the Geographical Imaginary', *Progress in Human Geography* 34, no. 1 (2010): 56–66.

Yates, Doug, *The Ungovernable City: The Politics of Urban Problems and Policy Making*, Cambridge, MA: MIT Press, 1977.

Zelinsky, Wilbur, 'Personality and Self-Discovery: The Future Social Geography of the United States', in Ronald Abler et al. (ed.), *Human Geography in a Shrinking World*, 108–21, Belmont: Duxbury Press, 1975.

About the author

Ben Campkin is the author of *Remaking London: Decline and Regeneration in Urban Culture* (2013), which won the Urban Communication Foundation Jane Jacobs Award (2015) and was commended in the Royal Institute of British Architects President's Awards for Research (2014). His other publications include *Engaged Urbanism: Cities and Methodologies* (co-editor, 2016), *Sexuality and Gender at Home: Experience, Politics, Transgression* (co-editor, 2017) and *Dirt: New Geographies of Cleanliness and Contamination* (co-editor, 2007). He is Professor of Urbanism and Urban History at The Bartlett School of Architecture, University College London, and Co-Director of UCL Urban Laboratory.

Index

Abramov, Alexander 137
The Ace of Clubs 37
ACT UP (AIDS Coalition to Unleash
    Power) London 36
aesthetics
    of groups and documents 34, 54,
        154, 168
    of venues 18, 22, 32, 74, 89, 98, 100,
        113, 124–125, 134, 143, 147,
        149, 158
Ahmed, Sara 19–20, 22, 79
AIDS. *See* HIV/AIDS
AIDS Memory UK project 4
Albion & East. *See* Ruth and Robinson
Allford Hall Monaghan Morris 154
al-Qaradawi, Sheikh Yusuf 52
The Alternative 91
ambisexual 115, 231 n.127
Ames, Mark 162, 164, 166–8
A & M Leisure 164
Andersson, Johan 22, 90, 100, 134,
        149–50, 238 n.86
Anglo-American discourse 15
anti-social thesis debate 17, 19, 22–3
Arana-Morton, Jonathan 124, 139
Architects Liaison Group 32
Ardill, Susan 40
Arthur, Benjamin 156
Arts Council England 172
Asset of Community Value (ACV) 111,
        119–26, 128, 135, 160
    The Black Cap 120, 122–4, 137–40,
        142, 143
    government recognition 129
    Heaven 111
    The Joiners Arms 147, 153, 160
    local authorities' responsibilities
        120–1
    nominees/nominations 128–9
    The Royal Vauxhall Tavern 120,
        124–8, 234 n.35
The Astoria 107–10, 115

Austin, J. L. 20

The Backstreet 147, 156–61, 164, 169
Bagleys Studios 101, 225 n.55
Baker, Kenneth 42
Bang! 107, 108
Banks, Tony 148
Beaumont, Dan 116
The Bell 6, 37, 96–101, 103, 111, 115,
        133, 224 n.47, 224 n.50, 225 n.51
Bell, David 12
Benjamin, Walter 13
Benjy's 156–7
Berlant, Laurent 19, 23, 24, 175
Bersani, Leo 17, 19, 185 n.81
Bickell, Brian 75–6
Big Society 122
Binnie, Jon 12
biphobia 4
Birmingham Gay Community Centre
        33
The Black Cap 3, 6, 9, 77, 119–26, 128,
        131, 135–45, 154
    acquisition 120
    ACV registration/status 120, 122–5,
        136–40, 142, 143
    business plan 140–1
    and Camden LGBT Forum/
        Forum+ 123, 124, 126, 128,
        137, 141, 232 n.2, 232 n.10
    closure 119, 137, 141–3
    Historic England, Pride of Place
        map 136
    social media campaign 137
The Black Cap Community Benefit
        Society 144
The Black Cap Foundation 137, 140,
        240 n.110
Black Lesbian and Gay Centre
        Project 44, 163, 194 n.82,
        250 n.118
Black Lesbians UK 55

Blake, Peter 152
Bloc Bar 143, 144
Bloch, Ernst 18, 19, 21, 186 n.92
Bloomberg, Michael 18
Blowing the Lid (Feather) 9
Boheme 156
Bohemian-Gay index 73
Boyfriend Joe 141. *See also* Parslow, Joe
The Breakfast Club 124, 139
Brexit 172
A Brief History of Neoliberalism
 (Harvey) 16
Brown, Gavin 24, 150
Brunskill, Richard 99
Buckland, Fiona 15
Budd, Carol 51
Bullus, Mark 112
Bundy, Reg 123
Burchiellaro, Olimpia 152
Burford, Ian 51
Busby's Disco 102
Butler, Judith 12, 20

Cable 251 n.125
Camden 91, 92
Camden Council 113, 120–1, 123, 128,
 142, 144
Camden LGBT Forum/Forum+ 123,
 124, 126, 128, 137, 141, 232 n.2,
 232 n.10
Camden Peoples' Theatre 101
Camden Securities 139, 241 n.126
Campaign for Real Ale (CAMRA) 62,
 153, 232 n.3
Campbell, Jane 98
Cannell, Alexander 51
Canvas. *See* Bagleys Studios
Casson, Simon 128, 130
Castells, Manuel 11
Castiglia, Christopher 21, 100
Centre News 34, 35
CgMs 139, 241 n.133
*Changing the World: the London Charter
 for Lesbian and Gay Rights* 33
chemsex 68–9
 club closures and 69
Chisholm, Dianne 13–14, 17, 21–2,
 183 n.50
city governments 49

Civil Partnership Act 51
Civil Partnerships Bill 55
clusters of venues 91
Coke, David 238 n.86, 239 n.91
Collins, Alan 24, 72
Community Benefit Society 135
community infrastructure 24
Company Limited by Guarantee Not
 Having Share Capital 30
Compco Holdings 108
Conservative Manifesto 42, 122
Conservatives 28, 39, 42, 47, 48, 55,
 59–60, 120, 122
The Conservatory and Vespa
 Lounge 115
Consolidated Developments 113–14,
 230 n.114, 230 n.117
Co-operative and Community Benefit
 Societies Act 2014 135
Corbyn, Jeremy 39
Coronavirus pandemic. *See* Covid-19
 pandemic
counselling services 38
Covid-19 pandemic 2, 6, 66, 171–7
 London Pride 65
Cream, Julia 12
The Cross 101
Crossrail 68, 106–11, 115, 116, 227 n.77
Crossrail Bill 108
Crossrail Tottenham Court Road 68
Cruising Utopia (Muñoz) 17
Cultural Infrastructure Map 24
Cultural Infrastructure Toolbox 63
Culture Recovery Fund 172
Curran, James 47, 48

Dalston Superstore 116, 173
Davey, Peter 30
de Certeau, Michel 48
decriminalization of homosexual acts
 between men 53
Delany, Samuel 14
Department for Transport 103–4
Derwent Valley 108
Deutsche, Rosalyn 15–16
Dindol, David 162
disidentification 17, 19, 133, 176
diversity 63–4, 78–9
 of clientele 78

policies and practices 20
of women 79
Doan, Petra 24, 74
Downey, Rob 54
Dragonfly Finance S.A.R.L. 137
Drama Queens Drag Theatre
	Company 122, 126
Duckie 128, 130, 131, 134, 135, 174–5
Duggan, Lisa 17, 22, 51, 57
Dyke (Campbell) 98

Eastern Coaldrops 102
Edelman, Lee 17, 19
The Edge 115
Edwards, John 156
Employment Equality (Sexual
	Orientation) Regulations
	(2003) 109
English Heritage/Historic England 106,
	119, 123, 126, 131–2, 134–6,
	140, 214 n.29, 231 n.125
Epistemology of the Closet (Sedgwick) 12
Equalities Act 2010 57
Equalities Impact Assessment
	(EqIA) 110
equality 49–66
	Johnson administration 51, 55–9
	Khan administration 51, 56, 60–6
	Livingstone administration 47, 50–7,
		65
Equality Act 2006 108
Equality Act 2010 103, 109, 114, 160,
	228 n.86, 249 n.100
Equality Act (Sexual Orientation)
	Regulations 55
Equality and Inclusion Policy Framework
	(Transport for London) 108
Estates Gazette 75
The Euston Tavern 99
Evening Standard 71, 74

The Fallen Angel 100, 104, 113
Family Fierce 136
The Farringdon Works 43
Farshéa, Kell 193 n.74
Faucet Inn 124, 136, 138, 240 n.105
Fear of a Queer Planet (Warner) 14
Feather, Stuart 9, 44
Feminist Sex Wars 41

financial crisis of 2008 68, 84, 90–1, 122
First Out Café 6, 89, 100, 111–16,
	208 n.127
Florida, Richard 73
Fluid 88
Foucault, Michel 10, 13, 16, 181 n.17,
	183 n.48, 186 n.92
Foundation for Future London 155
Frankfurt School 13, 16, 18
Friends of the Joiners Arms
		(FOTJA) 143, 153–5, 168
Friends of the RVT 120, 124, 128,
	234 n.35
Frolov, Alexander 137

Galliard Homes 156
Gasholder 102
Gates, Gary 73
The Gateways 97
G-A-Y 6, 106–11, 114, 116, 162, 174,
	227 n.80
Gay Bar (Atherton Lin) 152
gaybourhood 67, 69, 71–5
Gay Business Association 43, 68, 116
Gay Centre 27. *See also* London Lesbian
		and Gay Centre (LLGC)
Gay Index 73
Gay Liberation Front (GLF) 8–9, 15,
	41, 43–4, 56, 65, 99, 180 n.9,
	185 n.75
Gay's the Word bookshop 3, 35, 64, 97,
	99, 133
The Gay UK 88
Gelders, Mirik Milan 59, 61–3
Gender Trouble (Butler) 12
gentrification 69–74
	minority sexualities and 72
Ghaziani, Amin 72–4
The Ghetto 68, 107, 115–16, 231 n.131
Giuliani, Rudy 17
GLA Act 1999 48, 54
Glass, Ruth 72
The Glass Bar 103–6
Goldsmith, Zac 59–60, 206 n.106
Gomez de Villaboa, Fran 152
Gordon, Ian Richard 49
Greater London Authority (GLA) 47,
	119
	Culture at Risk team 144, 154, 172

diffuse mode of governance   48
Johnson administration   51, 55–9
Khan administration   51, 56, 60–6
LGBT Engagement Meetings   57
LGBT Forum   54
Livingstone administration   47, 50–7,
  65
sexual orientation and LGB
  equality   47, 50, 53
sustainable development   48
Visitors' Centre   51
Greater London Council (GLC)   27
abolition of   28, 30, 39, 42–3, 47
equalities policies   28
Gay Working Party   27
Grants Sub-Committee   29
sector-by-sector modernization
  plan   47–8
social policies   47
Green Carnation   115
Green Party   52
Grindr   85
The Guardian   131

Hakim, Jamie   68–9
Halberstam, Jack   16, 17, 20, 22, 53,
  185 n.72, 185 n.74, 185 n.79
Hall-Carpenter Archives   4, 32, 34, 35
Harris, Nigel   123
Harvey, David   15–16
hate crime   68
Hatherley, Owen   48
Haworth, Jann   152
Heaven   107, 111, 120
ACV nomination   111
as a pop-up vaccination centre   174
Hebbert, Michael   24
Heidegger, Martin   19
Heritage in Pride marches, New York
  64
Her Upstairs/Them Downstairs   143
Hibbitts, Thomas   69
Historic England. *See* English Heritage/
  Historic England
The History of Sexuality (Foucault)   10,
  16
HIV/AIDS   4, 21, 27, 30, 35, 36, 38, 39,
  41, 50, 54, 78, 100, 101, 123,
  133, 135, 144, 167, 174, 179 n.2,

188 n.117, 200 n.31. *See also*
  AIDS
Hobart, Simon   116, 231 n.128
Hollenbeck's   139
homonormativity   50–51, 57, 186 n.83
homophobia   27, 31, 171
Homos (Bersani)   17
'The Homosexual Role' (McIntosh)   9
Houlbrook, Matt   76
Hunt, R. Justin   69, 212 n.12
Husserl, Edmund   19

identity
attachment and   19
as a site of struggle   19
identity-based social movements   16
identity politics   17–18
consumer culture   16
gay   22
homonormative   17
radical   99
If Memory Serves (Castiglia and
  Reed)   21
Imaan   55
Imbiba   139
Immovate   120
infrastructures   23. *See also* queer
  infrastructure
infrastructures of the social   23
Institute for Contemporary Arts   30
intangible heritage   82
UNESCO's definition of   199 n.21
Islington   27, 91, 92

Jameson, Fredric   15–16
Jameson, Rex   136
Jarman, Derek   156–7, 246 n.64, 247 n.66
Jennings, Rebecca   97
Jessop, Brad   155
Johnson, Boris   37, 51, 55–9
Johnson, Darren   52
The Joiners Arms   77, 120, 147–55, 160,
  164, 168–9
ACV registration   147, 153
after-hours parties   150
FOTJA   143, 153–5, 168
inclusivity   150, 152
Pollard and   148–50, 152
Jones, Andy   115

Jo Purvis's tea dances   37, 98
Joseph, Jeremy   107, 110, 111, 174,
    228 n.96
Julien, Isaac   99

Kaveney, Roz   41
Keith, Michael   52, 53, 56
Kew Capital Limited   120
Khan, Sadiq   51, 56, 60–7, 77, 148, 160,
    165, 168, 206 n.106, 208 n.126,
    209 n.140, 210 n.150
Kicking Horse Limited   124, 136, 137,
    139, 142, 144
Kicking Horse Three   144
Kincaid, Robert   89–90, 113
King's Cross   91, 101–3
King's Cross Central   101, 102
King's Cross Remixes   101
King's Cross Story Palace   99
Knopp, Lawrence   11
Kolvin, Philip   60–1
Kotak, Ash   123–4

Labour Campaign for Lesbian and Gay
    Rights   36
Labour Left   52
Lamé, Amy   62, 63, 128, 154, 168, 171,
    207–8 n.126–8
Late Night Levy   60, 206–7 n.108
Lauria, Mickey   11
Lees, Loretta   72, 73, 138
Lefebvre, Henri   13, 14, 48, 183 n.48,
    184 n.59
Legislation for Lesbian and Gay Rights
    Campaign   37
Lesbian and Gay Youth Movement   36
Lesbians Against Sadomasochism
    (LASM)   40
Lesbians and Gays Support the Miners
    (LGSM)   97
Levine, Martine   10
Lewis, Gordon   231 n.125
Ley, David   73
LGBTQI+ COVID-19 Mutual Aid
    network   172
LGBTQ+ Venues Forum   173
LGBT Venues Charter   63
Licensing Act 2003   75
Lin, Jeremy Atherton   152

Livingstone, Ken   16, 33, 39, 47, 50–7, 65,
    108, 112, 114
Local Government Act 1985   42
Localism Act 2011   120, 122, 145
location-based apps   84–5
London
    2012 Olympics   52
    as a global city   47–9
    mayor/mayoralty   50–66
    postcolonial transformation   47
    sector-by-sector modernization
        plan   47
    terrorist bombings of 7/7   52
    Thatcher government   47
London Apprentice   91
London Co-operative Development
    Agency   112
London Gay Teenage Group Research
    Project   39
London Lesbian and Gay Centre
    (LLGC)   2, 4, 17, 27–45, 112,
    113, 153
    as an architectural project   31
    basement disco   37
    building   31–3
    Centre News   34, 35
    as a Company Limited by Guarantee
        Not Having Share Capital   30
    constitution   29, 34
    counselling services   38
    debt crisis   42
    elevation drawing   28
    funding   29, 39
    as ideological battleground for party
        politics   28
    Lesbian Strength marches   35
    Management Committee   30, 31
    members/membership   31
    nights at   37
    organizational structure   31
    Pride marches   35
    sadomasochist (S/M) groups   40–2
    self-help initiatives   30
    as a social enterprise   43
    staffing model   30
    Steering Committee   29–31, 44
    visual identity   34–5
    volunteering   38
    women and   30

as a workers' cooperative   28, 30
London Overground railway   91
London Partnership Register   51
The London Plan   23, 53–4, 58, 63, 65
London Pride   56, 65
London Residuary Body   42, 43
London School of Economics (LSE)   9
London's Grassroots Music Venues Rescue Plan   59, 60, 206 n.106
Looking for Langston   99

McCormack, Mark   172, 173
McDonnell, John   27
McGlynn, Nick   168
McIntosh, Mary   9, 10
McKenzie, Elaine   104–6, 226 n.71–5
McKenzie, Veronica   194 n.82, 250 n.118
McLaren, Malcolm   102
McLean, Fiona   31, 32
Madame JoJo's   70–1
MAMA   107, 110
Manifesto for the Night Time Economy (Kolvin)   60
Maples, John   39
Marshall, Bob   30
Marshall, Lo   68, 76, 89
Marshman, Tom   101
Massey, Doreen   41, 47–9, 52, 53
Mattson, Greggor   85
Measham, Fiona   172, 173
media representation   67–93
    chemsex   68–9
    digital technology   83–5
    gaybourhood   67, 69, 71–5
    Gay Business Association dataset   68
    gentrification   69–74
    safety and survival   78–81
    social media campaigns   76–8
Mellander, Charlotta   73
memory, affective power   21
men who have sex with men   68, 84
Meth Lab   136, 141, 143
Miles, Sam   84
Moss, Tommy   116
Mother Black Cap   136
Mowlabocus, Sharif   85
The Mud Club   102
Muñoz, José Esteban   16–22, 62, 63, 100, 133

Music Venues Taskforce   59

Nachtburgemeester   59
Nag Nag Nag   115
National Heritage List for England   119
National Historic Landmark   133
National Register of Historic Places   133
Native Land   163, 164, 167, 168
neoliberalism   22, 48, 69
Network Rail   103–4, 106, 107, 125, 163, 165, 251 n.125
New Labour   5, 47, 48, 56, 58, 73, 122, 148, 169
New Left   16, 28, 32, 39, 47–8
Night Commission   58–61
night-time governance   58–64
Night Time Industries Association   111, 172
No Future (Edelman)   17
NotTelevision   76

O'Grady, Paul   123
O'Sullivan, Sue   40
Otitoju, Femi   44–5
Out Now   68
Outrage!   36, 51, 52, 55
The Outside Project   63, 171–2, 175

PACE. *See* Project for Advocacy, Counselling and Education (PACE)
Parslow, Joe   141–3
Pateman, Rob   98
The Pigeons   92
Pink Jukebox   37
pinkwashing   56
Pistoni, Giuliano   150, 152
planetary urbanization   14, 184 n.59
Planning Inspectorate   121, 138, 241 n.123
PLP Architects   163, 251 n.126
Polari   55
Pollard, David   148–50, 152
Popbarz   116, 231 n.131
Popstarz   231 n.128
postmodernism   14–16
Power, Lisa   8–9, 44
Power, Vince   101
Preciado, Paul B.   173

Presland, Eric   97–100, 222 n.17
Pride marches/receptions   56
  as apparatus of place promotion   64
  institutionalization and
      commercialization of   64
  Johnson and   56–7
  Khan and   64–5
The Prince Albert   99
The Principles of Hope (Bloch)   18
The Production of Space (Lefebvre)   13
Project for Advocacy, Counselling and
      Education (PACE)   4, 35
Propaganda   107
Puar, Jasbir K.   53
Pulse, Orlando, Florida   60
Pulse, Southwark, London   147,
      161–8. *See also* XXL, Southwark,
      London
  closure   147
  as commercial/corporate event
      space   161, 163
  owners/operators   147, 161, 163–6
  railway arches   147, 161, 163
  Sampson and Ludgate House
      scheme   164
Pure Group   107

Queer, Trans and Intersex People of
      Colour (QTIPOC)   79, 87, 130,
      155, 218 n.87
Queer Constellations (Chisholm)   13
Queer Creatives Forum   173
queer heritage   2, 20–2, 82, 114, 144
Queer House Party   174
queer infrastructure   1, 6–8, 22–5, 83,
      145, 175–176, 189 n.131
Queer Phenomenology (Ahmed)   19
Queer Spaces Network (QSN)   76–8
A Queer Time and Place (Halberstam)   16

Railtrack   103, 104, 106
Ra-Orton, Simon   36
Raymond, Paul   70
Raymond Estates   70
RAZE Collective   76–8
recession   68, 83, 90, 100, 211 n.5, n.7
Reed, Christopher   21, 100
Regal London   155
REGARD   55

Remaking London (Campkin)   73
Resolution Foundation   90
Ritu (DJ)   97
Roberts, Allan   39
Robobond   147
Roestone Collective, University of
      Wisconsin-Madison   80
Rouge   109
Rough Sleeping Innovation Fund   171
The Royal Vauxhall Tavern (RVT)   6, 9,
      60, 77, 88, 99, 119, 120, 124–38,
      140, 142, 145, 175
  3D-laser scan   175
  ACV registration/status   120, 124–6,
      128, 129
  diversity   129–31
  Grade II listed building   131–133,
      235 n.52, 236 n.68
RuPaul's Drag Race   141
Ruth and Robinson   139–40
RVT Future   60, 77, 127, 128, 130–1, 135
Ryder-Tchaikovsky, Chris   97–98

Sadie Masie's   42, 197 n.119
sadomasochism (S/M)   40–2, 195 n.104,
      196 n.112
safe/safer space   36, 38, 79–81, 88, 104,
      123, 126, 153, 168
  for artistic experimentation   81
  creating conditions for   81
  feminist   79, 218 n.86
Sahara Nights   100
St Giles Circus   113, 114, 230 n.119
Salon, Philip   102
Samson and Ludgate House   147, 163–4,
      252 n.127
'Save Our Soho' protest   70
The Scala Cinema   99
Second World War   18
Section 28 of the Local Government Act
      1988   52, 157, 200 n.31
Section 106 agreement   155, 160, 166, 168
Sedgwick, Eve Kosofsky   12
Seijas, Andreina   61–3
sense of community   81–3
SeOne   251 n.125
Sexual Orientation Equality Scheme   54–5
Sexual Orientation Regulations
      2006   108

Shakti 37
Shenton, David 152, 154
Shires, Wayne 142–3, 232 n.131
Smith, Neil 72
social and cultural infrastructure 1, 24–5, 49, 58, 66
social constructionism 15
social infrastructure. *See* social and cultural infrastructure
social media campaigns 76–8
social reproduction 17
Society for the Protection of Ancient Buildings (SPAB) 156
Soho 69–71, 171
 clusters of venues 91
 commercialization 86
 gentrification in 70
Soho Estates 70–1
Soho Pride 57
Soho Society 71
Sommerville, Jimmy 99
South London Gay Community Centre 33
speech acts 20
Stansby, J. B. 103
Stephen Levrant Heritage Architecture Limited 156
sterile rezoning policies 17
Stonewall Equality Index 57, 202 n.41, 204 n.71
Stonewall Inn 132
Stonewall rebellion/uprising 17, 35, 56, 64, 132
Stryker, Susan 41
Sugar, Baron Alan 115
Summerskill, Ben 55
supergentrification 72, 138, 145, 165, 169
sustainable development 48

Tatchell, Peter 51–3, 55
Terrence Higgins Trust 35
Tesco Metro 92
Thame, David 75
Thatcher, Margaret 16, 27–28, 38, 42, 47
Them Downstairs. *See* Her Upstairs/Them Downstairs
Think Night (Night Commission) 61
Time Out 9, 92

Times Square Red, Times Square Blue (Delany) 14
Tonic Housing 64
Tory party 57
Tottenham Court Road Station 68
Tower Hamlets 52, 92
Transparency International 137
transphobia 4, 65, 80, 168, 171
Transport for London 107–9, 158
Trans Pride 65
Travers, Tony 49, 50
Tricky Dicky (DJ) 99

UCL Urban Laboratory 67, 76, 78, 85, 88–9, 95, 96, 107, 111, 129, 160, 162, 164, 175
UK Black Pride 65
UNISON 55
UNITE 173
Urban Aid 33
urbanization
 as a collective project 2
 heritage-driven processes 22
 neo-Marxian analyses 14
 planetary 14, 184 n.59
urban ungovernability 49

Valentine, Gill 12
van Loock, Frank 31
Vaughan, Steven 155
Vauxhall Pleasure Gardens 126, 133, 135, 238 n.86
venues 1–6. *See also* specific venues
Vice 44, 69
Vollin Holdings 137

Walker Court scheme 70–1
Walters, Ben 76, 78, 131
Warner, Michael 14–15, 17, 53
Watson, Oscar 42, 43, 197 n.119
#WeAreTheBlackCap 137
Weeks, Jeffrey 10
Weightman, Barbara 10–11
West Lodge of Euston Station 103–6
Westminster City Council 70, 71
Wilkinson, Linda 51
Wise, Valerie 42
Women's City 29–31, 96–7, 190 n.12, 222 n.8

women's spaces   11, 41, 86, 98, 104, 114
World City (Massey) 52–53
Wright, Jojo   70

XXL, Southwark, London   147, 161–9,
    249 n.110, 250 n.114, 252 n.135,
253 n.151. *See also* Pulse,
    Southwark, London

The Yard   115, 231 n.125
Yates, Douglas   49
YouTube   56, 98

Index

For the benefit of digital users, indexed terms that span two pages (e.g., 52–53) may, on occasion, appear on only one of those pages.

Achilleion, 342

Aiakes, father of Polycrates of Samos, 358, 388–89, 391

Aiakes, son of Syloson, tyrant of Samos, 394–95, 408–9

aisymnētēs, 328, 342–43, 386–87

Aeolian identity, 249–50

Aeolian Migration, 249–50, 303

Aeolic architecture, 346–47

Alcaeus of Lesbos, 300, 326, 327–29, 338–40, 342–44

Al-Mina, 190

Alyattes, king of Lydia, 279, 403–4, 553

Amarynthos, Euboea, 113, 187

Sanctuary of Artemis Amarysia, 105–6, 162–63, 204

Amasis, ruler of Egypt, 282–83, 393, 404–5, 416, 431

Ambracia, 550–52, 553–54, 556, 571, 582

Amorgos, 401–2

Amphiklos, ruler of Chios, 273

Anaia, 397

Anacreon of Teos, 392, 393, 410–11, 432–34

Anactorium, 550–52, 553

Antissa, Lesbos, 315–18

Aphra, Corfu, 524

Apollonia, 553–54, 555–56, 566, 571, 576–77

archaeohistory, xviii, 2–3

Archaic period, definition/temporal parameters of

Argos, 3

Chalcis and Eretria, 105

Chios, Lesbos, and Samos, 248

Corcyra, 491

Greek world as a whole, xxii–xxvi

Argive Heraion, 65–71

Argive plain, 11–12, 41–43, 52, 54

Argos

Apollo, Lykeios, 55–56, 58, 59–62

Apollo, Pythaeus, 15–16, 39–41, 58, 61–62

Aphrodite, Sanctuary of, 62

Aspis hill, 14–15, 40–41, 64

coinage, 55–56

Deiras ridge, 13–14, 15–16, 61–62

Dorians at, 58–59

Hypostyle Hall, 24–25

Larisa hill, 13–16, 23–25, 55, 59–60

Panoply Tomb, 21, 27–28

610   *Index*

Argos (*cont.*)
 phylai, 36–38
 Prophetes Elias hill (*see* Argos: Aspis hill)
 road network, 24
 slavery at, 37–38, 48–52
 Tomb 45, Argos (*see* Argos: Panoply Tomb)
 women, defend city, marry slaves, 48–51, 64–65
Arisba, Lesbos, 303, 313–15, 332
Arniadas, 534, 556
Artemis Amarysia, Sanctuary of. *See* Amarynthos, Euboea
Asine, Argolid, 39–41
Asius of Samos, 385, 421, 431–32
Atarneus, 279–80

Bacchiads, 545–46, 547–48, 549
Battle of the Champions, 46–47
Battle of Hysiae, 31, 45–46
Battle of Lade, 248, 269–70, 280, 285–86, 291–92, 331–32, 337–38, 358–59, 395, 408–9, 418–19
Battle of Sepeia, 3, 23–24, 47–50
Battle of Tegea, 53
Bouthrotos, 525–27
Butrint. *See* Bouthrotos

Calaurian Amphictiony, 42–43
Cape Phokas, Lesbos, 310–11, 340–41
Çatallar Tepe, 289–90, 396–97
Chalcidice, Euboean colonization of, 172
Chalcis
 army, 177
 Athenian cleruchy at, 101, 117, 152, 154–55, 179, 181, 197–98, 200
 attack on Attica, 506 BCE, 101, 139, 152–54, 180
 bridge at, 100
 divergences from Eretria, 101

Hippobotai, 150–52, 153–54
 relationship with Boeotia, 178–80
 settlement organization, 114–17
 settlement pattern, 117–20
 tyrants at, 154
Charaxos, brother of Sappho, 332, 333–34, 345–46
Charikrates, oikist of Corcyra, 537–38
Chios
 amphoras, transport, 284–85
 architecture, 298
 burial customs, 270–71
 Chios Town, 262–65, 271, 274, 293
 coinage, 285
 constitutional law, 274–76, 294
 Dophitis inscription, 277, 278
 Naucratis, role in foundation of, 282–84
 navy, 287
 olive cultivation, 262
 peraia, 279–80
 phylai, 277–78
 pottery, 271–73
 relationship with Lydia, 279
 relationship with Persia, 279–281
 sculpture, 298
 settlement pattern, 269–70
 similarities and differences from Lesbos and Samos, 248–49, 434–35
 slavery, 269–70, 277–78, 284, 286–88
 Strattis, 276–77
 wine production, 262, 281, 284–85
Cimmerians, 400, 401
Cleisthenes of Sicyon, 29–30, 32–33, 36–37, 72
Cleobis and Biton, 68, 72
Cleomenes, King of Sparta, 3, 23–24, 47–50
Cnidus, 283, 553, 555–56
Colonization
 Corinthian, 535–39, 549–52
 Greek, definition, xix

index 611

Euboean, 167–76
process of, 167–69
Corcyra. *See also* Corycra: urban center
of
amphoras, transport, 511–12, 560–61,
562
bull of, 558
burial customs, 528–34, 576–77
ceramic assemblage, 527–28
coinage, 566
colonization of, 502, 535–39, 545–46
colonization by, 547, 549–52, 555–56
Euboean colonization of, 175, 502,
538–39
Gulf of, 501, 503–5
indigenous population, 502–3, 534–35
navy, 555, 565–66, 567–68
peraia, 501, 525–27, 562, 565–67
Phaeacia, identified with, 494–96,
505, 507–8, 546–47, 555, 556–57, 575
phylai, 535, 541–42, 552
prytanis, 539, 547–48
relationship with Corinth, 535, 542,
545–54
settlement pattern, 523–25
slavery, 542–45, 561, 567–68
terminology for, 490–91
tuna fishing, 558
whips, 542–45
wine production, 559–60
Corcyra, urban center of. *See also*
Corcyra
acropolis, 503–5
agora, 494–96, 510–11
Alcinous harbor (*see* harbors and port
facilities)
Analipsis chapel/hill, 491, 496, 503–5
Apollo Corcyraios, cult of, 518–19,
570–71
Arniadas *stēlē*, 533, 556
Artemis Agrotera, cult of, 521–22, 570

Artemision (*see* Sanctuary/Temple of
Artemis)1
Bay of Garitsa, 507–8, 509, 510–11, 523
Chalikiopoulos lagoon, 503–5, 507–8
Figareto (modern district), 503–5,
511–12, 517, 560–61, 562–64, 569
fortifications, 506–7
Garitsa (modern district), 491, 505–6
harbors and port facilities, 491, 496–
97, 503–5, 507–9, 535–36
Hera, cult and temple of (*see* Mon
Repos Temple)
Hyllaic harbor (*see* harbors and port
facilities)
Kanoni peninsula, 491, 503–5
Kardaki spring and temple, 494, 496,
503–5, 519–20, 571–72, 581–82
Lion of Menecrates, 532, 533, 567,
576–77
Mon Repos villa, 491, 496
Mon Repos Temple, 496–97, 517–19,
572–74, 577–79
necropoleis, 494–96, 502–3, 505–6,
522–23
Palaiopolis, 503–5
road network, 506
sanctuaries in, 512–22
Sanctuary of Dionysus, 496–97, 520,
560, 574, 581–82
Sanctuary/Temple of Artemis, 496,
513–17, 569–70, 579–81, 583–84
shipsheds, 508–9
"small Artemis sanctuary," 521–22,
562–64, 570
Soter hill, 491, 494–96, 505, 506, 523,
528–55, 573
Stratia (modern district), 512, 517,
562–64, 570
Tomb of Menecrates, 531–32, 539–41
workshops, 511–12, 560–61, 562–64, 569
Xenwares *stēlē*, 533–34

612 *Index*

Corcyra Melaina, 555–56
Corfu, island of, 490–91, 499–501,
  564–65. *See also* Corcyra
Corfu Town, 490–91, 494–96
Corinth, 405–6. *See also* Cypselids
  relationship with Corcyra, 491, 535,
    542, 545–54
Croesus, king of Lydia, 47, 279, 330–31,
  403–4, 405, 428–29
Cumae, Italy, 173
Cydonia, Crete, 393, 407
Cynaethus of Chios, 295–97
Cynuria, 45–53
Cypselids, 516–17, 545–54
  chronology of, 493
Cypselus of Corinth, 535, 549, 550–52

Daskalopetra, Chios, 294
Delian League, 248, 281, 331–32
Delos, 143–44, 295, 296–97, 392, 407,
  421, 427
Democedes of Croton, 72, 432–33
Dikaiarcheia, southern Italy, 393, 407
Dorian identity, 249–50
Dörpfeld, Wilhelm, 494–96
Douloi, Argos, 48–53
Duris of Samos, 317–52
Dystos, Euboea, 138, 141

Emporio, Chios, 251–59, 262, 265–68,
  274, 293, 315
Ephesus, 288–89, 317, 397–98
Epidamnus, 547, 549–50
Erasinos river, Argolid, 11
Eresus, Lesbos, 318–20, 340–41
Eretria
  Apollo Daphnephoros, Sanctuary
    of, 105–6, 122–25, 127, 131–32, 192,
    201–2, 208
  Athens, relationship with, 177–78,
    197–98

chōroi, 132–38, 156–58
coinage, 182
demes, 132–38, 156–58
divergences from Chalcis, 101
dykes, 125–26, 130
fortification wall, 131
gold hoard, 192
harbor, 132
Heroon at West Gate, 126–27, 131, 146,
  150–51, 204
Hippeis, 150–52, 155–56
navy, 158–61, 176, 180
Persian siege of, 180–82
Persian Wars, involvement in, 182
phylai, 132–38, 140, 156–58
settlement organization, 120–32
settlement pattern, 132–38
West Gate burials, 146, 150–51,
  155, 163
Erythrae, 279–80
Euboea
  amphoras, transport, 191
  colonization of Corcyra, 502, 537–39
  horse-breeding, 187
  metallurgy, 191–94
  Mycenaean period, 100
Euboean Gulf, 97–100, 101
Euboic-Attic weight standard, 193, 194
Eupalinos of Megara, 360–61
Euripos
  Euboea, 97–100
  Mytilene, 304

Fikellura style pottery, 383
Fusco kraters, 21–22

Greek world, definition of, xviii–xix
Gulf of Corcyra, 501, 503–5

Hellanicus of Lesbos, 300
Heraion, Samos. *See* Samian Heraion

index

Histiaeus of Miletus, 280
Homer, 295–98
Homeridae, Chios, 295–98
homoeroticism, female, 338. *See also* Sappho

Ibycus of Rhegium, 388, 432
Inachus river, Argolid, 11
Ion (legendary Athenian), 259–60
Ion of Chios, 273
Ionian identity, 249–50, 288, 292–93
Ionian League, 279, 288–93, 403
Ionian Migration, 249–50, 259–60,
    385–86
Ionian Rebellion, 280–81, 292, 329,
    331–32, 394–95, 408–9, 418
    Euboean role in, 180

Kampos plain, Chios, 262
Kardamatika, Corfu, 523–24
Karaova plain, 397–98, 399, 401
Karion, 398–99
Kato Phana, Chios, 251–59, 262, 268–69,
    282, 293
Kelendris, Cilicia, 401–2
Klima, Samos, 382–83
Klopedi, Lesbos, 313–15
Koes of Mytilene, 329, 331
Kolaios of Samos, 370, 414–15, 424
Koldewey, Robert, 298–300
Kreophylos of Samos and Kreophyleioi, 430
Ksamil peninsula, 525–26

Lake Lerna, Argolid, 11–12
Lamb, Winifred, 251–59, 298–300,
    315–17
Latomi, Chios, 270
Lefkandi, 110, 113, 119, 149–50, 163
Lelantine plain, Euboea, 110, 117, 139, 162,
    183–84, 186, 200
Lelantine War, 106–7, 161–67, 396
Lelantos river, Euboea, 110, 111, 139

Lesbos
    amphoras, transport, 334–35
    burial customs, 320–21
    coinage, 335–37
    conquest by Polycrates of Samos,
        248–49, 329, 331, 404
    political history, 322–25
    population, 337–38
    pottery, 321–22
    relationship with Lydia, 330–31
    relationship with Persia, 330–332
    settlement patterns, 320
    similarities and differences from Chios
        and Samos, 248–49, 434–35
    wine production, 332
Leucas, 552
Lycophron, son of Periander, 535, 553–54
Lydia, 279, 330–31, 403–4, 553, 555–56

Maiandrios of Miletus (historian), 352,
    398–99
Maiandrios, tyrant of Samos, 358, 363,
    393–94, 395, 407, 408, 427
Maroneia, Thrace, 281
mastic (on Chios), 260
Meliac War, 289–90, 396–403
Melie, 289–91, 396–403
Menecrates, 531–32, 535–36
Messon, Lesbos, 338–40, 344
Methone, North Aegean, 170–72, 192
Methymna, Lesbos, 303–4, 311–13, 325,
    332, 337
Miletus, 48–49, 162, 165, 180, 279, 280,
    283, 289, 329, 331, 383, 397, 401, 404
Mycenae, 15, 35–36, 38–39, 41, 43–45,
    49–50, 52–53, 69–70
Myrsilus of Lesbos, 327–28
Mytilene, Lesbos. *See also* Alcaeus;
    Myrsilus; Pittacus; Sappho
    acropolis, 304, 306–7
    agora, 306

614   *Index*

Mytilene, Lesbos (*cont.*)
  burial customs, 307–8, 309, 321
  chōra, 309
  coinage, 335–37
  Euripos, 304, 309
  fortification wall, 308–9
  harbors, 304–6, 307, 308–9
  Koes, tyrant, 329, 331
  Naucratis, role in foundation of, 334
  necropoleis, 307–8, 309, 321
  peraia, 323–25, 333
  political history, 323–29
  population, 337–38
  pottery workshops, 308
  prytanis, 328
  Sanctuary of Apollo Maloies, 306
  Sanctuary of Cybele, 307, 340
  Sanctuary of Demeter and
    Persephone, 306–7
  settlement organization, 304–9

Nagidos, Cilicia, 401–2
Naucratis, 282–84, 334, 402, 416
Nauplia, Argolid, 42–43
Naxos, Sicily, 173

Oichalia, Euboea, 137, 140–41
Oinopion of Chios, 273, 284
Old Eretria, 121
Oroites, Persian satrap, 393–94, 407–8,
  432–33
Otomatik Tepe, 291–92, 396–97, 399
Oxford History of the Archaic Greek World
  (*OHAGW*)
  commensurability, xviii–xx
  comprehensive coverage, xvii–xviii
  convenience, xx–xxi
  rubrics, xix–xx, xxxvii
  site selection, xxi–xxii
  transliteration and spelling, xxvi–xxix
Paktyes of Lydia, 279–80, 293, 330–31
Panionia festival, 288–93

Panionion, 288–93, 396–97
Panionios of Chios, 287
Penthilidai of Mytilene, 325–26
Penthilos of Mytilene, 325–26
PEP Chios, 259
Perama, Corfu, 523
Periander of Corinth, 535, 542, 553–54,
  555–56, 583–84, 585
Perinthus, 386–87, 395, 402–3, 417
Persia, xxiii, 26–27, 50, 133, 180-183,
  276–281, 290, 292, 330–332, 393–394,
  404–405, 407–409, 557
Phaeacia(ns), 494–96, 505, 507–8, 546–
  47, 555, 556–57, 575
Phanai. *See* Kato Phana, Chios
Pheidon of Argos, 25, 29–34, 36–37,
  55–56, 69
Phocaea, 279–80, 283, 288–89, 328, 335–37
Phrynon of Lesbos, 324
Pithecusae, Italy, 173
Pittacus of Lesbos, 324, 327–29, 342–43
Polycrates, tyrant of Samos, 388–95
  activity at Delos, Rheneia, 296–97,
    392, 421, 427
  conquest of Lesbos, 248–49, 329, 331
  fall from power, 407–8
  focus of historical accounts of Samos,
    351–52
  house in Samos Town, 358
  piracy, 390–92, 401–2, 404, 407, 425–26
  public works, 355–56, 358–59, 377, 379
polygonal masonry, 347
Priene, 288–89, 352, 397–402
Psachna plain, Euboea, 119
Psammetichus, grandson of Cypselus,
  493, 535, 540–41, 553–54
Pyrrha, Lesbos, 309–10
Pythagoras of Samos, 430–31
Pythagoreio. *See* Samos Town

Rekini, Corfu, 525
Rhegium, Italy, 173

index   615

Rheneia, 296–97, 391, 392, 407, 421

Rhoikos of Samos, 373, 412–13, 428–29

Rhomaios, Konstantinos, 496

Rizari, Chios, 270

Roda, 524–25

Rodenwalt, Gerhart, 513

samaina (type of ship), 390, 391, 409, 413–14, 417–18

Samian Heraion, 364–80, 422–27
  cult practice at, 426–27
  Cypriot votives, 415–16
  Dipteros 1, 373–75, 376, 379
  Dipteros 2, 379
  excavations at, 349–51
  Geneleos Group, 387–88, 419–20
  Hekatompedon 1, 367–69
  Hekatompedon 2, 371, 373
  Imbrasos river, 364, 371, 373
  Isches Kouros, 376
  juniper stump, 369–70
  lygos tree, 364, 422–23
  monopteros, 379–80
  Nordbau, 377
  North Stoa, 376
  Rhoikos altar, 376
  Rhoikos temple (*see* Dipteros 1)
  Sacred Way, 364, 373
  ships and ship models, dedication of, 371
  South Stoa, 371, 373
  Southern Kouros, 376
  Südbau, 377
  temenos wall, 376
  Temple A, 375
  Temples B, C, D, 379
  Toneia festival, 422–23
  treasury, 376–77
  votives at, 364–65, 370

Samos. *See also* Aiakes; Polycrates; Samian Heraion; Samos Town; Syloson; Theomestor

amphoras, transport, 410–11, 415
burial customs, 380–83
coinage, 417–18
Geomoroi, 386–88
Kambos Khoras plain, 354–55
Naucratis, role in foundation of, 402, 416
olive oil, production of, 410–11
peraia, 394–95, 397–403
piracy at, 388–89, 390–92, 401–2, 404, 407, 425–26
political history, 385–96
pottery, 383
relationship with Lydia, 403–4
relationship with Persia, 393–395
relationship with Priene, 397–402
relationship with Sparta, 393, 403–4, 405–7
"Samian earth," 411–12
sculpture, 428
similarities and differences from Chios and Lesbos, 248–49, 434–35
slavery at, 418–19
tribes, 395
wine production, 409–10

Samos Town
  acropolis, 355–58
  agora, 355–56, 358–59
  Ampelos hill, 355–56, 359–60
  Eupalinos tunnel, 359–62
  excavations at, 349–51
  fortifications, 355–56, 359, 404
  harbors, 359, 362
  Kastro hill (*see* Samos Town, acropolis)
  laura (bazaar), 358–59, 392
  Megas tumulus, 382
  necropoleis, 356–58, 363, 380–82
  sanctuaries, 362–63
  Sanctuary of Artemis, 362–63
  settlement organization of, 355–63

Sappho of Lesbos, 300, 344–46

616   *Index*

Schliemann, Heinrich, 494–96
Semonides of Amorgos/Samos, 431–32
Sigeum, 324, 328, 342
slavery, 37–38, 48–52, 269–70, 284,
    286–88, 542–45, 567–68, 575
Sparta
    relationship with Argos, 45–53
    relationship with Croesus, 403–4, 405
    relationship with Samos, 393, 405–7,
       425–26
Strattis, tyrant of Chios, 276–77, 280–81
Styra, Euboea, 106, 138
Sybota, Corfu, 525–26
Syloson, brother of Polycrates of Samos,
    388–89, 391, 393–94, 408
Syloson, son of Kalliteles, 375, 386–87
Syracuse, 21–22, 25, 295–96, 502, 536–37,
    538–39, 545, 555

Tamynai, Euboea, 136–37, 140–41, 187,
    204–5
Telesilla, Argive poet, 40–41, 48–49
Theodorus of Samos, 373, 412–13, 428–29
Theomestor, tyrant of Samos, 394–95,
    409
Theopompus of Chios, 41, 284, 352

Thyrea(tis). *See* Cynuria
Tiryns, 15, 41, 43–45, 49–50, 52–53
Torone, North Aegean, 172
Tynnondas, Euboean tyrant, 152–53

Vollgraff, Carl Wilhelm, 8
Vrachos, Euboea, 117, 139, 179
Vrontados plain, Chios, 262

Wild Goat Style pottery, 271–73, 321–22,
    383
wine production, 284–85, 332, 409–10,
    559–60
women. *See also* homoeroticism, female;
    Sappho; Telesilla
    beauty contests on Lesbos, 339
    cross-dressing at Argos, 64–65
    cult activities of, 202–3, 346, 401, 424
    defend Argos, marry slaves, 48–51,
       64–65
    depictions of, 18–22
    grave goods associated with, at Argos,
       56–57
    height, 57–58

Zancle, Sicily, 173, 409